# Perspectives and Practices of Ed for Sustainable Development



Informed by theory and full of practical advice, this key title offers a clear route to education for sustainable development (ESD) whilst questioning how we reconcile participatory, inclusive processes and the urgency of global crises.

This handbook provides guidance for those with an interest in the purpose and direction of learning and the principles and practices of sustainability in universities in the UK and beyond. With critical analysis and useful case studies and recommendations, the book covers key topics such as:

- The need for sustainable development and the role that universities can play in this
- Showing how ESD should be part of a whole institution approach
- Development of relevant curricula with innovative and inspiring pedagogies to support sustainability competencies
- Transdisciplinary learning and pioneering forms of knowledge production
- Graduate futures and emerging priorities in the field of ESD

Through detailed case studies from experts in the field, this book demonstrates how ESD enables a critical interrogation of our world and strengthens the capacities of our universities to nurture future thinking leaders.

This is essential reading for all those interested in beginning or widening ESD in programmes, universities and the wider sector, including academic staff, university senior managers and support staff, students, policy makers, employers, and community leaders.

**Rehema M. White** is Chair of the Sustainability in the Curriculum Committee at the University of St Andrews, UK, and Chair of Learning for Sustainability Scotland.

**Simon Kemp** is Professor of Education for Sustainable Development, the University Lead in Education for Sustainable Development and Deputy Director of the Sustainability and Resilience Institute at the University of Southampton, UK.

**Elizabeth A. C. Price** MBE is Professor of Environmental Education and is Deputy Pro-Vice-Chancellor Sustainability at Manchester Metropolitan University, UK.

**James W. S. Longhurst** is Emeritus Professor of Environmental Science and, until retirement, was the Assistant Vice Chancellor for Environment and Sustainability at the University of the West of England, UK.

'It has become almost commonplace to say that education is needed if we are going to address the multiple ecological and social crises facing humanity. Yet too little thought is given to what form that education might take, what is needed for a deeper transformation, and indeed whether some forms may even be harmful for the cause. This book provides deep insights into this question in the context of higher education. Addressing multiple aspects of the question through its different chapters – on the meanings of sustainable development, curriculum design, assessment, research, leadership and many other areas – it brings together existing knowledge on the topic and provides fresh perspectives. As the introduction states, one of the key challenges is that ESD is often considered a 'worthy' cause, but one not relevant to all. Instead, it needs to be understood as part of the fabric of all learning, and inherent to disciplinary coverage, professional development and the broader learning experience on campus and beyond. This book provides essential tools for bringing this approach into being in contemporary higher education institutions. It presents practical steps for change in an accessible format, without losing theoretical depth or an appreciation of the tensions and complexities. An essential companion for those grappling on a day-to-day basis with the pressing task of transforming universities for sustainable, just and creative futures.'

**Tristan McCowan**, *Professor of International Education at the Institute of Education, University College London, UK*

'This book is a valuable addition to literature on Education for Sustainable Development from many of the team of experts behind the 2021 AdvanceHE/QAA guidance report on the subject. The academic book format enables the team to take a more expansive, critical and reflective take on the ESD agenda, exploring the practicalities, challenges and motivations around achieving transformative change for learners, universities and communities to make progress with sustainable development. The book is likely to be of great value to staff leading on ESD in universities, senior leaders seeking guidance on impactful strategic approaches, and anyone with an interest in the many topics explored in depth from pedagogy to research-informed teaching, on which ESD sheds challenging and inspiring light.'

**Andrew Reeves**, *Academic Lead, Education for Sustainable Development, De Montfort University, UK*

'This book makes a compelling case for higher education to be transformed through the implementation of Education for Sustainable Development (ESD). It successfully addresses a broad audience – scholarly in its approach but also provides practical tools and specific examples making it as valuable for theoretical consideration as for educators seeking to enhance their own practice. It opens by reminding us of the purpose universities serve, highlighting their impact as generators of new learning, driving industrial and technological revolutions – and therefore stressing universities' importance in catalysing potential solutions to the planet's sustainability. This is an urgent and essential call for partnership working across higher education institutions and within institutions, it is argued, ESD links theory and practice to support academic communities in developing the competencies needed to secure human existence. There is no expectation the book will be read in a linear format and its structure helps the reader to select those elements of most interest at any point in time. ESD affects all disciplines and all parts of higher education institutions – this point is successfully made in a manner accessible to all those with an interest in higher education and sustainability.'

**Ailsa Crum**, *QAA's Director of Membership, Quality Enhancement & Standards*

'At its heart, this book is a powerful call to action for everyone in, or interested in, higher education. By linking ESD to career development, interdisciplinary learning, and real-world impact, it invites readers to rethink the many ways institutions can drive a more sustainable future. Informative, thought-provoking, and deeply practical, it demonstrates how anyone – student, educator, or industry partner – can lead change and contribute to education as a force for good, fostering purpose-led graduates and a more equitable society. I have no doubt it will become essential reading for those determined to transform the purpose and impact of our institutions in response to an urgent and rapidly changing world.'

**Charlotte Bonner**, *EAUC, UK*

'This book is a compelling call to action which articulates the critical role of students and staff in leading sustainable change, both within and beyond the boundaries of a university campus. The book offers the reader a comprehensive reflection on the evolution of ESD within the Higher Education sector, and provides case studies and tools which inspire the reader to challenge current practices and identify opportunities to help embed sustainability within their institution.'

**Stephanie Todd**, *Strategic Operational Lead for Sustainability, Kingston University, UK*

'An eloquent summation of the importance of interdisciplinarity and intersectionality in Education for Sustainable Development. It is a necessity in a world where every single student and their chosen degree relates to sustainability, and has the power to create real, essential change. Climate crisis related issues often feel emotionally exhausting; this book acknowledges that, and provides much needed hope for students embarking on their higher education journeys.'

**Bitsy Pout**, *Ecologist*

'With it now having been several decades since the initiation of the ESD movement and its integration into higher education settings, this book offers a comprehensive and timely assessment of where the HE sector is up to with its efforts to support sustainability transformations. The criticality implied in the title is lived up to in the book's contents where the authors have been unafraid to probe at the uncomfortable and contentious questions that must be confronted by HE institutions if they are to meaningfully respond to the grave planetary conditions, and if they are to properly fulfil their obligations to both students and society. Careful attention is paid to whose voices are included in these efforts, and whose are not. The book's opening chapters also feature an in-depth exploration of how the underlying historical and political contexts of HE institutions may have contributed to some of the existential challenges we now face. The diligent critiques made within the book are accompanied by pragmatic and productive suggestions for alternative paths forward. The featured examples of activities would be particularly instructive for practitioners and stakeholders who are hoping to better align their institutional aims, strategies, and practices with a more authentic vision of sustainability. I consider this guide to be essential reading for anyone with a keen interest in the interface between sustainability and the HE sector.'

**Henry Finn**, *PhD Student, UK*

'Backed by rich research and compelling anecdotes, this book highlights the essential skills graduates need to be equipped with to keep up with the expanding green economy. It thoroughly explores how sustainability is woven into every degree programme, making it an invaluable resource for students, educators and advocates of sustainable development.'

**Manvir Rai**, *Undergraduate Student, UK*

'A must-read for anyone interested in the area of Education for Sustainable Development (ESD). The points raised on the importance of higher education and the need for collaboration in ESD lays the groundwork for everyone to do so much more. A very informative read.'

**Samuel Inkster**, *Undergraduate Student and Student Sustainability Champion of Year Finalist, 2024, UK*

'This book has so much potential to help guide future teachers and students in environment and sustainability-based courses. It concisely lays out the range of options for the associated issues regarding various aspects of the whole ESD subject area and analyses all strongly. I'm especially pleased that there's recognition how graduates are gravitating towards offers and sectors focused on worthy causes, not the stereotypical best paying job.'

**Aksel Conway-Forecast**, *Undergraduate Student, UK*

'A valuable guide that puts a clear emphasis on preparing students for careers in sustainability, while also educating on the importance of pulling sustainability into all facets of higher education.'

**Jack Dinham**, *Undergraduate Student, UK*

'This book ignites a great leap for new transformations that the area of ESD needs, connecting theoretical concepts and practices in education. Sustainability practices and their theory are holistically approached and assessed. This encourages students, educators, and others to become familiarised with ESD to break the barriers of anxiety around 'what is to come' and build on 'what can be done'. This book provides detailed insights without becoming inaccessible, empowering student readers to become the creators of change, and educators the enablers in moulding a future for sustainability. This book is vital for anyone who wants to change our world through educational routes.'

**George Banton**, *Undergraduate Student, UK*

# Perspectives and Practices of Education for Sustainable Development

## A Critical Guide for Higher Education

Edited by Rehema M. White,
Simon Kemp, Elizabeth A. C. Price
and James W. S. Longhurst

Routledge
Taylor & Francis Group
LONDON AND NEW YORK

Designed cover image: Getty Images

First published 2025
by Routledge
4 Park Square, Milton Park, Abingdon, Oxon OX14 4RN

and by Routledge
605 Third Avenue, New York, NY 10158

*Routledge is an imprint of the Taylor & Francis Group, an informa business*



*British Library Cataloguing-in-Publication Data*
A catalogue record for this book is available from the British Library

ISBN: 978-1-032-58803-2 (hbk)
ISBN: 978-1-032-58801-8 (pbk)
ISBN: 978-1-003-45156-3 (ebk)

DOI: 10.4324/9781003451563

Typeset in Sabon
by KnowledgeWorks Global Ltd.

To Hazel, Polly, Bagheera, Phoebe, Effie, Minnie, Skipper and Biscuit. Thanks also to our families for all the lost weekends.

# Contents

*List of Contributors* *xi*
*Preface and Acknowledgements* *xiii*
*Foreword* *xiv*
*Glossary* *xv*

1 **Introduction: A Book to Co-Create Sustainable Futures** 1
SIMON KEMP

2 **Education for Sustainable Development: Definitions, Debates and Design** 9
ELIZABETH A. C. PRICE AND REHEMA M. WHITE

3 **Towards a Sustainable University: People, Purpose and Paradigm Shifts** 36
ZOE P. ROBINSON, PETRA MOLTHAN-HILL AND PETER HIGGINS

4 **Education for Sustainable Development: From Disciplinary to Transdisciplinary Approaches** 59
REHEMA M. WHITE AND CHRIS PREIST

5 **Education for Sustainable Development: Curriculum Design, Content and Challenges** 87
GEORGINA GOUGH AND SIMON KEMP

6 **Critical Pedagogies to Engage Heart, Hand and Head in Education for Sustainable Development** 108
REHEMA M. WHITE, ELIZABETH A.C. PRICE AND CATHERINE HACK

7 **Innovating Assessment for Education for Sustainable Development** 129
SIMON KEMP AND REHEMA M. WHITE

8 **Sustainability Research, Teaching and Practice: Towards Transdisciplinary Knowledge Co-Production in Universities** 162
REHEMA M. WHITE, CLARE SAUNDERS AND ZOE P. ROBINSON

9 **Leadership and Governance for Education for Sustainable Development: Engagement, Strategy and Transformation** 189
JAMES W. S. LONGHURST, ZOE P. ROBINSON AND ELIZABETH A. C. PRICE

10 **Professional Development for All: Enabling Advocates for Education for Sustainable Development** 211
PATRICK BAUGHAN, ELIZABETH A. C. PRICE AND JAMES W. S. LONGHURST

11 **Monitoring and Evaluating Education for Sustainable Development: Co-Creating Quality Learning Experiences and Outcomes** 229
REHEMA M. WHITE, CAROLYN S. HAYLES AND GEORGINA GOUGH

12 **Graduate Futures: Embodying Education for Sustainable Development** 255
SIMON KEMP

13 **Conclusions: Creating Hope Through Education for Future Generations** 274
REHEMA M. WHITE

*Index* *289*

# Contributors

**Patrick Baughan** worked as Head of Education at The University of Law, leading education programmes and curriculum enhancement projects on Education for Sustainable Development. He has been working in educational development and research since 2005. His research activities span areas including sustainability, curriculum, assessment, feedback and academic integrity.

**Georgina Gough** is Professor of Education for Sustainable Development at UWE Bristol. Georgina is an elected member of the UK and Ireland Principles of Responsible Management Education (PRME) Steering Committee and UWE's Board of Governors. She leads UWE's MSc Sustainable Development in Practice.

**Catherine Hack** is Lead Consultant Education with Advance HE. She supports excellence in education by leading strategic leadership and change in HEIs. She developed the Advance HE Student Success Framework and led, in collaboration with the Quality Assurance Agency, the revision of sector guidance on Education for Sustainable Development.

**Carolyn S. Hayles** Professor Carolyn S. Hayles is Chair of Environmental and Sustainable Design for the Built Environment at Cardiff School of Art and Design at Cardiff Metropolitan University, UK. Carolyn's research focusses on the development and delivery of sustainable decision-making processes and frameworks, including approaches to climate change mitigation and adaptation.

**Peter Higgins** is Professor of Outdoor, Environmental and Sustainability Education at the University of Edinburgh, a Board member of the Scottish Government's nature agency NatureScot, chair of its Scientific Advisory Committee, and member of the UK Joint Nature Conservation Committee. He is a trustee of the educational charity, the Field Studies Council.

**Simon Kemp** is Professor of Education for Sustainable Development, University of Southampton ESD Lead, Sustainability & Resilience Institute Deputy Director, and co-Chair of the QAA/Advance HE ESD Guidance. His student-focused ESD work has been recognised through THE 'Most Innovative Teacher of Year', a National Teaching Fellowship, and Green Gown 'Sustainability Professional of the Year' awards.

**James W. S. Longhurst** is Emeritus Professor of Environmental Science and until late 2023 was Assistant Vice Chancellor for Environment and Sustainability at UWE. He chaired the 2014 and co-chaired the 2021 Advisory Group producing the QAA/

Advance HE guidance on ESD for HE. He is the former Chair of the EAUC and Vice President of the Institution of Environmental Sciences.

**Petra Molthan-Hill** is Professor at Nottingham Business School, Nottingham Trent University (UK), Co-Chair of the UN PRME Working Group on Climate Change, author of 'Handbook of Carbon Management', editor of 'Sustainable Management: A Complete Guide for Faculty and Students' and leads the 'Climate Literacy Training -CLT-ECOS'. From 2013 to 2021, she led the Green Academy at NTU integrating with her team the SDGs into the curriculum of every discipline across all faculties.

**Chris Preist** is Professor of Sustainability and Computer Systems at the University of Bristol, UK, and the Academic Director of Sustainability.

**Elizabeth A. C. Price** MBE is Professor of Environmental Education and Deputy Pro-Vice-Chancellor Sustainability at Manchester Metropolitan University, UK.

**Zoe P. Robinson** is a Professor of Sustainability in Higher Education at Keele University, UK, where she has worked for 20 years as a researcher, educator and practitioner, driving sustainability in the curriculum, research and wider institution, and working with communities on place-based decarbonisation and localised approaches to green skills development.

**Clare Saunders** is Professor in Environmental Politics in the Department of Humanities and Social Sciences, University of Exeter, Cornwall. She has decades of experience of research into the social innovators and activists who shape environmental thoughts and actions.

**Rehema M. White** is an academic in the School of Geography and Sustainable Development at University of St Andrews and Chair, Learning for Sustainability Scotland, who researches knowledge for sustainability and human nature relationships, drawing on the natural and social sciences, and gathers together academics, practitioners and policy makers to co-design collaborative solutions to specific sustainability challenges.

# Preface and Acknowledgements

The world seems to be waking up to the fact that higher education graduates have to address rather than exacerbate global sustainability challenges such as the climate and nature crises. In UK, the Quality Assurance Agency (QAA) and Advance HE thus supported an expert advisory group, ably led by James Longhurst and Simon Kemp, to refresh the 2014 Guidance for Education for Sustainable Development (ESD) in Higher Education in UK. The expert group met once in 2020 before Covid-19 caused them to convene online. The resulting new QAA/Advance HE Guidance was launched in 2021 and was received well, even with enthusiasm, from the existing ESD community and people expressing new interest. A conversation on critical pedagogy for sustainable futures started to spread into and across different groups and institutions. This book emerged after the positive reception to and greater interest in the 2021 ESD Guidance, and to fuel those conversations. Although there was some excellent writing on ESD in higher education, there was not a book that covered the areas of relevance in one volume, across all disciplines. The group thus decided to convene once more and to sketch out this volume.

Whilst all of the book authors were on the Guidance expert group, additional group members were not able to contribute to the book. We thus acknowledge Alex Ryan, Kate Mori, Quinn Runkle, Paul Warwick, Emma Wilcox and Meg Baker.

Thanks to Fritha West for valiant reference checking in the final stages.

Thanks to Quinn Runkle, Jennifer O'Brien and Pathik Pathak for case studies.

Rehema M. White, Simon Kemp, Elizabeth A. C. Price
and James W. S. Longhurst

# Foreword

We live in extraordinary times, a phase of human and planetary existence marked by daunting threats and widespread anxiety, but which *at the same time* is inspiring vision, creativity and renewal that together signal that a safe future *is* possible – if together we make it so.

In this setting, the purpose, role and impact of education are increasingly called into question. Does its net effect take us towards a more sustainable and viable future – OR reinforce society's current unsustainable trajectories? UNESCO calls for the 'transformation of education' – policies and practices which can empower and enable learners to develop a critical understanding of the systemic socio-ecological issues facing us, but also to engage in the generation of positive pathways offering hope and reassurance into the future. This is the responsibility of education in our volatile times.

The evolution of ESD over the last few decades offers a re-purposing of educational endeavour, a re-thinking of the nature and role of knowledge, and a promise of participatory pedagogies that any higher education institution can employ – to ground and inspire their work towards the realisation of personal fulfilment, social justice and coherence, economic viability and ecological health as mutually affecting goals.

As reflected in this most timely and richly informative book, ESD poses a radical and urgent challenge. But as the book makes clear, ESD is also an invitation to engage, a signpost to indicate a learning journey for all, and a proven vehicle for the educational re-thinking, rejuvenation and renewal this important journey involves. This transition is not easy, but it is possible and necessary for our shared future. It is time to be bold. With this 'critical guide' in hand – based on the authors' many years of deep experience and drawing on lessons from a worldwide movement in higher education – any university can, over time, become the pioneer that people and planet now need.

Stephen Sterling, Professor Emeritus of Sustainability Education, University of Plymouth, UK; Author of (2024) *Learning and sustainability in dangerous times*. Agenda Publishing, Newcastle-upon-Tyne, UK.

# Glossary

Most of the terms in this glossary are contested; there are different views on their meanings, and they are dependent on the context. We explain below the ways in which we understand these terms in this book, and we expand on the different views of these terms, drawing on literature, in the book chapters.

**Academic discipline** Academic disciplines came into being along with universities in the Middle Ages as knowledge accumulated, and there was a need to classify and organise information and to specialise in learning. Academic disciplines are intellectual domains linked to theories and methods but can also be seen as organisational structures around scholarly communities. Whilst we theorise academic disciplines within knowledge frameworks, learners tend to see them as subjects, courses or programmes.

**Academic staff** Academic professionals employed by higher education institutions to plan, lead and execute subject-specific teaching and assessment as part of their degree programme delivery requirements.

**Adaptation and resilience** Adaptation refers to adjustments in ecological, social or economic systems in response to actual or expected climatic stimuli and their effects. It refers to changes in processes, practices and structures to moderate potential damages or to benefit from opportunities associated with climate change. In this context, resilience is the ability of a system or individual to absorb, withstand and recover from an adverse environmental event.

**Advance HE** Advance HE is a member-led charity of and for the sector that works with partners across the globe to improve higher education for staff, students and society. Worked with QAA to produce the ESD Guidance for the Higher Education sector.

**Affective, practical and cognitive learning** ESD is often said to engage the heart, hand and head. The heart represents affective learning, in the socio-emotional domain, influencing values and attitudes. The hand represents practical or experiential learning, in the behavioural domain, supporting action competencies for sustainability. The head represents cognitive learning, in the intellectual domain, for knowledge and critical thinking skills. Pedagogies should support these different kinds of learning for a holistic ESD experience.

**Artificial General Intelligence (AGI)** Where computing develops near human-level intelligence with the ability to learn, adapt, conduct human intellectual tasks, and the possibility to go beyond human intellectual capacity (Suleyman and Bhaskar, 2023).

**Artificial intelligence (AI)** 'The capacity of computers or other machines to exhibit or simulate intelligent behaviour; the field of study concerned with this. In later use also: software used to perform tasks or produce output previously thought to require human intelligence, esp. by using machine learning to extrapolate from large collections of data' (Oxford English Dictionary, 2024).

**Assessment (of/for/through) learning – authentic, experiential** assessment forms the critical role of proving that students have a valid understanding of their programmes and strengthens learning through tasks of varying complexity, self-evaluation and crucially feedback to students. Assessment should be underpinned by pedagogy, academic discipline or interdisciplinarity, and uphold programme standards.

Assessment of Learning demonstrates the achievement of learning; Assessment for Learning provides feedback on teaching and learning; Assessment as Learning empowers students to self-regulate and critically evaluate (AdvanceHE/QAA, 2021).

**Authentic assessment** Authentic assessment measures how students apply their knowledge to real-world situations to prove the extent of their understanding and thinking. Authentic assessment can include professional training with competence-based tasks and a focus on preparing students for employment through assessed exercises of direct relevance to future professional practices.

**Blended learning** Learning and teaching that is delivered through a combination of different methods. Typically, this is the term used to describe technology-led delivery such as the use of videos (lecture capture, filmed case studies) and online literature combined with 'in-person' or 'face-to-face' delivery more generally associated with traditional lectures in teaching rooms and lecture theatres.

**Climate change** A change in the state of the climate that can be identified (e.g., by using statistical tests) by changes in the mean and/or the variability of its properties and that persists for an extended period, typically decades or longer.

*Climate* is usually defined as the average weather – or more rigorously, as the statistical description in terms of the mean and variability of relevant quantities – over a period of time ranging from months to thousands or millions of years. The classical period for averaging these variables is 30 years, as defined by the World Meteorological Organization (WMO). The relevant quantities are most often surface variables such as temperature, precipitation and wind. Climate in a wider sense is the state, including a statistical description, of the climate system.

*Climate change* may be due to natural internal processes or external forcings such as modulations of the solar cycles, volcanic eruptions and persistent anthropogenic changes in the composition of the atmosphere or in land use. Note that the United Nations Framework Convention on Climate Change (UNFCCC), in its Article 1, defines *climate change* as: 'a change of climate which is attributed directly or indirectly to human activity that alters the composition of the global atmosphere and which is in addition to natural climate variability observed over comparable time periods'. The UNFCCC thus makes a distinction between *climate change* attributable to human activities altering the atmospheric composition and *climate variability* attributable to natural causes' (Intergovernmental Panel on Climate Change, 2022: Impacts, Adaptation and Vulnerability. Summary for Policymakers, Technical Summary and Frequently Asked Questions. Glossary).

**Compassionate pedagogy** Compassionate pedagogy is a commitment by educators to be kind and to counteract institutional and class practices that ideologically disadvantage students who are in some way not being served by typical pedagogies, hence it supports diversity. It includes self-reflexive practices and empathy.

**Competencies** Competencies are suites of knowledge, skills and capacities that support actions and functions but also include abilities to value and reflect. They enable people to respond to complex demands and tackle uncertainty. There are eight cross-cutting key competencies for sustainability, in addition to discipline or learning specific competencies that may be supported.

**Co-production, co-creation and co-design** Sustainable development is a collaborative venture, and transdisciplinary scholarship, including work across academic and non-academic partners, is often involved. Co-production occurs when different actors undertake activities together to achieve a shared outcome (e.g. an event to engage students in a local community group). Co-creation occurs when different actors develop the idea for an initiative together (e.g. the inspiration for a master class seminar series that is subsequently run by a university department). Co-design is when different actors collaboratively brainstorm, pilot, reflect and develop a shared outcome through a design process (e.g. students work with local authority to increase sustainable transport use, pilot a bus pass then modify and implement the plan).

**Curriculum (including design)** The curriculum is how we structure students' learning across their degree programmes. There may be variations in terminology depending on the extent of reading and the language used within a university. For example, there is the UNESCO model of 'formal', 'non-formal' and 'informal' (UNESCO, 2017). 'Formal' refers to the curriculum including fieldtrips, 'non-formal' is learning away from the classroom and assessed work such as community group projects, and 'informal' is the wider cultural context that students live within such as media influences and societal norms. An alternative model of the curriculum across higher education comprises three distinct but complementary and overlapping areas of 'formal learning', 'informal learning' and the 'hidden curriculum'.

**Decolonising the curriculum** Decolonising the curriculum is the process of uncovering unconscious bias, challenging assumptions and including more diverse ethnic and cultural perspectives in formal learning.

**Degree** 'A protected term for a higher education qualification at one of several levels, determined by the depth and breadth of study and awarded only for achievement in full of the outcomes set out in the appropriate qualification descriptor in the relevant qualifications framework' (QAA Glossary, 2022).

**Degree level** Degree courses consist of a number of different 'levels' depending on the year of study. Each different level can lead to a separate qualification if the student decides to end their studies at the completion of a level (year of study). The degree levels are part of the nine government qualification levels. Degree levels commence at level 4 of the national qualification levels (after the completion of level 3 – A level and equivalent qualifications) and offer the award of Certificate of Higher Education (CertHE) after completion of the first year of studies. The second year is at level 5, with completion offering a Diploma of Higher Education (DipHE). The third and normally final year of a degree is level 6, with the award of a Degree with Honours [normally either Bachelor of the Arts (BA) or Bachelor of Science (BSc)]. Undergraduate students might complete a four-year 'Integrated Masters' degree which is at level 7, the same level as for a Postgraduate taught degree such as a Master of Arts (MA) or Master of Science (MSc) degree.

See 'Degree' for a definition of the term 'degree'.

**Doughnut economics** Doughnut economics recognises that humans need to live within the limits of planetary boundaries and over the social foundation. This means respecting resource and environmental limits rather than seeking unlimited economic growth.

**EAUC** Environmental Association for Universities and Colleges (EAUC) is the leading body for sustainability in the post-16 education sector in the UK and Republic of Ireland. It is primarily a membership body with over 300 member organisations; a charity and a company limited by guarantee; organiser of the UK and Ireland Green Gown Awards and the International Green Gown Awards.

**EDI** Equality, Diversity and Inclusivity comprise a set of policies and practices within higher education institutions. Equality is about ensuring that everyone has the same opportunities, and no-one is treated differently or discriminated against because of their personal characteristics. These are known as 'protected characteristics' under the UK Equality Act 2010. Diversity is about recognising, valuing and taking account of people's different backgrounds, knowledge, skills and experiences. Inclusion is where these differences between people and groups are seen as a benefit, and where people feel comfortable to share their perspectives and differences, knowing that their opinions and ideas are valued.

**Education for sustainable development** Education for Sustainable Development (ESD) in Higher Education supports learners in all disciplines to develop knowledge, skills and capacities for human wellbeing, with attention to those who are marginalised, whilst ensuring that we live within environmental limits to address interconnected global challenges, including climate change, loss of biodiversity, unsustainable use of resources and inequality. Such learning employs critical, reflexive and potentially transformative pedagogies and curricula to create a space for dialogue, innovation and openness and to support specific and generic competencies. It enhances the cognitive, socio-emotional and behavioural dimensions of learning and encompasses learning content and outcomes, pedagogy and the learning environment itself. A whole institution approach links a sustainability focus across disciplines, teaching and research, operations and community engagement. Staff and students need to collaborate in the co-production of curricula and to partner with external actors. Graduates are change agents in the sustainability transition.

**Educator** A person who teaches students (and others) through the different forms of curriculum and is viewed as a leading authority on their academic discipline.

**Employability** 'A set of achievements, skills, understanding and personal attributes that makes graduates more likely to gain employment and be successful in their chosen occupations' (QAA Glossary, 2022).

**Environmental education** Environmental education developed from the 1970s with different approaches, including education *in* the environment (experiential, often outdoor, education – engaging the heart); education *about* the environment (providing information – an intellectual exercise) and education *for* the environment (critical and political education that aims to develop active participation and a sense of responsibility in learners – enabling hands-on activity). It lacks the development context and long-term focus of sustainability, which for some people is positive, because it avoids neoliberal and colonial ideas of 'progress', but for other people is negative, because they argue that we need social justice to achieve environmental outcomes, and we need to address social and environmental issues concurrently because they are interdependent.

**Environmental stewardship** Environmental stewardship refers to the responsible use and protection of the natural environment through participation in environmental management and sustainable practices. Stewards may be individuals, groups, agencies, governments, firms or networks of actors.

**Epistemology** Epistemology is the theory of knowledge. Your view of the world influences your beliefs around knowledge and hence your interpretation of data. There are different theories of knowledge: rationalism suggests we can know things by applying logic and reasoning, and focuses on the intellect (a very philosophical approach). Empiricism suggests we need to appreciate our senses, gather data and evidence our assumptions (a typical scientific view). Existentialism preferences our personal experiences, emotions and morals (relates to experiential knowledge, art and religious frames). People often draw on a combination of these views to construct their assumptions about the world. In relation to education for sustainable development, we often discuss ways of reconciling a positivist epistemological position (aligning with empiricism) from science with an anti-positivist position that celebrates subjectivity and context (interpretivism) to study society.

**Formal curriculum** The formal curriculum is rooted in the universally accepted Bloom's Taxonomy (Bloom, 1956) with programme learning objectives based around knowledge, comprehension, application, analysis, synthesis, evaluation, which is in itself an order of increasing complexity. Through this structural approach to the curriculum, educators deliver teaching and assessment to students, with quality assurance structures and mechanisms in place to ensure the content meets formal regulated university requirements for the award of a degree.

**Formative assessment** Assessment where a numerical mark, letter grade and/or feedback comments are provided, but no mark is awarded as part of the degree. Formative assessment is for feedback and is important in supporting learners and helping them improve their work.

**Generative Artificial Intelligence** 'Artificial intelligence designed to produce output, esp. text or images, previously thought to require human intelligence, typically by using machine learning to extrapolate from large collections of data; (also) a system, piece of software, etc., used to create content in this way' (Oxford English Dictionary, 2024). Also referred to as 'Generative AI'.

**Graduate** 'A person who has attained a bachelor's or higher degree' (QAA Glossary 2022). The term graduate is also used to refer to a student who has recently left university having completed their degree programme and achieved their qualification.

**Graduate attributes** Graduate attributes are the personal and professional skills and qualities that a degree provider believes their graduates should possess through the completion of their programme and engagement in the hidden curriculum.

**Green skills** 'the knowledge, abilities, values and attitudes needed to live in, develop and support a society which reduces the impact of human activity on the environment' (CEDEFOP, 2010).

**Greenwashing** The use of public relations techniques to persuade an audience that a higher education institution's policies and practices are sustainable. Often used to hide the disconnect between the rhetoric of ambitious university sustainability statements and their insufficiently effective operational practices.

**Hidden curriculum** The 'hidden curriculum' is considered the dimension of student learning and experience that sits outside of formal and informal learning and assessment but is crucial in providing students with views and experiences that allow them to understand the place of their learnings in society and the workplace, whilst developing skills to prepare for life after graduation.

**Higher education** 'Education that comes after secondary and further education, leading to a qualification or credit awarded by a degree-awarding body. Typically, it involves working towards a degree, but some programmes may lead to a diploma, certificate or other award or qualification on the national Qualifications Frameworks' (QAA Glossary, 2022).

**Higher education institution** 'Universities, colleges or other organisations that primarily deliver programmes of higher education. An institution with the power to award degrees conferred by Royal Charter, or under Section 76 of the Further and Higher Education Act 1992, or under Section 48 of the Further and Higher Education (Scotland) Act 1992, or by Papal Bull, or, since 1999, granted by the Privy Council on advice from QAA, or, in England, granted by the OfS on advice from the QAAunder section 42 of the Higher Education and Research Act 2017' (QAA Glossary, 2022).

**Indigenous** Indigenous people have inhabited a land for generations, since before colonial times. They often still express traditional culture and practices, use Indigenous languages and hold ancestral ties to their land.

**Informal learning** 'Informal learning' is based around formal learning objectives but typically takes place away from regular compulsory learning provision and settings. A useful definition is provided by Coombs & Ahmed (1974) as organised and systematic education activities outside the formal framework to deliver specific types of learning. In the context of ESD, this can be through visits to community groups, immersive learning within society and experiential learning through non-assessed activities on field courses as just some of the examples of direct relevance to ESD and curriculum design. Informal learning is sometimes used interchangeably with 'non-formal learning'.

**Interdisciplinarity** Interdisciplinarity is integrative. For example, a learner may experience two or more disciplines but will synthesise plans, knowledge and outputs across them. This approach goes beyond *what* they learn to *how* they learn.

**Learner centred** A learner-centred approach places students at the heart of the education process where they determine the focus of what, how, where and the pace they learn. It may also include students deciding how they are assessed. The previous education experiences, strengths, weaknesses, opportunities and threats can be utilised to determine the techniques to be adopted.

**Learners** A term used to describe any individual seeking to gain knowledge, understanding and skills in a selected area or areas. Whilst the term 'learner' might be used interchangeably with 'student', it is distinctively different as a learner may be seeking knowledge, understanding and skills through their own research or presentations and is not necessarily following a programme of study at an institution.

**Learning for sustainability** Learning for sustainability has a similar meaning to education for sustainable development (ESD). It is the term often used in Scotland and is increasingly used across Europe and by UNESCO. It is preferred by some people because the term 'learning' implies active learning by learners rather than passive absorption of 'education'; it more readily includes non-formal and informal modes of learning and thus better represents the holistic and lifelong learning experience of individuals; it intends the goal of sustainability rather than the process of sustainable development; and in Scotland, it is a neutral term that combines the fields of ESD, global citizenship and outdoor learning in learning in schools.

**Living lab** A 'living lab' refers to the use of the university campus, facilities and areas the university interacts with for the delivery of teaching and/or assessment tasks. The term 'living lab' may also be applied to projects with partners in other countries due to the collaborative focus of the work.

**Module/unit** 'Module' or 'unit' are the terms used to refer to a defined group of teaching, reading, practical work and assessment activities for one specific focused area as part of a programme of study. Successful completion of the module or unit will result in credits being awarded at the level of study that contributes to the final award of the degree, certificate or diploma. The term 'unit' or 'module' will be applied depending on the accepted nomenclature used in the institution.

**Monitoring and evaluation** A part of the Quality Assurance process. Usually focused on quantitative data and often a closed constrained process. Used in this book to mean the navigation and mapping that enables dialogue, partnership and exploration of new knowledge and practice horizons through ESD.

**More-than-human** Humans are part of and interdependent with a wider world with plants, animals and other living and non-living entities. The term non-human is sometimes used to describe these entities, but this implies duality and the superiority of humans (e.g. humans versus 'the rest'). 'More-than-human' reminds us that humans constitute only one of many actors, and that other actors have their own capacities and powers.

**Multidisciplinarity** Multidisciplinarity combines different disciplines in an additive manner. For example, a learner experiences different disciplines but does not synthesise across them.

**Nature/ecological /biodiversity crisis** The terms 'nature crisis', 'biodiversity crisis' and 'ecological crisis' may be used interchangeably. Fundamentally, these terms collectively refer to the breakdown of natural systems that support biodiversity and health of all species. The word 'crisis' is important, as it indicates the collapse of species numbers, distribution and ecosystems at unprecedented recorded rates in excess of natural background levels. The nature/biodiversity/ecological crisis is mostly referred to as a consequence of climate change but is also associated with deforestation, land-use change for agriculture and urbanisation.

**Neoliberal** Neoliberalism is associated with the reduction of state regulation of labour and economic markets and reduced government spending, with a set of economic liberalisation policies, such as privatisation, globalisation, free trade and austerity.

**Non-formal learning** 'Non-formal' is learning away from the classroom and assessed work such as community group projects. Sometimes used interchangeably with 'informal learning', this is the preferred term adopted by UNESCO as part of the 'formal', 'non-formal' and 'informal' structure.

**Normative** ESD is normative, which means that it is concerned with social norms and is value oriented. It seeks to not only understand but also to change norms towards more sustainable ways of being and living; it has purpose and meaning.

**Ocean acidification** When carbon dioxide ($CO_2$) dissolves in sea water, it forms carbonic acid, decreasing the ocean's pH, a process collectively known as ocean acidification.

At present, ocean acidification is calculated as taking place approximately 10 times faster than any point in the last 300 million years. Ocean acidification jeopardises the ability of ocean systems to adapt to changes in ocean chemistry with the potential to change marine ecosystems and impact many ocean-related benefits to society such as coastal protection or provision of food and income. (IUCN, 2017: Ocean Acidification issues brief)

**Ontology** Ontology is a perspective on the nature of reality. Ontology is concerned with what is true or real. Scientists often believe that there is truth and a reality 'out there', whereas social scientists using qualitative research usually believe that reality is experienced differently by individuals. In education for sustainable development, we often have to reconcile these different perspectives.

**Paradigm shift** A paradigm shift means a change in perspective on the way the world works, a difference in worldview. ESD opens up possibilities for a paradigm shift by enabling learners to explore and critically reflect on alternative frames of view. ESD does not dictate an exact worldview that must be required but rather demonstrates that other paradigms exist and should be considered.

**Partnership** Partnership is a crucial term in ESD, referring to the collaborations that take place between academics, students, senior management, operations staff, business leaders, policy makers and community groups. Partnerships can take place within and across most settings such as within all forms of the curriculum, multi-organisation research projects, outreach work, fieldwork with regulators for example.

**Pedagogy** Pedagogy is the theory and practice of teaching, which influences the interactive process between educator and learner and with the learning environment. In education for sustainable development in higher education, pedagogies aim to support knowledge and skills, develop the core competencies for sustainability and facilitate transformation for sustainable development. Innovative pedagogies challenge existing approaches and seek new ways to facilitate learning. Critical pedagogies encourage learning with analysis and reflection, often through academic as well as practical lenses.

**Planetary boundaries** Defines the safe operating space for humanity. A set of nine planetary boundaries representing components of the Earth system critically affected by anthropogenic activities. Six of the nine planetary boundaries have been crossed.

**Postcolonialism and neocolonialism** Postcolonialism is the period after Western colonialism, when people subordinated under imperialism can transition to rethink their history and reclaim identity and agency. Neocolonialism is a form of colonial-like exploitation of a developing country through economic, political or cultural pressures, often by former colonial rulers, that reinforces capitalism and neo-liberal globalisation.

**Post-normal science** Post-normal science represents a constructivist notion of scientific knowledge, recognising that science choices and interpretations can be subject to political, moral and cultural influences and that science is not objective truth. Post-normal science is influenced by academic and non-academic actors and has social relevance and has value to society.

**Programme and/or course** A Degree 'programme' or 'course' is formed of a number of 'units' (or 'modules') with the number varying depending on the institution, but the number of credits remains consistent across the sector at 120 credit points. Students routinely refer to what 'course' they are studying rather than their 'programme', but the term 'programme' is the primary term used within pedagogic studies and university curriculum quality processes. The QAA Glossary (2022) use the term 'programme of study' and provides the following definition: 'An approved course of study that provides a coherent learning experience and normally leads to a qualification. UK higher education programmes must be approved and validated by UK degree-awarding bodies'.

**Progression** 'Progression' refers to the movement of a student from one level of their study to the next higher level of study upon completion of assessments that have led to award of sufficient credits to 'progress'. This can be referred as progression by year (e.g. year 1 to year 2), progression by 'part' which is synonymous with year (e.g. part 2 to part 3) or progression by level (e.g. level 6 to level 7 for integrated master's students).

**QAA** The Quality Assurance Agency for Higher Education (QAA) is an independent charity working to benefit students and higher education. It works to safeguard standards and improve the quality of UK higher education wherever it is delivered around the world. It worked with Advance HE to produce the ESD Guidance for the Higher Education sector in 2021.

**Quality assurance** The set of processes and procedures used by HEIs to assure stakeholders that the claimed quality and standard of provision is met in practice.

**Radical and reformist** ESD is essential for us to address global and local sustainability challenges. There are different opinions on the emphasis of ESD. Some actors believe we need reformist perspectives to bring people along with us; encouraging gentle shifts towards sustainability and modifying existing organisations, for example, encouraging green consumerism and recycling. Others believe that we need more radical change, and we need to reflect this in ESD. For example, radical views include the need to disrupt existing power hierarchies and constrain forms of capitalism. Individual educators and learners may align with different perspectives, but it is important to emphasise that we are addressing wicked problems and major responses are required.

**Relational and eco-pedagogies** Relational pedagogies explore relationships between humans and with more-than-human beings. Relational pedagogies recognise complexity and consider that the pursuit of sustainable development requires constitutive processes but also relationships and collaborative enterprise. Eco-pedagogies are often considered to be forms of relational pedagogy. People can hold different values with respect to nature, hence eco-pedagogies need to explore both practical consequences of natural resource use and more emotional connections with nature. 'Ecocentric education' goes further in placing nature at the centre of the learning process.

**Social constructivism** Social constructivism is a pedagogical approach that is teacher-guided and student-centred. It generates a collaborative learning process in a social context, for example, group work and dialogical approaches. Peer learning enables learners to go beyond the curriculum and share experiences and perspectives.

**Social responsibility** The expectation that organisations and individuals should not behave or conduct their business activities in a manner that is unethical, amoral and create harm to people and society. Instead, they should conduct their work with people and communities at the forefront of their intentions and should make a positive contribution to wider society.

**Subject Benchmark Statements** Each academic discipline in UK has to meet Subject Benchmark Statements requirements for their higher education degree qualifications to be recognised. This provides consistency across institutions and coherence to disciplines. ESD is not only supported but now required by all Subject Benchmark Statements, hence there is a statutory obligation to include ESD in all higher education programmes. Disciplines include ESD in their Subject Benchmark Statements in innovative ways.

**Students** 'All individuals studying a higher education course regardless of demographic, mode or level of study, subject area or geographic location. This includes current students on a course of study, recent former students and graduates (as defined by the provider's regulations), and people applying for a place at a higher education provider' (QAA Glossary, 2022).

**Sustainability** Sustainability occurs when there are respectful, relational interconnections between people and with nature, local communities prosper, there is social equity within and across countries and global partnerships enable fair trade. Sustainability is often easier to define as having overcome unsustainability, including environmental degradation, over-consumption and inequality resulting from turbocapitalist, extractive, colonial processes.

**Sustainability research and sustainability science** Sustainability research is considered here to be research *for* sustainability, which retains the normative impetus of Education *for* Sustainable Development. Research *on* sustainability implies a more neutral stance of providing information or knowledge without engaging with its use. All research could be relevant to sustainability. Sustainability science is seen here to be a limited subset of sustainability research, an emerging discipline that reconnects scientific and technological directions with social and political debates, focusing on several key research domains: usually climate, biodiversity, agriculture, fishery, forestry, energy and resources, water, economic development, health and lifestyle, but often focusing on technological solutions rather than underlying causes.

**Sustainability transition and sustainability transformation** Sustainability transitions are long-term, gradual, systemic and structural changes in society towards more sustainable options and outcomes. They involve socio-technological innovation, behaviour change and scaling of practices from local (niche) to national (landscape) levels. The urgency of the nature and climate crises causes many people to call for a more radical sustainability transformations that are faster and imply a new system rather than adjustment of the last. Sustainability transitions and transformations are also sometimes used in relation to institutions, organisations and businesses to demonstrate a journey towards sustainability; they should signal significant change and not merely greenwashing.

**Sustainable development** Definitions of sustainable development vary across time and sector, with different conceptions playing out even within the UN SDGs. We see it as being an aspiration and an organising principle for local and global development that supports the wellbeing of both people and the planet whilst recognising the interconnectedness of humans and nature; it is a journey towards sustainability.

**Sustainable university** An aspiration that requires a higher education institution to move from 'bolt-on' approaches to sustainability to one that embraces a fundamental commitment to whole institutional transformation encompassing teaching and research, operations and community engagement.

**Transdisciplinarity** Transdisciplinary learning can be understood in different ways. It occurs when different disciplines and non-academic stakeholders are involved and can lead to sharing or development of new paradigms across disciplines. Learners construct their knowledge from different elements. Transdisciplinarity can be a successful route towards transformative learning, but not all ESD needs to strive for multi-, inter- or transdisciplinarity.

**Transformative learning** Transformative learning enables learners to alter their frame of reference or perspective through critical reflection. Transformative learning is often seen to be necessary because of the scale of transformative change required in society to achieve sustainability.

**Transgressive** Transgressive learning is disruptive, causing paradigms, processes and practices to change to enable sustainability transformations.

**Turbocapitalism** Turbocapitalism is an accelerated form of capitalism, with a free-market economic system in which private enterprise is largely unregulated by the government, there are few or no trade unions, and concerns for employees or communities are minimal. This extreme form of capitalism is believed to be on the rise and can exacerbate social inequalities and environmental degradation.

**United Nations Sustainable Development Goals (UN SDGs)** The UN SDGs were launched in 2015 to create a global framework and impetus for action in transforming our world for a more sustainable future. They comprise 17 goals, 169 associated targets and 248 indicators. The SDGs are universal, applying to all countries, sectors and scales, and they incorporate a wide scope of intention.

**University** 'Independent, self-governing organisations that undertake research and teaching and are diverse in size, mission, history, and the range of subjects on offer. The first universities arose from colleges or institutions founded by groups of scholars, often with monastic connections and/or noble or royal patrons. Subsequently, universities have been established by a Royal Charter, Act of Parliament, Papal Bull or by Order of the Privy Council enabling them to develop their own programmes of study and award their own degrees' (QAA Glossary, 2022).

**Wellbeing** 'Well-being is a positive state experienced by individuals and societies. Similar to health, it is a resource for daily life and is determined by social, economic and environmental conditions' (World Health Organization, 2021: Health Promotion Glossary of Terms).

**Whole institution approach** A whole institution approach provides a sustainability focus and integration across disciplines, teaching and research, operations and community engagement.

Chapter 1

# Introduction

## A Book to Co-Create Sustainable Futures

*Simon Kemp*

### The Challenge

This is a book for a future. A future that offers hope for the young, and older, people with whom we are privileged to share our higher education institutions. Our students. We learn together with intelligent, energetic and passionate people. Our students offer us their minds and hearts when they join us for their education and the most transformative experience of their lives. This is a responsibility that we should not and must not take lightly. In this book, we accept that responsibility and provide inspiration and practical ideas to help create a more positive social, cultural, economic and environmental future through Education for Sustainable Development (ESD) in higher education.

Higher education, in the form of structured teaching and research institutions such as universities, has been in existence for close to a millennium with the University of Bologna recognised as the oldest university still in existence in this form (Paletta and Bonoli, 2019). This is an infinitesimal period of time in the context of the history of our planet but a time of unprecedented flux with profound consequences for all life on Earth, as rooted in the development and application of knowledge. In this relatively small window of time, we have seen the human population of our planet increase from an estimated 323 million to over 8 billion people (Our World in Data, 2024), with unparalleled resource demands associated with population increase and technology expansion and change. In this millennium of higher education and partly due to knowledge produced and shared by such institutions, humans produced the agricultural and industrial revolutions (O'Brien, 1977); built transport systems to move products, food and people around the world (Rodrigue, 2020); reduced child mortality in most but not all of the world (Ritchie, 2018); extended average human expectancy (Dattani *et al.*, 2023); created unparalleled wealth disparities within nations and across the globe (Estes, 2019); increased access to basic education (Ritchie *et al.*, 2023) and brought improved healthcare to more people but with remaining disparities to access globally (WHO, 2023).

However, humans have also caused unparalleled wealth disparities (IMF, 2022; World Bank, 2023), created and released long-lasting artificial pollutants (Caesar *et al.*, 2024), polluted our life-maintaining waters and atmosphere (Caesar *et al.*, 2024), developed terrifyingly powerful and more efficient ways of killing greater numbers of people, built a weapon that could wipe out most of life on the Earth (Diaz-Maurin and Gaulkin, 2022), changed our climate to the point of impending irreversible disaster (Ripple *et al.*, 2024) and are now developing information technology and pursuing artificial general intelligence which could turbocharge all of the above (Suleyman and Bhaskar, 2023).

DOI: 10.4324/9781003451563-1

All and more of these key inventions and societal changes across this period, with their associated environmental consequences, are associated with higher education. For example, three universities were leading contributors to the Manhattan Project (U.S. Department of Energy, n.d.), where academics holding the highest levels of education and research qualifications worked with the government and the military to develop the nuclear bomb and change the course of history and the future for us all. The partnerships we make in academia and how we collectively apply knowledge and research skills from our education matter.

Scientific research has proved the global consequences of emitting carbon dioxide to the atmosphere all the way back to the start of the industrial revolution, including the work of the (lesser recognised) female scientist Eunice Newton Foote in 1856 (Ortiz and Jackson, 2022). Yet academic knowledge, teaching and research have also been complicit in continually advancing technology and engineering techniques to require ever more energy consumption and associated carbon emission equivalent increases, with evidenced disastrous consequences for the majority of human and non-human life on Earth (Ripple *et al.*, 2024). Our changing climate causes a raft of unpredictable, interlinked, complex impacts. These include changes in food systems, sea level rises, ocean acidification, increased storm intensity, vast forest fires, fracturing human societies, climate migration, biodiversity crisis and ecosystem collapse being just some examples (IPCC, 2022). We have evidence and relatively reliable predictions of these impacts.

We also stand on the precipice of potentially the most profound changes in human history through the astonishingly rapid and mostly uncontrolled expansion of artificial intelligence (AI), with the development towards more powerful artificial general intelligence (AGI). In this case, computing develops near human-level intelligence with the ability to learn, adapt, conduct human intellectual tasks and likely go beyond human intellectual capacity (Suleyman and Bhaskar, 2023). AGI has the potential to change the world in unpredictable ways. We mostly understand the cause and effect of our current human-led technological and political decisions, but we do not understand and may not be able to control the turmoil resulting from AGI. We need to be resilient, to be adaptive and to consider new ways of thinking, teaching, assessing and supporting our students for unexpected futures in this new world.

Our universities provide evidence of anthropogenic impacts and develop some solutions, yet we also participate in the technological and political advances that cause those impacts. Our education systems must recognise their role in the harm leveraged upon our planet, historically, now and in the future. However, recognition is insufficient. It is our moral duty as educators to respond. This book is about leading and supporting changes to our higher education system through ESD. ESD is not being positioned here as *the* solution to all these challenges, but we have no doubt it sits at the centre of education contributing positively and not negatively to an unpredictable world.

## Education for Sustainable Development

The positioning of ESD is crucial. When one considers the complexity and scale of the interconnected challenges briefly outlined above, it is easy to consider this field of principles and practices to be negative and overwhelming. However, that is not the case. ESD is about challenging embedded norms, accepting uncertainty, embracing creativity and the possibilities of critical consciousness and viewing education and its intended outcomes through a distinctively different lens. It is a collaboration between academics, higher education professional services staff, the community, organisations and most crucially students. ESD is about providing quality education for our students. Education that is transdisciplinary through critical, futures and systems thinking coupled with pragmatic implementation and self-awareness.

Addressing the enormity of the sustainability challenges can be emotionally exhausting, especially when working in this field for extended periods of time. Sustainability can be, and frequently is, anxiety-inducing for us as university staff as well as for our students. We need to be cognisant of the mental health challenges which are demonstrated through the increasingly researched field of eco-anxiety or climate anxiety. We, as academic colleagues, need to support each other, as well as supporting our young people, many of whom are learning about the true depth and complexities of the challenges for the first time. ESD has always been formed around a compassionate, supportive community, and it is crucial that this continues.

ESD recognises the need for collaboration to address the challenges, not just within higher education institutions but also across the sector. In the world of academia, high-impact research is generally partnership-based, with many funding awards requiring international teams and multidisciplinary projects. This team-based endeavour is not replicated in the learning, teaching, assessment and student experience domain of university delivery. A primary institutional incentive for education activities is the recruitment of students for the receipt of fees, placing institutions in competition between one another rather than offering rewards for working together. An educational incentive purpose is to design distinctive, unique, impactful, employability-focused teaching, learning and assessment that can transform students' lives and to keep them to ourselves to attract the best and the highest number of students. The system is structured to disincentivise the sharing of innovative pedagogies, yet the need for collaboration sits at the heart of the sustainability challenge and the discipline of ESD.

Despite the structural challenges for collaborative education, it is the experience of the authors that the ESD community has a strong history of collegiality, recognising the need to work together and acting accordingly. This communal approach to pedagogies is vital for a variety of reasons. ESD requires inter- and transdisciplinary approaches, with the different perspectives offered by practitioners across the community a core component of the systems thinking necessary for tackling sustainability. The extracurricular activities that add richness to the student experience are more successful when actioned across the whole of the sector, and this can be achieved by colleagues in different institutions working with student support organisations such as Students Organising for Sustainability (SOS) to build and deliver impactful programmes that develop knowledge, skills, experience, employability benefits and positive sustainability impacts. Finally, we need to enthuse and support each other, not solely within our home institutions but across all institutions. We need to reignite the fires of jaded, worried and exhausted academics. These are the reasons why a collegiate approach must lie at the heart of everything we do in the challenging, emotional and rewarding field of ESD.

ESD offers a transformative agenda in which students and staff collaborate and explore not only *what*, but also *why* and *how* we must conceptualise and act on sustainability. Content and modes of the teaching and learning that occur within our higher education institutions will determine the fate of people and planet, as well as (re)defining the potential roles of universities.

Within ESD, there lies the risk that it is simply considered to be a 'worthy' cause, and this can easily isolate colleagues who mistakenly believe it is not relevant to them and their discipline. This book intends to bust these types of myths. Not only through the demonstration that ESD is often multidisciplinary, interdisciplinary or even transdisciplinary, but also that it is innovative and impactful with clear outputs that benefit graduates and universities, not only society and the environment (as if that isn't enough in itself). Put simply, ESD is high-quality education. It is good education, with the aspiration of being transformative education.

The aims of this book are to offer a critical debate on ESD, linking theory and practice, and to encourage those with an interest in higher education to explore or deepen engagement with principles and perspectives of ESD. With this book, we seek to develop an enhanced critical understanding of ESD and what it can achieve for the higher education community. We aim to shine the brightest of lights on this growing field of complex academic enquiry and transformative practice with the purpose of strengthening theory-action-impact links and also to stimulate a deeper critical conversation within the academic community.

The timing is right for this book. Most universities now have a committee to develop sustainability in the curriculum, learning for sustainability, social responsibility and environmental education or some other framing of ESD. The UK Quality Assurance Agency, with Advance HE, refreshed the new UK ESD guidance in March 2021 (QAA and Advance HE, 2021). We are now seeing an increase in requests for advice and resources by individuals, groups and institutions wishing to do more or deeper ESD. Student bodies have been demanding more ESD for years and are supporting the efforts of institutions to meet these needs.

## The Themes, Structure and Content of the Book

Throughout this book, we use the terms 'higher education institutions' and 'universities' almost interchangeably, depending on the topic of the chapter, but we recognise that higher education is also offered through colleges, degree apprenticeship programmes and vocational and creative arts institutions, such as colleges of art or conservancies. However, we will primarily use the terms 'higher education', 'higher education institution' and 'universities' for degree providers across the chapters. Degree providers differ in their use of terminology around curriculum design and delivery. A single defined unit delivering teaching, reading, practical work and assessment for one specific focused area may be termed a 'unit' or 'module' depending on the nomenclature used in the institution. These titles are used interchangeably throughout the book, reflecting the terms used in the institution of the author(s) and the case study or example being addressed. A curriculum formed of a number of 'units' (the number varies depending on the institution) is delivered as a degree 'course' or a 'programme', again depending on the prescribed terminology of the institution. We will also use these terms interchangeably to reflect that students normally refer to their 'course', but most institutions manage their curricula and quality infrastructure around 'programmes'. This mixed terminology approach is adopted, as we do not wish to isolate any reader from the academic, professional services or student community through alienating language.

This book will open with an in-depth critical investigation of ESD in Chapter 2. We will explore the evolution of principles and practices, its role within the higher education sphere, where it has come from, where it is now and where it may lead in future pedagogies and impact. The links with the United Nations Sustainable Development Goals will be introduced here, a focal point worthy of critique that we will return to at various junctures through the book.

The potential and execution of higher education institutions in the delivery of ESD as a whole institutional endeavour will be introduced in Chapter 3. We will question the purpose of higher education and universities, recognising the pressures on leaders and colleagues whilst also questioning if a truly sustainable university is achievable.

The middle part of the book will interrogate how we deliver our education within our institutions. Chapter 4 will investigate the position of ESD in terms of individual academic disciplines, considering the possibilities of single discipline methods whilst exploring multidisciplinary, interdisciplinary and transdisciplinary approaches. The structural and theoretical perspectives of delivering teaching, learning and assessment through our curricula will be addressed in Chapter 5, including how competencies provide the framework for impactful education for our students. Pedagogy is the driving force for teaching and learning. This will be examined from a critical perspective in Chapter 6 through an exploration of the variety of approaches that can be adopted and adapted through ESD. The transformative nature of innovative assessment will be explored in Chapter 7. This is the area of greatest personal investment for our students, so it is crucial that the book delves into the rich variety of assessment forms and case studies that are actioned across the higher education sector and with external partners.

Education does not exist without research enquiry and knowledge exchange. Chapter 8 will demonstrate the critical inclusion of teaching and research practice links whilst considering how and why academics and students engage with inter- and transdisciplinary investigation. ESD requires compassionate and impactful leadership in order to deliver its transformational potential. The links to equality, diversity, inclusion and well-being are clear and will be addressed in Chapter 9.

Without the requisite knowledge and skill set of staff within a higher education institution, there is little doubt that sustainability endeavours are set for failure. All staff, whether academic, professional services or operational, require support and resources if we are to achieve successful whole institution sustainability. The mechanisms for professional development will be studied in Chapter 10. The success or failure of this and all dimensions of ESD requires robust mechanisms of monitoring and evaluation for quality provision. Practical tools and frameworks for monitoring are explored in Chapter 11.

Arguably, the greatest indicator of success in ESD lies in the work and impact of our students after graduation. The future work of our graduates is where ESD can have the most profound of scalable and temporal contributions to society and the environment. Chapter 12 will dive deeply into how higher education institutions can support students pursuing sustainability (or 'green') jobs through competencies and skills development in the curriculum, with graduate stories to showcase how career paths are forged along with the diversity of opportunity available to our students upon their departure from our institutions. Finally, Chapter 13 will present a deep and enriching evaluation of the primary outcomes of each of the chapters, highlight the key themes for readers to reflect upon and identify crucial areas for future research.

## The Audience

The intended audience for this book is everyone with an interest and involvement in higher education. ESD is not a closed field of practice and enquiry, nor a closed community of scholars. It extends across every aspect of higher education, with tentacles reaching deep into every single nook and cranny. There is no part of higher education where

ESD is not important. Sustainability is crucial and of the utmost urgency for everyone, and with education being the focal point for potential solutions, it is of direct relevance to the whole community.

The most immediately obvious audience for the book is the educators who are responsible for curriculum design, teaching, learning and assessment, engaging with stakeholders and supporting students with emotional well-being and building employability portfolios for their future careers. Whilst this is the core audience, this is a rather restrictive view. The book also has direct relevance for professional services colleagues involved in curriculum quality and enhancement. It is also germane for operational teams to assist their understanding of the perspectives of academics during the design of curricula and how they may be able to develop collaborative teaching and assessments that also build positive sustainability impacts within the institutions, in addition to enhancing the employability prospects of students receiving the teaching and assessments.

This is also a book for all involved in leadership of any form in higher education. Senior management colleagues are crucial in driving the intellectual and structural change required for ESD. Without support from the top of an institution, and indeed the sector, the transformation needed will not be able to take place. The leadership requested by this book extends further from senior institutional management to faculty, school, programme, module, student unions, societies, outreach and individual students themselves becoming leaders.

Finally, this book intends to serve students. Our university students and graduates have enormous collective power. They are our future political, business, community and thought leaders who will enter a world that is rapidly changing, unpredictable and complex. Our higher education system must enable them to develop the skills, capacities and competencies to envisage and pursue more sustainable futures. We need to equip them for this world, to enable them to fulfil their potential and to develop specific skills for entrepreneurship, employment and civil society contributions with all sustainability implications (positive and negative) at the forefront of their minds. All students should have the opportunity to understand how curricula, teaching, assessment, professional development, skills enhancement and experience impact their studies and future prospects. This book opens the entire ESD process to students and invites their involvement throughout.

## The Authorship Group

The authors of this book work across different higher education institutions, each with distinct challenges that collectively reflect the complexities we face across the higher education landscape. Although we are not linked by geography and mission statements, we are unified by our collective, deep and lasting commitment to and expertise in ESD. Cumulatively, we have over 300 years of experience of thinking, researching, designing, implementing, teaching, assessing, practicing, publishing and reflecting in ESD.

The authorship group first convened to write the 2021 Advance HE and Quality Assurance Agency (QAA) Education for Sustainable Development Guidance (second edition), along with some other colleagues. As rewarding as that publication was, it became clear that there is a need for a far more substantial book, rooted in the academic literature but flourishing through our substantial combined expertise and practice. It is necessary to dive far deeper into the complexity of the academic and institutional issues that frame ESD and to provide examples, ideas and suggested solutions. This is the 'inspiration' for this book, both in terms of its totality and each of the component chapters, and we hope you find it to be of value to you, your students, your institution and the sector and that it prompts further critical analysis and publications from existing and new ESD practitioners.

## How to Use This Book

As with all books of this nature, we recognise that the majority of readers will not consume this book from the start to the end in sequential order. Although we obviously hope that you will. We recognise that some chapters are likely to be of greater interest than others depending on the focus of your role or what theme you would like to investigate deeper. Each chapter has been written to fit within the central premise of the book as outlined earlier in this particular chapter, but equally, each can be read independently as a stand-alone text.

To fit the collaborative ethos of ESD, we encourage readers to share this book with colleagues – academics, professional services, operational, external and of course students. We passionately advocate for debate on the many vital complex questions and systems thinking, with grounded possible solutions. It may be online, or it may be in person, but we hope discussions will engage wider than the immediate existing ESD community. We ask that you discuss the issues, questions and ideas with as many colleagues as possible. This might be as part of general pedagogic conversations, programme development meetings, curriculum design, quality assurance and enhancement, teaching design, assessment construction and student experience strategic development. The content of the book is of crucial importance and relevance for the whole of the higher education community and should not be wrapped up solely within the constraints of existing ESD colleagues.

Most of all, we hope readers will critically engage with the ideas, analyse the content, explore further within the references and apply the knowledge and practices to your own work. We hope you do so with renewed passion, energy, vitality and an invigorated sense that yes, we are in the midst of upsetting and challenging times but that collectively we can change the world for the better through ESD.

## References

Caesar, L., Sakschewski, B., Andersen, L.S., Beringer, T., Braun, J., Dennis, D., Gerten, D., Heilemann, A., Kaiser, J., Kitzmann, N.K., Loriani, S., Lucht, W., Ludescher, J., Martin, M., Mathesius, S., Paolucci, A., te Wierick, S. and Rockstrom, J. (2024) *Planetary Health Check Report 2024*. Potsdam Institute for Climate Impact Research, Potsdam, Germany. Available at: https://www.planetaryhealthcheck.org/storyblok-cdn/f/301438/x/a4efc3f6d5/planetaryhealthcheck2024_report.pdf [Accessed 31 July 2024].

Dattani, S., Rodés-Guirao, L., Ritchie, H., Ortiz-Ospina, E. and Roser, M. (2023) 'Life Expectancy', *OurWorldinData.org*. Available at: https://ourworldindata.org/life-expectancy [Accessed 31 July 2024].

Diaz-Maurin, F. and Gaulkin, T. (2022) 'Nowhere to hide: how a nuclear war would kill you – and almost everyone else', *Bulletin of the Atomic Scientists*. Available at:https://thebulletin.org/2022/10/nowhere-to-hide-how-a-nuclear-war-would-kill-you-and-almost-everyone-else/ [Accessed 31 July 2024].

Estes, R.J. (2019) 'The "Rich" and "Poor": The Widening Income and Development Gap Between Rich and Poor Nations Worldwide', in Brulé, G. and Suter, C. (eds.) *Wealth(s) and Subjective Well-Being*. Social Indicators Research Series, vol 76. Springer, Cham. DOI: 10.1007/978-3-030-05535-6_21

International Monetary Fund (IMF). (2022) *World Inequality Report 2022*. Available at: https://wir2022.wid.world [Accessed 31 July 2024].

IPCC (2022) *Climate Change 2022: Impacts, Adaptation and Vulnerability*. Contribution of Working Group II to the Sixth Assessment Report of the Intergovernmental Panel on Climate Change [H.-O. Pörtner, D.C. Roberts, M. Tignor, E.S. Poloczanska, K. Mintenbeck, A. Alegría, M. Craig, S. Langsdorf, S. Löschke, V. Möller, A. Okem, B. Rama (eds.)]. Cambridge University Press. Cambridge University Press, Cambridge, UK and New York, NY, USA, 3056 pp., DOI:10.1017/9781009325844.

O'Brien, P.K. (1977) 'Agriculture and the industrial revolution', *The Economic History Review*, 30(1), pp. 166–181. DOI:10.2307/2595506.

Ortiz, J.D. and Jackson, R. (2022) 'Understanding Eunice Foote's 1856 experiments: heat absorption by atmospheric gases', *The Royal Society Journal of the History of Science*, 76(1), pp. 67–84. DOI:10.1098/rsnr.2020.0031.

Our World in Data (2024) 'Population by country, available from 10,000 BCE to 2023, based on data and estimates from Hyde (2023); Gapminder (2022), UN WPP (2024)'. Available at: https://ourworldindata.org/grapher/population?time=1000.latest [Accessed 31 July 2024].

Paletta, A. and Bonoli, A. (2019) 'Governing the university in the perspective of the United Nations 2030 Agenda: The case of the University of Bologna', *International Journal of Sustainability in Higher Education*, 20(3), pp. 500–514. DOI:10.1108/IJSHE-02-2019-0083.

QAA (Quality Assurance Agency for Higher Education) and Advance HE (2021) *Education for Sustainable Development Guidance*. Available at: https://www.qaa.ac.uk/the-quality-code/education-for-sustainable-development [Accessed 31 July 2024].

Ripple, W.J. et al. (2024) 'The 2024 state of the climate report: Perilous times on planet Earth', *BioScience*, biae087. DOI:10.1093/biosci/biae087.

Ritchie, H. (2018) 'How child mortality has declined in the last two centuries', *OurWorldinData.org*. Available at: https://ourworldindata.org/child-mortality-global-overview [Accessed 31 July 2024].

Ritchie, H., Samborska, V., Ahuja, N., Ortiz-Ospina, E. and Roser, M. (2023) 'Global Education', *OurWorldinData.org*. Available at: https://ourworldindata.org/global-education [Accessed 31 July 2024].

Rodrigue, J.P. (2020) *The Geography of Transport Systems* (5th ed.). Routledge. DOI:10.4324/9780429346323.

Suleyman, M. and Bhaskar, M. (2023). The Coming Wave. Bodley Head. ISBN: 1847927483.

U.S. Department of Energy (n.d.) *The Manhattan Project: an interactive history*. Available at: https://www.osti.gov/opennet/manhattan-project-history/People/CivilianOrgs/university-of-california.html#:~:text=Three%20academic%20institutions%20stand%20out,and%20the%20University%20of%20California [Accessed 31 July 2024].

World Bank (2023) '2023 in Nine Charts: A Growing Inequality'. Available at: https://www.worldbank.org/en/news/feature/2023/12/18/2023-in-nine-charts-a-growing-inequality [Accessed 31 July 2024].

World Health Organisation (WHO) (2023) *Tracking universal health coverage: 2023 global monitoring report*. Geneva. Licence: CC BY-NC-SA 3.0 IGO. Available at: https://www.who.int/publications/i/item/9789240080379 [Accessed 31 July 2024].

Chapter 2

# Education for Sustainable Development

## Definitions, Debates and Design

*Elizabeth A. C. Price and Rehema M. White*

## Introduction

Education for Sustainable Development (ESD) has arisen in recognition of the need for people to develop the knowledge, skills and capacities to create a more sustainable world. Many different definitions and conceptualisations of sustainable development have been proposed, and there is vigorous debate about their relative merits (e.g. Robinson, 2004; Redclift, 2005; Springett, 2005; White *et al.*, 2023a; Martin et al., 2024). Such debate has extended to the form of underpinning education that will prepare people to envision and pursue sustainable futures. This debate is a mixed blessing for this field of enquiry and practice. Whilst a lack of clarity around the term can limit action, and impede collaboration, a degree of fluidity also enables different groups to develop their own contextualised understanding. Regardless, there is growing recognition of the value of ESD for all learners, and of the unique role that universities play in the transformation of individuals, institutions and societies towards more sustainable futures (Sterling, 2013; Price *et al.*, 2021). In the previous chapter, we outlined the need for ESD. In this chapter, we will describe sustainable development perspectives, explain some conceptual models and highlight the contemporary policy framework. We will then outline the history and framing of ESD, including topics, pedagogies and competencies, and consider what this means for education as a whole and for higher education specifically.

## Sustainable Development

### *The Emergence of Sustainable Development*

We face significant, interconnected global challenges, including biodiversity loss, climate change, pollution, extreme social inequality and health threats, with the vulnerable in society being most affected by the consequences of these issues, yet being least responsible for their impacts (UN, 2015; Oxfam International, 2023; Richardson *et al.*, 2023). The damage caused by human activities has long been felt by many Indigenous peoples and natural environments around the world, during centuries of colonisation and imperial expansion (Vásquez-Fernández and Cash Ahenakew pii tai poo taa, 2020), but large-scale human environmental damage was eventually also recognised in countries in the Global North. In 1962, Rachel Carson published a heartfelt call for change in '*Silent Spring*', lamenting the decline in bird populations caused by excessive use of chemicals and industrial agriculture (Carson, 1962). Since then, a clarion call for nature has highlighted

DOI: 10.4324/9781003451563-2

a continuous decline in biodiversity and the war for environmental protection has been waged (see Cowie *et al.*, 2022; Jarić *et al.*, 2022). Simultaneously, there was recognition of growing social inequality and the need to address increasing poverty caused by expanding human populations, colonial legacies, conflict and environmental change in ways that included local people rather than just donating aid (e.g. Chambers, 1983; Vásquez-Fernández and Cash Ahenakew pii tai poo taa, 2020; Martin *et al.*, 2024). The term 'sustainable development' first emerged globally in the 1980s in response to the growing awareness of the need to balance social and economic development with environmental stewardship (IUCN-UNEP-WWF, 1980; Tilbury, 1995; Robinson, 2004). The 1987 Brundtland Report, 'Our Common Future', defined sustainable development as 'meeting the needs of the present without compromising the ability of future generations to meet their own needs' (UN, 1987, p. 41). Sustainable development is now seen to be an aspiration and an organising principle for local and global development that supports the wellbeing of both people and the planet, and is a journey rather than a destination (UN 2015; UNESCO 2016). The evolution of sustainable development is integral to the emergence of ESD, but it is a contested concept with different definitions (see also Agbedahin, 2019; McCowan, 2023). We thus now consider some relevant frames and models.

### *The Interplay between Environmental, Social and Economic Goals*

There are different perspectives on sustainable development (e.g. Robinson, 2004; Redclift, 2005; Springett, 2005; White *et al.*, 2023a; Martin *et al.*, 2024; UNESCO, 2016), and it has been a contested concept and term (Robinson, 2004; Springett, 2005; Agbedahin, 2019; McCowan, 2023). Fundamentally, some actors, especially Indigenous groups and those seeking more radical sustainability transitions, argue that capitalist, extractive, colonial processes created unsustainability, and that in order to achieve human and planetary wellbeing, we need economic reform and respectful, relational interconnections between people and with nature (Springett, 2005; Datta, 2015; Vásquez-Fernández and Cash Ahenakew pii tai poo taa, 2020; Martin *et al.*, 2024). Others suggest that current dominant agendas around eco-efficiency and green growth have overridden a spiritual view and concepts regarding sufficiency and relationships and place (Robinson, 2004; Martin *et al.*, 2024). However, conceptualisations related to practical action for sustainable development often identify the need to integrate environmental, social and economic goals and strategies.

Many of the differences amongst models and between philosophies of sustainable development derive from diverse ways of understanding, prioritising or relating these aspects. The original idea of three pillars (environment, society, economy) has been largely refuted (Figure 2.1), due to recognition that these aspects interact, they are not of equal importance and they are static and not future facing (Adams, 2006; East and White, 2016). A Venn diagram then depicted environment, society and economy as overlapping arenas but suggested that each arena was of equivalent size and produced only a small desirable space. The notion of strong sustainability (Neumayer, 1999; Dietz and Neumayer, 2007) distinguished the characters of environment, society and economy and highlighted that natural capital cannot always be exchanged for financial capital; in other words, we cannot always buy ourselves out of an environmental problem. Various graphic illustrations have since shown how our actions are constrained by nature, natural capital, natural resources, environmental limits or ecological integrity, depending on the perspective of the author (Figure 2.1).

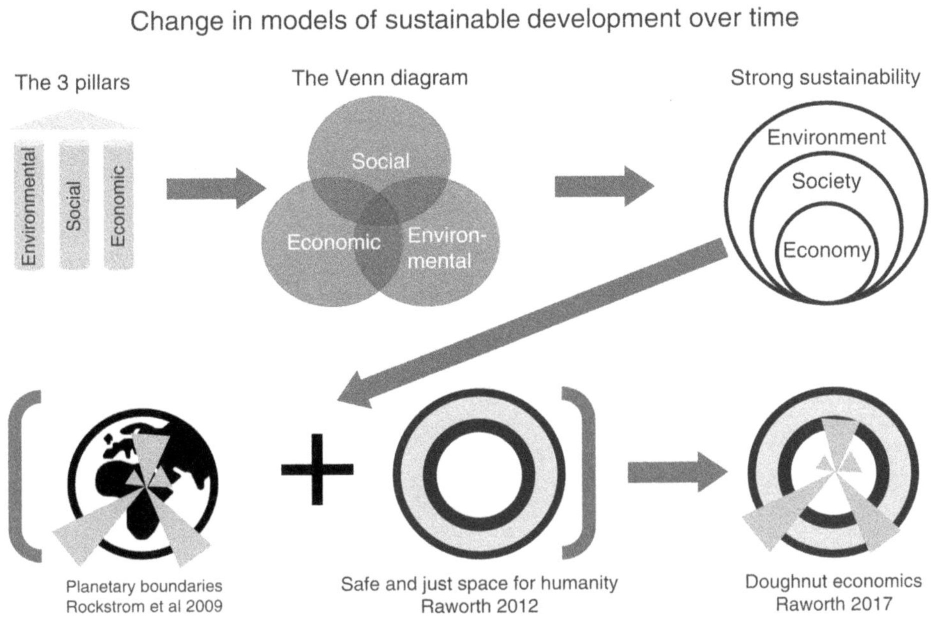


*Figure 2.1* Change in models of sustainable development over time, demonstrating a shift from the three pillars to the interacting Venn diagram and then strong sustainability. Evidence that we are overstepping planetary boundaries was demonstrated along with the need for a safe and just space for humanity within the environmental ceiling. (*Source*: Author drawn adapted from Rockström *et al.*, 2009; Raworth, 2012, 2017a,b.)

### *Planetary Boundaries*

The scale of human impacts was realised when the fragility of our small blue planet was captured in photographs of the Earth from space in 1968. Recent models recognise that we are overstepping the capacities of our planet to accommodate anthropogenic impacts. The concept of environmental stewardship that sustainable development seeks to achieve (IUCN-UNEP-WWF, 1980) was brought into sharp focus by the planetary boundaries model, which presents a set of nine planetary boundaries within which humanity can operate safely (Rockström *et al.*, 2009). The nine boundaries represent components of Earth system critically affected by anthropogenic activities and relevant to Earth's overall state, for example climate change and biosphere integrity. Recent updates indicate that society's activities have already crossed six of the nine planetary boundaries, while simultaneously pressure in all boundary processes is increasing (Richardson *et al.* 2023) (Figure 2.2).

### *Doughnut Economics*

Sustainable development must not only promote environmental stewardship, but must also balance this with socio-economic development, within the means of the planet (IUCN-UNEP-WWF, 1980; Tilbury, 1995). The debate around economic growth has been divisive (Robinson, 2004; Chankseliani and McCowan, 2021). More recent iterations of sustainable development models include alternative reframing of economics, including calls for

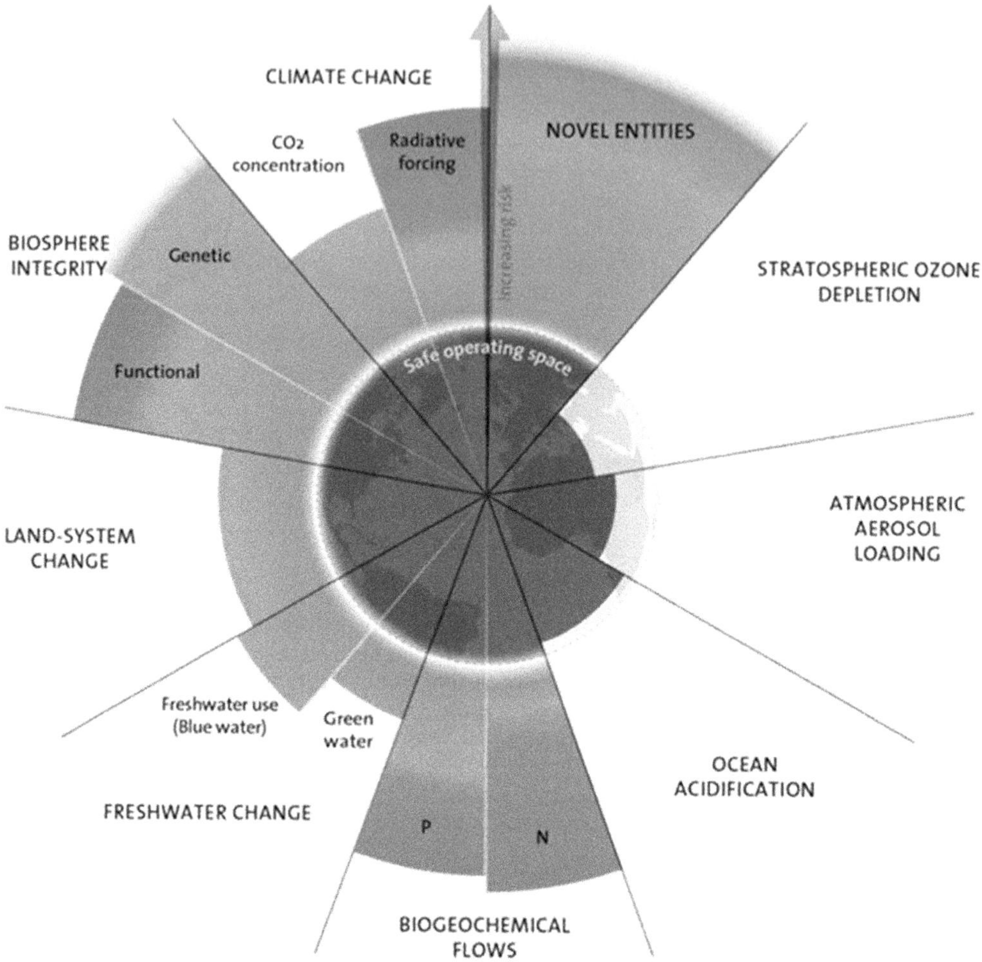


*Figure 2.2* Planetary boundaries 2023. Six of nine planetary boundaries are being crossed, while simultaneously pressure in all boundary processes is increasing. The central dark grey zone represents the safe operating space below the boundary, the lighter grey outside the safe operating space represents the zone of increasing risk. P = phosphorus, N = nitrogen, (Steffen *et al.*, 2015). Green water relates to the water available to plants (Wang-Erlandsson et *al.*, 2022). (*Source*: Azote for Stockholm Resilience Centre based on analysis in Richardson *et al.*, 2023; Wang-Erlandsson *et al.*, 2022; Persson *et al.*, 2022 and Steffen *et al.*, 2015, CC BY-NC-ND 3.0.)

degrowth, post growth, green economy and circular economies (Belmonte-Ureña *et al.*, 2021; Martin *et al.*, 2024), prosperity without growth (Jackson, 2009), sharing economies (Boar *et al.*, 2020) or some combination of these concepts. One effective way of depicting a new relationship between the three principal aspects (environment, society and economy), illustrates that a strong economy, sound science and good governance are merely drivers towards the principal goals of flourishing human societies and living within environmental limits, rather than being themselves the main objectives (Defra, 2005).

Doughnut economics is a conceptual model that links to the planetary boundaries perspective by defining a doughnut-shaped, safe and just space between planetary boundaries and social boundaries in which humanity can thrive (Raworth, 2017a, b). The doughnut is a space encompassed by two concentric rings: a social foundation, below which lie shortfalls in wellbeing, and an ecological ceiling, beyond which lies an overshoot of planetary boundaries (Raworth, 2017a, b) (Figure 2.3). The 12 social foundation indicators, such as health and education, are derived from the UN Sustainable Development Goals (SDGs; UN, 2015). The nine ecological ceiling indicators, such as climate change, are defined by the planetary boundaries framework. The doughnut thus highlights the dependence of human wellbeing on planetary health. The concurrent social shortfall and ecological overshoot highlighted by doughnut economics reflect deep inequalities (see also Oxfam International, 2023) and imply the need for a renewal of economic policymaking (Raworth, 2017a, b).

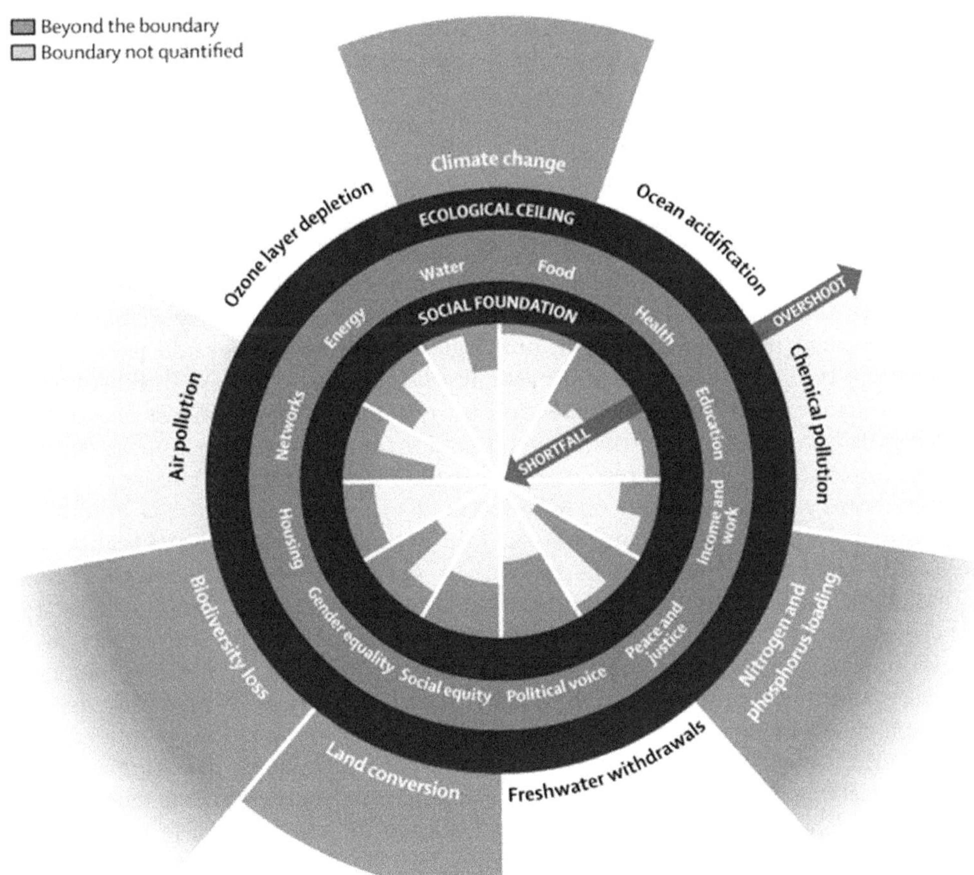


*Figure 2.3* The doughnut of social and planetary boundaries. Shortfalls and overshoot in the doughnut. Black circles show the social foundation and ecological ceiling, encompassing a safe and just space for humanity. Grey wedges show shortfalls in the social foundation or overshoot of the ecological ceiling. (*Source*: Kate Raworth and Christian Guthier CC-BY-SA 4.0, Raworth (2017a, b), Elsevier, CC BY 4.0.)

### *Sustainable Development Perspectives*

Universities may engage with sustainable development in ways that are projective, expressive or constructive (McCowan, 2023):

- Projective engagement reflects how educational institutions progress sustainable development, most notably through teaching students, research and community engagement.
- Expressive engagement highlights their impact on the environment and interactions in the community.
- Constructive engagement refers to scrutinising what sustainable development actually means, where sustainable development is understood as a *'terrain of debate'*. This process involves ontological dimensions (those relating to being and existence), epistemological ones (relating to the nature of knowledge) and axiological ones (relating to values and purposes) (McCowan, 2023).

The latter engagement recognises the plurality of perspectives that can be held on sustainable development (McCowan, 2023). Sustainable development is a moral and intellectual issue, reflecting differently for those who see the path via progress, economic growth and unfettered global capitalism (Chankseliani and McCowan, 2021) and those who perceive it to be a more rights-based approach in which wellbeing, rather than profit, is emphasised (Freire, 1970; Ferraro *et al.*, 2011). In its recognition of the unsustainability of current societal processes, critical theory suggests that it is a political as well as technological agenda (Robinson, 2004; Springett, 2005). The diversity of discourse can facilitate transitions towards sustainability if spaces for dialogue are generated (Hull, 2008). For example, dominant western paradigms around the duality of humans and nature can benefit from engaging with ontologies for a more integrated perspective as held by many Indigenous peoples and particular groups and cultures (Robinson, 2004; Vasquez-Fernandez and Cash Ahenakew pii tai poo taa 2020; Martin *et al.*, 2024). A shift towards human and more-than-human equity can acknowledge imperialist intentions to extract and use natural resources rather than live in and with nature.

Furthermore, varying positions on sustainable development derive from different ontologies and epistemologies, or conceptions of the nature of knowledge and reality. These positions broadly align, firstly, with a positivist position in which objective reality is paramount, scientific measurement and reason are required and technological solutions are believed to drive a route to sustainability. Secondly, an anti-positivist perspective suggests that much of what we see is socially constructed, that we need to understand experience and that we cannot measure all of the consequences of pursuing visions of sustainable development (Burrell and Morgan, 1979; Jackson, 2016).

In addition, views may differ on how transformative sustainable development should be. Civil society responses often favour radical change whilst governments tend to pursue iterative change, unless there is an ambitious leader or an external crisis that creates opportunity for change (Robinson, 2004).

> The different perspectives of sustainable development include viewing it as a model to improve current systems (endorsed by those focusing on viable economic growth), a call for major reforms (supported by those who advocate for a green economy and technological innovation) and an imperative for a larger transformation in power structures and embedded values of society (supported by transition movements).
>
> (UNESCO, 2016)

Despite ambiguities in the concept of sustainable development, 'it is better to engage with the notion than not to engage' since it offers 'an invitation to examine deeply and deliberately... the kind of society and planet that we would like and that can endure through time' (McCowan, 2023). Put simply, sustainable development is 'an aspirational ongoing process of addressing social, environmental and economic concerns to create a better world' (Advance HE/QAA, 2021). This dialogical process is also captured by Robinson (2004) 'sustainability is itself the emergent property of a conversation about what kind of world we collectively want to live in now and in the future' and Martin *et al.* (2024) 'we should accept that [sustainability] pathways are normative and political, intersecting debates about what should be done with the art of what is possible'.

### *Policy Frameworks and the UN Sustainable Development Goals*

Policy frameworks reflect the different perspectives on sustainable development articulated above. They have either privileged economic growth and extractive policies or supported a vision of human wellbeing and liberal rights where humans are stewards of the earth (Chankseliani and McCowan, 2021; McCowan, 2023). Examples of the latter include 'Buen Vivir', or 'Ubuntu', concepts that draw on Indigenous knowledge to offer a framework for living well (Costanza *et al.*, 2016). Perspectives embedded in place, culture and context can be more meaningful to local people (White *et al.*, 2023b). There are increasing calls to recognise such frameworks in efforts for decolonisation and restorative justice (Vasquez-Fernandez and Cash Ahenakew pii tai poo taa, 2020).

#### *The UN Sustainable Development Goals*

Other policy frameworks have grappled to combine potentially paradoxical approaches and come to an (uneasy at times) consensus over common goals and practices. For example, the United Nations (UN) SDGs were a compromise hammered out through committees and with consultation with seven million people across different nations and interest groups to clarify an agreed pathway (East and White, 2016; Chankseliani and McCowan, 2021).

The UN Agenda for Transformation for 2030 states ambitious aspirations for dignity for all and that nobody be left behind, along with visions of a healthy environment (UN, 2015). It denotes a strategy for people, planet, prosperity, peace and partnership, lays out specific goals and creates an action and evaluation plan to enact this transformation. The UN SDGs succeeded the UN Millennium Goals (MDGs, UN, undated a) and were launched in 2015 to create a global framework and impetus for action in transforming our world for a more sustainable future with 17 SDGs and 169 associated targets at its heart (UN, 2015; UN, undated b; UNESCO, 2016) (Figure 2.4). Unlike the MDGs, they are universal, applying to all countries, sectors and scales, and they incorporate a wider scope of intention (UN 2015; East and White, 2016; Chankseliani and McCowan, 2021). The transformative aspirations of the SDGs cannot be achieved without dialogue and learning processes between stakeholders (Sachs *et al.*, 2019).

Since they were first launched, there has been increased scrutiny of the SDGs. One challenge has been how to tackle the interrelationships and possible conflicts between goals. There are interlinkages, synergies and trade-offs between the different SDGs and their targets (Pradhan et al., 2017) (Figure 2.5). For example, SDG1: No poverty, has a synergetic relationship (where progress in one goal favours progress in another) with most

*Figure 2.4* United Nations Sustainable Development Goals. (*Source*: https://www.un.org/sustainabledevelopment/ The content of this publication has not been approved by the United Nations and does not reflect the views of the United Nations or its officials or Member States.)

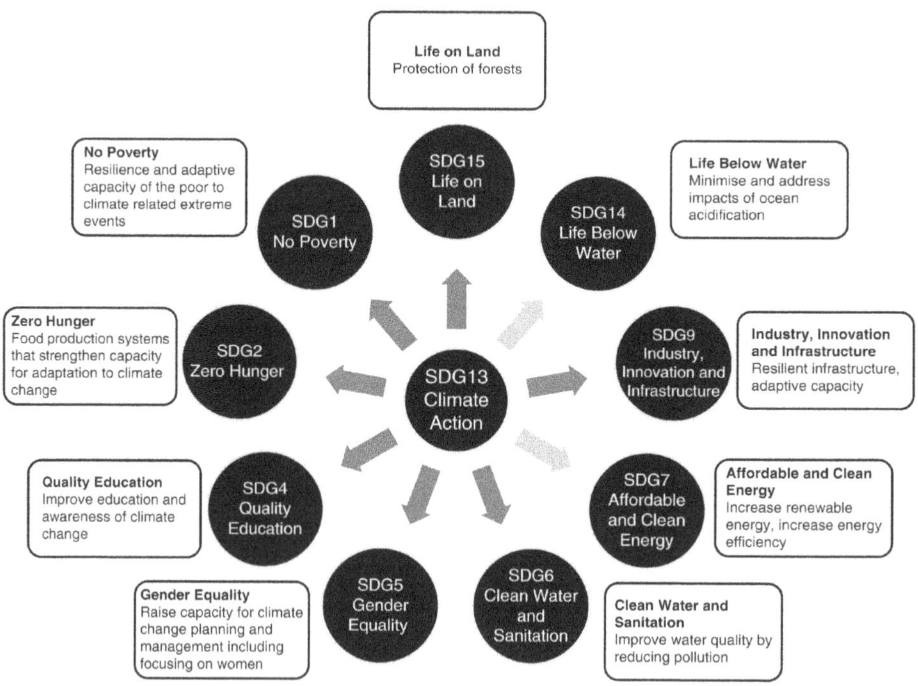


*Figure 2.5* An example of interlinkages between SDGs. Dark grey arrows represent explicitly linked SDGs, light grey arrows represent substantially linked SDGs. (*Source*: Redrawn from A Nexus Approach For The SDGs, UN undated c.)

of the others, whereas SDG12: Responsible consumption and production, is the goal most commonly associated with trade-offs (where progress in one goal hinders progress in another) (Pradhan *et al.*, 2017; Fonseca *et al.*, 2020). However, for most countries, positive correlations among the SDGs largely outweigh the negative ones (Pradhan *et al.*, 2017). Some of the most common trade-offs derive from tensions between environmental protection and economic growth (Eisenmenger *et al.*, 2020; Fonseca *et al.*, 2020). These relate to a paradox within Agenda 2030 in which there were some supporting groups favouring a post-World War II, international development mode of economic growth and others favouring more liberal forms of prosperity and possible consideration of degrowth models (at least within developed countries) (Chankseliani and McCowan, 2021). In fact, the SDGs are rejected by some researchers, who argue that the SDGs mostly maintain the current sustainability-through-growth paradigm, and thus exacerbate biodiversity loss, climate change and subsequent impoverishment of future generations (Kopnina, 2020).

A second issue relates to the diverse nature of each SDG. For example, SDG 16: Peace, Justice and Strong Institutions and SDG 17: Partnerships for the Goals clearly underpin all other SDGs and are essential to facilitate outcomes (Fonseca *et al.*, 2020). Furthermore, it has been recently suggested that SDG 13 (Climate Action) 'is the 21st century's greatest opportunity to drive forward all the Sustainable Development Goals' (UN, 2023). Thirdly, there are difficulties in obtaining quality data by which to evaluate and progress the goals (Sachs *et al.*, 2019).

Despite these potentially paradoxical characteristics, when considered as an indivisible whole, the SDGs are useful in representing a wide framing and scope of sustainable development, illustrating a holistic view of interconnected environmental, economic, cultural and social issues and dimensions and encouraging interdisciplinarity and systems thinking to recognise and understand relationships between them (Sterling, 2013; UNESCO, 2017; Price *et al.*, 2021). They are also useful in that they act as a common language to enable academics to engage with government, private sector and civil society actors more easily around sustainable development. If we tackle them critically in education, we can generate discussion on philosophy, aspiration and action.

This section has outlined perspectives and models of sustainable development as a basis for scrutinising what ESD means. Different worldviews, disciplinary perspectives and cultural values create diverse framings of sustainable development and hence ESD. The next sections explore the emergence of ESD and how it can become an integral part of higher education.

## The Emergence of Education for Sustainable Development

Sustainable development and ESD are global terms which provide a framework for responding to environmental, social and economic challenges, with sustainable development from local and global perspectives as the ultimate goal of ESD (Agbedahin, 2019). However, simply providing more education will not create a sustainable society (UNESCO, 2017), since the most educated societies can leave the deepest ecological footprints (McKeown, 2002). As Orr (2004) advocates, 'the worth of education must now be measured against the standards of decency and human survival – the issues now looming so large before us in the twenty-first century. It is not education, but education of a certain kind, that will save us'. Quality ESD is about what people learn, its relevance to global challenges and how learners develop the skills and attitudes to respond to such challenges to create a sustainable future (UNESCO, 2014, 2017). More than this, it is an expression of critical enquiry that can facilitate transformative learning (Springett, 2005).

The precursor of ESD was the concept of 'environmental education', which developed from the 1970s with three perspectives on and approaches to environmental education – education *in* the environment (experiential, often outdoor, education – engaging the heart); education *about* the environment (providing information – an intellectual exercise) and education *for* the environment (critical and political education that aims to develop active participation and a sense of responsibility in learners – enabling hands on activity) (Robottom, 1992; Fien, 1993; Tilbury, 1995; Huckle and Sterling, 1996; Springett, 2005; Tilbury, 2015). In the 1990s, there was a shift in environmental education going beyond immediate environmental outcomes to an emphasis on longer term sustainability (Tilbury, 1995). It was recognised that environmental education had to re-orientate to also consider quality of life of all humans and to integrate development concerns (see also Orr, 1992; Fien, 1993). The term ESD was first coined by the World Conservation Strategy of 1980 (IUCN/UNEP/WWF, 1980), which intended to more closely consider the root social, political and economic causes of the environmental challenges of the time (Tilbury, 1995). This strategy already highlighted tensions between economic growth and environmental conservation. It preceded the Brundtland Commission report (WCED, 1987) and was further supported by the 1991 World Conservation Strategy – Caring for the Earth: a strategy for sustainable living, which proposed that 'education programmes reflect the importance of an ethic for living sustainably' (IUCN/UNEP/WWF, 1991, p. 5). Later summits reinforced the importance of this re-oriented educational agenda. Tilbury describes how '[t]his form of environmental education differs significantly from the apolitical, naturalist and scientific work that was carried out under the environmental education banner in the seventies and early eighties' (Tilbury, 1995, p. 195). She defines this educational shift as representing holism, the intersections of environment and development programmes, requiring attention in the whole curriculum and of the whole person, teaching about values and with action in relation to real issues, including critical education and leading to socially critical skills, supporting political literacy with a futures perspective. The emergent education for sustainability called for a process of critical enquiry into the complexity of sustainability and its economic, political, social, cultural, technological and environmental dimensions (Huckle, 1996). It 'incorporates critical education goals within an issue-based pedagogy' (Tilbury, 2015, p. 207).

Subsequent to the World Conservation Strategies, calls to promote integration of environment and development concepts in all educational programmes and to reorient education towards sustainable development were made in Agenda 21 (Chapter 36), an action plan for governments and other relevant stakeholders towards sustainable development adopted at the United Nations Conference on Environment and Development (Earth Summit) in Rio de Janeiro, Brazil in 1992 (United Nations, 1992). UNESCO was identified as the Task Manager of Chapter 36 of Agenda 21 (UNESCO, 1997). Environmental education expanded to encompass wider engagement with development issues such as market forces, cultural values, equitable decision-making, government action and the environmental impacts of human activities in an interdependent manner in the broader concept of ESD (UNESCO, 1997; McKeown and Hopkins, 2005; UNEP, 2008).

The relationship between environmental education and ESD has been contested (Lotz-Sisitka, 2007). Some authors consider that sustainable development continues a process of capitalism, neoliberalism, neocolonialism and extractivism, threatening nature and

Indigenous peoples, and privileging human development without respecting environmental limits (Kopnina, 2020; Bonnett, 2007; Meadows *et al.*, 1972). The need to focus on re-establishing respect for nature and our dependence on the environment along with decolonial approaches have led some countries and scholars to prefer to retain the concept of 'environmental education' rather than 'education for sustainable development'. In some regions of the world, there remains a distinction between ESD and environmental education, and in others, there has been a merging of the terms (Agbedahin, 2019; Castellanos and Queiruga-Dios, 2021). For example, in Latin America, research centres on environmental education, while in Europe the focus is on ESD, and in North America, there has been a convergence in the use of the terms environmental education and ESD (Castellanos and Queiruga-Dios, 2021). However, UNESCO has moved beyond the use of environmental education as a term to focus on ESD (Agbedahin, 2019), and ESD should be a process of critical enquiry that interrogates societal norms and challenges political hegemonies (Robinson, 2004; Springett, 2005; Martin *et al.*, 2024). Recently, the term Education for the SDGs (or ESDGs) has been used to mean providing learners with the knowledge, skills and mindsets to address the SDGs through their current or future roles (SDSN, 2020). Given the critiques and limited lifespan of the SDGs, we would agree with Kopnina (2020) that this term could potentially miss the wider holistic framing and critical enquiry of ESD. We thus adopt the term of ESD, and we now further unpack meanings and practices of this term.

## What Is ESD?

As with sustainable development, there are different perspectives and definitions of ESD (Box 2.1).

### Box 2.1 Evolving Definition of ESD Reflecting Changing Emphasis and Dynamic Thinking in the Area

'Education for sustainable development is the process of equipping students with the knowledge and understanding, skills and attributes needed to work and live in a way that safeguards environmental, social and economic wellbeing, both in the present and for future generations.

*Education for sustainable development means working with students to encourage them to:*

- *consider what the concept of global citizenship means in the context of their own discipline and in their future professional and personal lives*
- *consider what the concept of environmental stewardship means in the context of their own discipline and in their future professional and personal lives*
- *think about issues of social justice, ethics and wellbeing, and how these relate to ecological and economic factors*
- *develop a future-facing outlook; learning to think about the consequences of actions, and how systems and societies can be adapted to ensure sustainable futures'* (QAA and HEA, 2014).

> Education for Sustainable Development is the process of creating curricula, including subject-relevant content and pedagogy to support sustainable development.
>
> (Advance HE/QAA, 2021)

Advance HE/QAA (2021) advocated a framing of ESD by UNESCO (UNESCO, 2019a) which captures many aspects:

> ESD empowers learners to take informed decisions and responsible actions for environmental integrity, economic viability and a just society, for present and future generations, while respecting cultural diversity. It is about lifelong learning, and is an integral part of quality education. ESD is holistic and transformational education which addresses learning content and outcomes, pedagogy and the learning environment. It achieves its purpose by transforming society.
>
> (UNESCO, 2019a)

Subsequent UNESCO definitions reflect the dynamic nature of thinking in the area and highlight periods of emphasis on certain aspects:

> Education for Sustainable Development is a lifelong learning process and an integral part of quality education. It enhances the cognitive, social and emotional and behavioural dimensions of learning. It is holistic and transformational, and encompasses learning content and outcomes, pedagogy and the learning environment itself.
>
> (UNESCO, 2021)

More recently, ESD was defined as:

> Education for sustainable development (ESD) gives learners of all ages the knowledge, skills, values and agency to address interconnected global challenges including climate change, loss of biodiversity, unsustainable use of resources, and inequality. It empowers learners of all ages to make informed decisions and take individual and collective action to change society and care for the planet. ESD is a lifelong learning process and an integral part of quality education. It enhances the cognitive, socio-emotional and behavioural dimensions of learning and encompasses learning content and outcomes, pedagogy and the learning environment itself.
>
> (UNESCO, 2024)

A dialogical process in Scotland led to a definition:

> Learning for sustainability enables visioning of culturally and place-specific futures and contributes to the creation of a fair and flourishing society and empowerment, particularly of the currently disempowered, whilst ensuring we live within ecological limits. Such learning uses innovative, reflexive and potentially

transformative pedagogies and curricula to enable skills development and resilience and encourage people to explore value based worldviews. Learning promoted action requires a systems based, interdisciplinary, partnership approach with strong leadership and integration across formal education and informal (such as community, business) and non-formal (such as media, culture) sectors.

(White *et al.*, 2023a)

However, sustainable development and ESD are dynamic concepts (UNESCO, 2014), and it is important to remain open to future possibilities and to adopt a definition relevant to the people and place at a given point in time.

In this book, we have adopted the following definition:

Education for Sustainable Development (ESD) in Higher Education supports learners in all disciplines to develop knowledge, skills and capacities for human wellbeing, with attention to those who are marginalised, whilst ensuring that we live within environmental limits to address interconnected global challenges including climate change, loss of biodiversity, unsustainable use of resources, and inequality. Such learning employs critical, reflexive and potentially transformative pedagogies and curricula to create a space for dialogue, innovation and openness and to support specific and generic competencies. It enhances the cognitive, socio-emotional and behavioural dimensions of learning and encompasses learning content and outcomes, pedagogy and the learning environment itself. A whole institution approach links a sustainability focus across disciplines, teaching and research, operations and community engagement. Staff and students need to collaborate in co-production of curricula and to partner with external actors. Graduates are change agents in the sustainability transition.

Essentially, ESD is not merely learning *about* sustainable development, but rather learning *for* sustainable development. It can, in fact, be a route to overall enhanced forms of learning, emphasising transformative rather than transmissive approaches, employing experiential learning and critical pedagogy and using real-world examples to support action as well as learning (Springett, 2005; Thomas, 2009; Sterling, 2012; Price *et al.*, 2021, 2024). This requires a *reframing* of teaching and learning and should not be considered as an add-on to existing curriculum. Integrating sustainability into core curricula is most associated with the transformative goals of ESD because it treats sustainability as part of the discipline (UNESCO, 2014; Vogel *et al.*, 2023). Such teaching does not dictate a set ideology, but rather develops capacities for critical analysis and opens up skills and spaces for debate about what sustainable development means in a particular context. ESD will have an impact in supporting learners across all academic disciplines in developing the subject relevant knowledge, skills and competencies to create and pursue visions of a better world and to recognise their current and future social, cultural, economic and environmental impacts, from a local and a global perspective (UNESCO, 2017; Advance HE/QAA, 2021). Moreover, it can inspire critique of modern society and contribute to wider debates regarding current forms of capitalism and globalisation (Springett, 2005) along with more difficult decolonial agendas (Vasquez-Fernandez and Cash Ahenakew pii tai poo taa 2020). As we can see from the discussion of sustainable development above, ESD is not merely about environmental issues but rather about how we can achieve human wellbeing within environmental limits. Whilst it is possible to explore ESD in one academic discipline, much ESD is enabled through real-world problems and framing, which often requires a transdisciplinary approach across disciplines and across academic and non-academic actors, as will be discussed further in Chapters 4 and 8.

### The Whole-Institution Approach

The whole-institution approach is a way of thinking about ESD that aims to integrate sustainability into all aspects and agendas of an institution (Price *et al.*, 2021, 2024). UNESCO (2019b) advocates a whole-institution approach to ESD: 'the whole-institution approach should be strengthened with emphasis on the necessity for education institutions and communities to work together'. ESD lends itself to student projects on local issues and the use of real-world examples in teaching, thereby strengthening community engagement (Sipos *et al.*, 2008). Furthermore, sustainability capability aligns with priority skills demanded by employers (Drayson, 2015; Holdsworth *et al.*, 2018). To effectively take action towards achieving the SDGs, we need professionals and citizens who have the skills, knowledge and mindsets to tackle the complex sustainable development challenges articulated by the SDGs through whichever career or life path they take (SDSN, 2020). By engaging directly with entrepreneurs, employers and industry, ESD can add value to the student journey (Advance HE/QAA, 2021). ESD may therefore be supported through a continuum covering formal, non-formal and informal learning (Rogers, 2019). Non-formal learning is understood to be structured and intentional and can include learning in and with communities, while informal education is unstructured and mainly comprises media and cultural influences (White *et al.*, 2023a). Formal and non-formal learning can mesh well together to increases students' understanding and motivation to take action for sustainable development (Price *et al.*, 2024).

### ESD in Theory and Practice

ESD has evolved as a field of practice in education and extra-curricular contexts but also as an interesting theoretical area of contestation. The prescriptive impetus has led to much emphasis on practice, and although this has been accompanied by conceptual insights, they have not always been picked up because of the sense of urgency to provide knowledge and skills to address global challenges. This book is one effort to demonstrate and encourage stronger engagement between theory and practice. Formal ESD, in nurseries, schools, colleges and universities, has been increasingly promoted by departments of education and national governments (e.g. DfE, 2022), supported by an active UNESCO suite of programmes and international higher education coalitions. After the UN Decade of ESD, Regional Centres of Expertise were encouraged (United Nations University, undated), and they supported the Global Action Programme that preceded the SDGs (Vaughter *et al.*, 2022), and now engage critically with globalising narratives whilst supporting local projects (Lotz-Sisitka *et al.*, 2010). Individuals, communities, local government and private sector entities thus all have a role to play in the active pursuit of a better world.

### *ESD in Higher Education*

Much of the theory and practice of formal ESD has been focused in schools, with a growing body of literature recently examining how we can support ESD in higher education. Whilst the underpinning concepts are the same, there are particular aspects to consider in higher education. First, this more advanced level of education permits a deeper critical analysis of social theory and more thorough unpacking of concepts such as decolonisation, modes of capitalism and relational ontologies (Datta, 2015; Vásquez-Fernández and Cash Ahenakew pii tai poo taa, 2020; Martin *et al.*, 2024). Second, learners can not only engage with real-world problems, but also develop solutions, especially in advanced projects and postgraduate research. Third, most higher education learners are young adults, beginning their independent lives away from families, and hence are open to transformative learning and to development of the norms they will take forward in life through a whole institution approach. Fourth, ESD in higher education occupies a unique frame in relation to knowledge production, exchange and implementation, because it opens new spaces between ways of teaching and learning, research and enquiry, practice and possibility. Higher ESD traverses the spectrum from early awareness of sustainable development for those not much exposed at school or in community contexts, to active leadership of sustainable development theory and innovation in research and engagement roles.

## Curriculum, Competencies and Pedagogies

Different sustainability issues and educational priorities have been emphasised in different countries, leading to a rich variety of ESD concepts and practices (UNESCO, 2014). Yet ESD is a holistic approach that typically focuses on three elements (UNESCO, 2017; SDSN, 2020; Advance HE/QAA, 2021; Price *et al.*, 2021, UNESCO, 2021):

- Subject-relevant learning objectives for the SDGs
- Key competencies for sustainability
- Transformational pedagogies to support sustainable development

ESD learning content includes discipline specific knowledge and skills; an understanding of how sustainability challenges are relevant to a particular discipline or profession; and cross-cutting understanding of key sustainable development issues (Advance HE/QAA, 2021). The SDGs are relevant to all disciplines and provide a valuable starting point for embedding ESD across academic disciplines (Advance HE/QAA, 2021; Price *et al.*, 2021 and see above). However, there are many other examples and ways of framing that could be relevant to particular disciplines, in the humanities and social sciences as well as the sciences.

### *Learning Domains*

Learning content can be framed in cognitive, socio-emotional and behavioural domains (UNESCO, 2017). Such framing extends back to the ideas of Patrick Geddes, whose triad Heart-Hand-Head (Geddes, 1919, 1949) has underpinned calls for a more outdoors, experiential and practical approach to education (Higgins and Nicol, 2010). The cognitive domain (head) includes knowledge and thinking skills necessary to better understand sustainability challenges. The socio-emotional domain (heart) includes social skills that enable learners to collaborate, negotiate and communicate to promote sustainable development as well as self-reflection skills, values, attitudes and motivations for sustainability. The behavioural domain (hand) describes action competencies that allow learners to take practical action for sustainable transformation (Sipos *et al.*, 2008; UNESCO, 2017; UNESCO, 2021; Toro-Troconis *et al.*, 2023).

### Key Competencies for Sustainability

A competence can be seen as 'a functionally linked complex of knowledge, skills, and attitudes that enable successful task performance and problem solving' (Wiek *et al.*, 2011), but it can also include abilities to value and reflect. Hence, 'a competence is defined as the ability to successfully meet complex demands in a particular context' through the mobilisation of psychological and social elements (Rychen, 2009). Cross-cutting key competencies for sustainability drawn from Wiek *et al.* (2011) were articulated by UNESCO in 2017 (systems thinking, anticipatory, critical thinking, strategic, collaboration, integrated problem-solving, self-awareness and normative competencies) (Table 2.1). The sustainability key competencies represent what learners need to deal with complex challenges. These competencies have been categorised as 'ways of

*Table 2.1* Key competencies (KC 1–8) for sustainability.

| | |
|---|---|
| | *Ways of thinking* |
| Systems thinking (KC1) | The abilities to use a holistic perspective; to recognise and understand relationships; to analyse complex systems; to think of how systems are embedded within different domains and different scales; and to deal with uncertainty. |
| Anticipatory (KC2) | The abilities to understand and evaluate multiple futures – possible, probable and desirable; to create one's own visions for the future; to apply the precautionary principle; to assess the consequences of actions; to learn from history and the past; and to deal with risks and changes. |
| Critical thinking (KC3) | The ability to question norms, practices and opinions; to reflect on own one's values, perceptions and actions; to collate, synthesise and analyse literature and data; and to take a position in the sustainability discourse. |
| | *Ways of practising* |
| Strategic (KC4) | The abilities to plan, develop and implement innovative strategies and actions that further sustainability at the local level and further afield. |

*(Continued)*

*Table 2.1* (Continued)

| | |
|---|---|
| | *Ways of practising* |
| Collaboration (KC5) | The abilities to learn from others; to understand and respect the needs, perspectives and actions of others (empathy); to understand, relate to and be sensitive to others (empathic leadership); to deal with conflicts in a group; and to facilitate collaborative and participatory problem solving. |
| Integrated problem-solving (KC6) | The overarching ability to apply different problem-solving frameworks to complex sustainability problems and develop viable, inclusive and equitable solution options that promote sustainable development, using interdisciplinary and transdisciplinary approaches where relevant |
| | *Ways of being* |
| Self-awareness (KC7) | The ability to reflect on one's own role in the local community and (global) society; to continually evaluate and further motivate one's actions; and to deal with one's feelings, desires and resilience. |
| Normative (KC8) | The abilities to understand and reflect on the norms and values that underlie one's actions; to recognise and understand the perspectives and cultures of others and to negotiate sustainability values, principles, goals, and targets, in a context of conflicts of interests and trade-offs, uncertain knowledge and contradictions. |

*Source*: Adapted from UNESCO (2017), AdvanceHE/QAA (2021) and CoDesignS ESD (2021).

thinking', 'ways of practising' and 'ways of being' (AdvanceHE/QAA, 2021) (Table 2.1) and can be adopted and adapted within higher education through alignment with appropriate learning outcomes (Figure 2.7).

Although the competencies approach is increasingly being adopted in ESD in higher education, it is not the only way to view ESD outputs. The whole person approach sees how individual people have identities, motivations and higher order learning. It can help us support development of higher moral consciousness and yield individual and societal benefits (Podger *et al.*, 2010). These authors suggest that dispositional thinking can enable reflection and critical integration across multiple experiences in relation to one's own values and societal norms. Others have also suggested that spirituality, compassion and the ability to see different perspectives are required to enable a sustainable world (Orr, 2002). A new ecological and humanist worldview must develop (Sterling, 2001) that recognises interconnectedness and relationality (Escobar, 2011; Datta, 2015). Hence, whilst we recognise the emphasis on competencies, we also retain awareness of individual human experiences, emotions and educational contexts. These aspects will be discussed further in Chapter 6.

### *Transformative Pedagogies and Learning Methods*

Transformative pedagogies can support learners to address the complexity, uncertainty, ambiguity and contradictory nature of sustainability challenges since the goal of transformative learning is to empower learners to change their frame of reference or perspective through critical reflection (Sipos *et al.*, 2008). Transformative ESD embeds knowledge and information about sustainability issues and solutions and delivers it in such a way that learners are able to engage practically and apply their learning in a way that allows them to see how they can make a difference (Sipos *et al.*, 2008; Price et al., 2020). Transformational learning can be participatory and experiential and can be implemented within formal, non-formal and informal systems of education to motivate and empower both learners and educators to take action for sustainable development (Sipos *et al.*, 2008; UNESCO, 2014; Agbedahin, 2019; Advance HE/QAA, 2021). Transformational higher education requires constructively aligned teaching, learning and assessment activities designed to meet key ESD competencies and learning outcomes (Advance HE/QAA, 2021) and can help shift transgressive norms (Lotz-Sisitka *et al.*, 2017). Examples of transformative approaches include object based learning, learning landscapes and storytelling (Nicholson et al., 2024). Transformative pedagogies will be explored further later in the book (Chapter 6).

## Putting ESD into Practice: The CoDesignS ESD Framework

A recent model for ESD learning and curriculum design links the key aspects of ESD and offers a practical guide to support initial and deeper engagement with ESD. The CoDesignS ESD framework is structured around three pillars of ESD (Figure 2.6) (Ahmad *et al.*, 2023; Toro-Troconis *et al.*, 2023):

a *Pillar A*: Specific learning objectives for the SDGs targeting the cognitive domain (head) aiming to develop knowledge and thinking skills, the socio-emotional domain (heart) aiming to develop values, attitudes and motivations, and the behavioural domain (hands) aiming to promote action competencies (Sipos *et al.*, 2008). The specific learning objectives for the SDGs emphasise the interconnectedness of the SDGs, fostering an interdisciplinary and systems framing of ESD.
b *Pillar B*: The key competencies for sustainability identified by UNESCO (2017) as being relevant for people to act for sustainability.
c *Pillar C*: Transformative pedagogies and teaching methods which are central to the design of future-focused curricula.

An example of how the framework can be used in practice is shown in Figure 2.7. The example is based on three activities:

1 Firstly: identify with students potential job roles and related activities associated with a discipline.
2 Secondly: consider with students how the job roles identified in Activity 1 might relate to one or more SDGs.

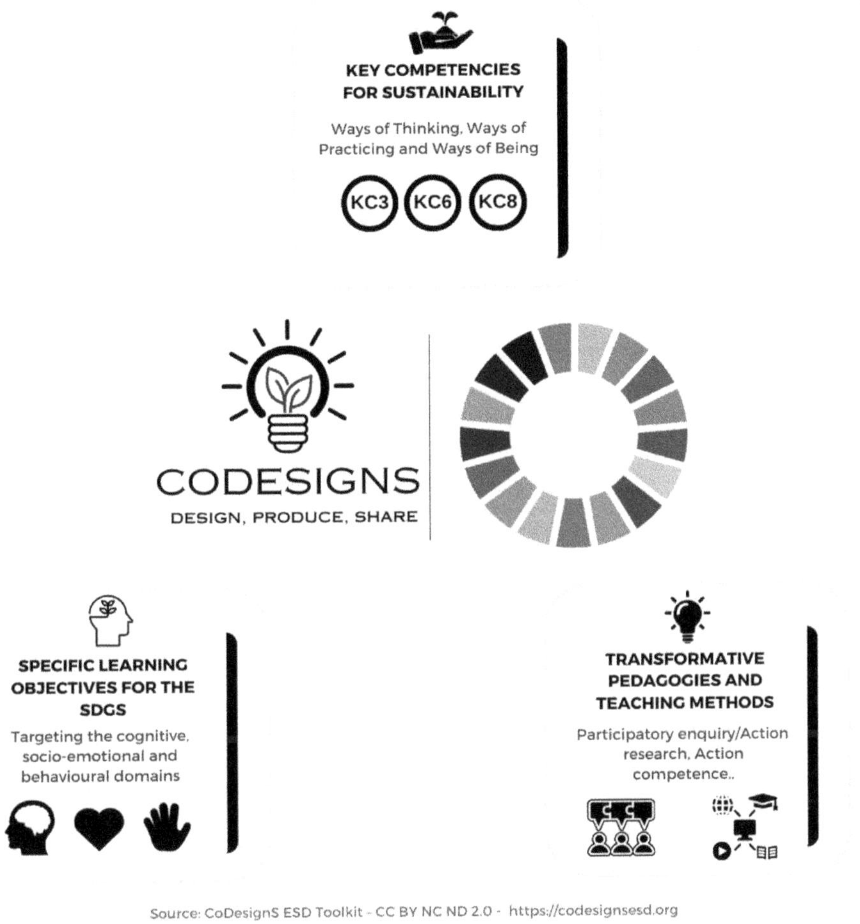


*Figure 2.6* Structure of the The CoDesignS ESD Framework. (*Sources*: CoDesignS ESD, 2021 – CC BY-NC-ND 2.0; Ahmad *et al.*, 2023; Toro-Troconis *et al.*, 2023.)

3 Thirdly: plan learning activities associated with these job roles by:

- Identifying specific learning objectives for the associated SDGs (Pillar A).
- Identifying key competencies for sustainability associated with the learning activities (Pillar B).
- Identifying transformative pedagogies associated with the learning activities (Pillar C).

Figure 2.7 illustrates an example of how the SDGs, learning activities, transformative pedagogies, learning domains and key competencies for sustainability may be embedded in first year Geography module (adapted from Nicholson *et al.*, 2024). Further examples in a range of contexts are available in a CoDesignS ESD Toolkit which includes cases of best practice that can be applied to different scenarios (CoDesignS ESD, 2021).

**Activity 1:** Identify with students potential job roles and related activities associated with a discipline.
**Activity 2:** Consider with students how the job roles and activities identified in Activity 1 might relate to one or more SDGs.
**Activity 3:**
- Plan learning activities associated with these job roles and specific learning objectives for the associated SDGs (Pillar A, specific learning objectives for the SDGs).
- Identify key competencies for sustainability associated with them (Pillar B, key competencies for sustainability).
- Identify learning activities and transformative pedagogies (Pillar C, transformative pedagogies and teaching methods).

**Activity 1:** Example: One of the job roles identified by first year Geography students: Transport and Town Planning and Development

**Activity 2:** Example: Key SDG identified by first year Geography students associated with Transport and Town Planning and Development:
**SDG11** Sustainable Cities and Communities.
Other related SDGs identified by students:
SDG1 No Poverty
SDG3 Good Health and Wellbeing
SDG5 Gender Equality
SDG6 Clean Water and Sanitation
SDG9 Industry, Innovation and Infrastructure
SDG10 Reduced Inequalities
SDG12 Responsible Consumption and Production
SDG16 Peace, Justice and Strong Institutions
SDG17 Partnership for the Goals

**Activity 3:** Example: Learning activities and transformative pedagogies associated with job roles and associated SDGs identified for a first year Geography module.
**Introduce learning landscapes:** (1) Consider use of sustainability trail to physically go to places, reflect, solve problems. (2) Use Google Earth to explore places associated with sustainability challenges.
**Storytelling:** Students write about some aspect of their life that links to a named SDG, and tell it in the form of a story, with a beginning, a middle and an end.
**Enhance emotional engagement:** (1) Use video to humanise problems rather than focus only on academic knowledge. (2) Teach 'constructing an argument' through practice by using debate to select group project topic.
**Highlight workplace competencies:** Role of teamwork – importance of tackling team working problems, learning to work with each other, enhancing diversity awareness.
**Hands-on activities:** (1) Object based learning. (2) Groups prepare large mind map of their topic, and use world cafe to share, peer learning. (3) Have talks from industry, alumni. (4) Introduce group infographic to the assignment.

**Activity 3:** Example: Head-Hands-Heart (Cognitive-Behavioural-Socio-Emotional) learning domains and key competencies for sustainability associated with learning activities identified for a first year Geography module:
**Head:** Activities: storytelling, highlight workplace competencies. Key competencies: critical thinking, systems thinking, anticipatory competencies.
**Hands:** Activities: introduce learning landscapes, highlight workplace competencies, hands-on activities.
Key competencies: collaboration, integrated problem solving, strategic competencies.
**Heart:** Activities: enhance emotional engagement, highlight workplace competencies. Key competencies: normative, self-awareness competencies.

*Figure 2.7* Implementing the CoDesignS ESD framework. (*Source*: Adapted from Nicholson *et al.*, 2024.)

## Alignment of ESD with Other Agendas in Education

Academics are often busy and time pressured, with high workloads and multiple competing tasks to complete (White, 2014). There is a barrage of ongoing agendas that have to be addressed in higher education. How can academics add ESD to this mix without contradicting other approaches or creating another thing to add to the list of things to do? The recent guidance (Advance HE/QAA, 2021) suggested that:

> There is an opportunity for ESD to reinforce other institutional objectives such as internationalisation and developing global perspectives; decolonising learning; promoting interdisciplinary and transdisciplinary learning; promoting employability and enterprise, and civic engagement; and championing equality, diversity and inclusion. In this respect, ESD offers an opportunity to frame curricula, harmonise

> such activities and provide the context in which all of these institutional priorities can find expression.
>
> (Advance HE/QAA, 2021)

For example, interrogation of the purpose of education and close attention to the curriculum and pedagogies can enhance understanding and practices in teaching and learning. The quest for quality education and avoidance of greenwashing can strengthen programme and institutional processes. Critically engaging with inequalities and global and environmental injustices supports efforts to decolonise the curriculum. The focus on innovation and future thinking for a sustainable world creates entrepreneurial students with awareness of global citizenship.

## Conclusions

Sustainable development is a recognition that human wellbeing and the health of nature are interdependent, but that the journey towards these twin goals is difficult. Different worldviews, disciplinary perspectives and cultural values create diverse framings of sustainable development and hence ESD. Supporting ESD is not merely about provision of factual knowledge, but rather about supporting development of specific and generic competencies using innovative pedagogies and the deepening of critical enquiry about the world in which we live and the sustainable futures we envision. In strengthening ESD in higher education, we need to traverse specific and generic needs, open up the radical whilst enabling the iterative, and create safe spaces of respect and trust for dialogical interrogation of what kind of futures we want and how to get there, including a plurality of perspectives but emphasising rigorous and critical study. We need to produce theory to underpin effective sustainable development whilst supporting practical change. This chapter has explored what ESD is and might be, and as noted above, adopts the following definition:

> Education for Sustainable Development (ESD) in Higher Education supports learners in all disciplines to develop knowledge, skills and capacities for human wellbeing, with attention to those who are marginalised, whilst ensuring that we live within environmental limits to address interconnected global challenges including climate change, loss of biodiversity, unsustainable use of resources, and inequality. Such learning employs critical, reflexive and potentially transformative pedagogies and curricula to create a space for dialogue, innovation and openness and to support specific and generic competencies. It enhances the cognitive, socio-emotional and behavioural dimensions of learning and encompasses learning content and outcomes, pedagogy and the learning environment itself. A whole institution approach links a sustainability focus across disciplines, teaching and research, operations and community engagement. Staff and students need to collaborate in co-production of curricula and to partner with external actors. Graduates are change agents in the sustainability transition.

Subsequent chapters explore learning and teaching, research, leadership and a whole-institution approach to transition towards an authentic learning environment for ESD. Following Chankseliani and McCowan (2021), we need to see higher education as a common good that builds on values such as social justice and solidarity, and develop liberation approaches to teaching and learning.

## References


Adams, W.M. (2006) *The future of sustainability: re-thinking environment and development in the twenty-first century*. Report for IUCN. Available at: https://portals.iucn.org/library/sites/library/files/documents/Rep-2006-002.pdf [Accessed 31 July 2024].

Advance HE/QAA (2021) *Education for Sustainable Development Guidance*. Available at: https://www.qaa.ac.uk/quality-code/education-for-sustainable-development and https://www.advance-he.ac.uk/knowledge-hub/education-sustainable-development-guidance [Accessed 31 July 2024].

Agbedahin, A.V. (2019) 'sustainable development, education for sustainable development, and the 2030 agenda for sustainable development: Emergence, efficacy, eminence, and future', Sustainable Development, 27, pp. 669–680. DOI:10.1002/sd.1931.

Ahmad, N., Toro-Troconis, M., Ibahrine, M., Armour, R., Tait, V., Reedy, K., Malevicius, R., Dale, V., Tasler, N. and Inzolia, Y. (2023) 'CoDesignS education for sustainable development: A framework for embedding education for sustainable development in curriculum design', Sustainability, 15, p. 16460. DOI:10.3390/su152316460.

Belmonte-Ureña, L.J., Plaza-Úbeda, J.A., Vazquez-Brust, D. and Yakovleva, N. (2021) 'Circular economy, degrowth and green growth as pathways for research on sustainable development goals: A global analysis and future agenda', Ecological Economics, 185, p. 107050. DOI:10.1016/j.ecolecon.2021.107050.

Boar, A., Bastida, R. and Marimon, F. (2020) 'A systematic literature review. Relationships between the sharing economy, sustainability and sustainable development goals', Sustainability, 12(17), p. 6744. DOI:10.3390/su12176744.

Bonnett, M. (2007) 'Environmental education and the issue of nature', Journal of Curriculum Studies, 39(6), pp. 707–721. Doi:10.1080/00220270701447149.

Burrell, G. and Morgan, G. (1979) Sociological paradigms and organisational analysis. London: Heinemann, pp. 1–9.

Carson, R. (1962). Silent spring. New York: Houghton Mifflin.

Castellanos, P.M.A. and Queiruga-Dios, A. (2021) 'From environmental education to education for sustainable development in higher education: A systematic review', International Journal of Sustainability in Higher Education, 23, pp. 622–644. DOI:10.1108/IJSHE-04-2021-0167.

Chambers, R. (1983). Rural development: Putting the last first. London: Routledge.

Chankseliani, M. and McCowan, T. (2021) 'Higher education and the sustainable development goals', Higher Education, 81(1), pp. 1–8. DOI:10.1007/s10734-020-00652-w.

CoDesignS ESD (2021) *CoDesignS Education for Sustainable Development*. Available at: https://codesignsesd.org/toolkit/ [Accessed 31 July 2024].

Costanza, R., Daly, L., Fioramonti, L., Giovannini, E., Kubiszewski, I., Mortensen, L.F., Pickett, K.E., Ragnarsdottir, K.V., De Vogli, R. and Wilkinson, R. (2016) 'Modelling and measuring sustainable wellbeing in connection with the UN sustainable development goals', Ecological Economics, 130, pp. 350–355. Doi:10.1016/j.ecolecon.2016.07.009.

Cowie, R.H., Bouchet, P. and Fontaine, B. (2022) 'The sixth mass extinction: Fact, fiction or speculation?, Biological Reviews, 97(2), pp. 640–663. DOI:10.1111/brv.12816.

Datta, R. (2015) 'A relational theoretical framework and meanings of land, nature, and sustainability for research with indigenous communities', Local Environment, 20(1), pp. 102–113. DOI:10.1080/13549839.2013.818957.

DEFRA (2005) Securing the Future—Delivering UK Sustainable Development Strategy. Available at: https://www.gov.uk/government/uploads/system/uploads/attachment_data/file/69412/pb10589-securing-the-future-050307.pdf [Accessed 31 July 2024].

Department for Education (DfE) (2022) Sustainability and climate change strategy. Available at: https://www.gov.uk/government/publications/sustainability-and-climate-change-strategy [Accessed 31 July 2024].

Dietz, S. and Neumayer, E. (2007) 'Weak and strong sustainability in the SEEA: Concepts and measurement', Ecological Economics, 61(4), pp. 617–626. DOI:10.1016/j.ecolecon.2006.09.007.

Drayson, R. (2015). Employer attitudes towards, and skills for, sustainable development. Executive summary: Employers. York: The Higher Education Academy.

East, M. and White, R.M. (2016) Reflecting on the Emergence of the UN Sustainable Development Goals: A Call for Action in Scotland. Report for Scottish Government and COSLA. Available

at: http://learningforsustainabilityscotland.org/wp-content/uploads/2019/09/Reflection-SDGs-Scotland_15April2016.pdf [Accessed 31 July 2024].
Eisenmenger, N., Pichler, M., Krenmayr, N., Noll, D., Plank, B., Schalmann, E., Wandl, M.T. and Gingrich, S. (2020) 'The sustainable development goals prioritize economic growth over sustainable resource use: A critical reflection on the SDGs from A socio-ecological perspective', Sustainability Science, 15(4), pp. 1101–1110. DOI:10.1007/s11625-020-00813-x.
Escobar, A. (2011) 'Sustainability: design for the pluriverse', Development, 54(2), pp. 137–140.
Ferraro, E., White, R., Cox, E., Bebbington, J. and Wilson, S. (2011) 'Craft and sustainable development: Reflections on Scottish craft and pathways to sustainability', Craft + Design Enquiry, 3, pp. 1–26.
Fien, J. (1993). Education for the environment — Critical curriculum theorising and environmental education. Geelong: Deakin University Press.
Fonseca, L.M., Domingues, J.P. and Dima, A.M. (2020) 'Mapping the sustainable development goals relationships', Sustainability, 12(8), p. 3359. DOI:10.3390/su12083359.
Freire, P. (1970). Pedagogy of the oppressed. New York: Seabury Press.
Geddes, P. (1919). 'Final lecture at the University of Dundee' [published in 1949 reprint of cities in evolution]. London: Williams and Norgate.
Geddes, P. (1949). Cities in evolution. New and revised edition. London: Williams and Norgate.
Higgins, P. and Nicol, R. (2010) 'Sir Patrick Geddes: "Vivendo Discimus"—By Living We Learn', in Sourcebook of experiential education key thinkers and their contributions. Abingdon: Routledge, pp. 87–92.
Holdsworth, S., Thomas, I. and Sandri, O. (2018) 'Assessing graduate sustainability attributes using a vignette/scenario approach', Journal of Education for Sustainable Development, 12, pp. 120–139. DOI:10.1177/0973408218792127.
Huckle, J. (1996) Education for sustainability. Earthscan: London.
Huckle, J. and Sterling, S. (Eds.) (1996) Education for sustainability. Earthscan: London.
Hull, Z. (2008) 'Sustainable development: Premises, understanding and prospects', Sustainable Development, 16(2), pp. 73–80. DOI:10.1002/sd.312.
IUCN-UNEP-WWF (1980) World Conservation Strategy: Living resources conservation for sustainable development. IUCN-UNEP-WWF. Available at: https://portals.iucn.org/library/efiles/documents/wcs-004.pdf [Accessed 31 July 2024].
IUCN-UNEP-WWF (1991) Caring for the earth: A strategy for sustainable living. IUCN-UNEP-WWF. Available at: https://portals.iucn.org/library/node/6439 [Accessed 31 July 2024].
Jackson, E.A. (2016) 'Ontological and epistemological discourse(s) on sustainable development: Perspective on Sierra Leone in the aftermath of a decade of civil unrest', Management of Sustainable Development, 8(1). Available at SSRN: https://ssrn.com/abstract=2811522 [Accessed 31 July 2024].
Jackson, T. (2009). Prosperity without growth: Economics for a finite planet. London: Routledge.
Jarić, I., Roll, U., Bonaiuto, M., Brook, B.W., Courchamp, F., Firth, J.A., Gaston, K.J., Heger, T., Jeschke, J.M., Ladle, R.J. and Meinard, Y. (2022) 'Societal extinction of species', Trends in Ecology & Evolution, 37(5), pp. 411–419. DOI:10.1016/j.tree.2021.12.011.
Kopnina, H. (2020) 'Education for the future? Critical evaluation of education for sustainable development goals', The Journal of Environmental Education, 51(4), pp. 280–291. DOI:10.1080/00958964.2019.1710444.
Lotz-Sisitka, H. (2007) 'Think piece—An opening dialogue with think pieces and feature articles on learning in a changing world in this journal', Southern African Journal of Environmental Education, 24, pp. 8–18. Available at: https://www.ajol.info/index.php/sajee/article/view/122734 [Accessed 31 July 2024].
Lotz-Sisitka, H., Mukute, M., Chikunda, C., Baloi, A. and Pesanayi, T. (2017) 'Transgressing the norm: Transformative agency in community-based learning for sustainability in southern African contexts', International Review of Education, 63, pp. 897–914. DOI:10.1007/s11159-017-9689-3.
Lotz-Sisitka, H., O'Donoghue, R. and Wilmot, D. (2010) 'The makana regional centre of expertise: Experiments in social learning', Journal of Education for Sustainable Development, 4(1), pp. 73–92. DOI:10.1177/097340820900400114.
Martin, A., Gomez-Baggethun, E., Quaas, M., Rozzi, R., Tauro, A., Faith, D.P. and Pascual, U. (2024) 'Plural values of nature help to understand contested pathways to sustainability', One Earth, 7(5), pp. 806–819.

McCowan, T. (2023) Tertiary Education and the Sustainability Agenda. Centre for Global Higher Education Working Paper series, Working Paper 90. University of Oxford, Oxford. Available at: https://www.researchcghe.org/publication/tertiary-education-and-the-sustainability-agenda/ [Accessed 31 July 2024].
McKeown, R. (2002) Education for sustainable development toolkit. Available at: https://unesdoc.unesco.org/ark:/48223/pf0000152453 [Accessed 31 July 2024].
McKeown, R. and Hopkins, C. (2005) 'EE and ESD: Two paradigms, one crucial goal', Applied Environmental Education and Communication, 4, pp. 221–224. DOI:10.1080/15330150591004616.
Meadows, D.H., Randers, J. and Meadows, D.L. (1972) The limits to growth: A report for the club of Rome's project on the predicament of mankind, pp. 158–175. New York: Universe Books.
Neumayer, E. (1999). Weak versus strong sustainability. Cheltenham: Edward Elgar Publishing.
Nicholson, D.T., Vargas, V.R., Price, E.A.C., Himatlal, K., Campen, L., Hartley, M. and Hewitt, T. (2024) 'Transformative learning design for ESD in a skills-based module', Open Scholarship of Teaching and Learning, 3, pp. 21–36. Available at: https://osotl.org/index.php/osotl/article/view/76/96 [Accessed 31 July 2024].
Orr, D. (1992) Ecological literacy: Education and the transition to a postmodern world. Albany: State University of New York Press.
Orr, D.W. (2002) 'Four challenges of sustainability', Conservation Biology, 16(6), pp. 1457–1460.
Orr, D.W. (2004) Earth in mind: On education, environment, and the human prospect. Washington, DC: Island Press.
Oxfam International (2023) Climate equality: a planet for the 99%. Available at: https://www.oxfam.org/en/research/climate-equality-planet-99 [Accessed 31 July 2024]. DOI: 10.21201/2023.000001.
Persson, L., Carney Almroth, B.M., Collins, C.D. and Cornell, S. et al. (2022) 'Outside the safe operating space of the planetary boundary for novel entities', Environmental Science and Technology, 56, pp. 1510–1521. DOI:10.1021/acs.est.1c04158.
Podger, M.D., Mustakova-Possardt, E. and Reid, A. (2010) 'A whole-person approach to educating for sustainability', International Journal of Sustainability in Higher Education, 11(4), pp. 339–352.
Pradhan, P., Costa, L., Rybski, D., Lucht, W. and Kropp, J.P. (2017) 'A systematic study of sustainable development goal (SDG) interactions', Earth's Future, 5, pp. 1169–1179. DOI:10.1002/2017EF000632.
Price, E., Longhurst, J., White, R., Preist, C., Mori, K., Robinson, Z., Baughan, P., Gough, G., Hayles, C., Higgins, P., Molthan-Hill, P., Hack, C. and Kemp, S. (2020) 'Education for sustainable development in higher education', Environmental Scientist, 29(4), pp. 38–45. Available at: https://www.the-ies.org/resources/value-environmental-science [Accessed 31 July 2024].
Price, E.A.C., Nicholson, D.T., Dunk, R., Lawler, C., Carney, M., Vargas, V., Veitch, S., Leigh, S., Singleton, M. and Mottram, S. (2024) 'Enabling change agents for sustainable development: A whole-institution approach to embedding the UN sustainable development goals in higher education', International Journal of Sustainability in Higher Education. DOI:10.1108/IJSHE-02-2024-0112.
Price, E.A.C., White, R.M., Mori, K., Longhurst, J., Baughan, P., Hayles, C.S. and Gough, G. (2021) 'Supporting the role of universities in leading individual and societal transformation through education for sustainable development', Discover Sustainability, 2, p. 49. DOI:10.1007/s43621-021-00058-3.
QAA and HEA (2014) Education for sustainable development: Guidance for UK higher education providers. Gloucester: QAA. Available at: https://www.advance-he.ac.uk/knowledge-hub/education-sustainable-development-guidance-uk-higher-education-providers [Accessed 31 July 2024].
Raworth, K. (2012) A safe and just space for humanity: can we live within the doughnut? Oxfam.
Raworth, K. (2017a) 'A doughnut for the Anthropocene: humanity's compass in the 21st century', The Lancet Planetary Health, 1, pp. e48–e49. DOI:10.1016/S2542-5196(17)30028-1.
Raworth, K. (2017b) Doughnut economics: Seven ways to think like a 21st century economist. London: Penguin Random House.
Redclift, M. (2005) 'Sustainable development (1987–2005): An oxymoron comes of age', Sustainable Development, 13(4), pp. 212–227.

Richardson, K., Steffen, W., Lucht, W., Bendtsen, J., Cornell, S.E., Donges, J.F., Drüke, M., Fetzer, I., Bala, G., von Bloh, W., Feulner, G., Fiedler, S., Gerten, D., Gleeson, T., Hofmann, M., Huiskamp, W., Kummu, M., Mohan, C., Nogués-Bravo, D., Petri, S., Porkka, M., Rahmstorf, S., Schaphoff, S., Thonicke, K., Tobian, A., Virkki, V., Wang-Erlandsson, L., Weber, L. and Rockström, J., (2023) 'Earth beyond six of nine planetary boundaries', Science Advances, 9(37). DOI:10.1126/sciadv.adh2458.

Richardson, K., Steffen, W., Lucht, W., Bendtsen, J., Cornell, S.E., Donges, J.F., Drüke, M., Fetzer, I., Bala, G., von Bloh, W., Feulner, G., Fiedler, S., Gerten, D., Gleeson, T., Hofmann, M., Huiskamp, W., Kummu, M., Mohan, C., Nogués-Bravo, D., Petri, S. and Robinson, J. (2004) 'Squaring the circle? Some thoughts on the idea of sustainable development', Ecological Economics, 48(4), pp. 369–384.

Robinson, J. (2004) "Squaring the circle? Some thoughts on the idea of sustainable development", Ecological Economics, 48(4), pp. 369–384.

Robottom, I. (1992) 'Matching the purposes of environmental education with consistent approaches to research and professional development', Australian Journal of Environmental Education, 8, pp. 133–146.

Rockström, J., Steffen, W., Noone, K., Persson, Å., Chapin, F.S. III, Lambin, E., Lenton, T.M., Scheffer, M., Folke, C., Schellnhuber, H., Nykvist, B., De Wit, C.A., Hughes, T., van der Leeuw, S., Rodhe, H., Sörlin, S., Snyder, P.K., Costanza, R., Svedin, U., Falkenmark, M., Karlberg, L., Corell, R.W., Fabry, V.J., Hansen, J., Walker, B., Liverman, D., Richardson, K., Crutzen, P. and Foley, J. (2009) 'Planetary boundaries: Exploring the safe operating space for humanity', Ecology and Society, 14(2), p. 32. Available at: https://www.ecologyandsociety.org/vol14/iss2/art32/ [Accessed 31 July 2024].

Rogers, A. (2019) 'Second-generation non-formal education and the sustainable development goals: Operationalising the SDGs through community learning centres', International Journal of Lifelong Education, 38(5), pp. 515–526.

Rychen, D.S. (2009) 'Key competencies: Overall goals for competence development: An international and interdisciplinary perspective', in International handbook of education for the changing world of work: Bridging academic and vocational learning. Dordrecht: Springer Netherlands, pp. 2571–2583.

Sachs, J.D., Schmidt-Traub, G., Mazzucato, M., Messner, D., Nakicenovic, N. and Rockström, J. (2019) 'Six transformations to achieve the sustainable development goals', Nature Sustainability, 2(9), pp. 805–814.

SDSN (2020) Accelerating education for the SDGs in universities: A guide for universities, colleges, and tertiary and higher education institutions. Sustainable Development Solutions Network, New York. Available at: https://resources.unsdsn.org/accelerating-education-for-the-sdgs-in-universities-a-guide-for-universities-colleges-and-tertiary-and-higher-education-institutions [Accessed 31 July 2024].

Sipos, Y., Battisti, B. and Grimm, K. (2008) 'Achieving transformative sustainability learning: Engaging head, hands and heart', International Journal of Sustainability in Higher Education, 9(1), pp. 68–86. DOI:10.1108/14676370810842193.

Springett, D. (2005) 'Education for sustainability in the business studies curriculum: A call for a critical agenda', Business Strategy and the Environment, 14(3), pp. 146–159.

Steffen, W., Richardson, K., Rockström, J., Cornell, S.E., Fetzer, I., Bennett, E.M., Biggs, R., Carpenter, S.R., de Vries, W., de Wit, C.A., Folke, C., Gerten, D., Heinke, J., Mace, G.M., Persson, L.M., Ramanathan, V., Reyers, B. and Sörlin, S. (2015) 'Planetary boundaries: Guiding human development on a changing planet', Science, 347(6223), p. 1259855. DOI:10.1126/science.1259855.

Sterling, S. (2001). Sustainable education: Re-visioning learning and change (Vol. 6). Totnes: Green Books for the Schumacher Society.

Sterling, S. (2012). The future fit framework: An introductory guide to teaching and learning for sustainability in HE. York: Higher Education Academy.

Sterling, S. (2013) 'The sustainable university: challenge and response', in Sterling, S., Maxey, L. and Luna, H. (eds) The sustainable university: Progress and prospects. London: Routledge, pp. 17–50.

Thomas, I. (2009) 'Critical thinking, transformative learning, sustainable education, and problem-based learning in universities', Journal of Transformative Education, 7, pp. 245–264. DOI:10.1177/1541344610385753.

Tilbury, D. (1995) 'Environmental education for sustainability: Defining the new focus of environmental education in the 1990s', Environmental Education Research, 1(2), pp. 195–212. DOI:10.1080/1350462950010206.

Tilbury, D. (2015) 'Student engagement and leadership in higher education for sustainability', in Routledge handbook of higher education for sustainable development. Routledge ed M. Barth, G. Michelsen, M. Rieckmann and I. Thomas. PLace of publication London and New York, pp. 273–286.

Toro-Troconis, M., Inzolia, Y. and Ahmad, N. (2023) 'Exploring attitudes towards embedding education for sustainable development in curriculum design', International Journal of Higher Education, 12, pp. 42–50. DOI:10.5430/ijhe.v12n4p42.

United Nations (UN) (undated a) The Millennium Goals. Available at: https://www.un.org/millenniumgoals/ [Accessed 31 July 2024].

United Nations (UN) (undated b) The 17 Goals. Available at: https://sdgs.un.org/goals [Accessed 31 July 2024].

United Nations (UN) (undated c) A Nexus Approach for the SDGs: Interlinkages between the goals and targets. Available at: https://sdgtoolkit.org/tool/a-nexus-approach-for-the-sdgs-interlinkages-between-the-goals-and-targets/ [Accessed 31 July 2024].

United Nations (UN) (1987) Report of the World Commission on Environment and Development: Our common future. United Nations-WCED-World Commission on Environment and Development. Available at: https://sustainabledevelopment.un.org/content/documents/5987our-common-future.pdf [Accessed 31 July 2024].

United Nations (UN) (1992) Agenda 21. In United Nations Conference on Environment and Development. Available at: https://sdgs.un.org/sites/default/files/publications/Agenda21.pdf [Accessed 31 July 2024].

United Nations (UN) (2015) Transforming our world: The 2030 Agenda for Sustainable Development. Available at: https://sdgs.un.org/2030agenda [Accessed 31 July 2024].

United Nations (UN) (2023) Climate Action Synergies. Available at: https://sdgs.un.org/topics/climate-action-synergies [Accessed 31 July 2024].

United Nations Educational, Scientific and Cultural Organization (UNESCO) (1997) Education for a sustainable future: A transdisciplinary vision for concerted action. Available at: https://unesdoc.unesco.org/ark:/48223/pf0000110686 [Accessed 31 July 2024].

United Nations Educational, Scientific and Cultural Organization (UNESCO) (2014) Shaping the future we want: UN Decade of Education for Sustainable Development (2005–2014) final report. Available at: https://unesdoc.unesco.org/ark:/48223/pf0000230171 [Accessed 31 July 2024].

United Nations Educational, Scientific and Cultural Organization (UNESCO) (2016) Global education monitoring report-place: Inclusive and sustainable cities. Available at: https://unesdoc.unesco.org/ark:/48223/pf0000246230 [Accessed 31 July 2024].

United Nations Educational, Scientific and Cultural Organization (UNESCO) (2017) Education for Sustainable Development Goals: Learning objectives. Available at: https://unesdoc.unesco.org/ark:/48223/pf0000247444 [Accessed 31 July 2024].

United Nations Educational, Scientific and Cultural Organization (UNESCO) (2019a) What is Education for Sustainable Development? Cited in QAA/Advance HE (2020). Available at: https://www.qaa.ac.uk/quality-code/education-for-sustainable-development and https://www.advance-he.ac.uk/knowledge-hub/education-sustainable-development-guidance [Accessed 31 July 2024].

United Nations Educational, Scientific and Cultural Organization (UNESCO) (2019b) Framework for the implementation of education for sustainable development (ESD) beyond 2019. Available at: https://unesdoc.unesco.org/ark:/48223/pf0000370215.locale=en [Accessed 31 July 2024].

United Nations Educational, Scientific and Cultural Organization (UNESCO) (2021) Education for sustainable development: A roadmap. Available at: https://unesdoc.unesco.org/ark:/48223/pf0000374802.locale=en [Accessed 31 July 2024].

United Nations Educational, Scientific and Cultural Organization (UNESCO) (2024) What is Education for Sustainable Development? Available at: https://www.unesco.org/en/sustainable-development/education/need-know?hub=72522 [Accessed 31 July 2024].

United Nations Environment Programme (UNEP) (2008) Mainstreaming environment and sustainability in African Universities Partnership (2004–2008 report). Available at: https://www.unep.org/resources/report/mainstreaming-environment-and-sustainability-african-universities-partnership-2004 [Accessed 31 July 2024].
United Nations University (UN) (undated) RCE Vision and Mission. Available at: https://www.rcenetwork.org/portal/rce-vision-and-mission [Accessed 31 July 2024].
Vásquez-Fernández, A.M. and Ahenakew pii tai poo taa, C. (2020) 'Resurgence of relationality: Reflections on decolonizing and indigenizing "sustainable development"', Current Opinion in Environmental Sustainability, 43, pp. 65–70. DOI:10.1016/j.cosust.2020.03.005.
Vaughter, P., Noguchi, F. and Li, S. (2022) 'Minding the GAP: An overview of five years of education for sustainable development (ESD) projects under the Global Action Programme (GAP) within regional centres of expertise (RCEs) on ESD', Frontiers in Sustainability.
Vogel, M., Parker, L., Porter, J., O'Hara, M., Tebbs, E., Gard, R., He, X. and Gallimore, J.-B. (2023). Education for sustainable development: A review of the literature 2015-2022. York: Advance HE.
Wang-Erlandsson, L., Tobian, A., van der Ent, R., Fetzer, I., te Wierik, S., Porkka, M., Staal, A., Jaramillo, F., Dahlmann, H., Singh, C., Greve, P., Gerten, D., Keys, P., Gleeson, T., Cornell, S., Steffen, W., Bai, X. and Rockström, J. (2022) 'A planetary boundary for green water', Nature Reviews Earth and Environment. DOI:10.1038/s43017-022-00287-8.
White, R.M. (2014) 'Who Am I? The role(s) of an academic at a "Sustainable University"', in W. Leal Filho, L. Brandli, O. Kuznetsova and A. Paço (eds), Integrative Approaches to Sustainable Development at University Level. World Sustainability Series. DOI:10.1007/978-3-319-10690-8_46.
White, R., King, B., Leask, K. and Higgins, P. (2023a) Supporting Environmental Education in the United Kingdom of Great Britain and Northern Ireland: Context, Status, Lessons Learned and Recommendations for Japan. Unpublished report.
White, R.M., Kockel, U., King, B., Leask, K., Higgins, P. and Samuel, A. (2023b) 'The future starts in the past: Embedding learning for sustainability through culture and community in Scotland', Frontiers in Sustainability, 4, p. 1128620. DOI:10.3389/frsus.2023.1128620.
Wiek, A., Withycombe, L. and Redman, C.L. (2011) 'Key competencies in sustainability: A reference framework for academic program development', Sustainability Science, 6, pp. 203–218. DOI:10.1007/s11625-011-0132-6.

Chapter 3

# Towards a Sustainable University

## People, Purpose and Paradigm Shifts

*Zoe P. Robinson, Petra Molthan-Hill and Peter Higgins*

### Introduction

This book focuses on education within universities. Yet, 'education' sits within a wider context of the whole institution – the messages it conveys through its estate, its practices and its explicit 'messaging'. It is questionable whether truly effective Education for Sustainable Development (ESD) could ever be achieved without being located in the context of a holistic sustainable university. Education does not just involve the formal curriculum, nor does it just involve traditional student learners. The student experience and therefore learning is much wider than the formal curriculum, and university staff and the university estate contribute to the student experience and learning in diverse ways – from placements and careers support, to leisure, catering and learning facilities, to accommodation and communications. The informal curriculum – the opportunities that students have that exist outside of their formal courses, the hidden, implicit/subliminal or null curriculum (Eisner, 1985) – the unintentional learning from the environment or what is omitted, all play a role in learning in the university setting.

Formal curricular learning opportunities are increasingly diverse, from traditional degrees, to continuing professional development short courses, corporate and executive education; full-time or part-time courses; and in-person, remote, online and blended learning delivery, amongst others. Staff and visitors to universities are also all learners, with universities both intentionally and unintentionally contributing to the learning of these different stakeholders. With the breadth of learning environment and learners it embraces, it is clear that for all universities with an explicit 'sustainability purpose', all staff, whether with responsibilities for delivering education or contributing to the wider university setting, need an understanding of both the sustainability implications of their roles and relevant links to education and learning.

Such a university must not just look to the sustainability of its own direct activities but to its potential to catalyse sustainability transformation beyond its physical boundaries. Universities are increasingly discussed as 'anchor institutions' in their regions (Birch et al., 2013) with significant impact and potential to influence the region. These connections can be as a major employer in the local area, a provider of an educated workforce, a key stakeholder in local economic agendas, a key influencer on infrastructure developments such as travel, and an advisor on policy for local, regional and national governance institutions. As beacons of sustainability within their local area, with a substantial staff and student population able to approach both their professional and personal lives with a sustainability lens, universities can also become much wider society influencers.

DOI: 10.4324/9781003451563-3

*Table 3.1* A sample of extracts from UK universities' mission and strategy statements. What is the mission statement of your university? To what extent do you see that played out in the everyday?

| *University* | *Strategy excerpt* |
|---|---|
| University of Bristol | 'Our mission is to make a positive impact locally, nationally and globally by addressing society's greatest challenges through our distinctive education, innovative research, and the value we place on excellence, inclusivity and partnership'. (https://www.bristol.ac.uk/university/strategy/mission/) |
| University of Edinburgh | 'We aim to ... make a significant, sustainable and socially responsible contribution to Scotland, the UK and the world, promoting health, economic growth and cultural well-being'. (https://governance-strategic-planning.ed.ac.uk/content-to-be-reused/vision-and-mission) |
| University of Exeter | 'Our purpose is to use the power of our education and research to create a sustainable, healthy and socially just future'. (https://www.exeter.ac.uk/media/universityofexeter/aboutusresponsive/strategy2030/documents/University-of-Exeter_Strategy_2030.pdf) |
| Keele University | '...making a difference in society by providing innovative, high-quality education for students from all backgrounds and by undertaking world-leading research that transforms understanding and brings benefit to society, communities and individuals' (https://www.keele.ac.uk/about/strategicplanandmission/) |
| Nottingham Trent University | 'Established in 1843, Nottingham Trent University has a long history of unlocking potential, breaking down barriers and making a real difference to lives around the world'. (https://www.ntu.ac.uk/about-us) |
| University of West England (UWE) | 'At UWE Bristol, we're focused on solving future global challenges through outstanding learning, world-leading research and a culture of enterprise'. (https://www.uwe.ac.uk/about/values-vision-strategy) |

Indeed, many universities state ambitions of influencing and supporting societal change at a regional or wider level (Table 3.1). To read the mission statements of many universities would be to assume that they are at the heart of societal transformation towards a sustainable future. Yet, experiences within these institutions might speak to disconnect between the articulation of mission, vision and strategy and the reality of the extent to which sustainability is core to the different sub-systems within a university. In the day-to-day activities and language of the university, is the purpose espoused in mission statements really enacted?

Moving 'towards a sustainable university' (Sterling et al., 2013) requires shifting from 'bolt-on' approaches to sustainability to those that embrace a fundamental commitment to whole institutional transformation (Sylvestre and Wright, 2015). Some writers attest that such transformation necessitates the complete re-envisioning of the norms and structural relations that culturally define contemporary universities (Cortese, 2003; Sterling et al., 2013) while others define a pragmatic approach that attempts to utilise the mechanisms of the neoliberal university to achieve sustainability goals (Bessant et al., 2015; 2017).

The complexity within universities in the context of sustainability transformation is sub-divided by authors in different ways from the four different 'domains' of activity of Robinson and Laycock Pedersen (2021) – campus and operations, research and innovation, teaching and learning, and partnerships and outreach; to the seven sub-systems of Lozano et al. (2015) covering institutional framework, campus operations, education, research, outreach and collaboration, on-campus experiences and assessment and reporting. This chapter extends the first and condenses the latter to focus on the following sub-systems of research and innovation, partnerships and outreach, campus and operations, university administration and leadership, and education and student-facing activities – each one with the ability to shape the educational environment, and intersect and overlap in myriad ways, and with sustainability needing to run through each in the process of becoming a sustainable university.

This chapter will explore what a 'sustainability purpose' looks like across the different university sub-systems starting first with a historical view of 'university purpose' as a whole and the tensions that exist between more incremental and radical visions of what sustainability transformation in higher education entails, before exploring different sub-systems with a focus on how stakeholders in every part of the university can find meaning and purpose in their work, whether in research, teaching, management or operations, and influence the university's journey towards becoming a 'sustainable university'.

## The Purpose of a University – Different Traditions Revisited

The characteristics of the universities that we see today are the result of several hundred years of history through which universities have served different purposes and developed. The term university comes from the Latin phrase '*universitas magistrorum et scholarium*', first used at the beginning of the 13th century, translated as a 'community of teachers and students'. Universities were originally initiated either by students or teachers for themselves and their students as local initiatives before seeking permission to operate as a university, while others were founded through a top-down approach by an emperor or by the Pope (the first university charter was granted to Naples in 1224). Initially, universities' 'sole purpose was to protect the men of letters against external threats' (Kivinen and Poikus, 2006: 189). Kivenen and Poikus (2006: 196) highlight that that the 'aims such as the advancement of learning and dissemination of knowledge and education on one hand, and an adaptable qualification and competence among the graduates for service in the public sector on the other are repeated in the charters for 800 years', with scholars and everyone who completed a degree at one university allowed to teach at any other university in the 'Christian world' since 1233.

While many universities prepared their graduates for service in public sectors, there was also a strong focus on argumentation (called 'disputes') and the search for truth through debate and co-creation of knowledge between students and professors, which influenced the wider community and sometimes had a strong impact on society. For example, the protestant reformation started as a dispute in a local university initiated by Martin Luther, then the youngest Professor in the University of Wittenberg, Germany. Luther writing in 1517 to his bishop his 'Disputation on the Power and Efficacy of Indulgences' questioned the authority of the Catholic Church, leading to a profound change in European societies (Cummings, 2002).

Wilhelm von Humbold (1767–1835) is credited with developing principles of the modern university. For von Humboldt, a modern university rested on four pillars: (1) the integration of teaching and research, including the obligation to foster the creation of knowledge as well as its preservation and transmission; (2) the complementary principles of Lehrfreiheit (freedom to teach) and Lernfreiheit (freedom to study); (3) the demand for Einsamkeit (solitude) and Freiheit (freedom) in the autonomous pursuit of truth (leading to the idea of academic freedom); and (4) the introduction of the seminar system as the backbone of a community of teachers and students (Krull, 2005: 99).

These historical vignettes highlight the changing nature of universities, with others labelling different stages of universities' development. For example, Barnett (2010) outlines an ongoing progression from the *metaphysical* university to the *scientific* university, *entrepreneurial* university and *bureaucratic* university, describing the entrepreneurial university as ill-matched to the challenges of the day. Barnett goes on to propose the *ecological* university, which is better suited to the *unfolding demands of the future* and acts in the collective interest. Mbah (2014: ii) suggests combining this with the *interconnected* university capturing voices from different sectors of the local community, 'operating accessible community centres; researching local concerns such as water supply, agricultural systems and electricity generation and customising educational programmes to demonstrate local and global relevance'.

This short discourse into the development of universities and their purpose through the centuries shows that the purpose of a university is not predefined but continues to be open to new interpretations. While decisions may be necessary to 'make business sense', it behoves those working in universities to continue to question the purpose of the university and alignment of activities to a purpose beyond the university as a business. Habermas (1985) pointed out in his 'Theory of Communicative Action' that the business system and any other system can be framed as a social system with its own inherent logic. Actors in this system perceive their way of thinking and acting as 'morally neutral' without questioning the system itself (Instrumental reason), whereas Habermas argues we need to apply a system of thinking which continues to question '*what* is to be preserved' (Communicative reason). Applying this theory of Communicative Reason, Table 3.2 outlines some fundamental questions we might ask ourselves relating to the purpose implicit in the different university 'domains' outlined in this chapter.

*Table 3.2* Examples of 'communicative reasoning' and fundamental questions of different university 'domains'.

| *University sub-system* | *Fundamental questions* |
|---|---|
| Education and student-facing services | What should be taught at a university? Does it need to lead to employment? Do we need forms of transdisciplinary learning? Could current content be replaced? Is the current curriculum fit for the purpose of tackling society's biggest challenges? |
| Research and innovation | Does research need to lead to solutions to society's grand challenges? Is there such a thing as value neutral research? What do we do with research that might lead to negative consequences? Should we accept funding from corporations with a vested interest? |

(*Continued*)

*Table 3.2* (Continued)

| *University sub-system* | *Fundamental questions* |
|---|---|
| Partnerships and outreach | What do universities mean for the 'places' in which they are situated? Should the university prioritise societal challenges in their own areas or faced by society in general? Do students need international experience in other countries? Should we prioritise the climate emergency over certain forms of internationalisation and avoid anything where academics and students have to fly? |
| Campus and operations | Can timetables be arranged to minimise travel for students? Can university buildings be used to learn about sustainability? Can the university estate provide resources for local communities? |
| University governance and leadership | Can decision making be more democratised? Can staff and students have more of a voice? Do structures enable diversity in decision making? |

## Radical versus Incremental Change

Since the 1980s, western universities, like broader western society, have been strongly rooted in the context of neoliberalism and its association with economic liberalisation and decentralisation (Bessant at al., 2015). This wider political context has been translated into western universities through the increasing use of quasi-markets to drive competition between institutions (e.g. through university league tables), increases in audit culture (e.g. Sparkes, 2007) and an increasingly managerialist framing of higher education leading to increased articulation of priorities focused towards income generation, innovation and business engagement and the language of business (e.g. students as consumers) (Bessant et al., 2015). For those advocating for sustainability transformation within universities, these neoliberal forces are often viewed as antithetical to and undermining the purpose and responsibilities of higher education, with calls from critical pedagogy theorists to seek alternative models to the neoliberal university (Amsler et al., 2010). Many writers argue that if we simply operate within the paradigm we seek to shift, we both help to sustain it and compromise the potential for other radical models of education, with some writers going so far as to describe ESD discourse as fundamentally implicated as part and parcel of the neoliberal regime (Irwin, 2008; Blewitt, 2013) and that 'ESD is only possible with a radical paradigm change' (Jucker, 2014: 41).

In this chapter, we take a more incremental approach to change exploring what shifts we as individuals whatever our roles can make, while acknowledging the desirability of a radical paradigm change with sustainability at the heart of a university's purpose. While for practicality in this chapter we discuss separately single 'domains' in the university system, we aim to avoid the pitfalls of addressing only single issues, which will be inevitably unsuccessful in driving holistic change, through considering the interactions between all domains and looking at not just *what* is done, but how it is done (Rieg et al., 2021). This incremental and pragmatist approach towards a sustainable university acknowledges that universities, along with the rest of society, must go through a transition process over a period of time, and that requires using levers for change within the existing system and sub-systems (domains), steered by a clear direction towards sustainability. What a 'sustainable university' looks like in the context of the existing sub-systems, and how we lever change to get there is the focus of the rest of the chapter.

## Leveraging Change for Sustainability within University Sub-Systems

The concept of leverage points to catalyse systems change is well established in the emerging field of sustainability science (e.g., Meadows, 2008; Abson et al., 2017). This section explores levers for change across five intersecting university sub-systems (or domains) – research and innovation, campus and operations, partnership and outreach, governance and leadership, and finishing with education and student facing services – and considers how these levers impact the educational setting and learner, and hence ESD. The focus throughout is on considering different actors' agency to pull these levers of change.

### *Research and Innovation*

This section considers research on and about ESD and the implications of the pervading research culture on ESD research, and the university's research environment on broader sustainability research, the sustainability *of* research and the implications to ESD and students as researchers.

#### *Research on Education for Sustainable Development*

One of Humboldt's four pillars for a modern university was the integration of teaching and research, and the obligation to foster the creation of knowledge and its preservation and transmission. Yet tensions between the research and education missions of a university generate challenges. This includes pressure on academics working in the field of ESD to focus on disciplinary research areas at the expense of ESD practice or research, as well as a perception of the lower status of educational and pedagogical research (Cotton et al., 2018). Within the UK, this pressure comes from the way in which research is rated and rewarded (the Research Excellence Framework, or 'REF'), which in many ways is at odds with the aims of ESD (Bessant and Robinson, 2019). For example, inter- or trans-disciplinarity, sustainability, higher education for sustainable development research, which by definition do not fit within an established 'disciplinary area' and are relatively new, lack established theoretical foundations, and are not well recognised or accommodated in the REF. There are criticisms suggesting that ESD research is often of poor quality (Corcoran et al., 2004), but this is not surprising given the implicit disincentives to undertake research in the field, hindering the development of researchers.

The rating and rewarding systems of research has driven much of the language of research in universities to be around quantitative metrics of research income and publication number and 'quality' (linked to contested uses of publication ranking and citation indices), rather than a language of purpose. These metrics-driven and marketised approaches may create ideological contradictions, for those interested in ESD. As Sterling et al. (2016, p.89) state, '... for many ESD researchers, their primary purpose and motivation operates at a deeper level and relates to the grand challenges of securing a more sustainable societal and planetary future'. Whether an increasing consideration within the REF rating and rewarding system of the 'impact' on society of research has implications to ESD research and its 'impact' on our educational systems remains to be seen.

### *Research on and about Sustainability*

Although the transdisciplinary requirements of much sustainability research are still problematic in many ways for the research rating systems in the UK, recent years have seen an increase in sustainability-focused research funding opportunities, with sustainability issues across all disciplines moving to be seen as mainstream rather than marginal, and increasing requirements for more solutions-orientated, interdisciplinary research, co-produced with non-academic stakeholders. These changes in the funding landscape are therefore signalling to the research-focused academic community the importance of these issues, as well as increasing opportunities to meet other research metrics such as research income, and meeting research 'impact' requirements and the move towards research needing to demonstrate its direct societal value and contribution. These trends have a positive impact not just on achieving a 'purpose' of research activities in line with the major sustainability challenges our society faces but engaging different communities of academics and professional services staff whose careers and job roles have a focus on research activity. For some, a pivot of research focus to researching sustainability issues opens up new curriculum development opportunities aligned to current research activities. Universities pride themselves on education reflecting the cutting edge of knowledge (aligning with von Humboldt's first pillar of the modern university), hence an increased focus on sustainability issues and solutions in research, supports the development of a curriculum that starts to meet the needs of a sustainable future.

### *Sustainability of Research*

Until recently, there has been little consideration of the sustainability of *how* research is carried out in universities, beyond considerations of the 'carbon footprint' of academic travel particularly associated with the academic conference industry (e.g. Jäckle, 2022) for which good practice and guides have been developed (e.g., Taylor and Molthan-Hill, 2023). In the UK, a 'Concordat for the Environmental Sustainability of Research and Innovation Practice' has been developed. This has drawn attention to the potential impacts of *doing* research, including impacts from research infrastructure and equipment procurement to data storage, and travel. This sends important messages that no part of a university is 'exempt' from considering sustainability implications and will heighten research-focused academic and professional services staff awareness and engagement with the sustainability implications of their practices. As universities and staff researchers start to have to articulate the sustainability implications of the research they do, student researchers will inevitably also be asked to consider, articulate and minimise the impacts of their research activities as part of learning about good research practice.

Other considerations about how research is done, relate to the publication of research, the use of open access platforms for research papers as well as data sets, as well as starting to consider different ways of measuring the impact of articles beyond academic citations, to impact in other sectors and influence on policy and practice, as well as considering other means of disseminating research to more diverse audiences and user communities.

### *Students Doing Research*

Just as for many academic staff who might have professional lives as both educators and researchers, the majority of degree courses also train students to be researchers. This therefore provides opportunities for students to research sustainability-issues linked to their disciplines and consider how to do research in a sustainable way. There are also opportunities for students to carry out research projects with non-academic stakeholders, either in the local community, or research projects with students from different disciplinary courses. The use of university campuses or their local surroundings has gained significant traction in the sustainability education community as 'living labs' to research sustainable solutions, educate students in sustainable solutions and provide students with the opportunities to work on applied problems with non-academic stakeholders (see Box 3.1). While 'living labs' or/and external student consultancy projects are time consuming and need to be set up very well to achieve genuine sustainable impact (Molthan-Hill et al., 2020), they do highlight the benefits to be had by linking different domains of activity. Students can also be encouraged to critique the less sustainable aspects of current research practices, such as the uneven distribution of voices in academic research

**Box 3.1 Universities as Living Labs for Sustainability: University of Leeds (UK) and Taylors University, Malaysia**

The University of Leeds Living Lab was launched in 2017. The Living Lab brings together students, academic and operational staff to research and test sustainable solutions, enhance the curriculum and solve real world challenges, using the University and local area as both a testbed for innovation and a space for co-created research-led teaching. The Living Lab is structured into four different (but interrelated areas): Living Lab for Net Zero; Living Lab for Biodiversity; Living Lab for Air Quality; and Living Lab for Food Waste. A range of different projects sit under each heading. The Living Lab team at Leeds University facilitate interdisciplinary projects on any element of the university's Sustainability Strategy and involve any subject areas. The Living Lab team have also developed a toolkit to support the development of new living lab projects. See more at: https://sustainability.leeds.ac.uk/get-involved/leeds-living-lab/

Taylors University in Malaysia has a programme of eleven 'Impact Labs', which are used to fulfil the university's purpose of positively impacting different societies and ensuring progress on societal problems by integrating research, education and advocacy to deliver practical solutions and shape new policies and practices through solutions-focused teams of academic, professional staff, practitioners, partners and students. Each impact lab engages students, staff and wider stakeholders to address real problems. There are 11 different impact labs aligned to the sustainable development goals, including eradicating poverty, education for all, digital innovation and smart society, clean technology and food security and nutrition.

See more at: https://university.taylors.edu.my/en/discover-us/taylors-impact-labs.html#empowering-for-a-better-world.

and issues of research access, encouraging students to question systems and paradigms and view these as changeable.

Research and education are often pitted against each other as competing university missions, with HE pedagogical research falling in the 'borderland territory' between teaching and research (Cotton et al., 2018). Yet considering the synergies between research and education and other domains can help leverage institutions towards becoming truly sustainable universities. Some academics are more research-focused, and large numbers of professional services staff are engaged in supporting research. The majority of academics start their careers through research – and exploring the research-sustainability-education implications of their research provides another route to engage different groups of university stakeholders, and to ensure sustainability considerations are aligned across research and education.

### *Partnerships and Outreach*

The role of partnerships with non-academic stakeholders has become so important for universities that in addition to supporting the other domains (e.g., placement opportunities for students and co-producing research), it can be considered an important domain of activity in its own right. While teaching and research are generally considered a university's first and second missions, respectively, the 'third mission' has been articulated in different (but overlapping) ways, including universities' contribution to society (e.g., Compagnucci and Spigarelli, 2020), entrepreneurial/economic performance-based (Etzkowitz et al., 2000; Trencher et al., 2014) and commercial enterprise and business engagement focused. This 'third mission', however it is exactly articulated, aligns with ideas of 'civic universities' (see the Civic University Network for example) where universities become actors of positive societal change or 'anchor institutions' (Lewis, 2020) within their local areas.

Universities are large organisations and consequently have important impacts on their local areas in terms of employment, the infrastructure assets they own or influence, their spending power and the way they interact with the local community. Many universities have sizable Science and Technology Parks on their campuses and provide support programmes for local businesses. Despite the co-location of such initiatives on university sites, the degree of university involvement can be variable, with Science Park activity sitting almost entirely separate to the research and education domains of the university. Yet, a journey 'towards a sustainable university' comes with imperatives to embed sustainability ambitions into such activities. This can include tenancy requirements where the university leverages its position as landlord to drive sustainable practices within its Business Park tenants, as well as opportunities for staff and students to engage with them to support sustainability-focused projects.

Universities also have significant responsibilities as 'honest brokers', with important roles to play due to the perceived rigorous research and dispassionate analysis they are well positioned to supply (Bogenshneider, 2020). The role of honest broker can also include local convening power as has been seen in the recent role of universities in the development of local 'Climate Commissions' bringing together different sectors, in an attempt to create innovative, place-based governance structures to help tackle place-based climate action. The role of universities as anchor institutions in their local area relies on local networks and local relationships, and staff invested in the local area over time. This requires an institutional culture, which supports long-term career development in one place.

Universities also pride themselves on their global impacts and international influence as well as their relationship with significant global corporate partners. Yet, this comes with important questions of who to partner with as well the purpose of partnership, and the equality of the relationship. A truly sustainable university should ensure that these questions are considered across a full suite of sustainability considerations, being clear about where tensions exist.

### *Campus and Operations*

The recent history of considering sustainability in universities lies in the university estate, and traditional considerations of environmental management, including the efficient management of energy, waste and water. These 'environmental[1]' management practices have themselves evolved over time, for example, with changing discourse from waste to resource management, and changing national targets.

Beyond compliance, there are financial reasons for addressing environmental management and becoming energy and waste efficient, as well as increasingly reputational reasons, as current and prospective students are able to scrutinise 'green credentials' through national and international award schemes and league tables. As part of their strategy, many universities now have prominent sections on their websites highlighting their commitment to 'Sustainability and Social Responsibility' (SSR) and its many synonyms, often including major institutional commitments such as climate emergency and 'net zero' declarations or commitments to international initiatives such as the Sustainable Development Accord – a public commitment to act and report on educational institution's actions towards the UN's Sustainable Development Goals. The challenge for universities to meet such targets and commitments is not insignificant, as many have estates that are old and in need of considerable sums to upgrade to modern sustainable standards, as well as the challenge of more behavioural and systemic changes required.

There are also significant new challenges in terms of procurement, the growing energy demands of computing systems (including super-computers), staff travel for conference attendance, etc., and student travel, particularly in the context of the growing financial reliance on international students.

Some universities are also addressing the deficit in their $CO_{2e}$ budget by transforming their on-campus energy systems, investing in onsite or offsite renewable generation through wind or solar, and investing in sequestering projects such as woodland planting and peatland restoration, often in collaboration with partners. Doing so offers potential opportunities for both research and experiential learning by students and staff. Any such projects require careful discussion with local communities to avoid the negative impression that the university is a just another wealthy landowner, but rather one that is sensitive to the relationships local people have with the area, and ideally involving them in decision making and providing employment and engagement opportunities.

In the past decade or so, there has been a significant shift in the consideration of the university estate in terms of its links with other university domains, not least education. For example, many now have 'sustainability' departments that bridge the management of the university's estate and operations and aspects of teaching and research. Such activities can include running courses for staff on sustainability and supporting student projects and internships. However, the development of these separate 'sustainability' departments can also be problematic, potentially reducing a sense of responsibility and empowerment to drive sustainability transformation from outside of these structures, and raising questions of legitimacy in influencing change in education and research from non-academics.

The university estate, and the way that it is managed, and used to communicate sustainability, has implications for the 'implicit curriculum'. The degree to which the university is or is not aligned in its approach with curriculum content and wider institutional messaging about sustainability commitments will be noted consciously or sub-consciously by students and staff. David Orr, writes in 1993 (p. 226), 'we've assumed, wrongly I think, that learning takes place in buildings but that none occurs as a result of how they are designed or by whom, how they are constructed and from what materials, how they fit into their location, and how the operate and how well', challenging us to consider more deeply the implications to learning of our built environment and the processes by which decisions are made.

The university estate also offers significant opportunities as a 'living lab for sustainability' (e.g., Verhoef et al., 2020). Not only do universities have the opportunity to experiment with new ways of doing things that may not be of commercial benefit, but there are also opportunities to maximise benefits to other domains through integrating education and research. Additional sustainability benefit can be accrued through explicit communication of sustainability elements of the Estate, where sustainable buildings become positive learning tools for sustainability, and building users can learn from the sustainability decisions and processes embedded in the design and operation of the building or infrastructure itself (Box 3.2). However, for this to be the case, then these 'demonstrator' attributes need to be designed into the process and maintenance (and assessment and reporting) of estate developments from the start.

**Box 3.2 Learning from the Built Environment, Oberlin College, USA**

The Adam Joseph Lewis Centre at Oberlin College, USA, is an example of a radical building project to 'design with nature', which came from trying to address the gap between learning and the design of educational facilities. The project aimed to inspire students, designers and the wider community that we can design our neighbourhoods to enhance the biosphere. In 1992–1993, a course was run in the Environmental Studies programme on the emerging field of ecological design, during which students wrote articles on the class for the newspaper to build solid support for the project and interest in 'green' architecture. Two years later, College Trustees approved the project. Then followed 13 design charrettes (participatory design and planning workshops) to build a knowledgeable constituency for the project and calibrate the design to the purposes of the Environmental Studies programme. Embedding principles of ecological design, the project involved on-site water purification, solar technology, use of non-toxic materials, gardens, land restoration and accurate feedback on building performance, with the aim of making various aspects of sustainability visible to building users and visitors. The building was intended to be not just a place where classes were held but a place that educated by its design, operation and evolution. The building makes an important statement about the hidden relationship between architecture, landscape design and learning, and that long-term net costs should include long-term benefits to reputation, admissions, educational value and its role as a catalyst for other things. The building helped to launch the Oberlin project, an eight-year effort to influence sustainability across the City of Oberlin (Orr, 2015).

Orr, D. 2021. Building as Pedagogy: Oberlin's Adam Joseph Lewis Centre. Accessible at: https://www.buildingsandcities.org/insights/research-pathways/building-pedagogy.html.

### *University Administration and Leadership*

Leadership is an essential part of driving, enabling and maintaining, organisational change. Chapter 9 explores Leadership in more detail, including different models and tools of leadership. An important aspect of leadership for whole institution change for sustainability is the different 'levels' of leadership, often described as 'top-down', 'bottom-up' or 'middle-out' to describe the different centres of leadership within the university hierarchy. Who exerts leadership and their leadership style will have an important influence on the nature of whole institution change.

This short section focuses on the senior leadership in the context of university administration and governance structures. Senior leadership is important to sustainability in setting vision and strategy that leaders at 'lower' levels must respond to, and setting the conditions and culture of the organisation through the language and processes adopted.

The *process* of whole institution change, and the way it is done, is as important to sustainability as the content of change, and *what* is done (Rieg et al., 2021). This includes consideration of diversity within leadership positions and diversity in participation contributing to decision making. A shared understanding of what sustainability means for an organisation is needed to enable and maintain organisation-wide transformation (Rieg et al., 2021), and this requires ongoing consultative approaches and communication to fit the transient population of a university. Participation from students in high-level decision making is typically through elected student representation on committees. However, often these representatives may be new to committee structures, protocols and language reducing ability for effective participation. Or situations may arise where decisions and discussions take place outside such meetings, rendering participation a formality rather than a genuine forum for discussion. Such (un)participative systems lead to the maintenance of hierarchies and existing power dynamics (Robinson and Laycock Pedersen, 2021). Instead, efforts should be taken to elicit diverse participation at different stages (see Arnstein, 1969), and for different purposes (see Collins and Ison, 2009), and alternative approaches may be needed to bring underrepresented views into decision making. Creating processes to increase the diversity of voices in decision making is essential due to the lack of diversity in senior management of universities (Croucher et al., 2020). Box 3.3 demonstrates an example of a structure of 'shadow leadership' that increases the diversity of voices influencing decision making.

**Box 3.3 Increasing Diversity in Decision Making: A 'Shadow' Governance System, Nottingham Trent University (UK)**

The 'University Shadow Executive Team' (USET) was established at Nottingham Trent University with an aim of embedding equity, diversity and inclusion at the heart of the University. The USET is deliberatively diverse in its demographic profile in order to hear a range of views based on lived experiences. Collectively, these views inform considerations about strategic initiatives; it is not however a decision-making body. The University Shadow Executive Team first met formally in August 2021 after a series of earlier induction meetings and now meets monthly, chaired by the Vice Chancellor, with its agendas typically mirroring those of the Extended University Executive Team. Each member of the Extended University Executive Team is represented by a 'shadow' member on USET possessing a particular protected characteristic (disability, ethnic and racial diversity (inclusive of international and/or white minority profiles), LGBTQ+, gender identities that may be expressed in non-binary terms inclusive of transgender. Their role both individually and collectively as a group is to review the agenda items of business through the lens of Equity, Diversity and Inclusion and advise the Vice-Chancellor of any issues arising from the agenda items from an EDI perspective.

See more at: https://www.ntu.ac.uk/__data/assets/pdf_file/0036/1539981/EDI-Annual-Report-2020-21.pdf page 8.

Assessment and reporting is viewed as a separate sub-system of organisational change for sustainability by Lozano et al. (2015), but can equally be viewed, as here, as part of leadership and administration. Assessment and reporting is seen by Rieg et al. (2021) as key to initiate and drive change. Sustainability Reporting, Environmental Management Systems, which incorporate education and research domains and go beyond traditional 'environmental' management of the Estate, are all mechanisms that can create interconnections between different domains and create opportunities for reflection and further change. There are a number of different assessment tools to audit whole-institution approaches to sustainability, yet there are tensions about the amount of time that collating information for these tools requires, versus time spent 'doing' change, as well as challenges in gathering data which is fit for long-term sustainable decision making. For example, monitoring and evaluation data usually focuses on quantitative data, missing the depth of understanding which can come from qualitative data. Changes in the system such as underpinning values, goals and world views are where the greatest leverage for change lies (Meadows, 1999; Abson et al., 2017) yet are not easily reflected in short-term or quantitative metrics.

Creating positive change for sustainability is not enough, we need to ensure we have the leadership, administrative, assessment and reporting structures to *evaluate* and *maintain* such change. Robinson and Laycock Pedersen (2021) discuss the importance of building in resilience to new systems to reduce the chance of backsliding on positive changes made. Most of those working in the field of sustainability change management will recognise the experience of making change in systems, only for those systems to have reverted a few years later, or for technological solutions to fail to function effectively after a period of time. Thus, 'maintenance' must be an essential part of any assessment and reporting and administration process.

The effectiveness of assessment and reporting in contributing to driving and maintaining whole institution change is therefore likely to be determined by how this is carried out as part of the organisational system, and the building of processes which enable auditing and reporting to drive further change and allow honest and transparent assessment of progress, impact and effectiveness. Further detail on monitoring and evaluation for ESD is covered in Chapter 11.

Ultimately, if our students are to become society's future leaders and they learn implicitly from what happens around them, seeing and experiencing leadership which embraces an effective collaborative process for change is another essential link between whole institution change, leadership and education for sustainable development and the opportunity to learn about enacting change.

### *Education and Student-Facing Services*

Each of the sections above links different university 'domains' to the education 'mission', and specifically education for sustainability. But education, through both the curriculum and co/extra-curriculum, and student-facing support requires its own consideration here as part of a whole institution approach to sustainability. Whilst in the public mind universities are institutions of learning that balance teaching and research, the task for senior leaders and indeed all staff is much more complex.

The demands of a competitive marketplace resulting from the UK Government's 2012 introduction of a free market requiring universities in England and Wales to charge fees, and other funding issues can lead to a dilution of these core responsibilities, and in the specific context of curriculum to a range of perceived or real constraints. For example, pressures and time spent around research and income generation reduce time available for teaching and providing feedback for students. In recent decades, this has led to a trend towards forms of instrumentalism in curriculum design, larger classes, reductions in staff student contact time, reduction in time allocation for teaching preparation and administration, and increased use of online and blended learning. The implications for sustainability education are significant, in that complex interdisciplinary 'wicked' issues are not straightforward matters of content but rather demand consideration and thoughtful discussion (McCune et al., 2021, 2023), and hence the time and settings to enable this. Likewise, effective ESD pedagogies, such as experiential learning, require more time and resource than traditional content-based lectures and essay-based assignments, creating tensions when time allocations for teaching activities are constrained.

Talk of 'education' often implies a focus on the formal, taught curriculum, yet opportunities within the co- (or extra- or informal) curriculum also have the required transformational opportunities of sustainability education, and potentially even more so, with increasing limitations and pressures on the formal curriculum. It may be easier to develop some sustainability competencies through the co-curriculum than the formal curriculum due to the experiential nature of learning in the co-curriculum, hence a need to view the role of the co-curriculum as part of the core education process (Sanusi, 2019) (while acknowledging that different student circumstances will give different access to co-curriculum opportunities). Joyner Armstrong et al. (2016) describe how in a truly holistic approach to sustainability, there is a blurring of the informal and formal curriculum, while

Robinson and Laycock Pedersen (2021) describe how the formal curriculum can catalyse learning within the co-curriculum.

The potential co-curriculum opportunities to support education for sustainability are only bounded by the imagination. Some opportunities may be more structured and university-led, for example, formal volunteering programmes, opportunities to engage with university-led sustainability events such as 'green weeks' and roles such as student auditors for university-wide schemes such as the SOS-UK Green Impact scheme (SOS-UK, undated). However, students also create their own opportunities, for example through the formation of sustainability societies, and other student-led initiatives, which may even arise as a response to students' views on the 'unsustainability' of certain actions of the university. In the authors' own experiences, students have led, amongst others, the development of circular economy initiatives in response to the 'waste' produced when students move out of halls, campus food growing initiatives, and even organic veg box schemes for the campus to improve access to organic food. A formal curriculum, which encourages development of a sense of agency to drive change, can help provide a catalyst for action and learning within the co-curriculum space (Robinson and Laycock Pedersen, 2021).

Students' Unions can be one of the key student-facing organisations in relation to co-curriculum activities in a students' time at university. Where necessary to increase the profile of and knowledge about sustainability within Students' Unions, staff and student officers within Students' Unions can be supported by the University through University provision of annual sustainability training for new sabbatical officers, as well as collaborative working across sustainability initiatives. Mechanisms including funding, and staff resources to support students with ideas to drive their own sustainability initiatives within a co-curriculum context, can help empower and develop agency in students, giving them their first taste of driving change.

In much the way that a lack of sustainability in the university's campus and operations comes with it implicit messages of the lack of importance of sustainability, the message received by students if sustainability does not feature in their courses is that it becomes as Eisner (1985) argues, the 'null curriculum', or if it is allocated limited time and resources it becomes part of an 'implicit curriculum' wherein it is not properly valued. Similarly, the management of the estate, its buildings, cafes, travel policies, etc., tend to be conducted with little or no consultation or involvement of staff and less so with students, ironically as these are the users of such facilities and systems. Such decisions result in 'signals' which are picked up by staff as well as students, and can lead to a sense that the institution is not committed to sustainability as a primary purpose (despite espoused mission statements). The corollary is of course that those institutions that do commit to more participative approaches and build sustainability into curriculum design and co-curriculum opportunities generate a reinforcing, positive sense of direction towards a more sustainable university, society and future.

Given the increasing awareness of students that the prospect of a sustainable future is slipping away from them, there is a clear need to convey positive messages through the university estate and functions, supported by a curriculum that enables them to develop the knowledge, skills, attitudes and values that will be helpful in enabling them to work towards such a future. The need to authentically reduce 'eco-anxiety' and convey a sense of hope through positive action should clearly be as central to the mission of universities as the development of core learning skills and subject-specific knowledge. The rest of the book focuses on more specific educational activities, but it should always be remembered that education can be influenced, both positively and negatively, by every part of the university and its different domains and missions.

## Bringing It Together: Whole Institution Change

The literature about sustainability in higher education has been criticised for being largely piecemeal in its approach, focusing separately on estates or educational aspects (Corcoran et al., 2004; Rieg et al., 2021). The complexity and breadth of higher education institutions has led us to address each domain separately within this chapter, but of equal importance is bringing these elements together to consider genuine whole institutional change. Senge's (1990) seminal work on 'Learning Organisations' provides a useful lens for considering whole institution change in the context of sustainability in higher education institutions. Senge defines learning organisations as 'organisations where people continually expand their capacity to create the results they truly desire, where new and expansive patterns of thinking are nurtured, where collective aspiration is set free, and where people are continually learning to see the whole together' (1990: p.3). Senge levels similar criticism at management literature, of a tendency to apply simplistic frameworks to what are complex systems, a tendency to focus on parts rather than seeing the whole, and failing to view organisation as a dynamic process. Creating a shared vision for a 'sustainable university' has the potential to create a lodestone by which coherence and purpose can be brought to the process of change.

Seeing the whole helps us to understand the wicked problems and areas which act in tension, whether competition for resources between teaching and research, or intransigent problems between the financial drive for international students and associated carbon emissions. Engaging in open and honest dialogue about the tensions across the institution as a whole, and embracing the journey to a sustainable university as a process and transition, can help unlock impasses driven by a fear of not being perfect. It can also help identify current paradigms and the paradigm shifts[2] needed.

Understanding universities as complex, adaptive systems can help us to identify different leverage points for change. The sections above identify different domains in the university system as points of leverage, with connections between the different domains, contributing to whole institution change. Box 3.4 outlines an exercise that can be carried out to consider the current paradigms and the paradigm shifts needed in each domain.

### Box 3.4 Paradigm Shift Exercise

This exercise is designed to help you consider current paradigms that exist in how things are done in your university under the different domains and to consider future desirable paradigm shifts and specific actions that can help lever change. For each domain consider:

1 what are the current paradigms limiting sustainability?
2 what desired new paradigms could support sustainability?
3 what is needed to achieve the desired paradigm shift?

Examples are given below.

Shifts to new paradigms or ways of working may require changes in mindset. At the heart of changing mindsets is thinking about how things could be done differently, starting with questioning how things are done at the moment.

### Domain 1: Research and Innovation

For example

#### *Current Paradigm*

Research is largely talked about by university management in terms of income and publication metrics.

#### *Desired Paradigm*

Research is encouraged and celebrated in terms of the positive impact that it has on society.

#### *Mechanisms to Shift Paradigms*

Those involved in research at all levels use the language of purpose rather than metrics and openly challenge language solely about income or publication metrics.

### Domain 2: Partnerships and Outreach

For example

#### *Current Paradigm*

University Science Park tenants have little interaction with university educators and academics and might be at odds with university sustainability aspirations.

#### *Desired Paradigm*

As a requirement for tenancy on the Science Park, business values must align with a sustainability mission, with an expectation to engage with staff and students, supported through regular engagement events.

#### *Mechanisms to Shift Paradigm*

Catalyse a shift in policy through communication to senior management of best practice elsewhere; direct engagement with science park tenants and communication to senior management of benefits to staff and students to encourage up-scaling.

### Domain 3: Campus and Operations

#### *Current Paradigm*

Sustainable technology solutions are not evaluated or monitored to see lasting impacts.

#### *Desired Paradigm*

Data collection on solutions is embedded into formal assessment and reporting. Data collection and analysis is supported by students where appropriate.

#### *Mechanisms to Shift Paradigm*

Develop policies to require new technology to be evaluated and reported at the senior level.

### Domain 4: University Administration and Leadership

#### *Current Paradigm*

The student voice is included in decision making largely through elected representatives and formal committee structures only.

#### *Desired Paradigm*

Shadow structures (see Box 3.3) in place for all decision making to increase diversity of voices informing decision making.

#### *Mechanisms to Shift Paradigm*

Policy shift

### Domain 5: Education and Student-Facing Services

#### *Current Paradigm*

The built (or natural) environment is not seen as an important source of learning, so there is no communication of sustainable decisions in the built environment.

#### *Desired Paradigm*

The built (or natural) environment is seen as an important source of sustainability learning; sustainability is built into new builds and renovations and communicated effectively long-term to users as a source of learning.

***Mechanisms to Shift Paradigm***

Inclusion of education and learning potential included in sustainable building design guides, and included in governance, monitoring and evaluation processes for built (or natural) environment developments.

However, the theory of leverage points for systems change highlights that the greatest leverage is in cultural and mindset shifts (Meadows, 1999; Abson et al., 2017; Rimanoczy and Llamazares, 2021). This is strongly influenced by shifting external contexts (e.g., the increasingly neoliberal context and new public management practices within universities (Bessant et al. 2015, 2017) and requires time and consistency to change. Mindset shift requires developing a shared vision of a sustainable university, ongoing communication of the importance of sustainability, distributed responsibility and leadership, and monitoring and accountability systems that embed true reflection on the state of progress.

There remains debate (e.g., Irwin, 2008; Blewitt, 2013; Jucker, 2014: 41) as to whether the required shifts in our higher education settings to create 'sustainable universities' can be achieved through small incremental shifts or whether dramatic change is needed. The COVID-19 2020/2021 lockdowns saw perhaps the most sudden and dramatic change to our education systems with a sudden switch to online teaching, combined with the hopeful, but ultimately unfulfilled, mantra of 'build back better'. The changes in working patterns during COVID-19 have led to some embedded change, in terms of increased use of online platforms for meetings and teaching. Whether these practices are 'better' (and better for *whom* in the context of our education settings and for *what*) still remain to be truly assessed in the long-term. COVID-19 provides a useful reflection point on the sort of catalyst needed to create a transformational shift towards sustainability in our education systems. Such catalysts by their nature mean that their impacts cannot be planned for, suggesting that their impacts for sustainability are as likely to be negative as they are positive. Therefore, maybe the radical shift required lies not in a shock event but through shifting the mindsets of all those working across all domains of our education settings. Everybody will have different triggers to a shift in mindset, but leaders, in whatever part of an education setting they work, can help create the conditions for transformation, through encouraging a language and culture supportive of a sustainability transition. As we see more and more universities start to clearly articulate the links to sustainability in what they do, maybe we are seeing signs of that paradigm shift, which will only become apparent as we look back in the rear-view mirror of the history we are creating.

It may seem that this chapter implies that all universities should be the same in how they transform to be 'sustainable universities' and embrace a whole institution approach. Yet we know that differentiation in universities is important. For example, some are more closely embedded in their local communities, some more focused on elite international research, and different disciplinary strengths and focus will be found in different institutions. A sustainable university may look different in different cultural settings, as

**Box 3.5 Key Readings for Those Seeking to Explore a Whole Institution Approach**

1 Sterling, S., Maxey, L., & Luna, H. (Eds.). (2013). The sustainable university: Progress and prospects.
Includes many leading UK writers on different aspects of sustainable transformation in universities
2 Sterling, S. (2024). *Learning and sustainability in dangerous times.* Newcastle on Tyne: Agenda Publishing. p. 234.
Compiles the writings of Stephen Sterling, one of the pioneers of sustainability education.

so clearly articulated by the International Islamic University Malaysia, which combines a focus on the SDGs through Islamic teachings and concepts, linking the fundamental teaching of Islam with society's current needs (Sanusi, 2019). A whole institution lens to sustainability education enables these differences to be maintained, through ensuring that sustainability is woven through the priorities for each institution, while also considering new opportunities for sustainability developments and the implications to sustainability education (Box 3.5).

If universities don't seriously tackle the sustainability implications across all their missions and operations, then the alternative is to contradict the espoused mission statements of universities, which position themselves at the heart of societal transformation towards a sustainable future, and to acknowledge the current reality of the '*unsustainable* university'. Anything less than whole institution change and a realignment of each domain of the university to support sustainable outcomes implies both a denial of the twin climate and biodiversity emergencies we face, and also a failure to realise the 'duty of care' universities have to their current and future generations of students. It is not just *what* universities do, but the *way* they do it, and how they *demonstrate* sustainability values that will impact both students and staff learning for sustainability, and in the 'not so long-run' the measure of universities' contribution towards a sustainable future.

## Notes

1 Environmental appears in scare quotes to draw attention to (in the authors') view the problematic use of this term which evades connection to the, inter alia, economic, social, cultural and political elements of both its causes and impacts, and how the use of 'environmental' as a badge has enabled these issues to be sidelined by those not considering themselves or their roles as concerned with 'environmental issues'
2 A paradigm shift is defined as 'an important change that happens when the usual way of thinking about or doing something is replaced by a new and different way' (Ref. https://www.merriam-webster.com/dictionary/paradigm%20shift)

## References

Abson, D.J., Fischer, J., Leventon, J., Newig, J., Schomerus, T., Vilsmaier, U., … & Lang, D.J. (2017). Leverage points for sustainability transformation. *Ambio*, *46*, 30–39.

Amsler, S., Canaan, J.E., Cowden, S., Motta, S., & Singh, G., eds. (2010). Why Critical Pedagogy and Popular Education Matter Today. Higher Education Academy Subject Centre for Sociology, Anthropology and Politics. [Online]. http://www.lulu.com/gb/en/shop/joyce-canaan/why-critical-pedagogy-and-popular-education-matter-today/paperback/product-6318961.html

Arnstein, S.R. (1969). A ladder of citizen participation. *Journal of the American Institute of Planners*, *35*(4), 216–224.

Barnett, R. (2010). *Being a University*. Routledge.

Bessant, S. E. F., Robinson, Z. P., & Ormerod, R. M. (2015). Neoliberalism, new public management and the sustainable development agenda of higher education: history, contradictions and synergies. *Environmental Education Research*, *21*(3), 417–432.

Bessant, S.E., Robinson, Z.P., & Ormerod, R.M. (2017). Neoliberalism, New Public Management and the Sustainable Development Agenda of Higher Education: History, Contradictions and Synergies. In *Neoliberalism and Environmental Education* (pp. 129–144). Routledge.

Bessant, S.E., & Robinson, Z.P. (2019). Rating and rewarding higher education for sustainable development research within the marketised higher education context: Experiences from English universities. *Environmental Education Research*, *25*(4), 548–565.

Birch, E., Perry, D.C., & Taylor, H.L. Jr. (2013). Universities as anchor institutions. *Journal of Higher Education Outreach and Engagement*, *17*(3), 7–16.

Blewitt, J. (2013). EfS: Contesting the Market Model of Higher Education. In *The Sustainable University* (pp. 51–70). Routledge.

Bogenschneider, K. (2020). Positioning universities as honest knowledge brokers: Best Practices for communicating research to policymakers. *Family Relations*, *69*(3), 628–643.

Collins, K., & Ison, R. (2009). Jumping off Arnstein's ladder: Social learning as a new policy paradigm for climate change adaptation. *Environmental Policy and Governance*, *19*(6), 358–373.

Compagnucci, L., & Spigarelli, F. (2020). The third mission of the university: A systematic literature review on potentials and constraints. *Technological Forecasting and Social Change*, *161*, 120284.

Corcoran, P.B., Walker*, K.E., & Wals, A.E. (2004). Case studies, make-your-case studies, and case stories: A critique of case-study methodology in sustainability in higher education. *Environmental Education Research*, *10*(1), 7–21.

Cortese, A.D. (2003). The critical role of higher education in creating a sustainable future. *Planning for Higher Education*, *31*(3), 15–22.

Cotton, D.R., Miller, W., & Kneale, P. (2018). The Cinderella of academia: Is higher education pedagogic research undervalued in UK research assessment? *Studies in Higher Education*, *43*(9), 1625–1636.

Croucher, G., Wen, W., Coates, H., & Goedegebuure, L. (2020). Framing research into university governance and leadership: Formative insights from a case study of Australian higher education. *Educational Management Administration & Leadership*, *48*(2), 248–269.

Cummings, B. (2002). *The Literary Culture of the Reformation: Grammar and Grace*. Oxford University Press.

Eisner, E.W. (1985). The three curricula that all schools teach: The educational imagination. *New York: Macmillan Publishing Company. (1992)'A Reply to Gabriele Lakomski', Curriculum Inquiry*, 22, 205–209.

Etzkowitz, H., Webster, A., Gebhardt, C., & Terra, B.R.C. (2000). The future of the university and the university of the future: Evolution of ivory tower to entrepreneurial paradigm. *Research Policy*, *29*(2), 313–330.

Habermas, J. (1985). *The Theory of Communicative Action: Volume 1: Reason and the Rationalization of Society* (Vol. 1). Beacon Press.

Irwin, R. (2008). After Neoliberalism': Environmental Education to Education for Sustainability. In *Environmental Education* (pp. 171–193). Brill.

Jäckle, S. (2022). The carbon footprint of travelling to international academic conferences and options to minimise it. *Academic Flying and the Means of Communication*, 19–52.

Joyner Armstrong, C.M., Hustvedt, G., LeHew, M.L., Anderson, B.G., & Hiller Connell, K.Y., 2016. When the informal is the formal, the implicit is the explicit: Holistic sustainability education at Green Mountain College. *International Journal of Sustainability in Higher Education, 17*(6), 756–775.

Jucker, R. (2014). *Do We Know What We Are Doing? Reflections on Learning, Knowledge, Economics, Community and Sustainability*. Cambridge Scholars Publishing.

Kivinen, O., & Poikus, P. (2006). Privileges of Universitas Magistrorum et Scolarium and their justification in charters of foundation from the 13th to the 21st centuries. *Higher Education, 52*, 185–213.

Krull, W. (2005). Exporting the Humboldtian University.

Lewis, R. 2020. Unpacking the role of universities as civic anchor institutions. Available at: https://yorkshireuniversities.ac.uk/2020/02/20/unpacking-the-role-of-universities-as-civic-anchor-institutions/

Lozano, R., Ceulemans, K., Alonso-Almeida, M., Huisingh, D., Lozano, F.J., Waas, T., … & Hugé, J. (2015). A review of commitment and implementation of sustainable development in higher education: Results from a worldwide survey. *Journal of Cleaner Production, 108*, 1–18.

Mbah, M. (2014). *Rethinking university engagement to address local priority needs within the context of community development: a case study* (Doctoral dissertation, Canterbury Christ Church University).

McCune, V., Tauritz, R., Boyd, S., Cross, A., Higgins, P., & Scoles, J. (2021). Teaching wicked problems in higher education: Ways of thinking and practising. *Teaching in Higher Education, 28*(7), 1518–1533.

McCune, V., Scoles, J., Boyd, S., Cross, A., Higgins, P., & Tauritz, R. (2023). Academic identities and teaching wicked problems: How to 'shoot a fog' in a complex landscape. *Higher Education Research & Development*, 1–14.

Meadows, D. (1999). Leverage points. *Places to Intervene in a System, 19*, 28.

Meadows, D.H. (2008). *Thinking in Systems: A Primer*. Chelsea Green Publishing.

Molthan-Hill, P., Robinson, Z.P., Hope, A., Dharmasasmita, A., & McManus, E. (2020). Reducing carbon emissions in business through responsible management education: Influence at the micro-, meso-and macro-levels. *The International Journal of Management Education, 18*(1), 100328.

Orr, D.W. (1993). Architecture as pedagogy. *Conservation Biology*, 7(2), 226–228.

Rieg, N.A., Gatersleben, B., & Christie, I. (2021). Organizational change management for sustainability in higher education institutions: A systematic quantitative literature review. *Sustainability, 13*(13), 7299.

Rimanoczy, I., & Llamazares, A.M. (2021). Twelve principles to guide a long-overdue paradigm shift. *Journal of Management, Spirituality & Religion, 18*(6), 54–76.

Robinson, Z.P., & Laycock Pedersen, R. (2021) Activist Learning. In: Gamage, K. and Gunawardhana, N. (Eds). *Wiley Handbook of Sustainability in Higher Education Learning and Teaching*. Wiley

Robinson, Z.P., & Laycock Pedersen, R. (2021). How to repurpose the university: A resilience lens on sustainability governance. *Frontiers in Sustainability*, 2, 674210.

Sanusi, Z.A. (2019). Case study—Humanising higher education: Transforming the co-curriculum as the core-curriculum at the international Islamic university Malaysia (IIUM). *Higher Education in the World*, 7, 206.

Senge, P. (1990) The Fifth Discipline: The Art and Practice of the Learning Organization.

SOS-UK (undated) Green Impact. Available at: https://www.sos-uk.org/project/green-impact Accessed on: 10th August 2024

Sparkes, A.C. (2007). Embodiment, academics, and the audit culture: A story seeking consideration. *Qualitative Research*, 7(4), 521–550.

Sterling, S., Maxey, L., & Luna, H. (Eds.). (2013). *The sustainable university: Progress and prospects*. Routledge. London and New York.

Sterling, S., Warwick, P., & Wyness, L. (2016). Understanding Approaches to ESD Research on Teaching and Learning in Higher Education. In Barth, M., Michelsen, G., Rieckmann, M., & Thomas, I. (Eds.), *Routledge Handbook of Higher Education for Sustainable Development*. Chapter 6, pp it is Routledge, Abingdon and the DOI: 10.4324/9781315852249.

Sylvestre, P., & Wright, T. (2015). Organisational Change and Organisational Learning for Promoting Higher Education for Sustainable Development. In *Routledge Handbook of Higher Education for Sustainable Development* (pp. 301–314). Routledge.

Taylor, H., & Molthan-Hill, P. (2023). PRME Sustainable Travel and Events Guidance. Available at: https://d30mzt1bxg5llt.cloudfront.net/public/uploads/PDFs/Virtual-First.pdf

Trencher, G., Yarime, M., McCormick, K.B., Doll, C.N., & Kraines, S.B. (2014). Beyond the third mission: Exploring the emerging university function of co-creation for sustainability. *Science and Public Policy*, *41*(2), 151–179.

Verhoef, L.A., Bossert, M., Newman, J., Ferraz, F., Robinson, Z.P., Agarwala, Y., ... & Hellinga, C. (2020). Towards a learning system for university campuses as living labs for sustainability. *Universities as living labs for sustainable development: Supporting the implementation of the Sustainable Development Goals*, 135–149.

Chapter 4

# Education for Sustainable Development

## From Disciplinary to Transdisciplinary Approaches

*Rehema M. White and Chris Preist*

### Introduction

The purposes of education at a university require us to prepare learners in all programmes for a complex, uncertain future, and to address inter- and intra-generational justice and environmental limits, whatever the subject, vocation or employment options (see Chapter 2). How do we prepare our learners – who have different interests, priorities and perspectives – to understand and play a positive role in the required societal transformation and planetary rescue? How do we encourage higher education academic and professional staff to cross the boundaries of structure, organisation and intellectual debates?

Academic disciplines shape the ways we seek and understand knowledge, the type of knowledge generated and shared and the goals of such knowledge (Aram 2004). Disciplinary context is thus critical in the ways we portray views on the world, what content is taught and how such knowledge might be employed beyond academia. Disciplinary context is important in our consideration and practice of education for sustainable development (ESD). The aims of this chapter are, therefore, to explore the meanings and consequences of academic disciplines; to assess sustainability-focused disciplines; to discuss practical aspects, benchmarks and other required content for university programmes in particular disciplines; to examine epistemological differences; and to explore multi-, inter- and transdisciplinarity.

Global challenges, including the climate and nature crises, social inequality and globalisation, have manifested and will continue to cause change in people's lives and throughout their careers (Raworth 2012; Rockstrom *et al.* 2023; UN 2015). Education in all disciplines needs to adapt to this changing reality, to ensure that all graduates can address risks now and in the future, and become change agents for a more sustainable world (Sterling 2001). Many universities have now made a commitment to integrate sustainability into all of their degree courses, although the extent and form of this integration differs (Price *et al.* 2021). ESD supports the development of specific and generic sustainability competencies, such that graduates gain the skills and capacities to adapt and respond to change, through provision of relevant curricular content and innovative pedagogies (Wiek *et al.* 2011; Giangrande *et al.* 2019; see Chapter 2). Disciplinary context can also highlight, demonstrate and support responsibility for institutional, personal and professional behaviours. The broad commitment to ESD involves considering, in the context of each academic discipline, what content is appropriate for that discipline, how it should be included in a given degree programme curriculum and what pedagogical

DOI: 10.4324/9781003451563-4

approaches can be used to do this. Curriculum (Chapter 5), Pedagogy (Chapter 6) and Assessment (Chapter 7) are essential in this implementation.

ESD requires a whole institution approach (see Chapter 3), and therefore, staff and learners in different disciplinary units should also be encouraged to engage with institutional efforts to phase out fossil fuel use, reduce waste, conserve biodiversity and other operational priorities. Institutional practices may include, for example, recycling, cup re-use schemes, the availability of vegetarian/vegan options and sustainable transport routes. Such behaviours will be informed through inductions but can be reinforced in subject discipline programmes and departments, the unit at which learners mostly engage. Personal choices can be explored through collaborative learning, dialogical pedagogies and other approaches. If staff have appropriate professional development, they can explicitly include professional responsibilities in disciplinary programmes (see Chapter 10). Teaching, research, practice and engagement for sustainable development are inter-linked, within and beyond disciplines (see Chapter 8).

Whilst we theorise academic disciplines within knowledge frameworks, learners tend to perceive them as programmes in degree subjects, located at institutions of their choice, for their study. Learners have a mix of different aspirational and pragmatic motivations to begin and continue such study. Some learners are passionate about their discipline or subject. Others might be more motivated by the career options that their disciplinary education opens up for them. Others may be living out the expectation of being a student at university or exploring future options. In all cases, sustainability challenges can respond to or potentially stimulate their motivation.

Research with engineering learners identified three broad categories of motivation for their engagement with the programme (Alpay *et al.* 2008). Learners sought to have a positive impact in the world, pursue academic interest and excellence, or prepare for personal and professional success. Integration of ESD into a disciplinary programme can respect and work with these different motivational frames. Rather than assuming that all learners have a pre-existing passion for sustainable development, we can understand their various priorities and engage them in different ways. These may include moral arguments, question provocation, highlighting employment needs or merely through pedagogies that engage and excite learners.

Disciplines differ in the extent of vocational emphasis and practical application for sustainable development. Whilst all programmes can be linked to real-world problems, the link may be more tenuous for theoretical fields such as Pure Mathematics and more tangible for vocational degrees such as Engineering or Conservation.

## Disciplining Academia

Academic disciplines came into being as knowledge accumulated, and there was a need to classify and organise information and to specialise in learning. The concept of a 'discipline' (cf disciple) arose in the Middle Ages when universities were first founded. However, it was perhaps only in the 1970s in the Western world that organisational disciplinarity was heavily subscribed to by academics (Chettiparamb 2007). Disciplines have also been viewed through an intellectual frame as 'thought domains – quasi-stable, partially integrated, semi-autonomous intellectual conveniences – consisting of problems, theories, and methods of investigation' (Aram 2004, p.380). This definition also captures the sense that disciplines coalesce around particular topics and modes of research. Finally, academic disciplines imply scholarly communities and can thus be seen as a social construct.

Disciplines thus serve three main purposes: they boundary intellectual domains, they enable organisational structures within which people can work and for which budgets can be allocated; and they facilitate communication and exchange between academic staff and learners and external stakeholders with common interests, permitting fluidity across institutions and from academia across to professions, especially for vocational disciplines. Subdisciplines exist; for example, Genetics, Zoology and Botany are all overlapping aspects of Biology. Disciplines overlap; and there are diffuse and dynamic boundaries between disciplines. For example, Art History overlaps both with History and with Art.

Learners often do not see these academic disciplines when they enrol, and the depth of knowledge and approach within each academic discipline becomes apparent to them as they progress through their degree programmes.

## ESD in Different Academic Disciplines

Educator and learners can explore how their discipline interacts with the sustainability agenda and its priorities. Some learning is specific to and valuable for a given disciplinary programme. Such learning can be practical (around use of materials and methods), experiential (such as fieldtrips), professional (in relation to career implementation), intellectual (concepts and ideas) and supporting a range of key competencies (such as future, critical or systems thinking, strategic or collaborative, normative or self-awareness competencies – see Chapters 2 and 6). Assessment is critical in enabling learning for sustainable development (Nicholson and Vargas 2021; see Chapter 7), and many disciplinary forms of assessment link to accreditation or represent disciplinary norms.

There are many ways by which a discipline can interact with sustainability agendas and priorities. These can be multiplied and deepened in practice by individual academics, in modules and across programmes, by conducting a curriculum review to integrate ESD (also see Chapter 11). The examples below, of how disciplines could develop approaches to respond to sustainability challenges, demonstrate rich opportunities for ESD interventions to be embedded in modules or programmes.

- Physics develops more effective photovoltaic materials and battery storage solutions.
- Physical Geography predicts changing climatic conditions to advise adaptation strategies.
- English explores old and new stories with regards to our relationship with the earth and each other.
- Human Geography highlights questions of ecological justice.
- Biology explores ecosystem restoration and nature-based carbon sequestration approaches (including assessment of their effectiveness).
- Law develops the concept of attributing legal personhood to entities within nature, such as rivers (Clark *et al.* 2018).
- Economics provides insight into 'negative externalities' as drivers of environmental degradation, and the contested relationship between economic growth and environmental impact – such as the 'environmental Kuznets curve' (Stern 2017).
- History analyses past colonial injustices and extractive practices which have impoverished countries in the global south.

In all cases, these illustrate the value of each discipline in applying its theoretical frames and practical methods to sustainability challenges. The diverse ways in which academic disciplines engage in ESD are surprising and imaginative. Table 4.1 demonstrates some real examples to inspire novel ideas. In some cases, this ESD engagement also leads to enhanced potential employment opportunities for graduating students.

*Table 4.1* Examples of how different academic disciplines are demonstrating ESD in several higher education institutions across UK.

| *Discipline* | *Institution* | *Example of how ESD is embedded in different disciplines* |
|---|---|---|
| Medicine | University of Bristol | Sustainability is a helical theme within the UoB Medicine programme, so it is returned to and built on year on year. Specific topics covered include the impact of poverty on health; health impacts of climate change including heat stress and increased range of vector-borne diseases; the impacts of extreme weather events on healthcare systems; and approaches to mitigate the environmental impacts of healthcare provision. |
| Political Science | University of Bristol | The compulsory 'Thinking Politically' first-year unit introduces core political ideas. Climate change is used as one motivating example to explore tensions arising both in national politics and international relations. Learners have the option of focusing on climate change in their assessments and have the option to engage in a policy 'hackathon' based on local examples. |
| Economics | University of Bristol | The optional third year 'International Trade' unit has been revised to incorporate 'trade and the environment' as one theme. Learners explore readings linked to relevant theories, gather data focused on environmental factors and assess different approaches and indicators to measure the environmental impacts of trade. |
| Materials Chemistry | University of Bristol | The Materials Chemistry pathway extensively explores the sustainability implications of materials and research to attempt to reduce impacts. This includes understanding the impacts of plastics pollution, the properties of biopolymer alternatives, upcycling techniques, advances in materials chemistry to improve the economics of solar cells and the development of polymeric gels able to absorb pollutants such as heavy metals or carbon dioxide. |

*(Continued)*

*Table 4.1* (Continued)

| *Discipline* | *Institution* | *Example of how ESD is embedded in different disciplines* |
|---|---|---|
| Art History | University of St Andrews | A module on community heritage and sustainability explores issues, including climate change, decolonisation, Indigenous knowledge and well-being. Taking its cue from Scottish polymath Sir Patrick Geddes's maxim '"Think global, act local' (1915), learners examine sense of place and belonging, adaptation and capacities for sustainable futures. Learners investigate climate emergency case studies, many led by researchers in the institution. A focus on competency development is strengthened through seminars, SDG exercises, museum visits and reflective essays. |
| Film Studies | University of St Andrews | A module on Ecocinema examines cinema's relationship to the natural environment. The module makes learners sensitive to the ways that a variety of media have contributed to the environmental crises we now face. Learners gain critical knowledge about theories of nature, the environment and landscape and adopt an interdisciplinary approach to explore connections between aesthetics, culture, politics and nature. They watch films, read texts and engage in discussions with various historical contexts. Films explore tourism in national parks in North America; impacts of dam building in Northern Thailand; the oil industry's use of film to associate petroleum use with modernisation in Scotland and Iran. |
| Computer Science | University of St Andrews | A module on digital preservation and promotion of heritage explores how digital technologies can create representations of and engagement with heritage items. Topics include cultural landscapes, intangible heritage and natural heritage, with discussion of organisations such as UNESCO, ICOM, Network of European Museums, Europeana, Historic Environment Scotland and analysis in relation to the SDGs. They investigate digitisation processes and create audio, photographs and videos and Virtual Tours 360, and cover creative commons, intellectual property and Wikis with discussion of legal and cooperative frameworks for sharing and supporting citizen science. |

Employer needs and expectations from a given discipline can change, requiring curricular adaptation to ensure relevance. For example, mechanical engineers pursuing a future in vehicle design now need a solid understanding of electro-mechanical systems because of the transition to electric vehicles. Accounting and finance learners increasingly need to understand climate and sustainability-related financial disclosures (Monasterolo *et al.* 2017).

Learners studying a discipline must understand the positive and negative ways in which their future employment and knowledge can impact the world. For example, learners studying Geology and mining should have some understanding of the social and ecological consequences of mining, and the ways in which these can be mitigated and reduced. This could include questions of land rights in the Global South and postcolonial critiques of the behaviour of global mining companies. This allows them to be better informed, to engage in debates on these topics, and also to understand and work with professionals who have a more direct responsibility for areas such as community engagement. Computer science learners should have an understanding of the energy use of algorithms, how to make them more energy efficient and how to design services to avoid unnecessary computation. They should be aware that some applications (such as blockchain and the training of large machine learning models) can be very energy intensive. Medical and health sciences learners should understand diverse health needs in the Global South and failures of current practice. This may include debate regarding the impact of patents on the availability and cost of drugs in the Global South and (at times illegal) uses of generic drugs.

Disciplinary debates of relevance to sustainability are often associated with pioneering ideas or discipline boundary areas and can be exciting for learners to consider during their studies as well as leveraging new career options. Such debates also expose educators and learners to interdisciplinary thinking, as will be explored in detail later in this Chapter. For example, in Pharmacology and Biochemistry, an understanding of debates around biopiracy and the patenting of indigenous knowledge by multinationals (Hamilton 2006) is now important. For Conservation and Ecology, an understanding of harms caused to Indigenous communities by neo-colonial conservation strategies, and exploration of more collaborative and participatory approaches is critical (White *et al.* 2023).

Whilst many of these examples demonstrate how disciplines look to the past, assess current contexts and explore emerging possibilities, academic disciplines can also provide deep insights into the nature of the challenges we face and predictions for the future. These include, for example, natural science disciplines predicting future trends in climate change, economics assessing radical strategies for redistribution of wealth to address inequalities at global scales, social sciences studying how we can make redress for colonialism and humanities studying underlying worldviews, relationship between humans and nature and the impacts of AI on human visions for the future. Sustainability challenges create wicked problems – each of which is unique, with no ‘correct’ answer, demanding adaptive responses – in an uncertain, complex future (Rittel and Weber 1973). Disciplines need to prepare learners not only through development of sustainability competencies (Wiek et al. 2011; Giangrande *et al.* 2019) but also with disciplinary-specific contexts for this complexity. Examples include the shift towards circular economies and the resource, process and partnership consequences across Economics, Law, Chemistry and Management. Supply commitments for ‘sustainable products’ require consideration of technical approaches to supply chain monitoring, slavery, mining, human rights and land reform issues across disciplines such as Management, Law, Economics, Social Anthropology, Philosophy and Geography. Such examples demonstrate the need for holistic, systems thinking across the curriculum, especially when embedding ESD.

Not all academic learning is pro-sustainability, and the practices adopted by a particular discipline and the careers associated with it might actually cause environmental or social harm. Such cases need careful critical reflection, and often action learning, in ESD to enable learners to analyse trade-offs and adopt or develop mitigating approaches. For example, science laboratories are often significant consumers of energy (for ventilation and equipment) and resources. Learners who use such laboratories could be trained in environmentally responsible techniques, for example, using the LEAF scheme (University College London 2024). Such practices can be embedded in learning, such as forming part of a practical assessment, rather than simply being a 'tick box' briefing given at the beginning and then forgotten.

Another example of potential sustainability detriment could be learners travelling significant distances on fieldtrips. Such activities have immense pedagogical value but bear a carbon cost and possible impacts on local cultures and places. Disciplines such as Anthropology or Geography may emphasise the need for cultural norms to be respected and disciplines such as Biology or Geology can emphasise carbon trade off options, but all disciplines should explore the wide scope of sustainability costs and benefits. Again, such learning could constitute a formal part of the assessment.

Hence, disciplines can link to the rich and diverse ESD agenda in a number of different ways. Curriculum design should provide appropriate content in each discipline. Authentic educational experiences can then be designed around this content, using innovative pedagogies to support sustainability competencies in a way which is engaging and valuable to learners, educators, employers and wider society. In this way, every academic discipline can offer high-quality ESD. In addition, consideration of how to embed ESD within academic disciplines enhances the general quality of education. This process encourages academics and learners to be creative, to push disciplinary boundaries, to reflect on how their daily practices influence sustainability, to look back to the past and forwards to a more sustainable future, and to consider how they can contribute to sustainable development through disciplinary knowledge and practice.

## Benchmarking and Professional Requirements

Academic staff in any discipline rarely have the freedom to teach exactly what they wish. Each academic discipline in UK, for example, has to meet requirements of Subject Benchmark Statements (SBS) (QAA/AdvanceHE 2021) for their higher education degree qualifications to be recognised. This means that much of the curricular content is broadly pre-determined, that content is broadly shared across institutions and that programmes can feel packed with all of the curricular expectations. However, as we have seen above, there is still enormous scope to teach and enhance benchmark material through ESD. Importantly, ESD is not only supported but also now required by all SBS (Price *et al.* 2021).

Benchmark statements refer to ESD in a variety of different ways (Table 4.2). The selection shown deliberately excludes the obvious disciplines contributing to ESD, such as Geography, Biology or Environmental Science. Many of these example statements demonstrate an over simplistic relationship with ESD. In some of the benchmark

*Table 4.2* QAA Subject Benchmark Statements – selected examples from 2022, 2023 and 2024. Full benchmark statements are available at QAA (2024).

| *Academic discipline* | *Year* | *Example benchmark statement text* |
|---|---|---|
| Anthropology | 2024 | *Comprehensive education for sustainable development (ESD) .... ensures that students:*<br>a *have an understanding of the political, social and economic conditions and dependencies that support human communities around the world*<br>b *are aware of the impact of human economic activity on the climate, ecology and biodiversity of the planet*<br>c *have a well-informed sense of how to prioritise and enact collaborative and sustainable forms of development, action and organisation with, and for, present and future human communities.*<br>*The various pathways to anthropological knowledge and practice provide students with a comparative framework ....especially as conceived by the 2015 United Nations Sustainable Development Goals (SDGs). In its empirical and comparative focus on human behaviour, biology, culture and society, Anthropology emphasises the diversity of human interactions with one another and the environment, unpacks the obstacles to just, strong and sustainable global relations, and develops key competencies required to make development and institution-building inclusive, sustainable and equitable* |
| Archaeology | 2022 | *The core skills provided by all Archaeology degrees align with the learning outcomes suggested by the Education for Sustainable Development Guidance produced by Advance HE and QAA (March 2021). ... Archaeology both encourages and embeds partnerships and interdependence between economic, social and environmental factors. By developing a deep understanding of what life was like in the past for people and non-humans, archaeology can actively contribute to the narratives about how we create a vision of a better world. Indeed, as the only subject that deals with the entirety of the human past, archaeology offers a critical perspective on how we now shape that future. In particular, the discipline is uniquely placed to foster an appreciation of the fragile and finite nature of the archaeological resource and the need for sustainable approaches to its use and conservation. Moreover, archaeology is directly involved with the development of sustainable and ethical heritage and tourism industries across the world. Emphasis should be placed on conveying this value to a wider society, both within local and regional communities and government organisations who are in a position to determine future outcomes.* |
| Biomedical Science and Biomedical Sciences | 2023 | *It is important to note that sustainability is not solely about the environment. It is an ongoing process of addressing social, environmental and economic concerns to create a better world, and, as such, has particular relevance to Biomedical Science and/or Biomedical Sciences. Practical considerations might include reducing paper use, the LEAF initiative for improving the sustainability and efficiency of laboratories and discussion* |

(*Continued*)

Table 4.2 (Continued)

| *Academic discipline* | *Year* | *Example benchmark statement text* |
|---|---|---|
| | | *of ethics and environmental impact of laboratory work, replacing chemicals with sustainable alternatives if possible, and consider glassware in place of disposable plastic. An awareness of waste reduction, bioremediation, careful use of all non-renewable resources, alternative energy sources and pollution control can be explored in the curriculum. Where applicable, consideration could also be given to assessment design. ... An understanding of the United Nations Sustainable Development Goals (SDGs) is essential to this vision.* |
| Classics and Ancient History | 2022 | *The contemporary study of Classics and Ancient History (and Byzantine Studies and Modern Greek) presents significant opportunities for education on issues of sustainability. Moreover, in the discipline, there is a recognition that academic studies do not exist in isolation from the world in which people live: the immediate context and the issues that face contemporary society shape the way in which the curriculum is approached. Many modern values relevant in discussions on sustainability can fruitfully be problematised or put into perspective through dialogue with the ancient world, for instance values of consumerism or materialism, the virtue of economic growth (and the imperative on government to sustain it), secularism, liberalism, fundamentalism. In addition, various approaches, such as eco-criticism, post-humanism and the Anthropocene, or different attitudes to the natural world in antiquity, as they emerge from literary and material remains, are currently debated in scholarship and influence teaching.* |
| Communication, Media, Film and Cultural Studies | 2024 | *Sustainability is not only about climate change and other environmental questions, but an intellectual framework and ethical principle that informs contemporary social practice. It encompasses a broader range of goals and aspirations to improve social justice, poverty, health and education at local and global levels, often drawing on external reference points such as the United Nations' Sustainable Development Goals (SDGs).*<br>*Sustainability agendas offer new lenses through which to view the relationships between social, cultural, economic and environmental challenges.... Course design processes should use these lenses in considering content, assessment, employability, delivery practices and facilities, and the role of higher education in changing rather than reproducing or perpetuating unsustainable social practices. Communication, Media, Film and Cultural Studies subjects are .... concerned with media representation of sustainable development, holding governments and organisations to account, and raising awareness and informing debates. Degrees in this field may also be concerned with how creative and media industries affect or contribute to the climate crisis, for example through practices, consumptions, facilities or infrastructure.* |

*(Continued)*

*Table 4.2* (Continued)

| *Academic discipline* | *Year* | *Example benchmark statement text* |
|---|---|---|
| | | *ESD offers vital opportunities to challenge established approaches and assumptions not only within higher education in these subject areas, but also within the industries and sectors employing their graduates. ... ESD to ... offers an opportunity to reflect on and challenge established approaches to Communication, Media, Film and Cultural Studies. As such, it should be integrated throughout degree courses and not be simply confined to specialist modules.* |
| Computer Science | 2022 | *Computing courses ... should enable students to develop core personal and professional competencies to address the key societal challenges highlighted by the United Nations Sustainable Development Goals for 2030 in their future working lives. The Education for Sustainable Development Guidance (QAA and Advance HE, 2021) outlines pedagogic approaches for implementation in UK higher education institutions.... There will be places where environmental sustainability can be discussed, for example, the resource consumption of massive data centres used for cloud computing, and more generally, the environmental costs of both building hardware to support computing and disposing of electronic waste. Sustainable development also links with equality, diversity and inclusion; therefore, issues around social justice and economic prosperity can also be brought into the discussion in many areas of computing, alongside developing curricula that are global in outlook and that support inclusive lifelong learning and economic prosperity for all.* |
| Creative Writing | 2024 | *In developing students' ability to communicate, collaborate, create and think critically, Creative Writing works towards these [ESD] goals. Creative Writing courses can link creative practice to sustainability and environmental issues by exploring the relationship between the human and non-human across different creative genres, and between different modes and methods of story-making and writing. As a discipline, the creative, speculative and imaginative aspects of Creative Writing engage directly with critical thinking; with self-awareness through reflective practices; and with anticipatory thinking: three of UNESCO's Key Competencies for Sustainable Development.*<br>*Imaginative writing encourages students to explore place, planet, climate, community, habitat and the life of other species. Creative Writing students may engage with the natural environment through the study or practice of nature writing, environmental poetry, environmental journalism or plays, scripts and fiction on environmental themes, although this list is by no means prescriptive or exhaustive. Creative Writing cultivates qualities of attention and empathy, close observation of detail and imaginative evocation, which help students adopt an active and participatory relationship with the world. Sustainable development addresses social and economic concerns as well as the environment, and the interdisciplinary scope of Creative Writing can foster students' understanding of global* |

(*Continued*)

*Table 4.2* (Continued)

| *Academic discipline* | *Year* | *Example benchmark statement text* |
|---|---|---|
| | | *interdependencies and alternative perspectives. The emphasis on creativity, imagination and communication in Creative Writing means students are well placed to conceive sustainable futures, and to cultivate poetics, ritual, language and story as a medium of possibility, exploration, change and transformation. By working with and in response to historical and contemporary texts and other forms of cultural production, Creative Writing attends to issues of change and continuity, encouraging a critical, creative and reflexive attitude in relation to the past, present and future. The subject therefore equips students to respond flexibly, not only to current issues of sustainability but also to those not yet identified or yet to emerge.* |
| Criminology | 2022 | *Ultimately, university education, and criminology in particular, has a significant role to play in achieving the aims of the ESD -- transforming society and providing the foundation for a safer and sustainable world. Criminology should also offer students' knowledge across several subject areas, such as poverty, social justice, environmental and social harms, which enables learners to gain greater awareness of sustainable development and global citizenship and equip them with the skills and knowledge necessary to address 'social, environmental and economic concerns to create a better world'. Criminology students develop a range of skills, such as critical thinking, presenting effective arguments and the ability to listen to others; all crucial skills for global citizenship and criminal justice and security settings. When possible, students should be encouraged to pursue volunteering or work placements opportunities, which relate to sustainability of both educational development and the discipline within and beyond the academic realm. Such service and work learning can be embedded within modules.* |
| Land, Construction, Real Estate and Surveying | 2024 | *In the search for intergenerational equity, graduates can explore how they can contribute towards the UN Sustainable Development Goals (SDGs) and HABITAT Agenda, along with the targets these international agencies set for development to be sustainable. ...Discipline-specific and transferable skills shall be evenly cultivated, recognising that interdisciplinary knowledge and understanding are key to growth as recent studies of sustainable development have highlighted. The curricula for all the courses listed in this Statement can adopt the UNESCO key competencies for sustainable development: systems thinking, anticipatory studies, normative analysis and interpretation, strategic alliances, collaboration, critical reflection, self-awareness and integrated problem-solving..... Offering a programme of studies incorporating areas such as sustainable planning, design, construction, occupation and use of land and buildings, and green finance and investment equips graduates for their future practice. Applying this knowledge in practice, combined with being able to communicate and collaborate with others, supports movement towards a more sustainable present and future.* |

(*Continued*)

*Table 4.2* (Continued)

| *Academic discipline* | *Year* | *Example benchmark statement text* |
|---|---|---|
| Languages, Cultures and Societies | 2023 | *LCS courses offer students international and transnational perspectives, which invite reflection on questions of equality, peace and social justice in specific contexts and globally. LCS courses can stimulate debate and ethical reflection on cultural and social themes, such as gender roles, the impacts of colonialism or climate change, which are relevant to the UN's sustainable development goals. .... They also provide opportunities for comparative approaches to understanding attitudes to nature and climate change. They offer opportunities for students to analyse, evaluate, apply and reformulate knowledge on sustainable visions of the future. They encourage sensitivity to communication across cultures, and the need to understand the perspectives and values of others, in order to find common ground in working to solve global challenges.* |
| Optometry | 2024 | *Optometry is central to improving diverse health outcomes, and courses in Optometry should inspire future practitioners to engage with the ongoing process of addressing personal, human and global challenges to create better visual health and life experiences for all. Optometry courses may include topics drawn from the United Nations Sustainable Development Goals, particularly those associated with health and the environment. Education for sustainable development is thus an integral part of the study of Optometry, ensuring that graduates are equipped with the knowledge, skills and competencies that can enable them to generate innovative solutions to complex challenges and contribute to the improvement of community and global health. More information on education for sustainable development can be found in the QAA and Advance HE guidance.* |
| Politics and International Relations | 2023 | *ESD offers an opportunity to reflect on and challenge established approaches to Politics and International Relations. It should be integrated throughout degree courses and not simply confined to specialist modules. .... The United Nations Sustainable Development Goals (SDGs) can help to frame the Politics and International Relations curriculum in a way that reflects the rich and diverse context of ESD.... Establishing learning environments that encourage interdisciplinarity and focus on authentic approaches enables students to see their own experiences and challenges reflected throughout their studies. This includes developing in students a commitment to active community engagement, and the key skills and abilities which allow them to challenge sites of injustice, rethink established power structures and explore diverse ways of interpreting orthodox thinking ... Politics and International Relations ... consider the implications of climate breakdown and interconnected questions of economic and social well-being, gender, race and other forms of inequality, thereby developing critical insight into established narratives and hierarchies of power.* |

*(Continued)*

*Table 4.2* (Continued)

| *Academic discipline* | *Year* | *Example benchmark statement text* |
|---|---|---|
| | | *Technology, social media, cyber warfare and misinformation shape the conduct of both national and international politics today. Students need the skillsets to decode, interpret and reject, when necessary, the multitude of narratives and propaganda filling social media. Understanding how knowledge is managed, contested and evolving is therefore a key part of ESD within Politics and International Relations degrees.* |
| Psychology | 2023 | *The goal is to develop Psychology graduates as global citizens who have the motivation and ability to work towards environmental integrity (cognisant of limited, finite resources), social justice (equality, fairness, sharing), economic prosperity (constrained by economic integrity and social justice) and the factors that affect their inter-relationships.... [The] key competencies cover ways of thinking (systems, future, critical), ways of practising (strategically, collaboratively, integrated) and ways of being (self-awareness, normative, reflective).... Effective pedagogical approaches for ESD are designed to be transformative and focus on learning processes rather than products, transcending performative tendencies, building confidence and enabling action in addressing sustainable development. ... Assessments facilitate attainment and authentic demonstration of the key competencies.* |
| Theology and Religious Studies | 2022 | *In the context of Theology and Religious Studies (TRS), ESD means attending to the ways that interdependent social, economic, cultural and environmental concerns intersect with religion and spirituality. ESD enhances the public impact, societal currency and professional value of TRS, using an environmental lens to complement and extend its existing focus on cultural diversity, social justice and global development. ESD encourages the development of knowledge and insight in relation to sustainable development, and its application to support action towards fairer and greener societies. An active learning approach recognises the role that religious professionals, spiritual communities and the interfaith movement can play in driving positive change for sustainability. ESD can be promoted in TRS courses by aligning content, pedagogy and assessment with the eight UNESCO sustainability competencies.* |

statements, there appears to be an assumption that ESD is synonymous with sustainable development. These statements mainly focus on curricular rather than pedagogical or competencies aspects. In some cases, they refer to operational aspects (e.g. Biomedical Sciences laboratory work), potential pedagogical approaches (e.g. Criminology placements, Politics and International Relations activities), the SDGs (e.g. Computer Science) and employment and career consequences (e.g. Theology and Religious Studies). In addition, most statements explain the need to embed ESD across the curriculum and not only in specialist modules. Finally, a checklist of questions could enable deeper engagement with ESD in future benchmark statements (see Box 4.1).

The following checklist is a guide to help those involved in setting a Subject Benchmark Statement to consider how ESD might be included in effective and meaningful ways.

**Box 4.1 Checklist to Evaluate the Depth and Rigour of Engagement Found in the Subject Benchmark Statements in Relation to the Expectations Set Out in the ESD Guidance (Source: J. Longhurst)**

**Benchmark Statements: ESD Guidance Checklist**

1. Does the Benchmark Statement acknowledge the issues present in the ESDG Setting the Context section? E.g. UNSDGs, UNFCC, Biodiversity Convention, UK government policies, plans and strategies, student demand and expectation for ESD?
2. Does the Benchmark Statement acknowledge the importance and purpose of the ESD Guidance?
3. Does the Benchmark Statement discuss the SDGs as an interrelated system in the context of the disciplines in the statement or does the Benchmark Statement cherry pick one or more SDGs to illustrate their case without reference to the full set of goals?
4. Is the UNESCO ESD definition cited and the meaning explored?
5. Is reference made to UNESCO competencies in the context of the disciplines contained in the Benchmark Statement?
6. Does the Benchmark Statement explore how the discipline(s) can contribute to a more sustainable future?
7. Does the Benchmark Statement explore the potential or negative impacts of the discipline(s)?
8. Does the Benchmark Statement consider the opportunity provided by ESD for curriculum framing?
9. Does the Benchmark Statement make the connection between ESD and other agenda considered in the statement such as EDI, employability or enterprise?
10. Does the Benchmark Statement make reference to simulation activities, living labs, case studies, experiential learning or research projects that can contribute to an ESD experience?
11. Does the Benchmark Statement make reference to links with local or national communities that can promote ESD?
12. Does the Benchmark Statement interpret in the context of the discipline(s) how ESD *aims at developing competencies that empower individuals to reflect on their own actions, taking into account their current and future social, cultural, economic and environmental impacts, from a local and a global perspective.*
13. Does the Benchmark Statement interpret in the context of the discipline(s) how Ways of Thinking competencies are developed in the discipline(s)?
14. Does the Benchmark Statement interpret in the context of the discipline(s) how Ways of Practicing competencies are developed in the discipline(s)?
15. Does the Benchmark Statement interpret in the context of the discipline(s) how Ways of Being competencies are developed in the discipline(s)?

16 Does the Benchmark Statement align Learning Outcomes with the key competencies?
17 Does the Benchmark Statement consider learning environments, and if so, do the examples align with the examples in the ESD Guidance?
18 Does the Benchmark Statement make reference to or otherwise consider the teaching practices identified in the ESD Guidance for developing ESD competencies?
19 Does the Benchmark Statement make reference to annotated references and resources provided in the ESD Guidance?

In addition to benchmark statements that proscribe degree content, many professional bodies have specific expectations for knowledge and competencies in sustainable development. For example, the Institution of Environmental Sciences (IES) provides accreditation for approved further and higher education degree programmes, within their Community for Environmental Disciplines in Higher Education (IES 2024). Student graduates of accredited programmes can apply for student membership of IES. The Institute of Engineering and Technology (IET) supports academic accreditation in the discipline of Engineering (IET 2024). This includes recognition of the need to evaluate environmental and societal impacts and to minimise adverse impacts, and to make informed ethical choices. Their statements also mirror some of the attributes of sustainability competencies, such as the requirements for teamwork and communication, which contribute to the collaborative competency. A further example is offered by the British Computer Society, which is a professional body for the Information Technology sector that accredits degree programmes in computer science (BCS 2024). Graduates of accredited courses meet criteria for professional registration. The accreditation process is thorough and includes some sustainability requirements. For example, under Design and Innovation (C5), learners must be shown to "Design solutions for complex problems that meet a combination of societal, user, business and customer needs as appropriate. This will involve consideration of applicable health & safety, diversity, inclusion, cultural, societal, environmental and commercial matters, codes of practice and industry standards". Under The Engineer in Society (M7), learners must learn to 'Evaluate the environmental and societal impact of solutions to complex problems (to include the entire life-cycle of a product or process) and minimise adverse impacts' and (M8) 'Identify and analyse ethical concerns and make reasoned ethical choices informed by professional codes of conduct'. These professional body expectations demonstrate how disciplines linked to professional qualifications must include ESD to remain valid.

A recent consultation emphasised how Professional, Statutory and Regulatory Bodies could work with higher education to influence the benchmark standards towards sustainability (St George's House 2024). Organisation change could include engagement with the Professional Bodies Climate Action Charter as well as integration of sustainability into training provision. The consultation also identified the need for more student voice and for system change including challenging economic orthodoxy and alignment of sustainability measures with quality metrics.

## Sustainability-Focused Degrees

### *Sustainable Development and Sustainability Science Programmes*

There has been much debate about whether sustainable development is now an academic discipline. Although many UK universities are now working towards embedding ESD across all university teaching and learning, there are also degree programmes specifically focused on sustainable development (e.g. White and Harder 2013). Examples of such degrees include Sustainable Development programmes at Universities of St Andrews, Edinburgh and Warwick, and a Sustainability Science programme at University of York. There are also many other programmes specialising in some framing of sustainable development. Sustainable development is sometimes referred to as a field of enquiry and learning that spans disciplines (e.g. White 2013). However, whilst ESD and sustainability research can occur in and across all disciplines, sustainability science is also emerging as a discrete discipline, by some measures (Clark 2007; Kates 2011; Leventon *et al.* 2021).

Sustainability science was introduced as an emerging discipline through the early 2000s. It was framed as a research area attempting to reconnect social and political debates about sustainable development with scientific and technological directions, by integrating different disciplines towards sustainability (Kates *et al.* 2001). It was acknowledged that we live in 'a world put at risk by the unintended consequences of scientific progress' (Kates *et al.* 2001: p.643). It was proposed that this disciplinary area sought to understand interactions between nature and society, at global and regional levels and with different social actors across Global North and South. Key questions were identified for the proposed discipline to address. Over the next two decades, there developed an increasing body of literature in the area of sustainability science. The proud editorial of the first issue of the new journal of *Sustainability Science* reiterated the intention to build a new discipline and to strengthen the scientific and technological underpinnings of the concept of sustainable development, at global, social and human system levels (Komiyama and Takeuchi 2006). They recognised the complexity of unsustainability, through industrialisation, subsequent rapid economic growth, excessive consumption and pollution. A new transdisciplinary knowledge process was proposed, and they identified the key role of education in this process. Clark (2007) described how PNAS created a section specifically for sustainability science. He noted that 'sustainability science is a field defined by the problems it addresses rather than by the disciplines it employs' (p.1737). In addition, he refuted that it was only basic or applied science but rather called it an enterprise centred on 'use inspired basic research'. It was suggested that sustainability science contained several key research domains: climate, biodiversity, agriculture, fishery, forestry, energy and resources, water, economic development, health and lifestyle; and that it should explicitly pursue a rigorous approach of setting goals and indicators, indicator measurement, causal chain analysis, prediction and backcasting and problem–solution chain analysis (Kajikawa 2008). Others proposed that a sub-division still existed between 'the more traditional disciplinary-based science for sustainability and the transdisciplinary science of sustainability' (Spandenberg 2011). The former aligns more with Mode 1 knowledge production and the latter with Mode 2 knowledge forms supporting critical, discursive, transdisciplinary, post-normal science (Gibbons *et al.* 1994). A grassroots movement of scientists wanting to contribute sustainability solutions combined, with greater top down support for sustainability science as the field emerged (Kates 2011).

Despite the energy coalescing around this potential new academic area, there has been ambivalence around the validity of sustainability science as a discipline, and also of its capacity to manifest a new form of knowledge production (Kastenhofer *et al.* 2011). After a decade of exponential growth of research papers in the field, some authors called sustainability science a successful and 'unusual, inclusive and ubiquitous scientific practice' (Bettencourt and Kaur 2011, p.19540). However, others suggested that, along with the division between traditional science and transdisciplinary approaches (Spandenberg 2011), there remained a separation between science and specific social and policy recommendations, rhetoric around participatory processes was not matched by action and global analyses were lacking (Kastenhofer *et al.* 2011). Whilst evidence of disciplinary cohesion was apparent early on, a tendency was noted for sustainability science research to drift back into traditional disciplines around policy and engineering areas (Bettencourt and Kaur 2011). It had also not resolved the epistemological tensions that occur when scientific hypothetico-deductive methods are combined with value-based stakeholder subjectivities (Burns *et al.* 2006 in White 2013).

More recently, some maturation of sustainability science is evident, and deeper critical analysis is leading to greater engagement with concepts such as relational thinking (West *et al.* 2020). Relational approaches shift the focus from interactions between entities towards processes and relationships, and erode the boundary between social and ecological dimensions of sustainable development. In addition, there has been increased emphasis on systems thinking and the potential of leverage points to leverage sustainability transformation (Leventon *et al.* 2021). However, sustainability transformation requires not only transformation of sustainability science but also transformation of the structures and processes of knowledge generation and exchange in universities, research funders, policy makers and others (Shrivastava *et al.* 2020). The contribution of sustainability science and wider sustainability research will thus be limited until structural changes for the public good are made in higher education and associated research and knowledge exchange. It is also possible that these critically reflective and systemic perspectives are not only a change in sustainability science but are also indicative of a shift in the wider context of sustainability research.

Many underlying sustainability issues are of moral or ethical origins, and can be only partially addressed by science (Lubchenco 1998 in White 2013). A solutions-focused science approach can be beneficial to sustainable development, but we also need deeper and wider questioning by scholars in the humanities and social sciences and by stakeholders in other knowledge systems, such as Indigenous Knowledge (Kimmerer Sweetgrass; Mardero *et al.* 2023). Such enquiry transcends problem identification and seeks ontological frames for current modes of unsustainability science. If we focus only on 'sustainability science', we neglect the 'development' aspect of sustainable development. Another concern around locating a single discipline is that some scholars could assume that sustainability is addressed by 'others' and is not an issue for everyone (White 2013). Finally, there are concerns around how the operationalisation of sustainable development has occurred. Its transposition into regulatory and implementation frameworks has led to it often being perceived as a constraint rather than a hopeful aspiration that inspires innovation (Everard and Longhurst 2018). These authors call for reivigoration of broader societal purpose in the theories and practices of sustainable development, going beyond the minimal application of sustainability principles in science and policy. Hence, in this Chapter, the emerging discipline of sustainability science is recognised, but it is also suggested that a field of 'sustainability studies' may thrive. Despite these areas of focus on sustainability, there is also a need to continue to call for embedding of ESD and sustainability research in and from all disciplines in an all-embracing field of enquiry and learning for sustainability. In addition, sustainability can be strengthened in sub-disciplines, such as Environmental Sustainability or Ecological Economics.

The debates around the evolving discipline of sustainability science echo those of previous disciplinary areas. For example, Environmental Science emerged in the 1970s and 1980s, and the teaching and learning associated with this area became known as environmental education (Denman 1986), the precursor, and, for some, a parallel to ESD (Springett 2005). Denman (1986) reflects on changes in society, on the normative direction of the budding environmental science and on growing relationships between disciplines (he scorns discussion of 'areas').

Some learners are drawn to study in programmes enabling them to explicitly focus on aspects of sustainability, such as Development Studies, Environmental Science or Energy Engineering. Such degree programmes often have a normative goal and pragmatically include different disciplines to contribute to problem-solving. Such learners are likely to be interested in more sustainability-focused content, more interdisciplinary content and deeper educational experiences, which allow authentic learning regarding how groups of professionals and other stakeholders engage with sustainability challenges beyond academia.

Other learners may select a disciplinary degree because of an interest in that discipline and a wish to use the tools it offers to make a difference. They might pursue a degree in Biology because of an interest in ecological restoration, or Medical Science to tackle health inequalities. They might pursue a degree in English to understand how culture is shaped through literature, and to create new stories for the future. These learners will initially have a deeper interest in, and a desire to study, more details of the sustainability challenges we face; current understandings of ways forward; and critiques and debates associated with these. We can thus distinguish between the former challenge-led perspective, which seeks to use an appropriate combination of disciplines to understand and address a particular sustainability challenge, and a discipline-led approach to ESD, which seeks to use the focus and methods of a discipline.

Whether a discipline is normative, inherently interdisciplinary and focused on some aspect of sustainability (e.g. Development Studies), or whether a discipline is more tightly boundaried within theoretical academic constraints (e.g. Philosophy), opportunities to embed ESD can always be developed. In all programmes, ESD curricular material and pedagogies may be deployed in core modules, in optional modules, as interdisciplinary or transdisciplinary modules open to learners from different disciplines [such as the Vertically Integrated Projects (Strachan *et al.* 2019)], or with extracurricular learning [such as Transition projects (White and Harder 2013)].

## Ways of Interpreting the World

ESD can be expressed in different forms across academic disciplines because of the fundamental differences across them in ways of seeing and interpreting the world, including ways in which knowledge is perceived. Knowledge is not absolute, nor an opinion, but is a form of justified true belief (see Lehrer 1990). Knowledge is not ephemeral but is situated in people and contexts, and is intimately bound up in power relations, as Foucault (see Foucault 2019) and others have argued at length. Beliefs about how knowledge is constructed influence clusters of academic disciplines and individual disciplines.

An individual's *ontology* is their way of understanding the world, their *epistemology* is the way of interpreting the world, their *methodology* is the way of gathering data to explain the world and *methods* are the tools used to gather, analyse and interpret data (see Burrell and Morgan 1979, Flowerdew and Martin 2013, Bryman 2016, Jackson 2016).

An individual's epistemological position influences and is influenced by their disciplinary choice, and will reflect their relationship with and beliefs around sustainable development. Broadly, academics in disciplines in the humanities and some social sciences tend to hold a more anti-positivist epistemological position, accept subjectivity and embrace a pluralistic discussion within the curriculum. They do not believe in one objective truth, and education is thus built more on learning to develop a critical argument than it is on the creation of a pyramid of 'truth'. They thus seek different possibilities and perspectives on sustainability and critically explore the underlying issues that cause current symptoms of unsustainability. They argue that multiple realities are possible, depending on perspective (such as gender, profession, ethnicity).

Academics in the natural and physical sciences, and associated applied disciplines such as engineering, tend to hold a more positivist epistemological positionality. They seek objective truth through testing null hypotheses. They recognise that current knowledge builds on a solid foundation of previous research results to create hierarchies of knowledge production. The sciences are thus effective in understanding the natural and physical world and in pursuing technological solutions. For example, fundamental results in physics and chemistry are built on in chemical engineering research to develop new battery technologies which are more efficient and cause less environmental harms.

These different epistemological positions can conflict if we try to work across disciplinary boundaries. There is thus a potential epistemological incompatibility that can make it difficult to undertake interdisciplinary teaching and learning. This is similar to the debates undertaken in mixed methods research. Many mixed methods researchers adopt a pragmatist philosophical position, choosing to accept the benefits of each approach without fully addressing the incompatibilities (Creswell 2003). Others might take a purist view that such philosophical incompatibilities cannot be overcome, or adopt dialectical processes to navigate differences. Recognition of conditional incompatibility could kindle deeper conversations about philosophical stances of particular interdisciplinary approaches (Hathcoat and Meixner 2017). ESD and sustainability research can thus actively address this epistemological incompatibility and navigate profound philosophical territories to adopt novel interdisciplinary approaches.

## Towards Transdisciplinarity in ESD?

Real-world problems are not defined by a single discipline. Individual disciplines can contribute to understanding and solutions, but disciplinary curricula are likely to be constrained by vocational expectations, accreditation needs and benchmark statements. Disciplinary learning can be valuable for those beginner learners or those seeking specialisation (Ivanitskaya *et al.* 2002). However, combining disciplines can lead to added benefits for such learning outcomes. The contribution of multiple disciplines can expand the capacity to explain and resolve sustainability challenges in ESD. In addition, ESD in higher education needs to achieve different learning outcomes, including inter- and transdisciplinary problem-solving, dealing with complexity, self-directed, collaborative learning and competence development (Barth and Timm 2011).

## *Definitions of Multi, Inter and Transdisciplinarity*

Multi, inter and transdisciplinarity occur along a spectrum rather than being distinct forms of learning (Klein 2012). Learners may learn through multidisciplinarity, for example, in joint degrees, in which there is rarely connection between the different disciplines within the degree. In Scottish university education, learners normally take multiple subjects in the first one or two years, expanding the base of education but often without explicitly linking the disciplines selected.

Whilst multidisciplinarity combines inputs from different disciplines in an additive manner, interdisciplinarity is integrative (Klein 1990). Interdisciplinary learning can be encouraged, for example, through a compulsory interdisciplinary foundation programme, through an assessment or through teams of learners from different disciplines working in a vertically integrated project (e.g. Strachan *et al.* 2019).

## *Benefits and Practices of Interdisciplinarity*

When incorporating interdisciplinary education into a disciplinary degree programme, different approaches are possible. The extent of interdisciplinarity will depend on the discipline, the university context and structures, pedagogical approaches and the inclination and experience of the academic staff involved, and practical issues such as timetabling and mandatory course content.

Interdisciplinarity requires knowledge synthesis and hence builds skills in synthesis (Spelt *et al.* 2009). Interdisciplinary understanding includes a performance element (Spelt *et al.* 2009) in which individuals 'produce a cognitive advancement—such as explaining a phenomenon, solving a problem, or creating a product—in ways that would have been impossible or unlikely through single disciplinary means' (Mansilla *et al.* 2000, p.219). Such abilities need to be supported by knowledge and sub-skills, including knowledge of disciplines; personal characteristics such as curiosity, openness and respect; communication abilities; educator expertise; and appropriate pedagogy enabling iterative and action based learning (Spelt *et al.* 2009). Interdisciplinary learning also enables maturity of epistemological beliefs and advances critical thinking through higher order learning and cognition (Ivanitskaya *et al.* 2002). For example, *humility, sensitivity to bias* and *empowerment* are seen to be possible outcomes of such learning. Relational learning, across disciplines and across personal and academic domains, is enhanced through interdisciplinary teaching and learning (Ivanitskaya *et al.* 2002). Interdisciplinary learning can also support different forms of innovative responses, including idea generation, once learners have gained practice in interdisciplinarity (Braßler and Schultze 2021). Along with intercultural approaches, interdisciplinarity and transdisciplinarity can promote transformative learning (Sommier *et al.* 2022).

Interdisciplinary learning can be enacted effectively through problem-based learning (Stentoft 2017). However, for this pedagogical approach, Stentoft (2017) notes that it can be difficult to organise the curriculum, develop learner competencies for interdisciplinarity and develop educator skills for learner support in this area. In addition, context is important, and interdisciplinary higher education programmes do not always support more change in critical thinking and need for cognition than disciplinary programmes (Lattuca *et al.* 2017). However, some studies have recorded higher measures of epistemological reflection after interdisciplinary programmes (Schilling 1991).

Interdisciplinary learning can be understood in a constructivist paradigm in which learners construct realities through their experiences as well as new learning (Stentoft 2017). The higher order learning, beyond memorisation of facts, requires a shift from *what* they learn to *how* they learn (Ivanitskaya *et al.* 2002; Stentoft 2017). Because disciplines do not provide the scaffolding for learning, additional aspects such as reflective and active learning (Ivanitskaya *et al.* 2002; Klein 2006; Stentoft 2017) and the development of competencies (Giangrande *et al.* 2019) become more significant. Problem-based learning can also scaffold interdisciplinary learning (Stentoft 2017). Stentoft (2017) notes that such learning requires competencies to deconstruct and gain insights from different disciplines before the learner reconstructs meaning across potentially conflicting disciplinary epistemologies. She points out that this requires development of capabilities such as the abilities to construct new knowledge, adapt to change and develop. Interdisciplinarity thus transcends individual disciplinary specialisation, helping prepare learners for future complex and uncertain worlds through integrating disciplines – 'a pedagogy of breadth' (Sherren 2008, p.240).

One way of addressing challenges of time, complexity and contradiction is to see ESD as a process of critical self-discovery that leads educators and learners to identify their role within the complex interactions between academic disciplines and implementation of disciplinary knowledge. The world needs disciplinary 'experts', working alongside interdisciplinary/transdisciplinary 'experts' who can act as the 'glue' or 'bridge' within communities of such people to address real-world problems. Brand and Karvonen (2007) describe an 'ecosystem of expertise' for knowledge for sustainable development. They describe how different skills come together to support interdisciplinary linkages across disciplines, traverse theory and technical aspects, engage with the public and stimulate civic debate. Hence, academics and learners can find their individual specialism and strengths and pursue these in collaborative team contexts.

Not all forms of interdisciplinarity are equal, and weak and strong forms have been identified. Interdisciplinary programmes can offer strong interdisciplinarity, in which integrated interdisciplinary modules and educators appointed to the programme facilitate learning, as opposed to weak interdisciplinarity, in which learners are exposed to modules bolted on from different disciplines by educators from those areas, with less capacity for synthesis and reflection (see Augsburg and Henry 2009; Klein 2010). However, there are effective ways in which interdisciplinary education can be integrated into disciplinary degree programmes:

> *Discipline-centred interdisciplinarity education*: When studying a discipline and considering how it interacts with sustainability challenges, educators can consider what insights and perspectives from other disciplines would be of value to learners of this discipline. How can these be integrated into disciplinary education in a way which gives learners a transformative appreciation of their discipline and how it interacts with others? This approach has the advantage that it can be tailored to the priorities of a given discipline and the likely directions learners may take afterwards, and hence prepare them to play a more effective role as disciplinary representatives in Brand and Karvonen's (2007) "ecosystem of expertise". Content of this form is often taught by academics from within the discipline who have a strong interest in and experience of interdisciplinarity/transdisciplinarity.

**Box 4.2 An Example of Discipline-Centred Interdisciplinary Education**

The University of Bristol's Sustainable Computing unit for third-year computer scientists focuses primarily on understandings and techniques from within the discipline for assessing and reducing the impacts of digital technology. It also includes significant content from beyond the discipline. This includes looking at eWaste management and the circular economy from management science, legal, policy and psychological perspectives alongside a technical digital design perspective. It uses case studies such as the conflict between Apple and the EU over device repairability legislation to illustrate how these different perspectives can combine to yield fruitful insights and critiques. It also investigates the social impacts of the digital supply chain, focusing on poor conditions and conflict in the mining of Tantalum in the Democratic Republic of Congo. Learners engage in a critical consideration of attempts to improve this through digital tracing in the chain. They also consider a wider geopolitical perspective on critical mineral supply chains, the tensions between China and Western powers for access to these, and engagement through social science frameworks on questions of extractivism by these powers.

*Challenge-centred interdisciplinary education*: The challenge-centred approach gives the interdisciplinary education necessary to understand a given sustainable development challenge deeply, by drawing on perspectives from many disciplines. It can be taught by a team of academics from different disciplines, and will usually be an interdisciplinary course, taken by learners from across the institution as an option. It has the advantage that learners learn from, and alongside, people from other disciplines, with different ways of interpreting the world, which increases the scope for transformative learning (Box 4.2).

**Box 4.3 An Example of Challenge-Centred Interdisciplinary Education**

In the Sustainable Development programme at the University of St Andrews, a core Honours methodology module included teaching and learning material from academics from different disciplinary backgrounds. Learners from different pathways were asked to conduct small group research projects to identify and enhance aspects of operational sustainability within the institution, in partnership with local stakeholders. They had to negotiate different theoretical frameworks and methodological approaches and write both individual reflective essays on the process of transdisciplinary learning and a collective short report with recommendations for sustainability action.

People seeking deeper engagement with sustainability learning and action may prefer strong interdisciplinary experiences. Authentic educational experiences are thus offered which are not confined or constrained by any one discipline, and which can provide a transformative learning context for those who are most passionately engaged (Box 4.3).

### *Challenges of Interdisciplinarity*

In interdisciplinary academic endeavour, disparate groups of people with assorted skills come together to address different problems, working with different traditions and often employing different languages. There are thus many challenges and barriers to implementing interdisciplinarity in ESD in higher education. Curricula can already be packed full to meet professional or benchmark statement requirements. A balance needs to be struck with regard to provision of content and educational experiences from disciplinary content that educators and learners would need or expect in a given programme, versus that from other disciplines.

It can be difficult for academics to adopt interdisciplinary practices, because in higher education, people tend to be placed within disciplinary organisational structures, frames and learning outcomes. In addition, there needs to be focus on integration and depth as well as breadth. Sherren (2008) notes that 'The tendency to build environmental curricula from "environmentally tinged" subjects in a range of disciplines can create an eclectic assortment with little depth, no explicit integration and a lack of reflectivity about the normative nature of its content' (p.244). Disciplinary language and jargon can create challenges. Perceived risks of interdisciplinarity clash with drives for tenure and academic recognition, and with the financial burden of students paying heavy fees (Sherren 2008). The market model and commodification of education create further practical barriers to more complex and nuanced forms of learning (Sherren 2008).

### *Challenges of Transdisciplinarity*

Whilst interdisciplinarity can be considered more appropriate for ESD than mere multidisciplinarity, transdisciplinary learning is considered by many to be even more relevant. Transdisciplinarity can be understood in different ways. Transdisciplinary learning occurs when different disciplines and non-academic stakeholders are involved and can lead to sharing or development of new paradigms across disciplines (Tress *et al.* 2004; White 2013). This combination of academic and non-academic endeavour creates a partnership seeking to integrate knowledge forms for a common goal (Tress *et al.* 2004). However, it is sometimes also known as a synthesis across academic disciplines that causes paradigmatic changes within academia itself, creating new theory at the nexus of existing disciplines (CERI 1972, Sherren 2008; Klein 2010). Transdisciplinary learning is thus not defined by academic disciplines, and the learner can draw on multiple disciplinary debates or fragments to develop a synthesis. Hence, it is 'the ability of the learner to use and construct knowledge which shapes the boundaries and outcome of transdisciplinary learning processes' (Stentoft 2017, p.53). Examples of transdisciplinary learning are shown in Table 4.3.

Such in-depth learning is academically and personally challenging and time-consuming and requires advanced communication skills. It may thus be more suitable for academic staff or senior postgraduate research students than for undergraduates, in many contexts. Some taste of transdisciplinarity may be provided to undergraduates through the sharing of stories, case studies and workshops led by members of staff or guest lecturer-practitioners with deep transdisciplinary experience. Although transdisciplinarity is a route towards transformative learning, individual disciplines have significant potential contributions to make and strong interdisciplinary and transdisciplinary initiatives

*Table 4.3* Examples of undergraduate modules that enable transdisciplinary learning.

| | | |
|---|---|---|
| Vertically Integrated Project | University of St Andrews | This vertically integrated project (see Strachan *et al.* 2019) brings together researchers and learners from various disciplines who share an interest in the local Eden Estuary. This is a local nature reserve with SSSI, SAC, SPA and Ramsar status. Learners explore understanding of the estuary, assess action and exchange knowledge with stakeholders. Activities include a 'serious game', a 'resource' website and active collaboration with Sustainability Cupar and Green Shores. |
| Sustainable Development | University of St Andrews | A module on community, nature and governance explores how communities of place, interest, practice and value around the world can contribute to the transition(s) to sustainability. An action learning component includes a Transition University of St Andrews led community garden transect walk and activity (such as spreading compost and weeding). Learners undertake a field visit to a community project, and in return plant trees. An artist runs a participatory art therapy exercise. Assessment includes a critical essay, exam and group presentations reflecting on voluntary projects with community groups, e.g., making a short video running an event. |

are often grounded through feet in single disciplines. Not all ESD thus needs to strive for inter- or transdisciplinarity.

## Conclusions

Academic disciplines can thus be understood as overlapping and diffuse social constructs, intellectual domains and organisational conveniences. Many learners are largely unaware of disciplinary debates until they are well into their degree programmes. Whilst all disciplines can embed ESD, they are influenced by practicalities and regulations. These can both constrain and inspire ESD; for example, benchmark statements have set a minimum regulatory context in UK, although some of them could go further. The context and culture of the institution will also influence the capacity of academics within and across departments and disciplines to work with each other and with external stakeholders (Chapter 3). Exploring academic disciplines in relation to ESD enables academics to understand their purposes and contributions as well as theoretical and methodological frameworks. When academics work across disciplines, they see different perspectives and ways of interpreting the world. Although inter- and transdisciplinarity can be challenging, they can enable transformative learning for educators as well as learners and can engage higher education institutions more fully with the wider community. ESD can thus change academia itself, opening up new collaborations across academics, creating a new generation of more fluid knowledge generators and linking academia and practice more tightly. To achieve this, we will need transformative learning opportunities and support for both educators and learners. Staff development (Chapter 10) and enhanced integration of research, teaching and practice (Chapter 8) can help catalyse transdisciplinarity.

## References

Alpay, E., Ahearn, A.L., Graham, R.H. and Bull, A.M.J. (2008). 'Student enthusiasm for engineering: Charting changes in student aspirations and motivation', European Journal of Engineering Education, 33(5–6), pp. 573–585. DOI: 10.1080/03043790802585454.

Aram, J.D. (2004). 'Concepts of interdisciplinarity: Configurations of knowledge and action', Human Relations, 57(4), pp. 379–412.

Augsburg, T. and Henry, S. (eds.) (2009). The Politics of Interdisciplinary Studies: Essays on Transformations in American Undergraduate Programs. McFarland.

Barth, M. and Timm, J. (2011). 'Higher education for sustainable development: Students' perspectives on an innovative approach to educational change', Journal of Social Science, 7(1), pp. 13–23.

Bettencourt, L.M. and Kaur, J. (2011). 'Evolution and structure of sustainability science', Proceedings of the National Academy of Sciences, 108(49), pp. 19540–19545.

Brand, R. and Karvonen, A. (2007). 'The ecosystem of expertise: Complementary knowledges for sustainable development', Sustainability: Science, Practice and Policy, 3(1), pp. 21–31.

Braßler, M. and Schultze, M. (2021). 'Students' innovation in education for sustainable development—a longitudinal study on interdisciplinary vs. monodisciplinary learning', Sustainability, 13(3), p. 1322.

British Computer Society (BCS) (2024). Accreditation criteria and AHEP4 learning outcomes. Available at: https://www.bcs.org/deliver-and-teach-qualifications/academic-accreditation/ [Accessed 31 July 2024].

Bryman, A. (2016). Social Research Methods. Oxford University Press.

Burns, M., Audouin, M. and Weaver, A. (2006). 'Advancing sustainability science in South Africa', South African Journal of Science, 102(9), pp. 379–384.

Burrell, G. and Morgan, G. (1979). 'Assumptions about the nature of social science', Sociological Paradigms and Organisational Analysis, 248(1), pp. 1–9.

Centre for Research, Education and Innovation (CERI) (1972). Interdisciplinarity: Problems of teaching and research in universities. OECD report. 307 pages.

Chettiparamb, A. (2007). Interdisciplinarity: A literature review. Report for The Higher Education Academy. Interdisciplinary Teaching and Learning Group, University of Southampton. ISBN: 978-1-905788-36-1.

Clark, W.C. (2007). 'Sustainability science: A room of its own', Proceedings of the National Academy of Sciences, 104(6), pp. 1737–1738.

Clark, V.C., Emmanouil, N., Page, J. and Pelizzon, A. (2018). 'Can you hear the rivers sing? Legal personhood, ontology, and the nitty-gritty of governance', Ecology Law Quarterly, 45(4), pp. 787–844.

Cosme, I., Santos, R. and O'Neill, D.W. (2017). 'Assessing the degrowth discourse: A review and analysis of academic degrowth policy proposals', Journal of Cleaner Production, 149, pp. 321–334.

Creswell, J.W. (2003). Research Design: Qualitative, Quantitative, and Mixed Methods Approaches, 2nd edn. Thousand Oaks, California, USA: Sage.

Daly, H.E. (1994). For the common good: Redirecting the economy toward community, the environment, and a sustainable future. ISSR Library. Beacon Press.

Denman, D.R. (1986). 'Environmental learning: Some judgments of time and scholarship', in Barass, R., Blair, D.J., Garnham, P.H. and Moscardini, A.O. (eds.) Environmental Science: Teaching and Practice. Enjoc Press, pp. 440. ISBN 0 9506994 5 4.

Dryzek, J. (2021). The Politics of the Earth. Oxford: Oxford University Press.

Everard, M. and Longhurst, J.W. (2018). 'Reasserting the primacy of human needs to reclaim the "lost half" of sustainable development', Science of the Total Environment, 621, pp. 1243–1254.

Flowerdew, R. and Martin, D. (2013). 'Analysis of Data', in Methods in Human Geography. Routledge, pp. 189–286.

Foucault, M. (2019). Power: The Essential Works of Michel Foucault 1954-1984. Penguin UK.

Giangrande, N., White, R.M., East, M., Jackson, R., Clarke, T., Saloff Coste, M. and Penha-Lopes, G. (2019). 'A competency framework to assess and activate education for sustainable development: Addressing the UN Sustainable Development Goals 4.7 challenge', Sustainability, 11, p. 2832. DOI: 10.3390/su11102832.

Gibbons, M., Limoges, C., Scott, P., Schwartzman, S. and Nowotny, H. (1994). The New Production of Knowledge: The Dynamics of Science and Research in Contemporary Societies. London: Sage.

Hamilton, C. (2006). 'Biodiversity, biopiracy and benefits: What allegations of biopiracy tell us about intellectual property', Developing World Bioethics, 6, pp. 158–173.

Hathcoat, J.D. and Meixner, C. (2017). 'Pragmatism, factor analysis, and the conditional incompatibility thesis in mixed methods research', Journal of Mixed Methods Research, 11(4), pp. 433–449.

Institution of Environmental Sciences (IES) (2024). Accreditation application form. Available at: https://www.the-ies.org/accreditation [Accessed 31 July 2024].

Ivanitskaya, L., Clark, D., Montgomery, G. and Primeau, R. (2002). 'Interdisciplinary learning: Process and outcomes', Innovative Higher Education, 27, pp. 95–111.

Jackson, E.A. (2016). 'Ontological and epistemological discourse(s) on sustainable development: Perspective on Sierra Leone in the aftermath of a decade of civil unrest', Management of Sustainable Development, 8(1).

Jacobs, M. (2013). 'Green growth', in Falkner, R. (ed.) The Handbook of Global Climate and Environment Policy. DOI: 10.1002/9781118326213.ch12.

Kajikawa, Y. (2008). 'Research core and framework of sustainability science', Sustainability Science, 3, pp. 215–239.

Kastenhofer, K., Bechtold, U. and Wilfing, H. (2011). 'Sustaining sustainability science: The role of established inter-disciplines', Ecological Economics, 70(4), pp. 835–843.

Kates, R.W. (2011). 'What kind of a science is sustainability science?, Proceedings of the National Academy of Sciences, 108(49), pp. 19449–19450.

Kates, R.W., Clark, W.C., Corell, R., Hall, J.M., Jaeger, C.C., Lowe, I., McCarthy, J.J., Schellnhuber, H.J., Bolin, B., Dickson, N.M. and Faucheux, S. (2001). 'Sustainability science', Science, 292(5517), pp. 641–642.

Kimmerer, R. (2013). Braiding Sweetgrass: Indigenous Wisdom, Scientific Knowledge and the Teachings of Plants. Milkweed Editions.

Klein, J.T. (1990). Interdisciplinarity: History, Theory, and Practice. Wayne State University Press.

Klein, J.T. (2006). 'A platform for a shared discourse of interdisciplinary education', Journal of Social Science Education, 5(2), pp. 10–18.

Klein, J.T. (2010). Creating Interdisciplinary Campus Cultures: A Model for Strength and Sustainability. John Wiley & Sons.

Klein, J.T. (2012). 'A taxonomy of interdisciplinarity', in Frodeman, R., Klein, J.T. and Mitcham, C. (eds.) The Oxford Handbook of Interdisciplinarity. Oxford: Oxford University Press, pp. 15–30.

Komiyama, H. and Takeuchi, K. (2006). 'Sustainability science: Building a new discipline', Sustainability Science, 1, pp. 1–6.

Lattuca, L.R., Knight, D., Seifert, T.A., Reason, R.D. and Liu, Q. (2017). 'Examining the impact of interdisciplinary programs on student learning', Innovative Higher Education, 42, pp. 337–353.

LEAF Scheme (2024). Available at: https://www.ucl.ac.uk/sustainable/take-action/staff-action/leaf-laboratory-efficiency-assessment-framework [Accessed 31 July 2024].

Lehrer, K. (1990). The Theory of Knowledge. Boulder, Colorado: Westview Press.

Leventon, J., Abson, D.J. and Lang, D.J. (2021). 'Leverage points for sustainability transformations: Nine guiding questions for sustainability science and practice', Sustainability Science, 16, pp. 721–726.

Lubchenco, J. (1998). 'Entering the century of the environment: A new social contract for science', Science, 279(5350), pp. 491–497.

Mansilla, V.B., Miller, W.C. and Gardner, H. (2000). 'On disciplinary lenses and inter-disciplinary work', in Wineburg, S. and Grossman, P. (eds.) Interdisciplinary Curriculum: Challenges to Implementation. New York: Teachers College Press, pp. 17–38.

Mardero, S., Schmook, B., Calmé, S., White, R.M., Chang, J.C.J., Casanova, G. and Castelar, J. (2023). 'Traditional knowledge for climate change adaptation in Mesoamerica: A systematic review', Social Sciences & Humanities Open, 7(1), p. 100473.

McGregor, D., Whitaker, S. and Sritharan, M. (2020). 'Indigenous environmental justice and sustainability', Current Opinion in Environmental Sustainability, 43, pp. 35–40. DOI: 10.1016/j.cosust.2020.01.007.

Monasterolo, I., Battiston, S. and Janetos, A.C. et al. (2017). 'Vulnerable yet relevant: The two dimensions of climate-related financial disclosure', Climatic Change, 145, pp. 495–507.

Nicholson, D. and Vargas, V. (2021). 'Design principles for assessment of sustainability teaching', in Assessment and Feedback in a Post-Pandemic Era: A time for learning and inclusion. AdvanceHE, pp. 183–195. ISBN 9781916359352.

Price, E.A., White, R.M., Mori, K., Longhurst, J., Baughan, P., Hayles, C.S., Gough, G. and Preist, C. (2021). 'Supporting the role of universities in leading individual and societal transformation through education for sustainable development', Discover Sustainability, 2(1), p. 49.

QAA (2024) Subject Benchmark Statements. Available at: https://www.qaa.ac.uk/the-quality-code/subject-benchmark-statements [Accessed 30 September]

QAA Subject Benchmark Statements (SBS) (2024). Available at: https://www.qaa.ac.uk/the-quality-code/subject-benchmark-statements [Accessed 31 July 2024].

QAA/Advance HE (2021). Education for sustainable development guidance. Available at: https://www.qaa.ac.uk/quality-code/education-for-sustainable-development and https://www.advance-he.ac.uk/knowledge-hub/education-sustainable-development-guidance [Accessed 31 July 2024].

Raworth, K. (2012). A safe and just space for humanity: Can we live within the doughnut?. Oxfam.

Rittel, H.W. and Webber, M.M. (1973). 'Dilemmas in a general theory of planning', Policy Sciences, 4(2), pp. 155–169.

Rockström, J., Gupta, J., Qin, D., Lade, S.J., Abrams, J.F., Andersen, L.S., Armstrong McKay, D.I., Bai, X., Bala, G., Bunn, S.E. and Ciobanu, D. (2023). 'Safe and just earth system boundaries', Nature, 619(7968), pp. 102–111.

Schilling, K. (1991). Assessing models of liberal education: An empirical comparison. Washington, DC: Fund for the Improvement of Postsecondary Education. (ERIC Document Reproduction Service No. ED 359 864).

Sherren, K. (2008). 'A history of the future of higher education for sustainable development', Environmental Education Research, 14(3), pp. 238–256.

Shrivastava, P., Smith, M.S., O'Brien, K. and Zsolnai, L. (2020). 'Transforming sustainability science to generate positive social and environmental change globally', One Earth, 2(4), pp. 329–340.

Sommier, M., Wang, Y. and Vasques, A. (2022). 'Transformative, interdisciplinary and intercultural learning for developing HEI students' sustainability-oriented competences: A case study', Environment, Development and Sustainability, 1–18.

Spangenberg, J.H. (2011). 'Sustainability science: A review, an analysis and some empirical lessons', Environmental Conservation, 38(3), pp. 275–287.

Spelt, E.J., Biemans, H.J., Tobi, H., Luning, P.A. and Mulder, M. (2009). 'Teaching and learning in interdisciplinary higher education: A systematic review', Educational Psychology Review, 21, pp. 365–378.

Springett, D. (2005). 'Education for sustainability in the business studies curriculum: A call for a critical agenda', Business Strategy and the Environment, 14(3), pp. 146–159.

St George's House (2024) Delivering integrated climate education, skills and professional standards. A St George's House consultation 26-27 February 2024. Available at: https://www.stgeorgeshouse.org/wp-content/uploads/2024/02/20240227-St-Georges-House-consultation-EAUC-SOS-UK-PSRBs.pdf [Accessed 30 September 2024]

Stentoft, D. (2017). 'From saying to doing interdisciplinary learning: Is problem-based learning the answer?, Active Learning in Higher Education, 18(1), pp. 51–61.

Sterling, S. (2001). Sustainable Education: Re-visioning Learning and Change. Totnes: Green Books for the Schumacher Society.

Stern, D.I. (2017). 'The environmental Kuznets curve after 25 years', Journal of Bioeconomics, 19, pp. 7–28.

Strachan, S.M., Marshall, S., Murray, P., Coyle, E.J. and Sonnenberg-Klein, J. (2019). 'Using vertically integrated projects to embed research-based education for sustainable development in undergraduate curricula', International Journal of Sustainability in Higher Education, 20(8), pp. 1313–1328.

The Bridgetown Initiative (2024). Available at: https://www.bridgetown-initiative.org [Accessed 31 July 2024].

The Institute of Engineering and Technology (IET) (2024). Available at: https://www.theiet.org/media/10095/ahep4-the-small-print-for-heis.pdf [Accessed 31 July 2024].

Tress, G., Tress, B. and Fry, G. (2004). 'Clarifying integrative research concepts in landscape ecology', Landscape Ecology, 20, pp. 479–493.

United Nations (UN) (2015). Transforming our world: The 2030 Agenda for Sustainable Development. Available at: https://sdgs.un.org/2030agenda [Accessed 31 July 2024].

University College London (2024) LEAF – Laboratory Efficiency Assessment Framework https://www.ucl.ac.uk/sustainable/take-action/staff-action/leaf-laboratory-efficiency-assessment-framework

West, S., Haider, L.J., Stålhammar, S. and Woroniecki, S. (2020). 'A relational turn for sustainability science? Relational thinking, leverage points and transformations', Ecosystems and People, 16(1), pp. 304–325.

White, R.M. (2013). 'Sustainability research: A novel mode of knowledge generation to explore alternative ways for people and planet', in Sterling, S., Maxey, L. and Luna, H. (eds.) The Sustainable University: Progress and Prospects. Abingdon: Routledge.

White, R.M. and Harder, M. (2013). 'The journey towards sustainability via community: Lessons from two UK universities', in Sterling, S., Maxey, L. and Luna, H. (eds.) The Sustainable University: Progress and Prospects. Abingdon: Routledge.

White, R.M., Schmook, B., Calmé, S., Giordano, A.J., Hausser, Y., Kimmel, L., Lecuyer, L., Lucherini, M., Méndez-Medina, C. and Peña-Mondragón, J.L. (2023). 'Facilitating biodiversity conservation through partnerships to achieve transformative outcomes', Conservation Biology, e14057. DOI: 10.1111/cobi.14057.

Wiek, A., Withycombe, L. and Redman, C.L. (2011). 'Key competencies in sustainability: A reference framework for academic program development', Sustainability Science, 6, pp. 203–218.

Chapter 5

# Education for Sustainable Development

## Curriculum Design, Content and Challenges

*Georgina Gough and Simon Kemp*

### Introduction

This chapter is designed to illuminate the range of curriculum-related implications of Education for Sustainable Development (ESD). In particular, opportunities for ESD to inform the purpose of programmes of learning, and subsequent programme design (from process to outputs such as learning outcomes to curriculum content) are discussed. We explore ways by which the values and intentions of ESD can guide curriculum development. There is rationale for reviewing whether some individual higher education programmes should be offered considering the negative sustainability impacts when ESD is applied to its ultimate extent. However, this chapter concentrates on ways by which ESD and key educational and curriculum design principles and theories align to provide guidance for curriculum developers to strengthen ESD provision. Specifically, we consider notions of constructive alignment, learning journey, threshold concepts and learning outcomes. Further, we consider ESD as an impetus and framework for curriculum change.

The importance of the curriculum to ESD cannot be overstated. The curriculum sits at the very centre of the student experience of all aspects of ESD. Students learn, are assessed, gain skills, and experience of sustainability through the curriculum that forms their degree programme of study, and their opportunities for interactions with other disciplines when we correctly apply an inter-, multi- and transdisciplinary approach. The curriculum offers a structure where we can ensure critical core content is delivered and assessed, provides the framework that allows transformative authentic assessment to take place, and that the quality assurance requirements are consistently provided for all stakeholders. It allows us to hang a framework on ESD work that guides educators and ensures students understand what is being delivered and why. This latter point should not be overlooked, as students are not always told why their degree is being structured and delivered in a particular way, so communicating a conceptual structure that helps them understand the what, how and why of their degree programme is important, especially within the intrinsic complexity that is ESD.

How we construct, frame and deliver the curriculum matters. It is crucial. Sometimes it is mistaken for procedural quality assurance, but it is shaped by our philosophical approaches to structure and what we as educators want our students to achieve. It is how we weave all the different threads of ESD into delivery for students. By providing the backbone to ESD, curriculum development is a recipient of what constitutes ESD (Chapter 2), how a university can be a bastion of sustainability (Chapter 3) and how ESD is a discipline in its own right (Chapter 4). Curriculum then feeds out to pedagogy (Chapter 6),

DOI: 10.4324/9781003451563-5

innovative assessment (Chapter 7), research-led teaching and practice (Chapter 8) and enables important monitoring and evaluation to take place (as explored in chapter 11). Curriculum sits at the centre of this book.

## What Is the Curriculum?

There are different structural models and understanding of the curriculum. Chapters 3 and 8 present slightly different models, and it is worth noting there can be differences in terminology when conducting wider reading around curriculum development and structures. An example of one approach is the UNESCO model of 'formal', 'non-formal' and 'informal' (UNESCO, 2017). 'Formal' refers to the curriculum including fieldtrips, 'non-formal' is learning away from the classroom and assessed work such as community group projects, and 'informal' is the wider cultural context that students live within such as media influences and societal norms.

In this chapter, we are adopting one broadly accepted model of the curriculum across higher education that comprises three distinct but complementary and overlapping areas of 'formal learning', 'informal learning' and the 'hidden curriculum'. The formal curriculum is rooted in the universally accepted Bloom's Taxonomy (Bloom, 1956) with programme learning objectives based around knowledge, comprehension, application, analysis, synthesis, evaluation, which is in itself an order of increasing complexity. Through this structural approach to the curriculum, educators deliver teaching and assessment to students, with quality assurance structures and mechanisms in place to ensure the content meets formal regulated university requirements for the award of a degree.

'Informal learning', sometimes used interchangeably with 'non-formal learning' (Johnson & Majewska, 2022), is based around formal learning objectives but typically takes place away from regular compulsory learning provision and settings. A useful definition is provided by Coombs and Ahmed (1974) as organised and systematic education activities outside the formal framework to deliver specific types of learning. In the context of ESD, this can be through visits to community groups, immersive learning within society and experiential learning through non-assessed activities on field courses as just some of the examples of direct relevance to ESD and curriculum design.

Introduced as a concept by Philip Jackson in 1968 (Giroux & Penna, 1979), the 'hidden curriculum' is considered the dimension of student learning and experience that sits outside of formal and informal learning and assessment but is crucial in providing students with views and experiences that allow them to understand the place of their learnings in society and the workplace, whilst developing skills to prepare for life after graduation. It is the separation of what is formally delivered in the curriculum through quality assurance, and the totality of everything that students actually learn through all dimensions of their university experience. This may include the unintentional transmission of the sustainability values of the educators and the institution to students, impacting their overall learning (Winter & Cotton, 2012). Mickelsson *et al.* (2019) explore Dewey's (1938) theory of learning which recognises 'interconnections between our everyday experience and our environment in the learning process', which leads to considerations of learning happening outside of the classroom as well as within it. Thus, ESD becomes a whole institution endeavour within the hidden curriculum, not just the responsibility of educators.

It is important to state what is, and what is not, within the scope of curriculum discussions. The work of Paraskeva (2022) explores the relationship between university curricula, current social, political and environmental contexts, and the degree to which universities seek to inform and influence outcomes through the curriculum. Underlying ESD is a belief that curriculum can positively impact the world and that the outcomes of curriculum delivery include positive social, political, cultural and environmental change. There is also the vital recognition that university curricula can have a detrimental impact, and this needs to be at the centre of all planning and delivery to avoid a reductionist approach (Lozano *et al.*, 2013). The practical implications also need to be considered, such as questioning whether fieldwork can be conducted closer to home to reduce the direct travel emissions associated with curriculum delivery (McCowan, 2023), and ultimately whether activities within curricula perpetuate unsustainable ways (Orr, 1994)

## The Curriculum in Education for Sustainable Development

ESD needs to be holistically delivered (Holst *et al.*, 2024; Price *et al.*, 2024). UNESCO, as the lead UN agency for ESD, call for national leadership, multistakeholder collaboration and lifelong learning driven by a rethink of 'what, where and how we learn to develop the knowledge, skills, values and attitudes that enable us all to make informed decisions and take individual and collective action on local, national and global urgencies' (UNESCO, 2020, p.8).

It is not the task here to consider the rationale for the existence of individual university programmes. Rather, this chapter will detail some specific implications of taking an ESD approach in relation to the process and outputs of curriculum design which is conducted at various scales. This chapter primarily addresses design of whole courses of learning, with some reference to the planning of units within programmes.

## What Is Curriculum Design?

Higher education institutions (HEIs) differ in their use of terminology around curriculum design and delivery. A single defined unit delivering teaching, reading, practical work and assessment for one specific focused area may be termed a 'unit' or 'module' depending on the nomenclature used in the institution, and will be worth an approved number of credits to contribute to the final award. For this chapter, we will use the term 'unit'. A curriculum formed of a number of 'units' (the number varies depending on the institution, but the number of credits remains consistent across the sector) is delivered as a degree 'course' or 'programme', again depending on the prescribed terminology of the institution. This model of curriculum follows the curriculum-as-plan approach (Aoki, 1993). Despite students routinely referring to what 'course' they are studying rather than their 'programme', we will adopt the term degree 'programme' as that is the primary term used with pedagogic studies and university curriculum quality processes.

Curriculum design is the process of making decisions about the purpose, outcomes, structure, principles and delivery mode of a programme of learning and assessment. Morgan and Houghton (2011) identify nine components of curriculum design: aims, objectives, learning outcomes, academic & competence standards, syllabus, teaching methods, learning activities, assessment & feedback, and teaching & learning materials. ESD informs all of these components. This chapter will consider aims, objectives, learning outcomes, academic and competence standards and syllabus. Consideration of design at individual session level involves decisions and planning of specific learning activities which goes beyond the scope of strategic and structural curriculum design. Teaching methods, learning activities, assessment and feedback, and teaching and learning materials are part of, but not a specific focus of curriculum design, so are explored throughout the book but specifically in detail in Chapter 6 (pedagogies) and Chapter 7 (assessment).

Biggs and Tang's (2007) notion of constructive alignment is worthy of consideration here. Constructive alignment is an interactive system where teaching and learning activities and assessment tasks are aligned to the intended learning outcomes, and reinforce each other (Biggs *et al.*, 2022). Whilst the concept has been used to guide the process of curriculum design (e.g. Ruge *et al.*, 2019), it is most commonly used (and was devised) to guide the outcomes of curriculum design. The idea is that there are logical and coherent connections between the intended outcomes from a course of learning, with the teaching, learning and assessment activities facilitated with the group of learners (Trigwell & Prosser, 2014). In essence, does the teaching and learning enable students to achieve the outcomes, and does the assessment authentically measure whether students have achieved the set outcomes?

Curriculum design should also facilitate the inclusion of research-led teaching, as addressed in Chapters 3 and 8. Understanding the research process and working with their lecturers on research projects can provide opportunities for deeper learning through meaningful mentorship (Jiang & Roberts, 2011), which due to the values-led areas of ESD can be transformative for students. Positive role models are important throughout primary and secondary education, and higher education is no exception to this (Holt *et al.*, 2018), especially in the field of sustainability (Shephard, 2008).

As curricula are normally delivered at a university this offers the potential to use that physical space and local environments as a learning environment (as addressed in Chapter 3), or a 'living lab' (Favaloro *et al.*, 2019; Peker & Ataöv, 2019; Verhoef *et al.*, 2020), reducing the need for extended travel and additional carbon emissions where appropriate and not removing all the educational benefits from fieldwork and residential field courses (as addressed in Chapter 7). With the growth in remote and hybrid studying post-Covid, it should also be recognised that the application of real-world, place-based environments can help students interact with sustainability issues and assist a connection between students and the university for real-world sustainability learning despite not being on campus (Pretorius *et al.*, 2019).

## ESD and Programme Aims and Objectives

If curriculum were to be designed with the sole purpose of achieving sustainable development (SD), then the core programme aims, learning objectives and guiding principles then the UN sustainable development goals (SDGs) would provide a useful framework for the scope of SD and help challenge the common perception that SD is only about the environment. This is an interpretation of ESD advocated by Advance HE and Quality Assurance Agency for Higher Education (2021), and in the Mediterranean Strategy on Education for Sustainable Development (MSESD) (European Union, 2014). However, it is recognised that most academic programmes of study do not see their primary purpose as delivering SD. The curriculum scope and content should also recognise the contractions and tensions between the SDGs, and engage in the critique as addressed in Chapters 2, 6 and 8 of this book.

Consideration should be given to the appropriate balance of explicit vs implicit reference to SD (Armstrong & LeHew, 2011) at all points in the curriculum design process. Tassone *et al.* (2018) advocate that contemporary curricula should be interdisciplinary, engage with society and be centred on the responsible investigation required of researchers and stakeholders in society. Programme aim(s) may not explicitly reference SD. However, programme objectives might include, for example, 'commitment to ensure that students are provided with examples of application of their discipline to the challenges of sustainable development' or 'commitment to addressing the UN SDGs where relevant to the subject'. Rata (2019) and others (e.g. Bell *et al.*, 2017 and Carlone, 2017) consider academic and discipline identity as a part of curriculum development. However, drivers now commonly include purpose and application-driven concerns such as employability, inclusivity and sustainability as illustrated by the requirements of the Quality Assurance Agency (QAA) Subject Benchmark Statements. All programmes of learning might adopt a core objective of enabling learners to make a positive impact on the world through their professional practice as part of their curriculum design. This is now a requirement in QAA Subject Benchmark Statements. One example of the integration of sustainability into a Subject Benchmark Statement and programme requirement is offered by the History statement, a discipline some may not initially consider to be part of ESD: 'Environmental history in particular brings to the fore understanding of the interaction between nature and culture; how humans have affected the natural environments of the past; and how current problems are legacies of the past. However, public history, economic history and cultural history also focus on key aspects of sustainability' (QAA, 2022a). Further context of disciplinary contributions is analysed in Chapter 4.

There is also a growing movement towards SD-driven university curricula through Professional Statutory Regulatory Bodies (PSRBs) requirements for the accreditation of programmes. An example is the long-standing commitment of the Engineering Council to ensuring sustainability is a core component of accredited university degrees 'Sustainability of engineering practice is an issue of concern for the profession and HEIs are encouraged to make use of the United Nations Sustainable Development Goals, and Engineering Council Guidance on Sustainability in programme design and delivery' (Engineering Council, 2023). The embedding of sustainability into the sector, progressing directly from the curriculum is demonstrated by the requirement for all registered engineers and technicians to conduct their work so it contributes to SD, outlined in the UK Standard for Professional Engineering Competence (Engineering Council, 2023).

Programme purpose statements can inform programme learning outcomes that aim to embed ESD. Example outcomes include:

- *'Learners develop knowledge of health inequalities and skills to reduce these inequalities'* or,
- *'Learners can affect positive impact on climate change adaptation in the built environment.'* or,
- *'Graduates who can help to realise the potential for renewable energy to support net zero energy requirements.'*

These types of outcomes-based purpose statements serve as high-level programme objectives and, from an ESD-based approach, should explicitly identify SD contributions and benefits in order to drive programme-level integration and to make this commitment clear to students from the outset of their studies. Decisions on overall programme objectives and learning outcomes are informed by a variety of drivers. Such drivers may influence varies components of curriculum design. Table 5.1 identifies areas of curriculum

*Table 5.1* Drivers/criteria for curriculum design decisions (in UK HE) with example ESD-specific drivers.

| *Driver of curriculum design* | *Example ESD expectations and actions* | *Area of curriculum which is likely to need to respond to driver* | | | | | |
|---|---|---|---|---|---|---|---|
| | | *Programme aims and objectives* | *Learning outcomes* | *Academic standards* | *Curriculum coherence* | *Syllabus* | *Curriculum delivery and assessment & feedback* |
| Professional Statutory and Regulatory Bodies (PSRBs) | RIBA (Royal Institute of British Architects) criteria for architecture course accreditation: Graduates must understand 'the context of the climate emergency with an understanding of the relevant building physics informing zero carbon design standards' | x | x | x | | x | x |
| Benchmark statements | 'Course and module-level learning outcomes for ESD should interconnect subject-specific knowledge and skills in relation to housing studies, sustainability competencies and the 17 UN SDGs' (QAA, 2022b, p.8) | x | x | | x | | |
| Institutional focus on ESD in teaching and learning support | University of Southampton Academic Lead for ESD works with colleagues to embed sustainability across all programmes and working with students to develop programme-level SDG case study materials | | x | x | x | | x |
| Institutional graduate attribute framework | UWE Bristol states that all of its graduates will have the ability to contribute to 'the health and sustainability of future communities' | x | x | | x | | |
| Institutional strategy commitment | The University of Southampton Sustainability Strategic Plan has a requirement for ESD to be embedded across all curricula. | | x | | x | | x |

*(Continued)*

*Table 5.1* (Continued)

| *Driver of curriculum design* | *Example ESD expectations and actions* | *Area of curriculum which is likely to need to respond to driver* | | | | | |
|---|---|---|---|---|---|---|---|
| | | *Programme aims and objectives* | *Learning outcomes* | *Academic standards* | *Curriculum coherence* | *Syllabus* | *Curriculum delivery and assessment & feedback* |
| Employer requirements | Climate action planning, sustainability education, carbon emissions, carbon accounting and corporate sustainability were the fastest growing in-demand skills in job advertisements posted in LinkedIn in 2023 (LinkedIn, 2024) | | | x | | x | x |
| Government policy/ legislation | In Wales, the Welsh Government commits to education, which supports the ambitions of a globally responsible Wales and through ensuring that students understand the impact of Wales' industry (if not consumption) on global environment and climate | x | x | x | x | x | |
| Pedagogic principles | Core and threshold concepts of sustainable development | | x | | x | x | x |
| Social purpose of discipline/ profession | Fundamental purpose of nursing in society: 'leading the integration of emotional, physical, organisational, and cognitive nursing work to meet the needs of people, organisations, systems, and populations' (Royal College of Nursing, 2024) | x | x | x | | | |
| Societal values | 'The transformative ambition and universal applicability of the 2030 Agenda challenges the United Nations to remain steadfast in ensuring that the SDGs are implemented in accordance with international human rights law, eliminating gender inequalities and all forms of discrimination, reaching out to those that are furthest behind first, to ensure that no one is left behind' (UNSDG, 2024) | x | | | x | | x |

design which are likely to need to respond to specific driver requirements, with examples of sustainability expectations within each category.

These drivers can all variously be seen as barriers but most importantly as enablers for ESD practice. Since this book intends to support adoption of ESD as a framework for curriculum design, consideration has been given to ways by which these drivers of curriculum design can be seen as 'windows of opportunity' for guiding and justifying application of ESD to curriculum design.

## Learning Outcomes and Competences

Within the UK (QAA and Advance HE 2021) and internationally (UNESCO, 2017), guidance on ESD has emphasised competences as a core consideration. UNESCO (2017) identified 'competences for sustainability' (p.10). These are qualities and capabilities which would enable an individual to be able to act effectively for SD. Chapter 2 examines these in more detail. These competencies could be utilised as outcomes of a course of learning. For example, a student might be expected to have achieved/to embody/to be able to demonstrate:

1 Systems thinking competency
2 Anticipatory competency
3 Normative competency
4 Strategic competency
5 Collaboration competency
6 Critical thinking competency
7 Self-awareness competency
8 Integrated problem-solving competency (UNESCO, 2017)

In fact, UNESCO (2017) did advocate for the identification of cognitive, socio-emotional and behavioural learning objectives for students of programmes designed from an ESD approach Following an ESD approach, learner-centred outcomes focus on personal positive and negative impact on the environment and on society.

The relationship between curriculum and development of competencies needs further exploration. Keinänen *et al.* (2018) explore the relationship between competences, capacities and skills and state that 'a competence is formed by a set of capacities ...formed by several skills, all of which are required for a more complex professional performance' (p.31). The definitions of competencies are discussed in Chapter 2.

Higher education curriculum design and implementation should support the development of key sustainability competencies and programme-specific competencies throughout the education journey. A curriculum which supports competencies, attributes and values can enable transformative learning. In the academic education field, Dirkx *et al.* (2006) consider transformative learning as involving 'critical reflection of ...established beliefs' supporting epistemic assumptions' (p.100) and that will include 'emotional, intuitive, symbolic, imaginistic, and/or contemplative modes of learning' (Dirkx *et al.*, 2006). Obviously in this respect, curriculum is fully integrated with pedagogy and assessment processes.

## Competences in Curriculum Designers and in the Process of Curriculum Design

It is interesting to apply these same competences for ESD to those responsible for curriculum design, and to the process of curriculum design. Table 5.2 identifies example considerations in this regard.

*Table 5.2* Curriculum design process outcomes when curriculum designers have sustainable development competences.

| *Competency* | *Curriculum design practice enabled if educator has well developed competency* | *Probable outcome of curriculum design process if educator has well developed competency* | *Curriculum design example to support competency In learners* | *Outcome of curriculum design for the students* |
|---|---|---|---|---|
| Systems thinking competency | Takes the programmatic perspective into consideration<br>Includes relevant stakeholders<br>Brings insights from societal, industry and sectoral contexts | Holistic and meaningful curriculum<br>Development of programme community | Inclusion of wider context<br>Interdisciplinary or transdisciplinary curricular elements<br>Use of mindmaps or other tools to support system thinking | Capacity to understand interactions and consequences<br>Appreciation of leverage and tipping points |
| Anticipatory competency | Explores history and heritage<br>Future thinking approaches can be included<br>Manages the design process in a timely manner | Curriculum highlights past, present and likely future influences and consequences | Backcasting and historical examples used<br>Future thinking included through approaches such as modelling, scenarios or visioning | Ability to envision sustainable futures and plan towards these<br>Understanding of how history has influenced current sustainability issues and solutions |
| Normative competency | Is able to draw in relevant stakeholders in a manner which facilitates meaningful contribution and sense of purpose from all<br>Delivers a curriculum design which meets its core purpose | Development of programme community<br>Programme celebrates diversity and creates space for dialogue | Include perspectives from other stakeholders, including readings of films with voices of people we cannot access.<br>Examples of how change can occur for a positive world<br>Reflective approaches included | Capacity to understand a diversity of perspectives<br>Appreciation of different worldviews<br>Motivation for positive change |

(*Continued*)

*Table 5.2* (Continued)

| *Competency* | *Curriculum design practice enabled if educator has well developed competency* | *Probable outcome of curriculum design process if educator has well developed competency* | *Curriculum design example to support competency In learners* | *Outcome of curriculum design for the students* |
|---|---|---|---|---|
| Strategic competency | Understands the context for the design process and can facilitate a process which works effectively within this context | Efficient curriculum design<br>Curriculum enables complex assessments and group and independent work to be undertaken smoothly | Collaborative and independent work<br>Authentic assessment with clear tasks and timelines | Learners gain skills and capacities for organisation<br>Learners can enact aspirations |
| Collaboration competency | Works with other stakeholders effectively to ensure appropriate contribution from all<br>Works across disciplines and in teaching teams | Curriculum includes space for collaborative and experiential learning but also tools for collaboration e.g. sociocracy or conflict management | Group work<br>Work with external communities<br>Interdisciplinary or transdisciplinary work | Capacity to work well in teams or pairs<br>Ability to co-create solutions to sustainability issues |
| Critical thinking competency | Is able to prioritise and recognise the appropriate way forward in the face of all information which has been fed into the design process | Highlights relevant literature and theory<br>Critically presents issues, including underlying drivers and long-term consequences | Engagement with academic literature and theory<br>Tasks requiring critical analysis or critical reflection | Capacity to critically evaluate information, source and credibility<br>Ability to critically synthesise information<br>Critical decision making |
| Self-awareness competency | Acts in a manner which encourages relevant input from others and which does not exert undue influence on the process<br>Is personally resilient within pressures of work | Curriculum is sensitive to needs of diverse learners, including minority representation<br>Curriculum seeks self-awareness from learners | Curriculum includes discussion of reflection and tasks requiring reflection, such as reflective diaries<br>Dialogical spaces held for shared or collective reflection | Learners develop awareness of self-agency and potential as change agents<br>Capacity for personal resilience and adaptation in the face of personal challenges<br>Ability to manage emotional and mental health |

(*Continued*)

*Table 5.2* (Continued)

| *Competency* | *Curriculum design practice enabled if educator has well developed competency* | *Probable outcome of curriculum design process if educator has well developed competency* | *Curriculum design example to support competency In learners* | *Outcome of curriculum design for the students* |
|---|---|---|---|---|
| Integrated problem-solving competency | Negotiates complexity of drivers and components of, and opinions on curriculum design process to arrive at a coherent, timely curriculum | Curriculum includes authentic examples and case studies<br>Interdisciplinary and transdisciplinary approaches included | Examples of sustainability solutions provided to demonstrate solution potential<br>Authentic engagement to explore real-world issues<br>Collaborative work with external stakeholders | Ability to address (small) sustainability real-world challenges<br>Appreciation of local context and possibilities<br>Capacity to work in a team to collectively address issues |

Competencies can support good ESD curricular design, which in turn can support competencies in learning outcomes. Educators who themselves have well developed key sustainability competencies undertake enhanced curriculum design with better curricular outcomes. Curricula that are therefore designed to support key sustainability competencies in learners lead to enhanced learning outcomes.

Stakeholder engagement can support curriculum design in HE, addressing needs of communities and other stakeholders (Nelson, 2020). A collaborative process which brings together experienced curriculum designers with teachers is advantageous. Such inclusion enables identification of different world views, an ambitious curriculum and more robust achievement of intended learning outcomes.

It is widely recognised that curriculum design should incorporate student consultation as a minimum, and preferably student co-design (Chadha *et al.*, 2022). This is vital in ESD curriculum design when one considers the impact of our sustainability challenges on younger people. An additionally critical component of curriculum design is the need for reflection after a curriculum has been delivered. This is not a linear process but is rather a cyclical one (see Chapter 11). Again, this is important within ESD, as all academic components of the field of enquiry and practice are dynamic.

Here, we draw on two detailed case studies rather than several shorter example boxes to allow more detailed inspection of two different institutional approaches.

**Case Study 1: The University of the West of England, Bristol**

The University of the West of England (UWE Bristol) provides support to its academic community to embrace and deliver ESD through dedicated staff and clear guidance. Since 2019, a design note specifically focused on taking an ESD approach to curriculum design has supported staff to understand the principles and implications of such an approach. Programme teams are encouraged to be flexible in their curriculum design work and to consider the best way to embed ESD in their curricula, but are expected to make sustainability more explicit, tangible and accessible for students. Programme teams are asked to consider the following questions to ensure that ESD is embedded meaningfully into curricula and practice, as addressed by this case study from the University of the West of England.

- How does the programme engage with the sustainable development goals (SDGs)?
- How are climate action and sustainability being addressed by or affecting associated disciplines and professions, and how are these reflected in the programme content and delivery?
- How can sustainability opportunities provided in the programme be evidenced, e.g., to professional bodies, to prospective or current students, to employers?
- Can every member of the programme team articulate the overall ambition of the programme with regard to sustainability and/or the SDGs and do they understand their personal contribution?
- How is the programme team supporting the institution's Strategy 2030 ambition to create a sustainable university? This relates both to professional and personal behaviour.

Opportunities for enhancing practice may be identified through addressing the following questions:

- How can both the formal and informal curricular contribute to the delivery of ESD for students on your programme?
- How might induction be used to provide opportunities for programme leaders to talk about the ESD elements of the provision?
- What role might academic personal tutoring have in helping students to see the linkages between their discipline of study and the broader aims of ESD?
- What opportunities are there for including ESD in the programme through dissertations, projects and group work?
- What opportunities might be provided by placements and workplace learning in relation to their contribution to ESD?
- How might external speakers, field visits and extra-curricular events contribute to the overall ESD relevance of a programme?

Programme teams at UWE are supported to consider how every stage of curriculum design (new programme design, continuous improvement and periodic programme review) can be used to further enhance engagement of staff, students and external partners in ESD for better sustainability outcomes of the programme and its graduates. There is no expectation that *all* modules within a programme will explicitly include references to climate action and sustainability. However, in order to meet the expectation that every student will develop relevant skills, knowledge, capabilities and competencies for SD, every programme must provide a coherent ESD offer across all years of study. Examples of practice from across the institution are included in the internal guidance documents, as are templates used in quality assurance processes with ESD-guided responses provided for colleagues to take inspiration from in deciding the most appropriate curriculum design decisions for their programme of learning.

### Case Study 2: The University of Southampton

At the University of Southampton, all degree programmes are required to complete the Programme Approval and Review process every 5 years with the inclusion of prescribed documentation – SWOT analysis, programme specification, assessment strategy, learning & teaching philosophy, delivery mode & location, compliance frameworks, toolkits and action plan. The 'toolkits' consist of six compulsory or voluntary processes as part of the strategic or compliance priorities of the programme design. One of two compulsory toolkits is 'Sustainability', which is required to be completed for all new programme approvals and existing programme reviews. The toolkit is formed of support resources such as SDG curriculum mapping reports for all programmes and schools, the Southampton Sustainability Solutions e-module, the QAA/Advance HE ESD guidance and Academic Lead for ESD online support workshops to assist programme leaders in the completion of the mandatory 'Sustainability Programme Approval & Review Toolkit'. Programme leaders and teams are required to address the following questions, with supporting evidence:

- How do your programme learning outcomes relate to the SDGs?
- How are the SDGs addressed in the core and compulsory modules?
- How are the SDGs addressed in the optional modules?
- Is sustainability included in your PSRB or other programme accreditation requirements? If yes, how have you addressed this in the programme?
- How does sustainability fit into the programme in relation to the nature of study and academic standards expected of your graduates?

A crucial thread running through this process of curriculum design and reapproval is the involvement of students at each stage. As already mentioned, students are the recipients of the curriculum, and considering the impact it has on their future life prospects, students should be active participants in the process throughout.

## Curriculum Design Process Principles

In addition to outcomes for learners who undertake a course of learning, there are outcomes which can be derived from the process of curriculum design. These should inform the curriculum design process and, in the context of ESD, should be guided by principles of collaboration, co-creation, inclusion, equity, equality, reciprocity, responsibility and respect (Higgins *et al.*, 2019). Desirable outcomes of the curriculum process might include programme team cohesion and respect, individual and shared responsibility, meaningful work and staff wellbeing, consideration of expertise strengths and weaknesses amongst the programme team, and a more robust curriculum.

Collaborative curriculum design requires strong relationships and trust. Abbot and Cook-Sather (2020) identify the positive power of pedagogical disagreements, particularly between staff and student stakeholders as they assist in the clarification of differing perspectives for productive partnerships. Morgan and Houghton (2011) state that the inclusion of academics, professional services, students, industry, professional bodies, charities and government as stakeholder voices in curriculum design process supports holistic ESD outcomes for students and the wider curriculum team.

Collaborative curriculum design may be considered a difficult and potentially overwhelming prospect for educators new to both ESD and co-design. The CoDesignS ESD Framework Box 5.1) is grounded in UNESCO's (2017) key competencies for sustainability and the QAA and Advance HE (2021) ESD guidance and provides a guided structural approach to embed ESD in curriculum design using a co-design and co-creation approach.

### Box 5.1 CoDesignS ESD Framework for Curriculum Design (CoDesignS ESD 2021)

The CoDesignS ESD Framework for collaborative curriculum design is based on the CoDesignS Framework (CoDesignS, 2024; Ahmad *et al.*, 2023) and is a resource to support integration of ESD. It includes development of specific learning objectives for the SDGs, targeting the cognitive, socio-emotional and behavioural domains to support students in transformative learning (Cotton & Winter, 2010). In addition to this aspect of curriculum design, the toolkit supports key competencies for sustainability and key pedagogical approaches (see Chapters 2 and 6 for further information). The toolkit can be downloaded for free and applied to different contexts and encourages co-design by different actors (https://codesignsesd.org/toolkit/).

## Curriculum Quality Assurance Processes and the Opportunity for Embedding ESD

As much as we as educators may intend to develop our curricula based entirely on the academic domain, intellectual curiosity and advancing the subject area, the more functional reality is that we must build our curricula to meet quality control and enhancement requirements (Bath *et al.*, 2004; Bendermacher *et al.*, 2017; Stalmeijer *et al.*, 2022).

Again, it should be noted that the precise terminology adopted may differ between institutions, but the function and output remain consistent. The curriculum that forms the content of a degree programme is subject to inspection on a pre-determined cycle. Whilst this process will address the contemporary nature of the discipline, ensure the content meets the requirements of graduate employers and PSRBs (Day, 2018), and the institutional quality assurance procedures, this offers a crucially important opportunity to embed ESD within the curriculum of every programme in an institution and across the higher education sector. There is clear value in quality assurance processes supporting curricula related to the SDGs (Stukalo & Lytvyn, 2021).

Whilst curriculum approval procedures may be considered by some as a less exciting component of the ESD journey, mandatory process-driven quality assurance and enhancement requirements is the juncture where the actual embedding of sustainability into every curriculum of every programme across an institution can take place, and have the greatest transformative effect on all our students and graduates.

## Syllabus

In this section, implications of ESD for curriculum content, structure and flow are considered. A programme leader, or ideally stakeholder group, will need to settle on a curriculum which strikes the appropriate balance between explicit integration of sustainability content, skills and competence development into core and mandatory programme experiences, options for specialism and deeper engagement, and the primary academic content requirements for the discipline.

This chapter has already advocated for the inclusion of SD within core programme objectives and learning outcomes. If this position is accepted, then it becomes necessary to identify core knowledge which must be developed through the curriculum. Here, it is useful to review notions of core and threshold concepts. Once a unit of learning has been set with learning outcomes linked to SD, curriculum must be designed to ensure that users develop understanding of core and threshold concepts. The core concept acts as the foundation to progress subject understanding, whilst a threshold concept can be transformative, irreversible and integrative, showing how the world may be viewed as more problematic (Meyer & Land, 2006). Reeping (2020) suggests threshold concepts have been presented in the same manner as core concepts, but threshold concepts can have sequencing consequences for curriculum planning (Table 5.3). Subsequent curriculum concepts may only be understood once a solid understanding of threshold concepts is achieved. Referring to Bloom's taxonomy (Bloom, 1956), it could be stated that a threshold concept is one which a learner must have grasped in order to progress to higher levels of academic engagement with a topic (from understanding to analysis and evaluation).

In relation to ESD, core concepts which need to be understood for higher order engagement to be possible might include needs, limits, climate change, ecological footprint, inequality, intergenerational equity and justice, depending on discipline or programme. Concepts which are considered thresholds to facilitating a world view, which aligns with the principles of SD, include 'planetary boundaries' (Rockström *et al.*, 2009), 'safe and just Earth system boundaries' (Rockström *et al.*, 2023) and systems theory (Sandri, 2013).

Discipline-specific threshold concepts for SD should be considered by curriculum development teams. Timmermans and Meyer (2019) detail stages by which threshold concepts should be learnt in order to inform curriculum design and to enable ownership and

*Table 5.3* Summary of threshold concept attributes.

| *Quality* | *Description* |
|---|---|
| Bounded | May have only a specific purpose in a discipline |
| Discursive | Can involve an extended or enhanced use of language |
| Integrative | Brings together several disparate concepts, perhaps in an unexpected way |
| Irreversible | Can be difficult to 'unlearn' |
| Liminality | There is no straight path in learning the concept; involves a conceptual back-and-forth |
| Reconstitutive | May cause a shift in the student's subjectivity |
| Transformative | Changes the way the student sees/thinks about the discipline |
| Troublesome | Likely to be an issue for the student to learn, may be counterintuitive |

*Source*: Reeping, 2020 (p.60).

commitment from relevant curriculum stakeholders. In this way, the process embodies the values of ESD. Selecting and sequencing concepts to be learnt should be followed by identification of the knowledge and skills which students need to acquire, the ability to make appropriate judgements which students must develop, and the connections between these two outcomes (Rata, 2019; Winch, 2017). An ESD approach to curriculum also emphasises the application of knowledge and skills and consideration of the appreciation of a plurality of values as core learning outcomes.

There is a further need for curriculum developers to recognise that action for SD is relevant to all disciplines. Further to foundation concepts relating to what SD is, it may be appropriate to ensure student understanding of concepts linked to SD as a process. Inter and transdisciplinary approaches to SD, for example in using a nexus approach, may enhance understanding (Kurian, 2017). See Chapter 4 for further discussion.

The identification of core and threshold concepts provides direction for content coverage within mandatory programme learning units. Ensuring that foundation knowledge is obtained by all students on a programme, through core modules, opens the potential for optional modules to facilitate deeper exploration of concepts, further content or application of threshold concepts. ESD is a field known for its troublesome knowledge and wicked problems (Earle & Leyva-de la Hiz, 2021; Hull *et al.*, 2020). Disciplines should consider how they will offer students to engage with these more challenging concepts and issues. Bespoke specialist units within a programme can be useful, or interdisciplinary challenge-based formal, informal and hidden curriculum learning opportunities (Kłeczek *et al.*, 2020). This consideration of students' learning journey through the curriculum should ensure that ESD is embedded and authentic, rather than bolted on and isolated.

## Conclusion

Curriculum sits at the heart of ESD and this book. Without a contemporary, responsive, socially, culturally, economically and environmentally responsible curriculum, there is no ESD. There is scope for innovation within curricula through inter, multi and transdisciplinary approaches that reflect the urgency of systems thinking for ESD. Equally, the curriculum must be grounded in clearly structured quality assurance processes as a crucial step in embedding ESD across all curricula, a university and the higher education sector.

The curriculum offers a structure where we can ensure critical core content is delivered and assessed, providing the framework that allows transformative authentic assessment to take place. Equally, we must not lose sight of the need to ensures student understand what is being delivered and why.

Through this chapter, we have presented different structural models and understandings of the curriculum, addressing nuances between formal – non-formal – informal and formal – informal – hidden curriculum. We have explored how the curriculum drives ESD through curriculum design by academics, and the value of co-design. The central role of sustainability competencies within programme aims and objectives has been addressed, whilst also recognising the contradictions and tensions between the SDGs as a part of their inclusion.

The chapter has leaned heavily on the importance of a range of drivers with a deeper focus on quality assurance, sector guidance and the crucial inclusion of ESD in subject benchmark statements and PSRB requirements as the next phase in the evolution of ESD across the HE sector. The examples provided demonstrate the relevance of ESD to all disciplines by showcasing fields that break the constraining myths of sustainability being only a science and environment issue. Two extended case study examples from different universities are presented to illustrate the approaches that can adopted to ESD in the curriculum and how it is managed from a quality assurance perspective.

As is the case throughout the book, the application of competences provides our guiding star to transformative ESD. Their effective and imaginative use supports the most impactful ESD for all stakeholders. The curriculum is defined by and delivered through the syllabus, and this is explored in terms of not only sustainability content but also through the application of core and threshold concepts.

This chapter has provided rationale and justification for the consideration of ESD throughout the curriculum design process in relation to the stages of setting aims, objectives and learning outcomes and identifying core syllabus components. The principles and processes detailed here apply equally to new curriculum design and to review of existing, and likely well-established, curricula. All opportunities to review curricula in order to deepen engagement with ESD should be taken. Process and outcomes are as important as outputs. 'Curriculum is organic. It is responsive' (Sauntson and Hollis, 2023, p.13) and, as such, should be able to respond to the increasing and more urgent need for it to embody ESD.

## References

**Advance HE and Quality Assurance Agency for Higher Education (QAA)** (2021) Education for Sustainable Development Guidance, Quality Assurance Agency for Higher Education, Gloucester and Advance HE, York.

**Ahmad, N., Toro-Troconis, M., Ibahrine, M., Armour, R., Tait, V., Reedy, K., Malevicius, R., Dale, V., Tasler, N., and Inzolia, Y.** (2023) 'CoDesignS education for sustainable development: A framework for embedding education for sustainable development in curriculum design', *Sustainability*, 15(23), 16460–. DOI:10.3390/su152316460.

**CoDesignS** (2024) CoDesigns ESD Education for Sustainable Development. Available at: https://codesignsesd.org/.

**Coombs, P.H. and Ahmed, M.** (1974) *Attacking Rural Poverty: How Nonformal Education Can Help. A Research Report for the World Bank Prepared by the International Council for Educational Development.* International Council for Educational Development.

**Aoki, T.T.** (1993) 'Legitimating lived curriculum: Towards a curricular landscape of multiplicity', *Journal of Curriculum and Supervision*, 8(3), p. 255.

**Armstrong, C. and LeHew, M.** (2011) 'Scrutinizing the explicit, the implicit and the unsustainable: A model for holistic transformation of A course for sustainability', *Journal of Teacher Education for Sustainability*, 13(2), pp. 17–43. DOI:10.2478/v10099-011-0012-2.

**Peker, E. and Ataöv, A.** (2019) 'Exploring the ways in which campus open space design influences students' learning experiences', *Landscape Research*, 45(3), pp. 310–326. DOI:10.1080/01426397.2019.1622661.

**Bath, D., Smith, C., Stein, S. and Swann, R.** (2004) 'Beyond mapping and embedding graduate attributes: Bringing together quality assurance and action learning to create a validated and living curriculum', *Higher Education Research & Development*, 23(3), pp. 313–328. DOI:10.1080/0729436042000235427.

**Bell, D., Wooff, D., McLain, M. and Morrison-Love, D.** (2017) 'Analysing design and technology as an educational construct: An investigation into its curriculum position and pedagogical identity', *Curriculum Journal*, 28(4), pp. 539–558. DOI:10.1080/09585176.2017.1286995.

**Bendermacher, G.W.G., oude Egbrink, M.G.A., Wolfhagen, I.H.A.P. and Dolmans, D.H.J.M.** (2017) 'Unravelling quality culture in higher education: A realist review', *Higher Education*, 73, pp. 39–60. DOI:10.1007/s10734-015-9979-2.

**Biggs, J., Tang, C. and Kennedy, G.** (2022) *Teaching for Quality Learning at University* (Fifth edition). McGraw-Hill Education.

**Bloom, B.S.** (1956) *Taxonomy of Educational Objectives, Handbook: The Cognitive Domain.* New York: David McKay.

**Carlone, H.B.** (2017) 'Disciplinary identity as analytic construct and design goal: Making learning sciences matter', *The Journal of the Learning Sciences*, 26(3), pp. 525–531. DOI:10.1080/10508406.2017.1336026.

**Chadha, D., Inguva, P.K., Bui Le, L. and Kogelbauer, A.** (2022) 'How far do we go? Involving students as partners for redesigning teaching', *Educational Action Research*, 31(4), pp. 620–632. DOI:10.1080/09650792.2022.2058974.

**CoDesignS ESD** (2021) *CoDesignS ESD Framework for Curriculum Design.* Available at: https://codesignsesd.org/toolkit/ [Accessed 31 July 2024].

**Abbot, S. and Cook-Sather, A.** (2020) 'The productive potential of pedagogical disagreements in classroom-focused student-staff partnerships', *Higher Education Research & Development*, 39(7), pp. 1396–1409. DOI:10.1080/07294360.2020.1735315.

**Winter, J. and Cotton, D.** (2012) 'Making the hidden curriculum visible: Sustainability literacy in higher education', *Environmental Education Research*, 18(6), pp. 783–796. DOI:10.1080/13504622.2012.670207.

**Day, D.** (2018) *The Quality Assurance of Higher Education from the Perspective of Professional, Statutory and Regulatory Bodies (PSRBs).* Routledge. eBook ISBN: 9781315187518.

**Dewey, J.** (1938). *Experience and Education.* Macmillan: New York.

**Dirkx, J.M., Mezirow, J. and Cranton, P.** (2006) 'Musings and reflections on the meaning, context, and process of transformative learning: A dialogue between John M. Dirkx and Jack Mezirow', *Journal of Transformative Education*, 4(2), pp. 123–139.

**Engineering Council** (2023) *Guidance on Sustainability.* Available at: https://www.engc.org.uk/sustainability [Accessed 31 July 2024].

**European Union** (2014) *The Mediterranean Strategy on Education for Sustainable Development, Horizon 2020 Mediterranean Environment Programme.* Available at: https://medies.net/wp-content/uploads/2019/12/MSESD_brochure.pdf [Accessed 31 July 2024].

**Favaloro, T., Ball, T. and Lipschutz, R.D.** (2019) 'Mind the gap! Developing the campus as a living lab for student experiential learning in sustainability', in Leal Filho, W. and Bardi, U. (eds) *Sustainability on University Campuses: Learning, Skills Building and Best Practices.* World Sustainability Series. Springer, Cham. DOI:10.1007/978-3-030-15864-4_7.

**Higgins, D., Dennis, A., Stoddard, A., Maier, A.G. and Howitt, S.** (2019) '"Power to empower": Conceptions of teaching and learning in a pedagogical co-design partnership', *Higher Education Research & Development*, 38(6), pp. 1154–1167. DOI:10.1080/07294360.2019.1621270.

**Sauntson, H. and Hollis, E.** (2023). *Essential Guides for Early Career Teachers Understanding Your Role in Curriculum Design and Implementation* (Hollis, Ed.). Critical Publishing.

**Holst, J., Grund, J. and Brock, A.** (2024) 'Whole institution approach: Measurable and highly effective in empowering learners and educators for sustainability', *Sustainability Science*, 19(4), pp. 1359–1376. DOI:10.1007/s11625-024-01506-5.

**Holt, E.A., Ogden, T.H. and Durham, S.L.** (2018) 'The positive effect of role models in evolution instruction', *Evo Edu Outreach*, 11(11). DOI:10.1186/s12052-018-0086-6.

**Morgan, H. and Houghton, A.M.** (2011) *Inclusive curriculum design in higher education: Considerations for effective practice across and within subject areas.* Higher Education Academy (now Advance HE), York.

**Hull, R.B., Robertson, D.P. and Mortimer, M.J.** (2020) *Leadership for Sustainability: Strategies for Tackling Wicked Problems.* Island Press.

**Keinänen, M., Ursin, J. and Nissinen, K.** (2018) 'How to measure students' innovation competences in higher education: Evaluation of an assessment tool in authentic learning environments', *Studies in Educational Evaluation*, 58, pp. 30–36.

**Kłeczek, R., Hajdas, M. and Wrona, S.** (2020) 'Wicked problems and project-based learning: Value-in-use approach', *The International Journal of Management Education*, 18(1), p. 100324. DOI: 10.1016/j.ijme.2019.100324.

**Kurian, M.** (2017) 'The water-energy-food nexus: Trade-offs, thresholds and transdisciplinary approaches to sustainable development', *Environmental Science & Policy*, 68, pp. 97–106.

**Earle, A.G. and Leyva-de la Hiz, D.I.** (2021) 'The wicked problem of teaching about wicked problems: Design thinking and emerging technologies in sustainability education', *Management Learning*, 52(5), pp. 581–603. DOI:10.1177/1350507620974857.

**LinkedIn** (2024) *Global Green Skills Report 2023.* Available at: https://economicgraph.linkedin.com/content/dam/me/economicgraph/en-us/global-green-skills-report/green-skills-report-2023.pdf [Accessed 31 July 2024].

**Lozano, R., Lukman, R., Lozano, F.J., Huisingh, D. and Lambrechts, W.** (2013) 'Declarations for sustainability in higher education: Becoming better leaders, through addressing the university system', *Journal of Cleaner Production*, 48, pp. 10–19. DOI: 10.1016/j.jclepro.2011.10.006.

**Lozano, R., Merrill, M.Y., Sammalisto, K., Ceulemans, K. and Lozano, F.J.** (2017) 'Connecting competences and pedagogical approaches for sustainable development in higher education: A literature review and framework proposal', *Sustainability*, 9(1889). DOI: 10.3390/su9101889.

**Stukalo, N. and Lytvyn, M.** (2021) 'Towards sustainable development through higher education quality assurance', *Education Sciences*, 11(11), p. 664. DOI:10.3390/educsci11110664.

**Johnson, M. and Majewska, D.** (2022) *Formal, Non-formal, and Informal Learning: What Are They, and How Can We Research Them? Cambridge University Press & Assessment Research Report.*

**McCowan, T.** (2023) 'The crosscutting impact of higher education on the sustainable development Goals', *International Journal of Educational Development*, 103, p. 102945. DOI:10.1016/j.ijedudev.2023.102945.

**Timmermans, J.A. and Meyer, J.H.F.** (2019) 'A framework for working with university teachers to create and embed "integrated threshold concept knowledge" (ITCK) in their practice', *The International Journal for Academic Development*, 24(4), pp. 354–368. DOI:10.1080/1360144X.2017.1388241.

**Meyer, J. and Land, R.** (2006) *Overcoming Barriers to Student Understanding: Threshold Concepts and Troublesome Knowledge.* Routledge.

**Mickelsson, M., Kronlid, D.O. and Lotz-Sisitka, H.** (2019) 'Consider the unexpected: Scaling ESD as a matter of learning', *Environmental Education Research*, 25(1), pp. 135–150. DOI:10.1080/13504622.2018.1429572.

**Nelson, E.** (2020). Stakeholder engagement in curricular design. Addressing current and emergent community needs. *Journal of Nonprofit Education and Leadership*. 2020. Vol. 10, No. 1, pp. 25–48. https://doi.org/10.18666/JNEL-2020-V10-I1-8954.

**Orr, D.** (1994) *Environmental Literacy: Education as If the Earth Mattered.* Human Scale Education.

**Paraskeva, J.M.** (2022) 'The generation of the utopia: Itinerant curriculum theory towards a 'futurable future', *Discourse (Abingdon, England)*, 43(3), pp. 347–366.

**Giroux, H.A. and Penna, A.N.** (1979) 'Social education in The classroom: The dynamics of The hidden curriculum', *Theory & Research in Social Education*, 7(1), pp. 21–42. DOI:10.1080/00933104.1979.10506048.

**Pieters, J., Voogt, J. and Pareja Roblin, N.** (eds.) (2019). *Collaborative Curriculum Design for Sustainable Innovation and Teacher Learning* 1st edn. Springer Nature. https://doi.org/10.1007/978-3-030-20062-6

**Pretorius, R.W., Anderson, R., Khotoo, A. and Pienaar, R.** (2019) 'Creating a context for campus sustainability through teaching and learning: The case of open, distance and e-learning', *International Journal of Sustainability in Higher Education*, 20(3), pp. 530–547. DOI:10.1108/IJSHE-02-2019-0066.

**Price, E., Nicholson, D.T., Dunk, R., Lawler, C., Carney, M., Vargas, V.R., Veitch, S., Leigh, S., Singleton, M. and Mottram, S.** (2024) 'Enabling change agents for sustainable development: A whole-institution approach to embedding the UN sustainable development goals in higher education', *International Journal of Sustainability in Higher Education*. DOI:10.1108/IJSHE-02-2024-0112.

**Trigwell, K. and Prosser, M.** (2014) 'Qualitative variation in constructive alignment in curriculum design', *Higher Education*, 67(2), pp. 141–154. DOI:10.1007/s10734-013-9701-1.

**QAA (Quality Assurance Agency for Higher Education)** (2022a) *Subject Benchmark Statement: History*. Quality Assurance Agency for Higher Education, Gloucester. Available at: https://www.qaa.ac.uk/docs/qaa/sbs/sbs-history-22.pdf?sfvrsn=beaedc81_4 [Accessed 31 July 2024].

**QAA (Quality Assurance Agency for Higher Education)** (2022b) *Subject Benchmark Statement: Housing Studies*. Quality Assurance Agency for Higher Education, Gloucester.

**QAA (Quality Assurance Agency for Higher Education) and Advance HE** (2021) *Education for Sustainable Development Guidance*. Available at: https://www.qaa.ac.uk/the-quality-code/education-for-sustainable-development [Accessed 31 July 2024].

**Rata, E.** (2019) 'Knowledge-rich teaching: A model of curriculum design coherence', *British Educational Research Journal*, 45(4), pp. 681–697. DOI:10.1002/berj.3520.

**Reeping, D.** (2020) 'Threshold concepts as "jewels of the curriculum": Rare as diamonds or plentiful as cubic zirconia?', *The International Journal for Academic Development*, 25(1), pp. 58–70.

**Reeves, A., Gwilliam, J., Harrison, P., Price, E., Schantz, N., Ribchester, C., Hughes, T., Gretton, S., Strachan, S., Logan, L., Boxley, S., Lengthorn, E., Barrett, H. and Peres, S.** (2023). Education for Sustainable Development and Academic Quality: Principles and Processes for Higher Education Providers. Quality Assurance Agency (QAA).

**Jiang, F. and Roberts, P.** (2011) 'An investigation of the impact of research-led education on student learning and understandings of research', *Journal of University Teaching and Learning Practice*, 8(2), pp. 39–53. DOI:10.53761/1.8.2.4.

**Rockström, J., Gupta, J., Qin, D., Lade, S.J., Abrams, J.F., Andersen, L.S., Armstrong McKay, D.I., Bai, X., Bala, G., Bunn, S.E., Ciobanu, D., DeClerck, F., Ebi, K., Gifford, L., Gordon, C., Hasan, S., Kanie, N., Lenton, T.M., Loriani, S., Liverman, D.M., Mohamed, A., Nakicenovic, N., Obura, D., Ospina, D., Prodani, K., Rammelt, C., Sakschewski, B., Scholtens, J., Stewart-Koster, B., Tharammal, T., van Vuuren, D., Verburg, P.H., Winkelmann, R., Zimm, C., Bennett, E.M., Bringezu, S., Broadgate, W., Green, P.A., Huang, L., Jacobson, L., Ndehedehe, C., Pedde, S., Rocha, J., Scheffer, M., Schulte-Uebbing, L., de Vries, W., Xiao, C., Xu, C., Xu, X., Zafra-Calvo, N. and Zhang, X.** (2023) 'Safe and just earth system boundaries', *Nature*, 619, pp. 102–111. DOI:10.1038/s41586-023-06083-8.

**Rockström, J., Steffen, W., Noone, K., Persson, Å, Chapin, F.S., Lambin, E.F. and Foley, J.A.** (2009) 'A safe operating space for humanity', *Nature*, 461(7263), pp. 472–475. DOI:10.1038/461472a.

**Royal College of Nursing (RCN)** (2024) Definition and Principles of Nursing. Available at: https://www.rcn.org.uk/Professional-Development/Definition-and-principles-of-nursing.

**Ruge, G., Tokede, O. and Tivendale, L.** (2019) 'Implementing constructive alignment in higher education - cross-institutional perspectives from Australia', *Higher Education Research and Development*, 38(4), pp. 833–848. DOI:10.1080/07294360.2019.1586842.

**Sandri, O.** (2021) 'Providing a "point of entry": Approaches to framing sustainability in curriculum design in higher education', *Australian Journal of Environmental Education*, 37(1), pp. 56–68.

**Sandri, O.J.** (2013) 'Threshold concepts, systems and learning for sustainability', *Environmental Education Research*, 19(6), pp. 810–822. DOI:10.1080/13504622.2012.753413.

**Shephard, K.** (2008) 'Higher education for sustainability: Seeking affective learning outcomes', *International Journal of Sustainability in Higher Education*, 9(1), pp. 87–98. DOI:10.1108/14676370810842201.

**Stalmeijer, R.E., Whittingham, J.R.D., Bendermacher, G.W.G., Wolfhagen, I.H.A.P., Dolmans, D.H.J.M. and Sehlbach, C.** (2022) 'Continuous enhancement of educational quality – Fostering a quality culture: AMEE guide no. 147', *Medical Teacher*, 45(1), pp. 6–16. DOI:10.1080/0142159X.2022.2057285.

**Biggs, J.B. and Tang, C.** (2007). *Teaching for Quality Learning at University*. (3rd Ed.). Maidenhead: McGraw Hill Education & Open University Press.

**Tassone, V.C., O'Mahony, C., McKenna, E., Eppink, H.J. and Wals, A.E.J.** (2018) '(re)designing higher education curricula in times of systemic dysfunction: A responsible research and innovation perspective', *Higher Education*, 76(2), pp. 337–352. DOI:10.1007/s10734-017-0211-4.

**UN SDG (Sustainable Development Group)** (2024) *Universal Values*. Available at: https://unsdg.un.org/2030-agenda/universal-values [Accessed 31 July 2024].

**UNESCO** (2017) *Education for Sustainable Development Goals: Learning Objectives*, UNESCO: Paris.

**UNESCO** (2020) *Education for Sustainable Development: A Roadmap*, UNESCO: Paris. DOI:10.54675/YFRE1448.

**Verhoef, L.A. and Leal Filho, W., et al.** (2020) 'Towards a learning system for university campuses as living labs for sustainability', in Leal Filho, W. et al. (eds) *Universities as Living Labs for Sustainable Development*. World Sustainability Series. Springer, Cham. DOI:10.1007/978-3-030-15604-6_9.

**Winch, C.** (2017) 'Knowing "wh" and knowing how: Constructing professional curricula and integrating epistemic fields', *Journal of Philosophy of Education*, 51(2), pp. 351–369. DOI:10.1111/1467-9752.12245.

**Cotton, D. and Winter, J.** (2010) '"It's not just bits of paper and light bulbs": A review of sustainability pedagogies and their potential for use in higher education', *Sustainability Education*, pp. 39–54.

Chapter 6

# Critical Pedagogies to Engage Heart, Hand and Head in Education for Sustainable Development

*Rehema M. White, Elizabeth A.C. Price and Catherine Hack*

## Introduction

'Education for Sustainable Development (ESD) in Higher Education supports learners in all disciplines to develop knowledge, skills and capacities for human wellbeing, with attention to those who are marginalised, whilst ensuring that we live within environmental limits to address interconnected global challenges including climate change, loss of biodiversity, unsustainable use of resources, and inequality. Such learning employs critical, reflexive and potentially transformative pedagogies and curricula to create a space for dialogue, innovation and openness and to support specific and generic competencies. It enhances the cognitive, socio-emotional and behavioural dimensions of learning and encompasses learning content and outcomes, pedagogy and the learning environment itself. A whole institution approach links a sustainability focus across disciplines, teaching and research, operations and community engagement. Staff and students need to collaborate in co-production of curricula and to partner with external actors. Graduates are change agents in the sustainability transition (Chapter 2).

Education for Sustainable Development (ESD) arose from the need for education to address growing sustainability challenges and encourage learners to undertake transformative actions for sustainability to shape a different future (UNESCO, 2021) (Chapter 2). As the quote at the start of this chapter highlights, learning design for ESD encompasses learning content and outcomes, teaching methods and educational settings. Pragmatic concerns and constraints around class size, educator confidence, institutional systems and other issues may constrain possible approaches (Fiselier *et al.*, 2018), but there is an urgent need to equip educators with the tools and capacities necessary to deliver transformative ESD, regardless of discipline or mode of delivery (Varga-Atkins *et al.*, 2024). In Chapter 2, we presented a framing of ESD as subject-relevant learning objectives for the Sustainable Development Goals (SDGs), specific and key competencies for sustainability, and transformational pedagogies to support sustainable development (Advance HE/QAA, 2021). We discussed how education *for* sustainable development has a normative focus, in seeking to explore and pursue sustainable futures (see also Martin *et al.*, 2024). Hence, learning needs to go beyond information transfer to tackle the socio-political agenda of sustainable development and prepare learners for action. In higher education, this focus of ESD becomes particularly relevant, since students are developing their capacities as fulfilled individuals, responsible citizens, active community members, competent professionals and the leaders of tomorrow. The competencies they develop will not only include skills but also represent critical capacities (Wiek *et al.*, 2011) that enable them to challenge

DOI: 10.4324/9781003451563-6

contemporary dominant paradigms such as 'global turbocapitalism' (Hull, 2008), to develop new approaches (e.g. post-growth – Martin *et al.*, 2024) and even to create a new ethic for sustainability (Vásquez-Fernández and Cash Ahenakew pii tai poo taa, 2020).

In this chapter, we explore pedagogies for ESD in higher education. Fundamentally, these are defined as the theories and practices of teaching to develop the core competencies for sustainability and facilitate transformation for sustainable development. They refer to the interactive process between educator and learner and with the learning environment (Wall *et al.*, 2015). There are different approaches to teaching and learning (e.g. Learning Journals 2024). These can be broadly described as:

**Behaviorism** – This approach is teacher-centred. The class is taught by the teacher in a largely one-way transmission of information, for example, in a large lecture with no interaction. This approach is useful for the initial explanation of difficult ideas but limits learner engagement. Key proponents of this authoritarian approach included Thorndike, Pavlov and Skinner.

**Constructivism** – This approach is learner-centred. Learning occurs through experience and reflection, for example, through practicals, fieldtrips or project work. Learners are engaged more actively, but the curriculum is still directed and steered by educators. This approach originated from the research of Jean Piaget.

**Social constructivism** – This approach is teacher-guided and student-centred. It generates a collaborative learning process, for example, group work and dialogical approaches. Peer learning enables learners to go beyond the curriculum and share experiences and perspectives. Lev Vygotsky built on the ideas of Piaget, suggesting that learning is a collaborative process that occurs in a social context.

**Liberationist** – This form of critical pedagogy is student-centred and enables co-learning with the educator. It creates a more democratic and creative approach, for example, through student-led topics, and performance. This pedagogical approach aims to empower learners and educators. It was exemplified by Paulo Freire in Brazil in the 1970s (Freire, 1970), where it was important in enabling people to fight oppression and pursue a fairer future. It is liberating in that it demonstrates the possibility to think differently, to fulfil one's potential and to envision and pursue a better future.

In ESD in higher education, we employ a blend of these pedagogical approaches, often starting with some behaviourist undergraduate teaching (lectures), together with some social constructivist activities (tutorials) and perhaps some constructivist elements (practicals) and generally shifting more towards social constructivist learning in final year undergraduate and postgraduate teaching. It can be challenging to develop liberationist approaches in higher education, but such approaches can include strategies which enable transformative learning to take place and provide opportunities for the acquisition of knowledge, skills, attitudes and behaviours of learners. Such strategies can be instrumental or explorative, innovative or traditional, engaging technical learning or demanding deep self-reflection, or any combination of these possibilities. They can open up spaces to question whether we need radical or reformist approaches (Robinson, 2004) to address the current polycrisis. Many educators persist in teaching unproblematic truths and disciplinary discrete facts, and there is a rhetoric-pedagogy gap in ESD that needs to be overcome (Eilam and Trop, 2010), for example, through employing more liberationist approaches.

In order to address unsustainability, we need different paradigms and perspectives, which will in turn require transformative learning to enable us to explore alternative worldviews and transgress norms (Orr, 1994; Sterling, 2001; Springett, 2005; Hull, 2008; Lotz-Sisitka *et al.*, 2017). Transformative learning is uniquely adult, abstract and grounded in the nature of human communication (Taylor, 2007). It requires construction or revision of the interpretations of the meanings of one's experience (Mezirow, 1996). There is thus no single approach that will work for all learners, all disciplines or all institutions.

The aims of this chapter are to offer definitions of pedagogical approaches for ESD, to critically examine the rationale for compassionate pedagogy and approaches that support diverse learners (Hamilton and Petty, 2023), to examine transformative, active learning (Taylor, 2007) and relational pedagogies (Datta, 2015) and to provide practical ideas for different context and constraints, including institutional structures and systems, curricula and learning spaces.

## Compassionate Pedagogy and Supporting Diversity

Compassionate pedagogy can help to challenge tendencies of higher education to be overly competitive, grade focused and stressful for educators and learners (White, 2014; Gibbs, 2017). Compassion often includes awareness of self and of others, along with empathetic responses. It should not only be an obligation of care but rather authentic care for the wellbeing of others (Gibbs, 2017). Compassionate pedagogy has been defined as a commitment by educators to counteract institutional and class practices that ideologically disadvantage students who are in some way not being served by typical pedagogies, along with self-reflexive practices and pursuit of compassion (Hao, 2011). Such approaches fit well with ESD, which seeks to support intra-personal development and collaborative problem-solving along with safe spaces for transformative learning (Giangrande *et al.*, 2019). Creating space for compassionate pedagogies can, however, be challenging in a higher education context that is increasingly commodified and market driven (Hamilton and Petty, 2023). We can facilitate compassion in higher education institutions, but any attempt to contract or obligate it will have limited success (Gibbs, 2017). However, Gibbs (2017) argues that supporting compassionate and just approaches throughout the organisation can help everyone to flourish.

Compassionate pedagogy, along with active learning adaptations, can also support diverse student groups, including diversity in ways of seeing and interacting with the world. For example, increasing numbers of neurodivergent students are engaging in higher education (Bakker *et al.*, 2019). 'Neurodiversity can be understood as naturally occurring variation in the ways that humans perceive, experience and interact with the world, encompassing neurodevelopmental differences such as autism, attention deficit disorder (ADHD), dyslexia, developmental language disorder (DLD), dyscalculia, and developmental co-ordination disorder (DCD)' (Hamilton and Petty, 2023, pp. 1–2). We need cognitive diversity to help us address complex sustainability issues (Sulik *et al.*, 2021). Hence, including neurodiverse perspectives and experiences widens the possibilities for dialogical exchange and transformative learning for all learners, as well as being inclusive to learners who are often disadvantaged by overly neuro-normative pedagogical approaches. Hamilton and Petty (2023) call for adoption of more compassionate pedagogies, including universal design for learning and strengths-based approaches that enable all learners to achieve their potential. They suggest that this would provide better outcomes than merely offering bolt-on accommodations; whilst such plans can be useful, universal design incorporates flexibility and choice for all students, and compassionate approaches reduce anxiety and facilitate enjoyable learning spaces. Compassion and flexible pedagogies also enhance inclusion for other groups, enabling culturally responsive practices, listening to student voices and potentially creating a more welcome environment and a sense of community.

Teaching ESD can be emotional for educators, who may have strong values about their subjects, and for learners, who may feel sad, distressed or guilty and develop a sense of despair and powerlessness and possibly forms of eco-anxiety (Graham *et al.*, 2021). These authors discuss how it is important that educators can provide tools to support emotional awareness, to generate a positive ontological adjustment and to facilitate transformative learning. Such tools require trained educators and strong facilitation skills to tackle sustainability challenges realistically, yet offer pedagogies of active hope (Macy and Johnstone, 2012). A kinder, more inclusive and diverse environment in higher education can thus help to facilitate transformative learning and agency for more sustainable futures.

## Learning for All: Inter- and Transdisciplinary, Whole Institution and Community-Engaged Pedagogies

Reductionist approaches, that only recognise a part of the issues we face, threaten the movement towards sustainability (Baumgartner and Korhonen, 2010). There is thus a challenge for educators to deliver interdisciplinary pedagogical activities and experiences, either by considering interdisciplinary case studies within their own modules and courses, or by working together with other academics to co-create holistic, systems-based, complex pedagogical contexts – not just through curricula but via teaching and learning practices. Transdisciplinary approaches engage non-academics as well as developing pedagogies across academic disciplines (see Chapters 4 and 8).

The whole institution approach to ESD means not only that different parts of the institution need to pursue sustainability by relevant means, but also that integrated approaches are required. For example, group action pedagogies can address problems of operational sustainability and community engagement; reflection on learning can strengthen ESD pedagogies; student research projects can enhance aspects of institutional sustainability. Whole institution approaches also enable non-formal pedagogies through extra-curricular activities and informal learning through setting the tone of sustainability, for example, through actively informing students, staff and wider community about sustainability intentions, strategies and ongoing actions. Non-formal pedagogies can be driven by students themselves but also academic staff and others at the university. Informal pedagogy infuses university practices (e.g. supporting sustainable transport options, providing sustainable food choices) and principles (e.g. publicly declaring allegiance to sustainability policy and declarations).

The whole institution approach also increases focus on the importance of the educator and on educational processes in ESD. It aligns well with the notion of whole person learning (Podger *et al.*, 2010) and the need for staff, students and community members to co-learn through dialogue and practice.

## Relational and Eco-Pedagogies

In this section, we explore some of the theory behind relational and eco-pedagogies to strengthen rationale for and understanding of the need for some of these pedagogical approaches and learning activities.

We know that revealing and exploring different perspectives is essential for transformative learning, but that perspectives are associated with people, cultures and context, and hence pedagogies that recognise relationships are important. The plurality of paradigms on sustainable development (Robinson, 2004; Martin *et al.*, 2024) indicate that dialogical processes will be required for learners to understand and collaborate across different world views and deepen normative and cultural competencies. Relational pedagogies that explore relationships between humans and with more-than-human beings are critical in ESD. Relational pedagogies recognise complexity and consider that the pursuit of sustainable development not only requires constitutive processes but also relationships and collaborative enterprise (Walsh *et al.*, 2021). Such pedagogies develop the emotional intelligence of learners and also demand self-awareness and development of intra-personal competencies (Giangrande *et al.*, 2019). They facilitate learners to consider principled action through activating and deepening existing concerns (Glasser, 2004). The normative focus on action and complexity also demands pedagogies to develop awareness of scale and inter-scalar linkages (North, 2005).

Eco-pedagogies are often considered to be forms of relational pedagogy. Diverse values held in relation to nature align with different paths to sustainability action (Martin *et al.*, 2024). If sustainable development includes both utilitarian and more spiritual relationships with nature (Robinson, 2004), eco-pedagogies need to both explore practical consequences of natural resource use and more emotional connections with nature. 'Eco-centric education' goes further in placing nature at the centre of the learning process and exploring relationships from/with rather than just to nature (Kopnina, 2020, drawing on Shrivastava, 1994). Such perspectives establish a wider ethics, beyond human needs – a form of ecological justice that considers the rights of nature (e.g. Lecuyer *et al.*, 2018).

Relational ontologies help to break down divisions between individual, community and culture and thus shift worldviews from the mainstream modern ontology (Escobar, 2011). Not only human relationships but also the relationships between humans and more-than-humans are important. Such relationships are often built on emotional or spiritual links, and these spiritual interconnections can make actors responsible to each other and enhance ecological respect (Ingold, 2011). Meanings of traditional experiences, cultures and customs have been suggested to be important in demonstrating and reinforcing relationships between land, nature and sustainability (Datta, 2015). Such relationships are thus mediated partly through spiritual and experiential connections and not merely through utilitarian functions such as natural resource use or ecosystem services (Escobar, 2011; Datta, 2015). This realisation influences the pedagogies we need to employ to develop emotional intelligence and enable dialogue about spiritual frameworks.

Indigenous knowledge systems can be more holistic than the often reductionist Western education and can offer alternative ways of framing relationships between people and nature (Kopnina, 2020; Vásquez-Fernández and Cash Ahenakew pii tai poo taa 2020). Pedagogies grounded in Indigenous ways of knowing often engage with relational approaches. Reciprocity and respect are important (Kimmerer, 2013; Martin *et al.*, 2024; Vásquez-Fernández and Cash Ahenakew pii tai poo taa 2020), as is recognition of diversity, place and complexity (Kopnina, 2020). There can be difficult discussions about how diverse systems might be sympathetic to principles of sustainability (including respect for nature and all peoples). For example, authoritarian regimes have generated restrictive educational formats and excluded certain groups (e.g. women, minority groups) from the privileges and possibilities that education can provide. We must thus not totally refute Western knowledge but rather rebalance and reorient it towards a more critical yet compassionate direction.

Relational pedagogies also include intergenerational approaches that include 'all age reciprocity' (Mannion, 2012). Such pedagogies often involve connection to place and culture and can explicitly challenge contemporary paradigms by facilitating different generational lenses and highlighting diverse possible relationships with nature. Place-responsive pedagogies further develop connection with place and others (Mannion *et al.*, 2013).

What are the implications of eco- and relational pedagogies for ESD in higher education? First, this conceptual framework influences the pedagogies required to facilitate interaction between human and more-than-human actors and demands openness to different worldviews. Appropriate pedagogical approaches might include outdoor learning, nature connection, new materialism (Mannion, 2020; Walsh *et al.*, 2021). Second, eco- and relational pedagogies affect how we teach all topics, including sustainability, development, ecology, history and technical sciences, in requiring us to explore concepts such as hybridity, otherness, knowledge and relatedness. For example, we could engage our students more with community groups and through creative pedagogies (Podger et al., 2010). Third, they alter our relationships with and trust in policy, enabling us to develop and share more critical insights. For example, we may critically engage more with the SDGs (Kopnina, 2020) and with processes of decolonisation (Vásquez-Fernández and Cash Ahenakew pii tai poo taa 2020). Fourth, they emphasise relationship with place, promoting place-responsive pedagogies and thus also outdoor-based and intergenerational pedagogical approaches (Mannion, 2012; Mannion *et al.*, 2013). Fifth, they demonstrate that a one size fits all blueprint for ESD is not possible; the contextual, specific aspects of place-responsive, ecocentric and Indigenous pedagogies challenge uniform views of education for all (Mannion *et al.*, 2013; Kopnina, 2020). Finally, they shift positively how educators and learners work and become within our institutions, encouraging us towards relational approaches and embracing self-fulfilment, shifting away from individualism and competition towards collective action and collaborative working within more sustainable universities (White, 2014).

## Transformative, Active Learning

ESD is an integral part of quality education (UNESCO, 2024) and emphasises transformative rather than transmissive approaches (UNESCO, 2021). Innovative research methods, including action research, have revealed empirical insights on transformative learning in higher education and explored the nature and consequences of learning experiences (Taylor, 2007). These insights include difficulties in defining a perspective transformation and insufficient consideration of the effects of culture. There is also a tendency to overlook the possible negative personal and social consequences of a transformative learning experience (McDonald *et al.*, 1999). Transformative learning processes are often disruptive and can be accompanied by epistemological (involving a change in world view) and ontological (involving a change in ways of being in the world) change (Taylor, 2007), possibly permitting more relational ontologies as supported by Datta (2015) and others. Taylor (2007) notes that it is also important to identify 'pedagogical entry points' and how to work with students at the edge of their understanding.

A variety of tools for learner engagement can be employed in a range of contexts, including large lecture theatres, flexible learning spaces, online, outdoors and real world (Mannion *et al.*, 2013; Turner et al., 2020). Pedagogies supporting transformative learning include action learning, multi-media (including journalling and story-telling), personal challenges, reflection and emotional engagement (Taylor, 2007) and eco-, relational and place-based pedagogies (Mannion *et al.*, 2013; Walsh *et al.*, 2021). Authentic assessment, and active, learner-centred, experiential learning focusing on participation, collaboration and action that promote student engagement are more effective than transmissive approaches (Healey and Healey, 2019; UNESCO, 2021). Such approaches allow learners to be challenged and to themselves challenge contemporary paradigms, such as extractivist, growth-based, capitalist production and consumption models (Springett, 2005; Kopnina, 2020) and histories of colonisation (Vásquez-Fernández and Cash Ahenakew pii tai poo taa, 2020). Critical pedagogies (Freire, 1970) include assessment of alternative economic models such as degrowth, circular economy and ecological economics. Gradually, such ideas are ceasing to be radical and are becoming progressive, for example, Doughnut economics, a safe and just space between planetary boundaries and social boundaries in which humanity can thrive (Raworth, 2017a,b, Chapter 2) has attracted widespread interest (McManus *et al.*, 2022).

An innovative form of relational pedagogy is being undertaken in intercultural universities, which generally attempt to traverse ontological distance between Indigenous and western modes of learning and education. Such institutions not only undertake research and teaching but also work hard with local communities and contexts and aim to address inequalities of colonialism and ethnicity as well as vocational training (Schmelkes, 2009).

Learning and teaching in many contexts is increasingly adopting information and communication technologies (ICT) and higher education is changing rapidly as a result of digitalisation, artificial intelligence (AI), and subsequent to experiences during COVID-19. It may seem that digital pedagogies are the opposite of relational, eco- and place-based pedagogies, and they cannot replace these important learning approaches, but they do also play a role in supporting transformative learning and can enable ontological fluidity. Digital pedagogies and smart learning environments can help us rethink learning processes and, for example, support problem and project-based learning, case study and cooperative inquiry methods and provide personalised, adaptive learning support (Cebrián *et al.*, 2020). Digital developments can enhance educators' capacity to present learning opportunities and to offer and provide feedback on innovative forms of assessment (Ricard *et al.*, 2020). Virtual reality and international communication can support learning in class, whilst distance, online and hybrid learning, including MOOCs, can make learning more accessible and inclusive (Ricard *et al.*, 2020). As higher education students are usually digital natives, they interact with and use technology differently from previous generations and may, for example, prefer bite size teaching chunks rather than entire lectures.

Design thinking is gaining traction as an exciting, co-creative approach that links agendas such as entrepreneurial thinking together with ESD in higher education (Androutsos and Brinia, 2020). Design thinking comprises an approach, including brainstorming, piloting, iteration, refinement and implementation, and can be applied at the product level but also to develop socio-ecological innovation (White and van Koten, 2016).

Such pedagogical approaches can be empowering for students, because they inspire creativity, and they are solutions focused.

The pedagogical possibilities are thus exciting but can seem overwhelming to inexperienced or overworked educators in higher education. We thus now explore the practical implementation of such approaches.

Essentially, transformative learning design addresses two aspects of practice: firstly, learning activities and, secondly, constructively aligned transformative, active learning pedagogies.

### *Learning Activities*

The first aspect of transformative practice is about ensuring a good balance in the types of learning activities used. The Open University Learning Design Activity Types Framework (OU, 2021), consists of five activity types, focusing on observable student behaviour, and so puts students at the centre of learning and teaching. Assessment can involve any of the activity types or a blend of several (Chapter 7). The Framework acts as a prompt to develop active learning opportunities for students and can be used to review the balance of activity types in the curriculum. Learning design activity types can also be grouped into (1) Learning through experience, (2) Learning through others and (3) Learning through didactic methods (Arets *et al.*, 2016; Toro-Troconis *et al.*, 2019; OU, 2020, 2021) (Table 6.1). It has been suggested that an idealised breakdown of activities to move from 'know-what' learning towards more effective 'know-how' learning is 70% learning through experience, 20% learning through others and 10% learning through didactic methods; however, each discipline or situation may have a different profile

*Table 6.1* OU learning design activity types of framework

| *Activity type* | *Example terms to use when designing activities* | *Grouping* |
|---|---|---|
| **Assimilative**<br>Attending to information | Read, watch, listen, think about, observe, review, consider, study | Learning through didactic methods |
| **Communicative**<br>Discussing with others | Communicate, debate, discuss, argue, share, report, collaborate, present, describe, question | Learning through others |
| **Finding and handling information**<br>Searching for and processing information | Search, use, list, order, classify, analyse, select, evaluate, collate, plot, discover, manipulate, visualise | Learning through experience |
| **Productive**<br>Actively constructing an artefact | Create, build, write, make, design, construct, produce, draw, compose, record, remix | Learning through experience |
| **Practice**<br>Applying learning in a real-world or simulated setting | Practice, apply, mimic, experience, explore, investigate, perform, experiment, trial, model, simulate, improve | Learning through experience |
| **Assessment**<br>All forms of assessment, represented as a blend of the five activity types | | |

*Source*: Arets *et al.* (2016); Toro-Troconis *et al.* (2019); CoDesignS ESD (2021); OU (2021).

(Arets *et al.*, 2016; Toro-Troconis *et al.*, 2019; CoDesignS ESD, 2021). Essentially, this idealised breakdown promotes experiential learning (active methods such as problem-solving, analysis, production, creativity and practice) over didactic (learning by assimilation) and purely communicative (learning with and from others) activities, though it is recognised that experiential learning methods often also involve communication. For ESD, experiential learning is particularly important because it enables exploration of values and can support paradigmatic changes. Learning with others is also critical, to open up dialogical spaces and recognise different perspective on sustainability (Hull, 2008).

The form and extent of use of different activities will depend on the institution, academic discipline, programme, module, educator experience, student characteristics and wider curricular expectations and structures. Large educational shifts may need institutional direction and support, but there is always potential for individual educators to implement small steps and demonstrate the validity of such approaches.

## Learning Pedagogies

The second aspect of transformative practice is constructively aligned active learning pedagogies.

### *Constructive Alignment*

Constructive alignment for learning design provides a framework to create a learning environment that supports learning activities appropriate to achieving the desired learning outcomes. All components in the learning and teaching system – the curriculum and its intended learning outcomes, the teaching methods used and the assessment tasks – are aligned to each other (Biggs, 2003) (Figure 6.1) (see Chapter 5).

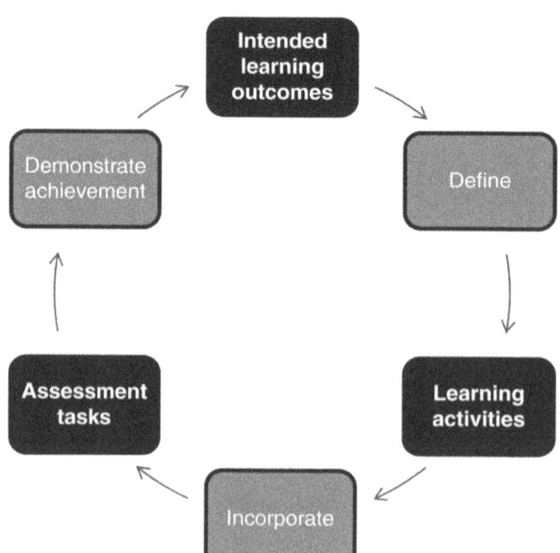


*Figure 6.1* Representation of constructive alignment (Biggs, 2003). Intended learning outcomes, teaching methods used and the assessment tasks are aligned to each other.

### *Transformative, Active Learning*

As described above, transformative learning refers to learning that goes beyond acquisition of knowledge, to that in which learners' values, behaviours and worldviews are transformed. This represents a move from purely knowledge-based learning, to learning that enables action and transformative agency. Transformative pedagogies are thus fundamental to ESD outcomes (UNESCO, 2021; O'Grady, 2023). We have seen in Chapter 2 how ESD develops a range of key competencies around ways of thinking, practising and being. To develop these competencies into action requires a transformative pedagogical approach based on experience and reflection that promotes collaborative enquiry, problem-solving and systems-based learning (O'Grady, 2023). This approach draws on active, student-centred, experiential learning.

Active learning often includes learners as participants and contributors, developing their agency and decision-making power over their learning. Active learning promotes student engagement and occurs at the level of the individual learner, or through cooperative (teacher centred) or collaborative (student centred) learning. Student-centred learning places learners at the centre of the learning process, where students may influence the content, activities and pace of learning (Michael, 2006). Experiential learning (Kolb, 1984) also engages students in meaningful learning activities that are in some way authentic. Experiential learning holistically immerses the learner cognitively, behaviourally and emotionally. As outlined in Chapter 2, the cognitive domain (head) includes knowledge and thinking skills necessary to better understand sustainability challenges. The socio-emotional domain (heart) includes social skills that enable learners to collaborate, negotiate and communicate to promote sustainable development as well as self-reflection skills, values, attitudes and motivations for sustainability. The behavioural domain (hand) describes action competencies that allow learners to take practical action for sustainable transformation (Sipos *et al.*, 2008; UNESCO, 2017, 2021; Toro-Troconis *et al.*, 2023). Table 6.2 shows the relationship between the head, heart and hands learning domains and learning activity types. Different verbs

*Table 6.2* Mapping transformative pedagogies with indicative verbs, learning activity types and learning domains.

| *Learning domain* | *Low level**<br>*Learning Design Activity Type: Assimilative (OU, 2021)* | *High level***<br>*Learning Design Activity Types: Finding and handling information; Communicative; Productive/ Creative; Practice (OU, 2021)* |
|---|---|---|
| <br>**Cognitive (Head)**<br>Comprises knowledge and thinking skills necessary to better understand the SDGs and the challenges in achieving them. | **Indicative verbs:** read, watch, listen, think about, observe, review, consider, study (Table 6.1).<br>**The verbs presented in this area are associated with the development of lower order cognitive skills: factual and procedural knowledge.* | **Indicative verbs:** communicate, discuss, analyse, evaluate, create, design, produce, investigate, experiment, improve (Table 6.1).<br>***The verbs presented in this area are associated with the development of high order cognitive skills. This means implementing transformative pedagogies that involve the cognitive, socio-emotional and behavioural learning domains.* |

*(Continued)*

*Table 6.2* (Continued)

| *Learning domain* | *Low level** <br> *Learning Design Activity Type: Assimilative (OU, 2021)* | *High level*** <br> *Learning Design Activity Types: Finding and handling information; Communicative; Productive/ Creative; Practice (OU, 2021)* |
|---|---|---|
| | **Indicative pedagogic approaches and teaching methods** <br> Reading, watching, listening, thinking about, accessing. | **Indicative pedagogic approaches and teaching methods** <br> *Participatory Enquiry/Action Research*: in participative inquiry/action research, students investigate an issue which is of importance to them personally. <br> *Action Competence*: in action competence, students are encouraged to envisage alternatives and solutions to unsustainable practices. <br> *Object-based learning*: focused on objects, instruction and student investigation assess and analyse some subset of the diverse physical, chemical, biological, ecological, social, ethical, political and economic associations between the object and the systems associated with it. <br> *Role/plays and simulations*: group discussions debates, digital storytelling, critical incidents, problem-based learning and team-based learning. |
|  <br> **Socio-emotional (Heart)** <br> Includes social skills that enable learners to collaborate, negotiate and communicate to promote the SDGs as well as self-reflection skills, values, attitudes and motivations that enable learners to develop themselves. | *Not applicable* | |
|  <br> **Behavioural (Hands)** <br> Describes action competencies. | *Not applicable* | |

*Source*: Adapted from CoDesigns (2021). ESD CC BY-NC-ND-SA 4.0.

map across to different learning activities and help to identify the relevant specific learning domain (head, heart, hands) and indicative pedagogical methods.

## Learning Environment

Learning environments encompass learner-educator-place interactions and provide an important basis for engaging in transformative pedagogies in higher education (Tasler and Dale, 2021; UNESCO, 2021). Tasler and Dale (2021) recognise three 'spaces' characterising a learning environment that can be considered in learning design. The first

*Table 6.3* Principles to underpin inclusive engagement

| |
|---|
| Respect the diversity of experiences and identities in the room. |
| Pay attention to each other, welcome feedback and think about the impact of what we say. |
| Reflect on our own learning, connections to the material and how our ideas and opinions are formed. |
| Consider the needs of others in terms of access to materials and discussions. |
| Stay curious. |

*Source*: Turner et al. (2020).

'space' recognises three components: learners, educators and places, since students and educators separately bring their varying experiences and expectations to the learning and teaching process (Healey and Healey, 2019), and learning and teaching places are also designed by people with different influences. The second 'space' defines the *interactions* between the first spaces: educators with learners, educators with virtual and physical places, and learners with virtual and physical places. Considering how learners interact with each other is also an important feature of learning design for transformative pedagogies (OU, 2021). The third 'space' is defined as where the learner, educator and place come together optimally to achieve transformational learning. Creative pedagogies seek to actively engage students in a way that has the potential to transform the learner. Effective approaches focus on the interaction between learner, educator and place through inclusive practice and include student-centred approaches in formal and informal physical places, and an enriched digital learning environment, promoting collaboration (Turner *et al.*, 2020; Tasler and Dale, 2021).

As noted above, engagement with learning can be influenced by existing social and educational inequalities. Inclusive practice considers the diverse needs, identities and engagement preferences of *all* learners to address barriers to participation in the learning environment (Hockings, 2010; Turner *et al.*, 2020) (Table 6.3).

As we saw in Chapter 2, learning environments can be formal, informal (such as community, business) and non-formal (such as media, culture) (White *et al.*, 2023). Furthermore, the whole-institution approach to ESD explored in Chapter 3 calls for learning environments where 'learners learn what they live and live what they learn', so that university governance, culture, facilities and operations embed sustainability practices, learners are engaged towards increasing their participation in sustainable development action, and the local community is seen as a valuable setting for learning and action for sustainability, enabling campus and community to become a 'learning laboratory' for sustainable development (UNESCO, 2021).

## Transformative Pedagogies in Practice

As we have seen, transformative, active learning methods engage the learner cognitively (head), emotionally (heart) and behaviourally (hands) (Sipos *et al.*, 2008), and learning design can include individual, cooperative or collaborative learning methods (Babić *et al.*, 2021).

Individual learning and reflection can stimulate the learner's interest and motivation and develop an understanding of how they learn best. This can be fostered through individual portfolios or personal reflective diaries or blogs.

Educator-centred cooperative learning involves the educator setting tasks, where individual learners are responsible for their own learning and assessment. Examples include jigsaw groups, where the educator assigns each group or person a piece of a problem to work on before bringing the pieces back together, a world café where students address a question in small groups and are invited to share insights from conversations with the whole group, role play, debate and cooperative problem-solving (Table 6.4).

*Table 6.4* Examples of effective active learning pedagogies.

**Debates and discussions:** Students develop theses and antitheses around example sustainability challenges (Kennedy, 2007; Turner *et al.*, 2020).

**Eco-pedagogies:** Engage students in nature-based activities and accompanying reflections, such as an afternoon in a community garden, self-guided fieldtrips or longer residential fieldtrips, adventure based modules such as canoeing down a river (White *et al.*, 2023).

**Enquiry-based learning:** (open-ended research question) and **problem-based learning** (closed question using problem-solving skills): Students encouraged to find alternative solutions focusing on futures thinking and action competence (Kahn and O'Rourke, 2005; Turner *et al.*, 2020).

**Gamification:** Integrate games into the classroom (Dunk *et al.*, 2021; Carbon Literacy for Universities: Man Met, undated).

**Group portfolio:** Students showcase critical thinking, problem-solving and collaboration skills by actively curating and reflecting on their work (Wakelet, 2023).

**Infographic:** Students create an infographic to represent key data pertaining to their topic (Jaleniauskiene and Kasperiuniene, 2023).

**Inter-generational learning:** Invite local community members from different generations to attend a discussion; set up interviews; or visit community places with different generational representation such as a community garden to explore wider perspectives on practice and place (Mannion, 2012).

**Jigsaw groups:** Assign each group or person an aspect or piece of a problem to work on before bringing the pieces back together (Turner *et al.*, 2020).

**Learning landscapes:** Use a physical or virtual space (e.g. an external open space or Google Earth) as a mechanism to promote collaborative problem-solving, learning and reflection on collective and individual sustainability behaviours (Dale *et al.*, 2022).

**Object-based learning:** Use sustainability implications of everyday items to stimulate discussion around systems thinking (Turner *et al.*, 2020; Dale *et al.*, 2022).

**Outdoor learning:** Engage students in activities such as field-based learning to enhance motivation and deeper connections, scavenger hunts to explore the sustainability implications of what they find or develop (or co-create with students) a sustainability trail on campus to make connections between sustainability and place (Fedesco *et al.*, 2020; Education Scotland, 2024).

**Relational pedagogies:** Watch a short documentary of life and sustainability issues in another part of the world and then discuss in class; explore role play; invite guest speakers from non-academic contexts; create safe dialogical spaces to express worldviews in tutorials; explore ontological diversity in relation to sustainability solutions (Walsh *et al.*, 2021).

**Storytelling:** Invite students to write a biography in a storytelling style, depicting an aspect of their life and/or values linked to a named SDG or sustainability issue ( Advance HE, 2024).

**Whole institution:** Students work on real issues of concern in their institution and wider community, including individual and group research projects, feeding into operational and policy concerns and aligning with sustainability research (White, 2013)

**World café:** Students address a relevant question and exchange perspectives in small groups, with opportunities to move between groups and to share insights from conversations with the whole group (World Café Community Foundation, 2015).

**Box 6.1 Examples of Whole Institution Pedagogies**

At the University of St Andrews, walking transects through university community gardens demonstrate the messiness and spontaneity of a community garden, explain processes of social organisation and provide active opportunities for students to 'give back' by undertaking gardening tasks for a short time. Hence, a combination of cognitive (knowledge about growing and community organisation), experiential (feeling soil quality, identifying weeds, the sensory experience of working in nature and possibly tasting and smelling garden produce) and socio-emotional (nature connection, collaborative action) learning is provided in an active fieldtrip that can also encourage students to contribute to community gardening projects and shift food consumption behaviour.

At the University of St Andrews, student dissertations have explored and provided recommendations for food choice and planning in university halls of residence catering, biodiversity action planning for the campus, Transition University of St Andrews projects and more.

Student-centred collaborative learning is where learners are accountable for their collective effort in learning and assessment. Examples include team-based learning, enquiry or problem-based learning, or a group portfolio (Table 6.4).

Babić *et al.* (2021) concluded that students prefer a mixture of collaborative, cooperative and individual work, and suggested that learners recognise the benefits of teamwork, but also the importance of individual, independent learning. In practice, a range of structured activities can enable students to successfully engage with their own transformative learning (OU, 2020; Turner *et al.*, 2020) (Table 6.4; Box 6.1).

## Putting Learning Design for ESD into Practice

In Chapter 2, we saw how the CoDesignS ESD Framework (CoDesignS ESD, 2021) links the key elements of ESD around three pillars:

A: Specific learning objectives for the Sustainable Development Goals (SDGs).
B: Key competencies for sustainability.
C: Transformative pedagogies and teaching methods.

Figure 6.2a, b summarises how these elements can be combined in a module, in this case, Professional Geographer, a core first-year undergraduate module delivered to Geography students. The front side of the card (Figure 6.2a) shows the SDGs (Chapter 2), learning domains, key competencies for sustainability (Chapter 2) and learning design activity types addressed in the module. It also provides a module description. The reverse side of the card (Figure 6.2b) describes how the specific learning objectives aligned to the head, heart, hands learning domains are achieved and assessed, how the SDGs are included (Chapter 2) and shows examples of transformative pedagogies and teaching methods used (CoDesignS ESD, 2021; Nicholson *et al.*, 2024). This example (Figure 6.2a, b)

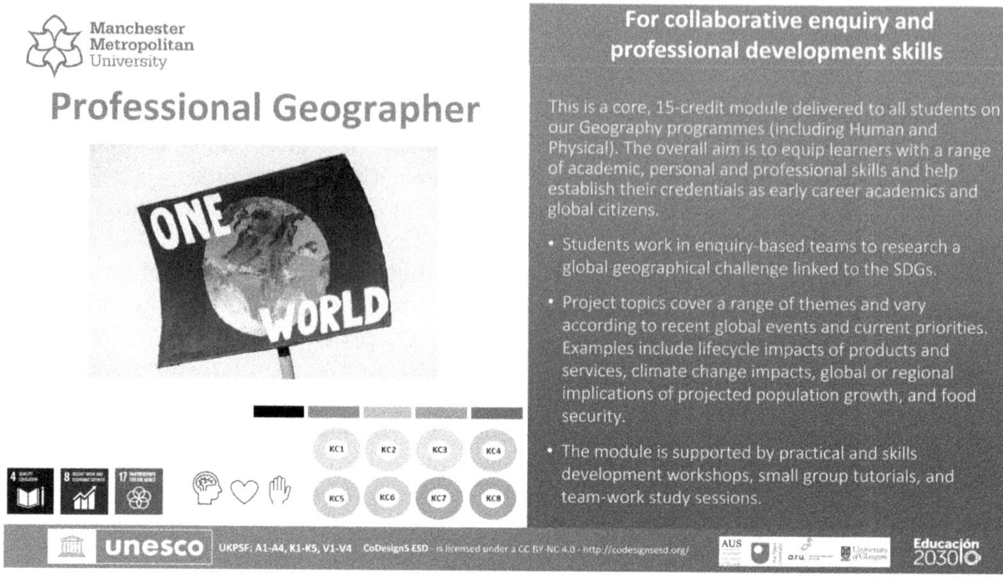


**How the Specific Learning Objectives have been achieved:**

At the end of this activity students were able to:

- Construct a critical academic argument based on evaluation and synthesis of appropriate sources, and recommend solutions to sustainability problems relating to geographical phenomena.
- Collaborate in a team, develop awareness of diversity, and reflect on personal responsibility for sustainability challenges. Demonstrate awareness of role as a global citizen.
- Build an online professional development portfolio, communicate (verbally, textually, and graphically) the outcomes of geographical enquiry.

**How the Specific Learning Objectives were assessed:**

- **Team presentation and infographic**: A 15-min presentation of of team projects exploring a global geographical challenge
- **Online Professional Development Portfolio:** Individual portfolio with evidence of goal-setting, career planning, self-assessment, and written critical review of an aspect of team project



**How the Sustainable Development Goals have been included:**

- Learning linked to obtaining quality education. Learners experience and understand the importance of inclusive and equitable quality education and promoting lifelong learning opportunities for all.
- Learning activity linking to professional development for the world of work. Learners apply learning to developing and demonstrating own potential for contributing to responsible futures.
- Learners are exposed to all SDGs and have developed systems thinking competence related to sustainability

**How have the designed teaching and learning activities been delivered?**

- **Enquiry-based learning:** Learners investigate an issue of personal relevance. Team project topics selected by students are authentic, real-world issues.
- **Learning landscapes:** Highly relevant to geography, sustainability issues are explored in specific places to develop understanding of concepts.
- **Object-based learning:** Physical objects in the classroom and on a sustainability trail stimulate systems thinking and personal reflection.
- **Collaborative debate and discussion:** Open discussion and debate promote peer learning and develop local and global diversity awareness

*Figure 6.2* (a, b) An example of a CoDesignS ESD module case study. The front side of the card (Figure 6.2a) shows relevant SDG icons, learning domains (head, heart, hands), learning design activity types (represented by different shades of grey horizontal bars), key competencies for sustainability (represented by circles labelled with KCs) and a module description. This side also makes reference to the Advance HE (2023) UK Professional Standards Framework (UKPSF). The reverse side of the card (Figure 6.2b) describes specific learning objectives, SDGs and teaching and learning activities incorporated into the module learning design (CoDesignS ESD, 2021; Nicholson *et al.*, 2024).

represents a skills module, illustrating learning design elements that are easily adaptable to a variety of disciplines. A range of example cases from different subjects, levels, modes of delivery and institutions across the world provides case studies showing how the elements of ESD learning design can be combined in a wide range of contexts and scenarios (CoDesignS ESD, 2021; Varga-Atkins *et al.*, 2024; Toro-Troconis *et al.*, 2024).

## Educators as Co-Designers

The adoption of different pedagogical approaches and activities can be challenging for educators. In higher education, many academics have had no or little formal training in teaching, although more support and quality control exists now than previously. Embarking on a social constructivist journey, for example, can be daunting if the educator has insufficient experience or training to provide competence and confidence. Liberationist and social constructivist approaches can enable educators to co-design curricula and solutions together with students and can thus empower educators through competency development and the possibility of their own transformative learning.

As student voice becomes stronger in higher education, we are seeing welcome inclusion of learners in co-design and participatory curriculum development (Nicholson *et al.*, 2024). Collaborative processes can include diverse perspectives and enhance quality of and buy in to curricula and learning processes (Boyle *et al.*, 2024). Student participation increases trust and satisfaction and generates co-creation (Perello-Marín *et al.*, 2018). Such partnerships can be very positive experiences for academic staff.

## Conclusions

Effective learning and teaching for ESD involves a move from purely knowledge-based learning, to learning that enables action and transformative agency (Lotz-Sisitka *et al.*, 2017; UNESCO, 2021; O'Grady, 2023). It enhances the cognitive (head), social and emotional (heart) and behavioural (hands) dimensions of learning and promotes inclusive student engagement by creating an enabling learner environment through learning design for transformative practice. There is a wide range of pedagogical approaches that can be adopted or enhanced by educators to facilitate quality ESD, and first steps towards such teaching or learning can include use of existing resources and adaptation of existing practice. It is widely accepted that we need a transition to a more sustainable future (Geels, 2010; UN, 2015) and that education will underpin and enable this. Transformative learning requires pedagogic practices that provide time and space for learners to make connections between their prior knowledge, experiences and perspectives and new knowledge and perspectives through social interaction and collaboration with others of diverse views and experiences, empowering them to critically examine evidence and challenge norms. Pedagogy for ESD should thus also critically interrogate existing paradigms and enable radical opportunities for new ontologies, ideas and practices. Such pedagogical innovation can be exciting and challenging, but fundamentally is also merely integral to quality education, regardless of context (UNESCO, 2021). Finally, if educators and learners are constrained by professional or practical limitations, we encourage pedagogical side steps such as including a new activity or adapting an assessment, trialling a new lecture or tutorial session, or bringing in a guest speaker, as these can all begin the journey towards transformational learning through innovative pedagogy.

## References


Advance HE (2023). Professional standards framework for teaching and supporting learning in higher education 2023. Available at: https://advance-he.ac.uk/knowledge-hub/professional-standards-framework-teaching-and-supporting-learning-higher-education-0?_ga=2.213367568.547873202.1720266851-1685358814.1720266851 [Accessed 31 Jul. 2024].

Advance HE (2024). Learning through storytelling. Available at: https://www.advance-he.ac.uk/knowledge-hub/learning-through-storytelling-0 [Accessed 31 Jul. 2024].

Advance HE/QAA (2021). Education for sustainable development guidance. Available at: https://www.qaa.ac.uk/quality-code/education-for-sustainable-development [Accessed 31 Jul. 2024].

Androutsos, A. and Brinia, V. (2020). Developing an innovative pedagogy for sustainability in higher education. In: A. Androutsos and V. Brinia, eds., Designing an Innovative Pedagogy for Sustainable Development in Higher Education. Boca Raton, FL: CRC Press, pp. 119–131.

Arets, J., Jennings, C. and Heijnen, V. (2016). 70:20:10 into action. Available at: https://702010institute.com/wp-content/uploads/2018/11/Primer-702010-into-action.pdf [Accessed 31 Jul. 2024].

Babić, T., Kolar, L. and Miličević, L. (2021). Individual, cooperative and collaborative learning and students' perceptions of their impact on their own study performance. 44th International Convention on Information, Communication and Electronic Technology (MIPRO), pp. 864–869. doi: 10.23919/MIPRO52101.2021.9596728. Available at: https://ieeexplore.ieee.org/document/9596728 [Accessed 31 Jul. 2024].

Bakker, T., Krabbendam, L., Bhulai, S. and Begeer, S. (2019). Background and enrollment characteristics of students with autism in higher education. Research in Autism Spectrum Disorders, 67, p. 101424. doi: 10.1016/j.rasd.2019.101424.

Baumgartner, R.J. and Korhonen, J. (2010). Strategic thinking for sustainable development. Sustainable Development, 18(2), pp. 71–75.

Biggs, J. (2003). Aligning teaching for constructing learning. Available at: https://www.advance-he.ac.uk/knowledge-hub/aligning-teaching-constructing-learning [Accessed 31 Jul. 2024].

Boyle, F.A., Buchanan, F.M., Ritchie, D. and Gamage, K.A. (2024). Exploring staff–student partnership in curriculum design. Education Sciences, 14(1), p. 61.

Carbon Literacy for Universities: Manchester Met (n.d.). Carbon literacy for universities. Available at: https://carbonliteracy.com/education/ [Accessed 31 Jul. 2024].

Cebrián, G., Palau, R. and Mogas, J. (2020). The smart classroom as a means to the development of ESD methodologies. Sustainability, 12(7), p. 3010.

CoDesignS ESD (2021). CoDesignS education for sustainable development. Available at: https://codesignsesd.org/toolkit/ [Accessed 31 Jul. 2024].

Dale, V., Tasler, N. and Sánchez-Jáuregui, L. (2022). Object-based learning: Active learning through enquiry. In: V. Dale, N. Tasler and L. Sánchez-Jáuregui, eds., 100+ Ideas for Active Learning. Sussex: Open Press. Available at: https://openpress.sussex.ac.uk/ideasforactivelearning/chapter/object-based-learning-active-learning-through-enquiry/ [Accessed 31 Jul. 2024].

Datta, R. (2015). A relational theoretical framework and meanings of land, nature, and sustainability for research with Indigenous communities. Local Environment, 20(1), pp. 102–113. doi: 10.1080/13549839.2013.818957.

Dunk, R.M., Mörk, J. and Price, E.A.C. (2021). Carbon literacy: Peer-to-peer training facilitates access for all staff and students. COP26 Universities Network Case Studies. Available at: https://uucn.ac.uk/wp-content/uploads/2022/07/Media_814591_smxx.pdf [Accessed 31 Jul. 2024].

Education Scotland (2024). Outdoor learning resources. Available at: https://education.gov.scot/resources/outdoor-learning-resources/ [Accessed 31 Jul. 2024].

Eilam, E. and Trop, T. (2010). ESD pedagogy: A guide for the perplexed. The Journal of Environmental Education, 42(1), pp. 43–64.

Escobar, A. (2011). Encountering Development: The Making and Unmaking of the Third World. Princeton, NJ: Princeton University Press.

Fedesco, H.N., Cavin, D. and Henares, R. (2020). Field-based learning in higher education: Exploring the benefits and possibilities. Journal of the Scholarship of Teaching and Learning, 20, pp. 65–84. doi: 10.14434/josotl.v20i1.24877. Available at: https://files.eric.ed.gov/fulltext/EJ1254300.pdf [Accessed 31 Jul. 2024].

Fiselier, E.S., Longhurst, J.W. and Gough, G.K. (2018). Exploring the current position of ESD in UK higher education institutions. International Journal of Sustainability in Higher Education, 19(2), pp. 393–412.

Freire, P. (1970). Pedagogy of the Oppressed. New York: Seabury Press.
Geels, F.W. (2010). Ontologies, socio-technical transitions (to sustainability), and the multi-level perspective. Research Policy, 39(4), pp. 495–510.
Giangrande, N., White, R.M., East, M., Jackson, R., Clarke, T., Saloff Coste, M. and Penha-Lopes, G. (2019). A competency framework to assess and activate education for sustainable development: Addressing the UN sustainable development goals 4.7 challenge. Sustainability, 11(10), p. 2832.
Gibbs, P. (2017). Higher education: A compassion business or edifying experience? In: P. Gibbs, ed., The Pedagogy of Compassion at the Heart of Higher Education. Dordrecht: Springer, pp. 1–15.
Glasser, H. (2004). Learning our way to a sustainable and desirable world: Ideas inspired by Arne Naess and deep ecology. In: P.B. Corcoran and A.E.J. Wals, eds., Higher Education and the Challenge of Sustainability: Problematics, Promise, and Practice. Dordrecht: Springer Netherlands, pp. 131–148.
Graham, P., Kuyvenhoven, C., Upitis, R., Arshad-Ayaz, A., Scheinman, E., Khan, C., Goebel, A., Brown, R.S. and Hovorka, A. (2021). The emotional experience of sustainability courses: Learned eco-anxiety, potential ontological adjustment. Journal of Education for Sustainable Development, 14(2), pp. 190–204.
Hamilton, L.G. and Petty, S. (2023). Compassionate pedagogy for neurodiversity in higher education: A conceptual analysis. Frontiers in Psychology, 14, p. 1093290.
Hao, R.N. (2011). Critical compassionate pedagogy and the teacher's role in first-generation student success. New Directions for Teaching and Learning, 2011(127), pp. 91–98. doi: 10.1002/tl.460.
Healey, M. and Healey, R. (2019). Student Engagement Through Partnership Guide. York: Advance HE.
Hockings, C. (2010). Inclusive Learning and Teaching in Higher Education: a Synthesis of Research. York: Higher Education Academy. Available at: https://www.advance-he.ac.uk/knowledge-hub/inclusive-learning-and-teaching-higher-education-synthesis-research [Accessed 31 Jul. 2024].
Hull, Z. (2008). Sustainable development: Premises, understanding and prospects. Sustainable Development, 16(2), pp. 73–80.
Ingold, T., ed. (2011). Redrawing Anthropology: Materials, Movements, Lines. Farnham: Ashgate Publishing, Ltd.
Jaleniauskiene, E. and Kasperiuniene, J. (2023). Infographics in higher education: A scoping review. E-Learning and Digital Media, 20, pp. 191–206. doi: 10.1177/20427530221107774. Available at: https://journals.sagepub.com/doi/epub/10.1177/20427530221107774 [Accessed 31 Jul. 2024].
Kahn, P. and O'Rourke, K. (2005). Understanding enquiry-based learning. In: T. Barrett, I. Mac Labhrainn and H. Fallon, eds., Handbook of Enquiry & Problem-Based Learning. Galway: CELT, pp. 1–12. Available at: https://www.researchgate.net/publication/258844946_1_UNDERSTANDING_ENQUIRY-BASED_LEARNING [Accessed 31 Jul. 2024].
Kennedy, R. (2007). In-class debates: Fertile ground for active learning and the cultivation of critical thinking and Oral communication skills. International Journal of Teaching and Learning in Higher Education, 19, pp. 183–190. Available at: https://www.isetl.org/ijtlhe/pdf/IJTLHE200.pdf [Accessed 31 Jul. 2024].
Kimmerer, R. (2013). Braiding Sweetgrass: Indigenous Wisdom, Scientific Knowledge and the Teachings of Plants. Milkweed editions.
Kolb, D.A. (1984). Experiential Learning: Experience as the Source of Learning and Development. Englewood Cliffs: Prentice-Hall.
Kopnina, H. (2020). Education for the future? Critical evaluation of education for sustainable development goals. The Journal of Environmental Education, 51(4), pp. 280–291.
Learning Journals (2024). What are the different pedagogical approaches to learning? https://learningjournals.co.uk/what-are-the-different-pedagogical-approaches-to-learning/
Lecuyer, L., White, R.M., Schmook, B., Lemay, V. and Calmé, S. (2018). The construction of feelings of justice in environmental management: An empirical study of multiple biodiversity conflicts in Calakmul, Mexico. Journal of Environmental Management, 213, pp. 363–373.
Lotz-Sisitka, H., Mukute, M., Chikunda, C., Baloi, A. and Pesanayi, T. (2017). Transgressing the norm: Transformative agency in community-based learning for sustainability in southern African contexts. International Review of Education, 63, pp. 897–914.

Macy, J. and Johnstone, C. (2012). Active hope: How to Face the Mess We'Re in Without Going Crazy. Novato: New World Library.

Mannion, G. (2012). Intergenerational education: The significance of reciprocity and place. Journal of Intergenerational Relationships, 10(4), pp.386–399. doi: 10.1080/15350770.2012.726601.

Mannion, G. (2020). Re-assembling environmental and sustainability education: Orientations from new materialism. Environmental Education Research, 26(9–10), pp. 1353–1372.

Mannion, G., Fenwick, A. and Lynch, J. (2013). Place-responsive pedagogy: Learning from teachers' experiences of excursions in nature. Environmental Education Research, 19(6), pp. 792–809. doi: 10.1080/13504622.2012.749980.

Martin, A., Gomez-Baggethun, E., Quaas, M., Rozzi, R., Tauro, A., Faith, D.P. and Pascual, U. (2024). Plural values of nature help to understand contested pathways to sustainability. One Earth, 7(5), pp. 806–819.

McDonald, B., Cervero, R.M. and Courtenay, B.C. (1999). An ecological perspective of power in transformational learning: A case study of ethical vegans. Adult Education Quarterly, 50(1), pp. 5–23.

McManus, M., Dooris, M. and Barry, J. (2022). Place-based climate action, community wealth building and Doughnut Economics: A rapid review. Available at: https://pcancities.org.uk/sites/default/files/RapidReview%20FINAL_0.pdf [Accessed 31 Jul. 2024].

Mezirow, J. (1996). Contemporary paradigms of learning. Adult Education Quarterly, 46(3), pp. 158–172.

Michael, J. (2006). Where's the evidence that active learning works? Advances in Physiology Education, 30(4), pp. 159–167. doi: 10.1152/advan.00053.2006.

Nicholson, D.T., Vargas, V.R., Price, E.A.C., Himatlal, K., Campen, L., Hartley, M. and Hewitt, T. (2024). Transformative learning design for ESD in a skills-based module. Open Scholarship of Teaching and Learning, 3, pp. 21–36. Available at: https://osotl.org/index.php/osotl/article/view/76/96 [Accessed 31 Jul. 2024].

North, P. (2005). Scaling alternative economic practices? Some lessons from alternative currencies. Transactions of the Institute of British Geographers, 30(2), pp. 221–233.

O'Grady, M. (2023). Transformative education for sustainable development: A faculty perspective. Environment, Development and Sustainability. https://doi.org/10.1007/s10668-023-03609-y [Accessed 31 Jul. 2024].

Open University (2020). Activity type cards. Available at: https://www.open.ac.uk/blogs/learning-design/wp-content/uploads/2020/09/activity-type-cards-August-2020.pdf [Accessed 31 Jul. 2024].

Open University (2021). OU Learning Design Activity Types framework. Available at: https://www.open.ac.uk/blogs/learning-design/wp-content/uploads/2021/10/OU-LD-Activity-Types-Framework-October-2021-FINAL.pdf [Accessed 31 Jul. 2024].

Orr, D. (1994). Earth in Mind: On Education, Environment, and the Human Prospect. Washington, D.C.: Island Press.

Perello-Marín, M.R., Ribes-Giner, G. and Pantoja Díaz, O. (2018). Enhancing education for sustainable development in environmental university programmes: A co-creation approach. Sustainability, 10(1), p. 158.

Podger, M.D., Mustakova-Possardt, E. and Reid, A. (2010). A whole-person approach to educating for sustainability. International Journal of Sustainability in Higher Education, 11(4), pp. 339–352.

Raworth, K. (2017a). A doughnut for the Anthropocene: Humanity's compass in the 21st century. The Lancet Planetary Health, 1(2), pp. e48–e49. https://doi.org/10.1016/S2542-5196(17)30028-1 [Accessed 31 Jul. 2024].

Raworth, K. (2017b). Doughnut Economics: Seven Ways to Think Like a 21st-Century Economist. London: Penguin Random House.

Ricard, M., Zachariou, A. and Burgos, D. (2020). Digital education, information and communication technology, and education for sustainable development. In: M. Burgos, ed., Radical Solutions and eLearning: Practical Innovations and Online Educational Technology. Singapore: Springer, pp.27–39.

Robinson, J. (2004). Squaring the circle? Some thoughts on the idea of sustainable development. Ecological Economics, 48(4), pp. 369–384.

Schmelkes, S. (2009). Intercultural universities in Mexico: Progress and difficulties. Intercultural Education, 20(1), pp. 5–17.

Shrivastava, P. (1994). Greening business education: Toward an ecocentric pedagogy. Journal of Management Inquiry, 3(3), pp. 235–243.

Sipos, Y., Battisti, B. and Grimm, K. (2008). Achieving transformative sustainability learning: Engaging head, hands and heart. International Journal of Sustainability in Higher Education, 9(1), pp. 68–86. doi: 10.1108/14676370810842193.

Springett, D. (2005). 'Education for sustainability' in the business studies curriculum: A call for A critical agenda. Business Strategy and the Environment, 14(3), pp. 146–159.

Sterling, S. (2001). Sustainable Education: Re-Visioning Learning and Change. Totnes: Green Books for the Schumacher Society.

Sulik, J., Bahrami, B. and Deroy, O. (2021). The diversity gap: When diversity matters for knowledge. Perspectives on Psychological Science, 17(3), pp. 752–767. doi: 10.1177/17456916211006070.

Tasler, N. and Dale, V.H.M. (2021). Learners, teachers and places: A conceptual framework for creative pedagogies. Journal of Perspectives in Applied Academic Practice, 9(1), pp. 2–7. Available at: https://jpaap.ac.uk/JPAAP/article/view/450/581 [Accessed 31 Jul. 2024].

Taylor, E.W. (2007). An update of transformative learning theory: A critical review of the empirical research (1999–2005). International Journal of Lifelong Education, 26(2), pp. 173–191.

Toro-Troconis, M., Ahmad, N. and Varga-Atkins, T. (2024). Learning design and education for sustainable development bootcamp: Background, framework and toolkit. Open Scholarship of Teaching and Learning, 3, pp. 1–20. Available at: https://osotl.org/index.php/osotl/article/view/112/95 [Accessed 31 Jul. 2024].

Toro-Troconis, M., Alexander, J. and Frutos-Perez, M. (2019). Assessing student engagement in online programmes: Using learning design and learning analytics. International Journal of Higher Education, 8(1), pp. 171–183.

Toro-Troconis, M., Inzolia, Y. and Ahmad, N. (2023). Exploring attitudes towards embedding education for sustainable development in curriculum design. International Journal of Higher Education, 12(4), pp. 42–59. https://doi.org/10.5430/ijhe.v12n4p42 [Accessed 31 Jul. 2024].

Turner, I., Norton, S. and Moody, J. (2020). #52etc – a Toolkit for Student Engagement. York: Advance HE.

United Nations Educational, Scientific and Cultural Organization (UNESCO) (2017). Education for Sustainable Development Goals: Learning Objectives. Available at: https://unesdoc.unesco.org/ark:/48223/pf0000247444 [Accessed 31 Jul. 2024].

United Nations Educational, Scientific and Cultural Organization (UNESCO) (2021). Education for Sustainable Development: A Roadmap. Available at: https://unesdoc.unesco.org/ark:/48223/pf0000374802.locale=en [Accessed 31 Jul. 2024].

United Nations Educational, Scientific and Cultural Organization (UNESCO) (2024). What is Education for Sustainable Development? Available at: https://www.unesco.org/en/sustainable-development/education/need-know?hub=72522 [Accessed 31 Jul. 2024].

Varga-Atkins, T., Toro-Troconis, M. and Ahmad, N. (2024). Editorial: Special issue on 'Learning design and education for sustainable development Bootcamp'. Open Scholarship of Teaching and Learning, 3, pp. i–xii. Available at: https://osotl.org/index.php/osotl/article/view/111/94 [Accessed 31 Jul. 2024].

Vásquez-Fernández, A.M. and Cash Ahenakew, P.T.P.T. (2020). Resurgence of relationality: Reflections on decolonizing and indigenizing 'sustainable development. Current Opinion in Environmental Sustainability, 43, pp. 65–70.

Wakelet (2023). The Future of Education: Empowering Students with Portfolios. Available at: https://blog.wakelet.com/the-future-of-education-empowering-students-with-portfolios [Accessed 31 Jul. 2024].

Wall, S., Litjens, I. and Taguma, M. (2015). Pedagogy in Early Childhood Education and Care (ECEC): An International Comparative Study of Approaches and Policies. London: Department for Education. Available at: https://assets.publishing.service.gov.uk/media/5a7f9ae4e5274a2e87db6dbc/RB400_-_Early_years_pedagogy_and_policy_an_international_study.pdf [Accessed 31 Jul. 2024].

Walsh, Z., Böhme, J. and Wamsler, C. (2021). Towards a relational paradigm in sustainability research, practice, and education. Ambio, 50(1), pp. 74–84.

White, R.M. (2013). Sustainability research: A novel mode of knowledge generation to explore alternative ways for people and planet. In: S. Sterling, L. Maxey and H. Luna, eds., The Sustainable University: Progress and Prospects. Abingdon: Routledge, pp. 165–178.

White, R.M. (2014). Who Am I? The role(s) of an academic at a 'Sustainable University'. In: W. Leal Filho et al., eds., Integrative Approaches to Sustainable Development at University Level. Cham: Springer, pp. 611–628. doi: 10.1007/978-3-319-10690-8_46.

White, R., King, B., Leask, K. and Higgins, P. (2023). Supporting environmental education in the United Kingdom of Great Britain and Northern Ireland: Context, status, lessons learned and recommendations for Japan. Unpublished report.

White, R.M., Möbius, K., King, B., Leask, K., Peres, S., Walker, J. and Higgins, P. (2023). A Handbook for Monitoring and Evaluating Education for Sustainable Development in Higher Education. Gloucester: QAA. Available at: https://www.qaa.ac.uk/docs/qaa/members/handbook-for-monitoring-and-evaluating-esd-in-universities.pdf?sfvrsn=ac42af81_12 [Accessed 31 Jul. 2024].

White, R.M. and van Koten, H. (2016). Co-designing for sustainability: Strategising community carbon emission reduction through socio-ecological innovation. The Design Journal, 19(1), pp. 25–46. Available at: http://www.tandfonline.com/doi/full/10.1080/14606925.2015.1064219 [Accessed 31 Jul. 2024].

Wiek, A., Withycombe, L. and Redman, C.L. (2011). Key competencies in sustainability: A reference framework for academic program development. Sustainability Science, 6(2), pp. 203–218.

World Café Community Foundation (2015). Café to Go! A Quick Reference Guide for Hosting World Café. Available at: https://theworldcafe.com/wp-content/uploads/2015/07/Cafe-To-Go-Revised.pdf [Accessed 31 Jul. 2024].

Chapter 7

# Innovating Assessment for Education for Sustainable Development

*Simon Kemp and Rehema M. White*

## Introduction

The importance of assessment is long established, and the multiple purposes of assessment have become more apparent. Assessment forms a critical dimension of proving that students have a valid understanding of their programmes (Wyse *et al.*, 2015) and strengthens learning through complex tasks, self-evaluation and feedback (Joughin, 2008). Assessment should be underpinned by theories of pedagogy and the subject discipline (Black and William, 2018) and should uphold programme and disciplinary standards (Joughin, 2008). Assessment, and its association with flexible pedagogies, are particularly important for learners in Education for Sustainable Development (ESD) (Ryan and Tilbury, 2013; Nicholson and Vargas, 2021). ESD is considered to be a route to enhanced learning overall, employing transformative rather than transmissive approaches, enabling experiential learning and future thinking, through critical and compassionate pedagogies, while engaging with real-world contexts (see Chapter 2: Springett, 2005; Thomas, 2009; Sterling, 2012; Gibbs, 2017; Price *et al.*, 2021, 2024). The transformative and other aspects of ESD can be supported through the deeper student learning experience of assessment in its myriads of forms (Nicholson and Vargas, 2021). We argue below that as the nature of ESD provokes innovative, authentic, interdisciplinary and self-actualising assessment, so does the challenge of assessment cause us to deepen our exploration into ESD.

Assessment matters to students, more so than any other component of their learning journey. It is the most direct and personal element of the university experience for students and needs to be handled the most sensitively. Concerns over a mental health crisis in university students are increasingly represented in mainstream media, and this is a worrying familiar part of student support that many of us educators regularly experience in our work. It seems that this is a long-established concern (Keyes *et al.*, 2012), and urgently needs deep, staff and student developed, whole university approaches (Cage *et al.*, 2021). There is thus a need to be cognisant of this student mental health crisis throughout assessment design, student support for assessment, and especially with respect to feedback. Words matter across the whole of the student journey, none more so than when staff comment on student work. The words of Robert Fulghum have real resonance and are relevant when setting, grading and providing feedback on assessment – 'Sticks and stones may break our bones, but words will break our hearts' (Fulghum, 1986).

In this Chapter, we will discuss the purposes of assessment, explore the meaning and forms of assessment in sustainability pedagogies, examine the value of assessment for interdisciplinary education and partnership building across disciplines, and illustrate how

DOI: 10.4324/9781003451563-7

innovative assessment can aid in developing solutions for a sustainable future. We will critically reflect on the possibilities of formative and summative assessment. The impact of feedback on learners will be considered, along with the implications of assessment on educator workload and training. We position this content within the recognition of the challenges we face as assessors by the exponential growth of artificial intelligence. We draw on Nicholson and Vargas (2021) to develop an analysis of the forms of assessment aligned with ESD. We offer an exploration of different assessment formats, including essays, discipline-focused reports, examinations, flipped classrooms, communications and digital technology led assessments, research projects, group assessments, peer assessment, authentic assessment, field work, skills development assessments, placement assessments. There will be a discussion of the deeper value possible from authentic assessment. Throughout the chapter, we present examples of innovative assessment practices that challenge, stretch and enthuse students in their quest for sustainability knowledge, skills and competencies in higher education institutions.

## The Purpose and Context of Assessment

Assessment is sometimes positioned at the top of the pedagogy iceberg metaphor as part of learning and teaching methods (Sandri, 2022), as it is seen to be towards the end of delivery. However, innovative and transformative assessment begins at the start of an educator's pedagogy. It informs the learning objectives, content, module and programme structure, and the delivery mechanisms. The assessment informs the entire pedagogy as much as the pedagogy determines the assessment. Assessment format influences whether students undertake a superficial approach to learning, acquiring only the knowledge they need to reproduce for assessment, or a deep approach in which they understand the underlying issues (Joughin 2008). The deeper social contexts of students' engagement with assessment are also crucial, as demonstrated in Box 7.1.

Assessment has multiple functions. It is partly about strengthening learning, as explained above, but also increasingly about judgement and grading of study completed, in addition to maintaining the standards of the discipline (Joughin 2008). For the first

### Box 7.1 Assessment as Social Interaction as well as a Grade

'Assessment is far from being a technical matter, and the improvement of assessment requires more than a redevelopment of curricula. Assessment occurs in the context of complex intra- and interpersonal factors, including teachers' conceptions of and approaches to teaching; students' conceptions of and approaches to learning; students' and teachers' past experiences of assessment; and the varying conceptions of assessment held by teachers and students alike. Assessment is also impacted by students' varying motives for entering higher education and the varying demands and priorities of teachers who typically juggle research, administration and teaching within increasingly demanding workloads. Pervading assessment are issues of power and complex social relationships' (Joughin, 2008, p. 4).

of these, assessments are set as learning tasks, normally longer and complex tasks rather than examinations; feedback is an important aspect in strengthening learning; learners develop capacity for self-evaluation; and assessment results can feed back into teaching. Joughin explains how, in the second context, early ideas of 'measurement' have been superseded by professional judgement of learner achievement against internal course expectations. Finally, external standards are upheld through assessment that is visible to professional bodies, often drawing on modes of assessment such as ongoing workplace challenges. Assessment in higher education needs to recognise a shift from assessment procedures used in schools, to which learners may have become accustomed, to more critical and reflective forms of assessment (Ecclestone, 2008; Joughin, 2008). Further to the transition from school to higher education, higher education assessment also needs to point beyond the university. Given that the work of graduates will be assessed in their future careers, assessment is thus partly about learners learning self-evaluation to strengthen future capacity for work (Boud 2008).

Many lecturers spend more time in a module setting providing feedback for assessments than in actual face-to-face teaching (Race, 2019). Assessment can be very difficult for staff, as it engenders high workloads, often working hard in short time periods to the deadline of the exam board, and can lead to the stress of dealing with disappointed or even angry students (Joughin 2008).

There is debate about the role of criteria in assessment. Whilst a good rubric can clarify assessment expectations, holistic rather than analytical assessment generates better learning for and by learners (Sadler, 2008). However, solid criteria can help learners develop a language to understand their progress and to emphasise learning in action (O'Riordan and Loacker, 2008). In good learning systems, learners may be involved in developing and agreeing the assessment criteria (Dochy, 2008). Dochy emphasises the benefit of *edumetric* rather than *psychometric* qualities of assessment; the former focus on evidence of learning rather than psychological attributes of the learner. The importance of supporting student voice and student engagement in flexible pedagogies (Ryan & Tilbury, 2013) and in ESD has been emphasised. In line with this has been the increasing recognition of the importance of student engagement in assessment design, implementation and evaluation, to empower them to appreciate and achieve high-quality work (Boud *et al.*, 2010 in Race p. 32).

Sadler (2013) argues that '[f]or students to become self-sustaining producers of high quality intellectual and professional goods, they must be equipped to take control of their own learning and performance' (Sadler, 2013, p. 54). To do this, they need to enhance their capacity to monitor the emerging quality of their work as they are producing it. He is in favour of a more holistic assessment that promotes mature independence in learning and moves away from very strict and over detailed preset criteria for grading.

There has been a trend towards more online learning and assessment in higher education, highlighting the need for support of learner expectations, readiness and participation; for staff training; and for content development, including multimedia provision (Kebritchi *et al.*, 2017). Covid hastened the onset of digital learning in higher education, and support is needed to support staff, students and institutions in developing appropriate pedagogies that take advantage of the potential of digitalisation whilst still offering authentic learning experiences (García-Morales *et al.*, 2021). With regards to assessment in the online context, collaborative activities can include assessment, or at least basic acknowledgement, of engagement and interaction. Group assessments can stimulate peer learning in such digital contexts but should include clear and pre-determined assessment criteria (Kebritchi *et al.*, 2017). These authors note the importance of formative and summative assessment even in online courses, although often formative aspects are neglected in this context.

Challenges for improved forms of assessment include agreement over the purposes of learning and education, and development of formats of assessment that can gauge competencies as well as curricular mastery (Joughin, 2008). Perceived current challenges around the ways that grading divert focus from learning to outcome number can be addressed. One solution is that learners undertake self-assessment for grades and these are then facilitated by educators (Yorke, 2008 in same book as Joughin).

There are questions about how much assessment to provide. There has been a clear shift in most contexts away from the classic, time-limited, constrained examination. It has been suggested that we should move towards 'assessment as learning not assessment of learning' (Race, 2019). Race discusses how this move has sometimes led to the opposite – concerns about too much continuous assessment. He notes that assessment becomes a significant stress on learners and educators if it occurs too often; it becomes repetitive if the same assessment form is used repeatedly; it causes students to focus on grades, and it is usually written, not assessing learning by doing. The conflicts around this continual drift to smaller, more frequent assessments is addressed in Box 7.2.

Several suites of principles for successful assessment have been developed. Boud and Associates (2010) produced seven general principles that could easily be adopted and then explored in depth in a given module, programme or institution. They promoted assessment as a tool to engage students in productive learning and highlighted the important of teacher and student but also the wider institutional culture in putting assessment at the centre of learning (Box 7.3). Also in 2010, the National Union of Students published the 'NUS Charter on Assessment and Feedback'. This contained 10 recommendations on assessment, each with explanatory detail as reproduced below (the full document can be downloaded from http://www.nusconnect.org.uk/asset/ news/6010/ FeedbackCharter-toview.pdf).

**Box 7.2 The Challenge of Assessment Quantity, Format and Frequency**

'By and large, higher education has replaced the stress of one final examination with the stress of multiple in-course assessments on top of a smaller exam. We have substituted one intense period of revision with the anxiety that comes from an insidious trickle of small assessments. Contemporary students always seem to have assessment on their mind, whether or not there is an assignment due, an online test to do, an essay, a short mid-term test, a laboratory check-out test and so on. At least the final exam was something that had to be dealt with sometime in the future and this allowed students more space and freedom to study as they wished until that time' (Harland, 2012, p. 114).

**Box 7.3 Seven Value Principles for Successful Assessment in Higher Education (Boud and Associates 2010)**

Assessment has most effect when:

1. assessment is used to engage students in learning that is productive.
2. feedback is used to actively improve student learning.
3. students and teachers become responsible partners in learning and assessment.
4. students are inducted into the assessment practices and cultures of higher education.
5. assessment for learning is placed at the centre of subject and programme design.
6. assessment for learning is a focus for staff and institutional development.
7. assessment provides inclusive and trustworthy representation of student achievement.

There was a further and more detailed iteration of such value principles by Race (2019). He focuses on deep underlying principles of validity, authenticity, transparency, reliability and inclusiveness, along with veracity, manageability and the potential to motivate and support deep learning (Box 7.4).

**Box 7.4 Assessment Value Principles (Race, 2019)**

- *Validity is about whether the particular assessment format under consideration is the most appropriate for the intended purpose. In other words, is it the best way of measuring evidence of achievement of the related intended learning outcomes?*
- *Reliability is about how well different assessors would agree on the mark or grade awarded for a particular piece of students' work. This is also, of course, about fairness and indeed justice as perceived by students and others.*
- *Authenticity is about how well the assessment correlates to the sorts of things students need to be able to do in their career after leaving the educational institution. It's about the real-world relevance of the assessment activity.*
- *Transparency is particularly about how well students can see how the assessment works in practice, and how marking occurs. Professional bodies also are keen to see this.*
- *Inclusiveness is about how well the assessment can be taken by a range of candidates with additional learning needs, including dyslexia, dyspraxia and so on. It is about minimising unfair discrimination towards candidates with particular needs.*
- *Manageability – how long it takes to mark etc*
- *Feedback – providing material for real change*

- *Veracity – to what extent can and would students submit material that is not their own honest material, perhaps including plagiarism [more recently AI not accredited)*
- *Potential for deep learning*
- *Motivate students to learn*

These principles underpin the importance of assessment in supporting a genuine learning experience. They also demonstrate some of the practical constraints. The need to support educators has been recognised by bodies such as QAA in UK. QAA note that:

> Assessment processes are implemented effectively when all staff involved have the necessary knowledge and skills, have received the appropriate development or training to fulfil their specific role, and are clear about their remit and responsibilities. Higher education providers identify what is appropriate for each role and how competence will be demonstrated, recognising that assessment involves different roles, each of which may be carried out by a variety of staff.
>
> (QAA, 2013, p. 11)

## Assessment and Education for Sustainable Development

Traditional pedagogies in higher education tend to support teacher-centred instruction, passive, individual and limited learning, abstract and fixed knowledge and cognitive outcomes. However, Nicholson and Vargas (2021) argue that ESD in higher education strives for more learner centred, experiential, active learning supported by diverse modes of teaching and assessment, with collaborative, interdisciplinary approaches, orientated towards the theory-practice nexus and supporting self-regulated learning and whole person outcomes. These authors recommend a shift from assessment *of* learning to assessment *for* learning and assessment *as* learning (see also Keamy *et al.*, 2007; Dann, 2014).

Building on the themes of pedagogies for ESD, the underlying concepts of assessment for and as learning, and the support of key sustainability competencies, Nicholson and Vargas (2021) proposed nine design principles for assessment for ESD. These include learner centred, flexible, future thinking, experiential, collaborative, interdisciplinary, authentic, affective and enquiry based. (see Table 7.1).

Nicholson and Vargas (2021) point out that this assessment framework aligns well with the concepts of flexible pedagogy (flexible in terms of pace, place and mode) outlined by Ryan and Tilbury (2013). The latter authors propose that new ideas for flexible pedagogy include learner empowerment, future-facing learning, curriculum organisation, boundary crossing, social learning and transformative capabilities. Flexible pedagogies not only require dynamic and innovative approaches from educators but also support learners to develop flexibility and capacity for adaptation and enhanced ability to tackle complex, unpredictable challenges. Many of the suggestions for ESD assessment offered in this Chapter are also compatible with notions of inclusive,

*Table 7.1* Design principles for assessment in education in sustainable development in higher education.

| *Design principle* | *Description* |
|---|---|
| Learner centred | Supports self-regulation and agency, permits individual learning according to their context and abilities and enables co-creation of curricula and experiences. For example, learners may co-create the boundaries or format of assessment. |
| Flexible | Better enables the diversity of students to achieve their potential; empowers and develops agency in learners by offering them more choice in their assessment possibilities. Examples include offering choice of assessment options such as presentation or report, curricular flexibility such as choice in essay topics or portfolios. |
| Future and global thinking | Supports learners to tackle uncertain, predictable challenges at global scales by encouraging adaptive, creative responses, scenario thinking and other approaches that develop capacity and confidence. Examples include scenario reports, creative writing on future imaginaries or socio-ecological modelling. |
| Active and experiential | Provides an iterative approach to a new experience or stimulus, including application of learning through, for example, living labs, learning portfolios and group *vivas*. |
| Collaborative | Promotes peer and social learning and changes students' awareness of diversity and self-recognition of agency. Enables teamwork and exploration of the dynamics of group learning and action. Examples include group projects with community organisations, followed by group presentations, or shared reports. |
| Interdisciplinary | Promotes systems thinking, multi- and interdisciplinary approaches, and relevance to real-world, complex problems. Can enable individual students to draw on different disciplinary frameworks, or enable groups of students from different disciplines to work collaboratively. Deepens disciplinary understanding and epistemological maturity. Examples include Vertically Integrated Project assessments, essays requiring integration of different disciplinary perspectives, or explicit interrogation of interdisciplinarity through essays, mind-mapping, posters or other means. |
| Authentic and situated | Engages with real-world contexts, possibly enables students to interact with stakeholders. Offers purpose, possibly leads to application of results of assessment and strengthens accountability and agency. Can be intensive, such as assessment of work placement activities, or lighter touch, using examples of practical situations in the classroom. Examples include policy briefs, reports detailing recommendations for action or posters presented at sessions to which stakeholders can be invited. |
| Affective | Develops heart, hand and head learning to engage affective as well as cognitive and physical domains. Encourages whole person engagement through experience and reflection, sometimes through challenging examples in collaboration with others. Needs to be facilitated with sensitivity. Examples include reflective essays, diary vlogs, role play. |

(*Continued*)

*Table 7.1* (Continued)

| *Design principle* | *Description* |
|---|---|
| Enquiry based | Builds from an open-ended question to research design, data collection and analysis and interpretation of empirical results in relation to theory. Problem-based learning develops from a more closed question. Can be collaborative and small or large in credits and emphasis. Examples include dissertations, storyboards, research enquiry reports. Assessment may be of a substantive output or of a specific task undertaken during the complex process of enquiry. |
| Creative | Enables learners to express themselves, to explore art, craft or design in representing, communicating or addressing sustainability challenges. Explores affective aspects of learning. Examples can include recognition of creativity in many assessment formats, such as posters (e.g. visuals), reports (e.g. graphic communication), powerpoints (e.g. photography) or standalone art-based or design assessments. |

*Source*: Adapted from Nicholson and Vargas (2021), with the addition of creative.

compassionate and even relational pedagogies (see Chapter 6). They are often pioneering and innovative, demanding commitment, imagination and courage from educators as well as learners. They enable learners to challenge themselves, develop agency and fulfil their potential, demonstrate evidence of learning achievement, comply with benchmark and professional standards and often contribute to real-world sustainability challenges. The exploration of this ESD assessment thus demonstrates that ESD is a flavour of quality education. We suggest that emphasis on ESD should go beyond discussions on curriculum, pedagogy and competencies and should encourage emphasis on assessment as the locus where student learning, experience and effort focus within modules and programmes.

## Feedback on Feedback

One of the most important aspects of the assessment journey for students is the support and feedback provided by academics on their work. Feedback needs to be compassionate and constructive, yet honest, valid and reliable, in line with the principles of assessment (Race, 2019). Feedback and assessment are not merely individual; institutional support and a partnership approach are required to support excellent learning (Boud and Associates 2010). Many lecturers spend more time in a module setting and providing feedback for assessments than in actual teaching (Race, 2019). Assessment can be very difficult for staff, as it engenders high workloads, often to the deadline of the exam board, and stress of dealing with disappointed or even angry students (Joughin 2008). There is a balance between the form and detail of feedback and the workload of educators (Race, 2019). As discussed above, feedback matters to learners and to educators.

## Formative and Summative Assessment

### *Formative Assessment*

Framed as assessments of knowledge and understanding, assessments can carry a grade in a predetermined standard range of values (e.g. a percentage score of 62 or a letter grade such as B), or carry no awarding mark at all. Where marks and/or comments are provided, but do not count towards a module grade or programme award, the assessment is termed 'formative assessment'. This form of work is for feedback only and is important in supporting learners, allowing them to understand what they are doing well and what they can do to improve their work. Formative assessments are considered a vital tool in assisting students in the development of their 'assessment literacy' (Advance HE, 2012). Bennett (2011) considers formative assessment to be an approach broadly described as 'assessment for learning', rather than testing of learning.

Formative assessments are an oft-overlooked component of the learning portfolio for students because the exercises do not lead to grades that count directly to a students' progression or degree award. Conversations with students suggest they will normally focus their efforts on work that leads to marks towards their final qualification and classification, raising concerns amongst academics over 'mark chasing'. Whilst traditionally it has been felt that students would strongly direct learning to assessment that counts for final grade, the actual evidence on this is mixed, and many students are 'cue-deaf' and pursue learning holistically across a course. Formative assessments require additional feedback and thus also increase the workload of staff (Joughin 2008).

Despite the challenges of student motivation and time for feedback, the opportunity to experiment, learn and possibly make mistakes in a 'safe-space' is of great value to students and is arguably one of the most important and valuable parts of a university education. Making mistakes is a good way to learn as the shock factor, or even embarrassment in some instances, has a lasting impact. Learners are able to develop their understanding and are less likely to repeat similar mistakes. This is especially the case in the interdisciplinary, holistic field of ESD. Students are frequently required to learn about topics and conduct work in areas in which they are unfamiliar, and they may not be attuned to the systems thinking aspect of ESD. This makes it all the more vital that students are provided the opportunity to experiment, learn and gain feedback with no fear of negative consequences in grading.

In addition, in ESD, students might find some sustainability issues distressing. 'Eco-anxiety' or 'climate anxiety' is a relatively well established yet new condition with students (e.g. Graham *et al.*, 2020), and first exposure to the more challenging discourse that can be presented when starting sustainability studies can be emotionally difficult. The complexity and potential impact of climate anxiety has a range of distressing impacts with clear evidence of the negative affect it is having on mental health and wellbeing on people of all ages across the world, particularly younger people, regardless of whether or not they are directly affected by climate change (Grantham Institute, 2021). We have a clear duty of care for our students and must be sensitive to them when addressing potentially difficult sustainability issues such as the effects of climate change or colonisation.

ESD requires a whole person commitment, including affective as well as cognitive and emotional engagement (Nicholson and Vargas, 2021). However, students can become emotional in assessment writing and struggle to articulate their feelings in relation to critical reflection. It is vital that students are given feedback without consequences when learning how to present emotionally challenging work in academic assessment frameworks for the first time.

Formative assessment also allows greater innovation from educators due to the low pressure on students. This opportunity for experimentation can allow practitioners to attempt more radical forms of assessment before applying them to a module where the students are awarded summative credit-bearing marks towards their degree. After all, academics as well as students need a safe place to experiment, and possibly make mistakes, without consequences.

## Formative Assessment Case Study: United Nations Sustainable Development Goals Summit at the University of Southampton

An example of an ESD formative assessment is the United Nations' Sustainable Development Goals Summit that forms part of the 'Global Sustainability Challenges' interdisciplinary cross-university module at the University of Southampton. The SDG summit is a global sustainability negotiation and collaboration game, designed to encourage students to think more deeply about each of, and the whole suite of, the SDGs through lenses of different parts of the world, and reflecting the challenges for the people who live there. Students are allocated to teams representing 'blocs of nations', or a single large nation. All students are then required to learn about the SDGs over the period of a week and to consider how they apply in different resource availability, social, cultural, religious, economic and environmental situations. In their teams, students agree on the SDGs that matter most to the people (and political leaders) of their allocated part of the world. All groups negotiate with the other blocs to reach agreement on which SDGs should be prioritised, in a scenario where the international community will only support a limited number of goals. A learning for this formative assessment is the greater challenge of which SDGs they may be prepared to sacrifice. The student groups then vote on their agreed SDGs, but with different voting power, depending on the strength of political influence held by that country or bloc of nations. Designed as an ice-breaker formative assessment, this exercise has the added value of students appreciating the importance of collaboration for sustainability, but also of normalising student participation in the classroom (Kemp *et al.*, 2015).

### *The Flipped Classroom as Formative Assessment*

The 'flipped classroom' is a well-established pedagogical approach, with the theory that students take responsibility for their learning. It can be seen as one form of formative assessment. In the flipped classroom, practical activities that were traditionally completed outside the classroom take place inside the classroom, whilst the learning associated with information dissemination (normally through class teaching) is conducted by students in advance of the timetabled class sessions (Låg and Grøm, 2019; Galindo-Dominguez, 2021). Flipped classrooms can be a valuable tool for ensuring students conduct research and complete required reading before lectures, seminars or workshops. Students should be able to develop deeper understanding of concepts that can be further enhanced in class. More class time can thus be spent on developing the intricacies of innovative, challenging assessment. The flipped classroom is an effective approach for students to learn about and to become more invested in sustainability (Buil-Fabregá *et al.*, 2019). In one study, over

90% of students found that the in-class exercises element of flipped learning made their classes more engaging, with the reflective learning being a valuable approach for ESD (Howell, 2021). The flipped classroom can also be applied to ESD in discipline-specific curricula as demonstrated by Rodríguez-Chueca *et al.* (2019) through their work in Environmental Management, Environmental Engineering, and Industrial Ecology.

The flipped classroom clearly relies on all students completing the required work in advance of the session. Whilst the majority of students are committed to their studies, there are no guarantees that all students will be of the same mindset or as organised as those who complete the pre-session reading. There is also the issue of equal access to time and resources. Students without reliable broadband in accommodation and living away from campus workstations may not be able to access materials such as data, stream videos, software packages, particularly if they are too data-heavy to access via mobile phone data. Equally, students with caring responsibilities or the time-intensive employment commitments to meet the general costs of living may not have sufficient time to complete additional tasks away from campus, especially if they are non-credit bearing formative exercises. At all points in the ESD journey, it is vital to remember that students have a multitude of different pressures, and there is no stereotypical student with a set amount of time to complete work away from the classroom.

It is these potential EDI concerns that raise queries over the wisdom of over-reliance on flipped classroom techniques as a pre-cursor for imaginative summative assessment tasks, even if time away from the classroom offers great opportunities to consider and digest systems-thinking learning. As with all ESD, and especially around innovative assessment, it is all about the right balance with all students in mind. Delivery of ESD without EDI at the heart of assessment provision lacks sustainability credibility.

### Summative Assessment

Once students have (preferably) completed formative assessment exercises, they can complete summative assessments to demonstrate their knowledge, understanding and achievement of the learning objectives. Summative assessments are assignments that are set at the end of a defined period of teaching and learning to test and measure the resultant outcome of the extent of student understanding from that period of learning (adapted from Kibble, 2017).

Summative assessments remain the dominant form of assessment for all traditional academic disciplines, including ESD. This takes place across a diverse range of formats, each allowing varying degrees of innovation around the interdisciplinary, systems-thinking requirements of ESD. The following subsections address the broad areas of traditional and emerging assessment approaches, with examples of innovative practices that educators may wish to embrace or develop further to meet the requirements of their students and programme learning outcomes.

### Learner Co-Production of Assessment

Learner empowerment and agency is strengthened when learners co-produce pedagogical elements such as assessment formats and processes (Ryan and Tilbury, 2013). Students are supportive of ESD content and approaches. The annual SOS-UK sustainability skills survey demonstrated that 85% of students think sustainability learning should be offered as placements or work experience; 80% wanted their coursework or dissertations to link to real-world issues; and 77% wanted to see sustainability widely integrated across their course content (SOS-UK, 2023).

### Students as Partners Case Study: The Students Organising for Sustainability UK (SOS-UK) SDG Teach In and Assessment

Through the annual SDG Teach In campaign, educators are encouraged globally, at all levels of education, to integrate sustainability through the SDGs, into their teaching, learning and assessment. When sustainability content is included in a course, but not assessed, it can be perceived as less important, and as 'optional' knowledge. The 2024 SDG Teach In saw over 1000 educators across 85 institutions pledge, reaching over 105,000 students.

Since 2018, SOS-UK have worked with 16 institutions and over 400 of their students to map current coverage of sustainability across the curriculum, identify opportunities to further integrate sustainability and climate justice into course content and assessment. Students across disciplines show that they want to be assessed on the real-world application of their knowledge – including hands-on, applied learning experiences, live research projects, community- and service-based learning, and creative and reflective activities.

Through such learning experiences, reinforced by innovative assessment metrics, students develop critical skills for sustainability. For example, 86% of students whose educators participated in the SDG Teach In reported improved communication, critical thinking and capacity for action. One student reported that, 'The Teach In supported me to make connection with what I am studying to climate change, equality and building a better future for everyone' SOS-UK, 2024).

### *The Benefits and Challenges of Different Assessment Formats*

The Chapter now explores exploration of different assessment formats, including authentic assessment, group assessments, essays, reports, communications and digital technology led assessments, and field work. There is no one assessment that is 'best' for ESD, but using a diversity of assessment throughout a module programme will help to support innovative pedagogies (see Chapter 6) and strengthen learning, deepen understanding and support development of the key sustainability competencies (see Chapter 2) as well as specific module learning outcomes. There is an extensive literature on assessment in higher education, as well as some practical toolkits to support assessment choice. The Quality Assurance Agency (QAA) has some resource guides especially for ESD along with several toolkits to support assessment development (QAA 2021). See a summary of some assessment formats in Table 7.2, and a more detailed analysis of some formats following. Some of these formats overlap with the principles discussed earlier in this Chapter.

### *Authentic Assessment*

Authentic assessment measures the ability of the students to apply their learning to real-world situations, and often professional contexts (Swaffield, 2011). Authentic assessment is a particularly effective measure of intellectual ability due to the need for students to prove the extent of their understanding and thinking (Koh, 2017). The complex,

*Table 7.2* Different assessment formats and their benefits and challenges, and particular relevance to education for sustainable development (ESD).

| *Assessment format* | *Benefits* | *Challenges* | *Particular relevance to ESD* |
|---|---|---|---|
| Authentic assessment | Links to real-world examples, can include experiential learning and even placements | Can be time-consuming and stressful for some learners; difficult to organise. | Fundamental to ESD to have at least some authentic assessment. Goes beyond the fieldtrip, which can be largely see and tell, into learning by doing and deep learning. |
| Fieldtrips | Can occur in flexible formats and be assessed in multiple ways and enable real-world engagement, nature connectedness, realisation of a plurality of perspectives, experiential learning | Can be costly, time-consuming and require significant staff and other resource. May be difficult for some learners with personal issues. | Align well with ESD through offering physical and affective as well as cognitive learning. Enable social and peer learning in a real-world context. Can provoke transdisciplinary and transformative learning. |
| Group assessments | Can enable understanding of plural perspectives, social and peer learning, develop learner agency | Can be complex and require support and mechanisms to ensure fair contributions whilst recognising learner agency, personal limitations of some learners and diversity of contributions | Support collaborative, strategic, normative and potentially interdisciplinary competencies and prepare learners for real-world contexts where issues are often tackled by teams |
| Critical essay | Enables deep and critical learning, familiar for social science and humanities learners | Can challenge science learners | Flexible – can be used across assessment portfolio and in coursework or exams; strengthens critical thinking and can be adapted to explicitly focus on, e.g., interdisciplinary debates or systems thinking |
| Reflective essay | Enables critical reflection on practical as well as theoretical contexts | Can be challenging for some learners and requires careful rubrics and sensitive feedback | Excellent mechanism to enable learners to reflect on implementation of sustainability practices or technologies. Can strengthen self-awareness and normative competencies as well as problem-solving and critical thinking |

(*Continued*)

*Table 7.2* (Continued)

| *Assessment format* | *Benefits* | *Challenges* | *Particular relevance to ESD* |
|---|---|---|---|
| Reflective journals | Enables continuous learning and analysis of practical experience | Can be challenging for some learners who fear personal exposure and requires careful support and feedback | Excellent route to develop understanding and cultural awareness of socio-technological sustainability transitions through personal learning, and to link practical and theoretical learning |
| Report | Strengthens data collection, analysis and interpretation and supports practical writing for diverse audiences | Can be challenging for some humanities and social science learners | Excellent for ESD in supporting learners to develop practical skills, strategic competencies and often future thinking in developing recommendations |
| Creative assessments | Inspire imagination and provoke interest, develop different skillsets | Very different forms of assessment can challenge some learners and require educators to be trained in assessment | Creative opportunities allow learners to develop imaginaries for sustainable or dystopic futures, to develop alternative ways of raising awareness and invoking sustainability action and to explore emotions of self and others |
| Posters | Can enable artistic representation and encourages very clear communication and synthesis of key messages for wider audience | Difficult to assess for groups. Need specific rubric and support and prior examples | Requires systems thinking to synthesise and contextualise complex issues into one poster; develops communicative competencies; can link with wider audience in transdisciplinary settings |
| Presentations | Can be individual or in groups; require communication skills; applicable to real life | Difficult for some learners who have anxiety around speaking; needs compassionate and constructive assessment | Excellent skill to develop communication, systems and critical thinking competencies. Can enable creative flair. Important to learn how to synthesise, communicate and debate verbally |
| Podcasts | Offer a creative opportunity to 'digital natives' to express themselves and communicate in ways beyond written word or numerical data to wider audiences | Can challenge educators to support and assess the outputs | Can be a creative way to link with external stakeholders, work in a team and produce an output with purpose, along with communication, collaborative, cultural and strategic competencies |

holistic problem-solving linked to systems thinking is especially relevant to the challenges faced in ESD.

Authentic assessment is frequently swept into the wider pedagogical basket of 'employability' and is directly related to the future of graduates (see Chapter 12). Gulikers *et al.* (2004) refer to authentic assessment as professional training incorporating competence-based curricula and assessment, with a focus on preparing students for the world of work through setting sector-relevant assessed exercises that directly relate to future professional practices. Such approaches are especially relevant to the futurity and impact dimensions of ESD. Authentic assessment provides practical approaches and experiences to support students transitioning from university-based simulations to workplace learning (Davidson *et al.*, 2019).

Authentic assessment supports many of the key sustainability competencies (Koh, 2017; QAA & Advance HE 2021) and can personalise the learning and assessment process for students, including navigation of sustainability values. Students can experience personal as well as professional growth. The confidence gained can enhance the ability of students to excel in other learning and assessment exercises. The professional experience can extend the opportunities available in terms of internships and employment.

Resilience building through authentic assessments (Dacre Pool *et al.*, 2019) helps prepare students for the challenges of working and developing careers in the sustainability field. Students will face many barriers, non-cooperation and frustration in their sustainability careers. Preparing for challenge through authentic experiences in the 'safe-space' provided through university studies and assessment is a vital element of study for the future.

## Case Study: The University of Manchester Living Lab

Professor Jennifer O'Brien, the architect of the University Living Lab, perfectly captures the philosophy behind and the relationship between ESD and authentic assessment with her comment 'If you have to do assessment, why not do something useful?'.

The University Living Lab (www.universitylivinglab.org) at the University of Manchester harnesses the skills of 44,000 students to the benefit of communities, through over 150 projects set by around 50 partners, local to global. The co-produced projects are framed with the United Nation's Sustainable Development Goals and are concept notes, or statements of the problem. Students from any discipline, at any level, including interdisciplinary groups, can adapt these challenges to their coursework, dissertation, or undertake them as the assessment on a taught unit. Once marked, the Living Lab platform returns the research to the organisation who set it. The organisation shares impact of the research, which the university links to the student. The University Living Lab enriches student experience whilst equipping graduates with skills for a sustainable future in an accessible way through authentic assessment in taught programmes, rather than co or extra-curricular activities. Students add value to organisation's operations with interdisciplinary approaches, a wealth of resources and innovative methodologies. The university is able to channel their commitment to sustainable development through the mainstay of assessment, whilst students make a positive difference.

The impact of University Living Lab is significant. As part of their core assessment, students have built sustainable urban infrastructure, informed council climate policy and foodbank strategy, enabled active travel, developed Widening Participation, strengthened health resilience and enhanced biodiversity – to name but a few benefits. Working with small NGOs and charities across the world connects knowledge and exchanges ideas. Co-production of research requires stakeholders to understanding each other's contexts. Knowledge is exchanged to enable broader authentic partnerships, local to global, to further priorities whilst enabling sustainability transitions and affecting change. The University Living Lab brings the full knowledge resources of universities to bear upon the most pressing global challenges, delivering replicable and scalable change whilst many of our students been employed by organisations they researched for, and many more attribute post-graduation employment to the University Living Lab.

### Case Study: Environmental Law and Management Systems (University of Southampton)

The Environmental Law and Management Systems (EMS) teaching and assessment at the University of Southampton has operated in a variety of guises over the years but with a consistent focus on industrial sustainability literacy and advanced-level professional skills development through working with external partners. The teaching is centred on understanding environmental impacts from organisational operations, application of environmental law and professional-level management systems development through the international standard for Environmental Management Systems (EMS) (ISO14001) which provides the framework. The module builds academic knowledge of the subject area, whilst providing professional practical experience of designing environmental management systems through discussion and group exercises as opposed to traditional lecture-based classes.

The assessment involves the creation of an EMS that meets the requirements of the international standard ISO14001 for a real-life client, not a hypothetical scenario. Previous clients have included large shopping centres, sports stadiums, national government organisations, local authorities, building firms, hospitals and an international airport amongst others.

Working in 'consultancy teams', students perform an environmental review of their client operations, identify the primary environmental legislation the company is required to comply with and prioritise management actions and structures to address the environmental impacts in order of significance. The consultancy teams then build an Environmental Policy Statement with objectives and targets, supported by a schedule of work based on auditing schedules and emergency preparedness. These project components are combined and submitted as a ISO14001 compliant EMS manual. The teams are assessed on this EMS Manual, a mock 1-hour ISO14001 Certification Audit with qualified auditors, and then present their EMS to the Board of the client where they are questioned and given bespoke (formative) feedback in the most authentic of assessments. The team skills, project management, professional standard environmental aspect and impact identification techniques, legislation application skills, client management, data significance and international standard certification manual creation are packaged and delivered in a way to give students the greatest opportunity for employment and career development.

### Case Study: Keele University Green Business and Consultancy Projects

A further example of small group work to deliver projects for clients with clear professional skills development for students comes from Keele University's 'Sustainability Consultant' and 'Greening Business: Employability and Sustainability' modules where students work with third-sector organisations and university departments. The creativity of students when presented with open opportunities to innovate in sustainability is demonstrated by the imagination of the submissions. These have included design of a climate escape room, development of a stand for a climate event and mapping of community groups involved in sustainability. Students work with staff on the Belbin team roles model to encourage student engagement with the employability transferable skills (Smith *et al.*, 2017) and to consider and build group working preferences through understanding themselves, with the careers-focused summative assessment including a client-led group report and an individual reflection.

The skills building and professional standard outputs from these forms of learning and assessment have led to a high number of graduates from these universities successfully gaining employment and building careers in global environmental consultancies, small local consultancies, industrial environmental support organisations, SMEs, local and national government, university sustainability and environmental roles, and environmental manager positions in multinational to small companies.

### *Work Placements and Assessment*

Transformative and authentic assessment is delivered through work placement modules, also referred to as work-integrated learning (WIL) (Ajjawi *et al.*, 2019). There is a wide spectrum of work placement opportunities in sustainability for students because of the increasing desire of organisations to tackle sustainability issues and the shortage of skilled individuals within current staff. Students benefit from completing subject-specific meaningful work placements and see their value in linking learning and employment (Yorke, 2010; Davidson *et al.*, 2019). Such placements offer skills development, real-world experience, enhanced communication and unparalleled networking opportunities. Informal conversations with hosts suggest that the placements act as unofficial extended job opportunities, and students who prove their worth are often offered employment at the end of the placement or the completion of their degree. However, the time invested in successful work-integrated learning and assessment should not be underestimated. Whilst some learners have richly transformative experiences, others have dissatisfying placements with little tangible benefit to themselves or their host organisation. It is complex to align the requirements of placement students, university module and placement leads, and the organisation partner (Ajjawi *et al.*, 2019). Mismatches between module assessment requirements and expectations of placement partners can occur.

The post-Covid move to 'hybrid working' where organisations accept staff working from home part or even full time has opened up a previously unavailable world of degree work placement opportunities for students. Organisations are increasingly comfortable with providing work placements for students where they can complete guided work tasks remotely, with no physical space and health and safety requirements. As part of the University of Southampton Environmental Science course, students can undertake a work placement module as part of their regular timetabled termtime week. The flexibility of being able to conduct work placement tasks in the same time period as attending classes allows students to obtain all of the academic and professional benefits provided by work placements, without needing to add an extra 'year in industry' to their time at university or take time away from potential paid work in summer vacation. Assessment tasks can include reflective portfolio analysis, data reporting and analysis, placement presentations to the work partner on project outputs and presentations to lower year students as a source of inspiration for future work placements.

### *Group Assessments*

Group assessments enable collaborative research and communication skills in a variety of settings. Collaboration is critical across local and national governments, civil society and the private sector, across topic sectors (e.g. health, transport, food, energy) across nations and across ontologies (e.g. Indigenous perspectives and scientific papers). Whilst group work in the classroom is beneficial, deeper, more transformative learning can take place through summative tasks including group assessments. The benefits for graduate employability from group assessments, and the importance of the resultant skills to employers, are well established (Arsenis *et al.*, 2021; Tumpa *et al.*, 2023, QS 2018). There are also benefits in terms of the ability to deal with the more complex wicked problems inherent within sustainability when there are more people contributing to a task, preferably in a 'brain-supporting environment', where people interact to help lead to better decisions (Hetzler, 2010).

This is especially powerful when students from different courses and academic expertise and perspectives collaborate. Inter and transdisciplinary work is key to tackling sustainability challenges (Horn *et al.*, 2023), and this is strengthened in higher education through group work (Knowlton *et al.*, 2014). However, group work can pose challenges, and these must be considered and fully accommodated into the development of all group work assessments.

It is vital that students feel supported in group work assessments if they are experiencing hidden difficulties, and their lack of ability to contribute is causing them anxiety. It needs to be clear to all students that group members may be experiencing a wide range of 'justifiable' problems such as personal or family physical illness, caring responsibilities, mental health issues or financial concerns requiring employment that prevent attending meetings. Students experiencing issues may not wish to divulge their personal circumstances to group members for understandable reasons, especially if the other students are essentially strangers. Students are often working on interdisciplinary group assessments from different subjects, which can create epistemological challenges. Therefore, students need to feel assured they can raise problems in an open manner to assessment leads, with confidence they will be treated fairly or even given an alternative assessment if necessary to provide them with the flexibility and support they need. Student welfare is paramount at all times. This is not only important for the struggling student but also for the other group members who should not be impacted.

Group assessments can be especially challenging and anxiety inducing for neurodiverse students (Clouder *et al.*, 2020). Fortunately, there is now greater awareness and sensitivity to the needs of increasing neurodiverse learners in higher education (Hillier *et al.*, 2018), and this awareness must extend to group assessment support. The internationalisation of the higher education community offers rich cultural benefits to our students, and the integration of different social and cultural perspectives is an important component of ESD in higher education (Catarci, 2021). However, international students may approach group assessments with trepidation because of language, culture or gender differences, and efforts must be made to ensure group assessment is inclusive and that all learners are sensitised to possible issues.

Group assessment can cause concerns that conscientious hardworking students could be let down by other students, who are frequently referred to by impacted students as 'freeloaders' (Weaver and Esposto, 2011). Student group assessment design thus needs to accommodate mechanisms to address contribution expectations and dynamics, such as division of total grade by learners, a conflict management process or oral viva. Some programmes have developed strict criteria to record contributions formally across the group, whilst other programmes allow learners to work through issues themselves, more like a real work situation, and only offer a facilitation process if requested.

### Group Assessment Case Study: Keele University

A group assessment is the Activist Project in a second-year module at Keele University. Students work in groups to deliver a sustainability activist project around a subject they are passionate about. They are given free rein to develop their activism ideas, with many finding it overwhelming initially. Examples of activist projects they have tackled include a climate cafe to address eco-anxiety, a wildlife calendar to raise awareness of biodiversity loss, student views about timetabling to reduce travel, a campaign tackling sustainability disinformation. Informal discussions with students indicate some experience an increasing sense of agency to drive change, whilst also developing their creativity, communication and team skills.

#### *Creative Assessments*

Creative assessments can be exciting for learners, allowing them to develop creative abilities that are often overridden by the focus on analytical, critical assessment. Work involving art, craft or design can help inspire imagination or visions of sustainable futures, realise emotional aspects of sustainable development or explore different ways to raise awareness and generate behaviour change.

### Creative Assessment Case Study: Sustainable Design Prototype (University of St Andrews)

This assessment linked theory to practice, offering student agency to select a topic in which they are interested, enabling students to be creative and to explore different media and presentation formats, all through a design process. Students were expected to develop key sustainability competencies such as critical thinking and strategic capabilities alongside specific skills for communication and innovation. Students were asked to create and draft a sustainable design and produce a prototype. The design could be of anything – a building, a process, an object for domestic use or anything else. There were no restrictions. Students were then required to produce a critical analysis explaining the rationale for their design, drawing on literature in relation to design principles and the topic of choice, and to illustrate the design outline or pilot, whether via a physical model, sketches, photos or other means.

The assessment proved effective in inspiring creativity and in increasing student motivation, but needed significant support. One of the learning outcomes was to develop an understanding of the concept of design for sustainability. Students enjoyed being able to choose their own topics, to be creative and to link academic learning to practical solutions.

Interesting sustainable designs produced by students have included:

- A design for a basic wrap shirt designed to fit different sizes, with a prototype made from organic cotton hand dyed with onion skin. The idea was to use organic materials and dyes, whilst reducing waste by creating a garment that would fit women who lost or put on some weight.
- A design for a new building in which to lecture sustainable development, with sketches and watercolour paintings illustrating the orientation to the south, a circular shape to encourage dialogue, crafted techniques using sustainable materials such as stone and wood.
- An art piece, designed to illustrate the dynamic processes of nature and need to be mindful and present in the moment. Photographs of a stone cairn sculpture captured the shape and colours against the sea and sky before the tide returned and subsumed the stones under waves, and scattered them back onto the beach.

### *Critical Essays*

The essay is one of the longest established forms of assessment. Utilised as a reliable pedagogical tool throughout the history of higher education, essays form a perennial component of a traditional staple diet across degree programmes. Assessment through essays facilitates deep learning approaches that can lead to attainment of positive learning outcomes, more so than examinations with short questions (Pereira *et al.*, 2016). The critical essay can be effective for the interdisciplinary learning and systems thinking that sit at the centre of ESD and requires learners to engage with literature and theory.

Sustainable development requires the natural and physical sciences and social sciences (e.g. Redclift, 2005). Essays can enable learners in the social sciences and humanities to develop deep learning using assessment approaches that are familiar to them, but science learners used to field data collection, or laboratory experimental work may find assessed essay writing intimidating. Supporting learners with unfamiliar learning and assessment approaches is especially important in ESD assignment design because learners come from different disciplinary as well as personal backgrounds.

Essays may be organised in the form of coursework or in timed examinations. The inherent flexibility of essays ensures they can be applied across a programme assessment portfolio to provide a balance of assessment types. There is a need for equity across assessment, as all students learn and execute work differently, and we have a responsibility to cater for all learning and assessment needs, especially with regards to the perennial tension of coursework or timed examination (see Harland, 2012).

### *Reflective Essays*

Reflective essays can be beneficial in helping learners link practical and theoretical learning with personal development. They can be used in different contexts. In ESD, it is useful to offer experiential learning, for example exploring sustainability action, working with external actors or placements. Such learning can be assessed not by the 'practical achievements', which would stifle experimentation and not account for influences of other actors, but by reflective essays that permit reporting of events plus analysis in terms of cognitive, physical and affective aspects. Examples of assessments concluding in reflective essays include measurement of carbon emissions.

## Reflective Essay Case Studies: Carbon Footprint Reflections (University of St Andrews, University of Southampton)

University of St Andrews first-year sustainable development students conducted a 'Behaviour change and carbon emissions' assignment. In brief, students were required to develop a plan to reduce their own and another's carbon emissions, to reflect on the consequences of actions in relation to climate change, and to critically interrogate how this relates to theories of behaviour change. There were two parts to this assignment. For the first part, students were asked to retrospectively calculate carbon emissions, using a bespoke carbon calculator, from the previous semester and to write a one-page plan proposing how emissions in semester two could be reduced by 10%. They were encouraged to focus on particular actions, for example, reduce shower time, walk or cycle more, eat more vegan meals. This part was a compulsory formative submission with feedback provided. For the second part, students submitted a report with carbon calculations for the second semester along with critical reflections on their experience. The learning and personal behaviour reflections were especially valuable with this assessment. Students could struggle to create an accurate carbon calculator, demonstrating difficulties in data collection design, and the intricacies in data recording.

Overall, this assessment generated good learning outcomes and positive student feedback. However, we had to be careful to not *enforce* sustainable behaviour changes and to emphasise their capacity to record data and to critically reflect on the carbon emissions associated with regular conditioned behaviours. If students resisted behaviour change or were already leading largely sustainable lifestyles, they could write about the societal norms or psychological barriers limiting behaviour changes and reduction in carbon emissions.

A similar exercise is applied at the University of Southampton as part of the interdisciplinary cross-university 'Global Sustainability Challenges' module in undergraduate year two or three. Students record their personal Carbon Emissions Behaviours in the areas of personal transport mode, dietary choices, music and podcast streaming, clothing purchases, water usage, waste generation, electrical appliances (e.g. laptops), along with qualitative data describing their actions and experiences every day for 28 days. Students record this data against the background of weekly lectures addressing the sustainability impacts and challenges of each of these themes to determine if increased knowledge affects their behaviours. Students are then required to submit a Reflective Analysis article about their behaviours, education interventions and the barriers, challenges and positive experiences around developing individual solutions for societal sustainability challenges. Assignment submissions and small group seminar discussions suggest that students find the process of monitoring their carbon emission behaviours over the period of a month to be personally challenging in terms of opening the eyes of even the most sustainability conscious students to their actual regular behaviours and the contributions they make to climate emissions. However, there is also evidence of (self-reported) sustainability-focused behaviour change, along with moves to get friends, housemates and family members to modify their daily activities across each of the categories.

### *Report Writing*

One of the most important aspects of ESD is the outcome for students to be able to effectively communicate sustainability issues, challenges and solutions to a diversity of audiences. The recipients of information and analysis may be policymakers, community groups, business colleagues, educators, or that widest of catch-all groups 'the general public'.

Different formats of reports provide critical skills for learners in ESD in all disciplines and are critical for those seeking to pursue a graduate career in the sustainability field. Report-based assessments should target relevant audiences, mirror the formats adopted across different sustainability sectors and require different modes of delivery. Reports can be designed for individuals or groups. For example, individual reports can assess student laboratory work, including the execution of a laboratory experiment, following methodological procedures, data management, data analysis and key outcomes, all set against a professional standard. An alternative example of an individual report is a review of literature in an area, such as dietary choices, set out in a report that can be read by a lay or policy audience, depending on the framing of the assessment.

### Individual Report Writing Case Study: Sustainability Legislation and Policy Brief (University of Southampton)

One of the challenges in successfully implementing sustainability legislation and policy is ensuring recipients understand how and why it applies to their role, organisation or sector. This assessment example tests student knowledge and understanding, along with their critical analysis skills as they demonstrate how case studies apply to areas of law and policy.

Students are required to research and develop a briefing document summarising an area of sustainability law and policy for a specific audience. Students select one audience (A) and one area of sustainability law and policy (B) for their submission. Please refer to the Supplementary Online Materials for a full breakdown of the audience and area example choices for students.

### *Communication and Digital Technology-Based Assessments*

For many years, educators have wrestled with the pace of change around all areas of digital technology and the ramifications for how we teach, engage and assess students in this rapidly changing education arena. Much has been made of the generation gap between young students who know nothing other than a world with full digital access and all the benefits and risks that entails, and the frequently older generation of educators who can feel as though they are always trying to catch-up with those who they are trying to teach and assess. The terms 'digital natives' and 'digital immigrants' are frequently used for learners and educators, respectively, when attempting to navigate this terrain in the higher education world (Evans and Robertson, 2020). This separation into two distinct groupings cannot be based purely on age, and this rather simplistic generational division can hide the nuances of how culture, technology access and levels of education can impact students' status as skilled 'digital natives' (Akçayır *et al.*, 2016) so educators should be wary of assumptions, especially when integrating digital technology into assessment. A risk is that educators can sometimes conflate the term 'innovation' with a requirement to use digital technology. However, providing educators are sensitive to skills, experience and financial access to digital technology, this is an area of considerable potential for enthusing students who may embrace these different types of assessment to traditional examinations and essays.

An example of using digital technologies as a tool for innovative assessment is the application of podcasts. The growth of podcasts as a cultural phenomenon continues unabated, with this information-based media format being equally embraced across generations, offering a rare option of an assessment form that speaks to both learners and educators. Data from Statista (2022) shows that estimated podcast listeners across the world are projected to rise to over 500 million in 2024, from 332 million in 2020, with UK listeners projected to rise to over 28 million people in 2026 from just under 9 million in 2017 (Statista, 2021). This is not a new pedagogical tool but builds on many years of analysis by Fernandez *et al.* (2009) who demonstrated such opportunities before podcasts became the ubiquitous presence they are today.

One of the advantages of podcast creation and assessment is the dissemination of sustainability knowledge beyond the physical university space. Unlike traditional knowledge exchange platforms such as paywall protected journals, podcasts are free to listen to, can be distributed globally and can be accessed by anyone with an internet connection on computer or smartphone. Podcast creation and release offer alternative sustainability learning opportunities for our students, but also for our staff and alumni, and transform the scale of reach of our extended sustainability knowledge exchange.

Examples of student-generated podcasts as an authentic assessment tool are offered by Wakefield *et al.* (2023) and Hall and Jones (2021), who discuss the engagement, creativity, active and deep learning offered as well as the challenges faced by students in tackling new techniques and technologies. The advantages of learner-generated digital media over teacher-generated digital media (Reyna and Meier, 2018) in developing creative skills for 21st-century graduates (Shrader and Louw, 2021) clearly speak to the competencies required for sustainability literate graduates.

Inclusivity is important in this form of assessment. If working in groups, different roles can be allocated to everyone in the podcast episode team, including speaking, research and episode script writing. The podcast process of presenting their work reduces pressure on the students as they can re-record their pieces if they stumble or are dissatisfied with their content – an opportunity not afforded to them in a one-off presentation, which is a growing concern for students with anxiety.

## Communication and Digital Technology-Based Assessments: Student podcasting as assessment

One example of how podcasts can be utilised as a valuable assessment tool as part of a sustainability pedagogy is offered by the 'Global Sustainability Challenges' cross-university interdisciplinary undergraduate module at the University of Southampton where the 'Meliora Podcast' (**https://meliorapodcast.buzzsprout.com**) has been adopted as a central part of the group assessment work. The 'Global Sustainability Challenges' module is available to most undergraduate students from across all faculties with a focus on teaching and assessing sustainability, informing sustainable behaviours, but also critically building creative industry employability skills for graduate futures through innovative assessment. Students are formed into interdisciplinary groups to break down the artificial education silos created by departmental structures and degree programmes, with the aim of enabling students to understand different disciplinary perspectives, social and cultural norms, and build systems thinking capacity. The student groups decide upon an interdisciplinary sustainability issue and conduct their research.

After completion of their group research, the students move to the development of new communication skills by developing their own episode script and then recording their podcast episode using professional quality microphones and podcast unit in a recording studio. The students then build further skills focused on future sustainability communication challenges, by taking all recording files to edit and produce an episode themselves using specialist software following the instruction document produced for students. Those episodes that achieve a high enough assessment mark (in this case 62% or above) are offered the opportunity to have their episode released on the Meliora Podcast, giving students an additional contribution to their CV and/or LinkedIn profile with credibility through association with the Sustainability & Resilience Institute at the University of Southampton. Being part of the Meliora Podcast is truly liberating for students and the sustainability research work that goes on in the higher education community because for once, students are given an equal platform to academics, an opportunity they have been keen to embrace.

First-year students at Keele University can produce an 'International podcast' as part of interdisciplinary groups for assessment. Students choose a country and create a podcast episode to discuss sustainability issues of relevance to that part of the world or globally – for example, response to the Paris Agreement, energy security breakdown, nature-based solutions, climate impacts and adaptations. The podcast format makes them go above and beyond past essay assignments for this theme.

### *Fieldwork*

Most higher education institutions recognise the pedagogical and experiential value of fieldwork, and that is especially the case with ESD where the real-world applications, place attachment and nature connectedness have particular relevance. The Royal Geographical Society (with IBG) (2020) Principles for Undergraduate Fieldwork is useful for planning and operation.

When developing and delivering fieldwork teaching and assessment, it is important to clearly align with achievement of ESD competencies. For example, fieldtrips can be excellent opportunities to explore self-awareness or normative competencies, to strengthen systems thinking or to build interpersonal competencies. All leaders must consider diversity and disability, being aware of different cultural expectations and norms. Leaders must ensure that those with hidden as well as visible disabilities, or with particular caring or other responsibilities, are accommodated. Inevitably, some students will experience extenuating circumstances so all fieldwork leaders must have an alternative experience or assessment that is not dependent on timings or physical accessibility issues, whilst not wishing any student to miss out on the 'real thing'. Whilst we defend the requirement for 'real' outdoor learning outside the classroom, we must recognise that sometimes we have to bring the outside in. It is crucial that these alternative provisions are not presented in a manner that makes students not only feel that are missing out, but also that they be an inferior student in any way.

In the time pressured world of students, you may find that greater engagement by students occurs if the fieldtrip is linked to summative assessment. The exact structure and content of the assessment is dependent on the location, content and time available on the fieldcourse. However, examples may include, but are not restricted to a field method report, a field data collection and analysis report, an examination that draws on the experience and content, a critical reflective article on the field research process and fieldwork results as a scientific presentation.

Residential fieldtrips take time and effort to organise well but also offer opportunity for deeper discussion and interaction, building a sense of cohort and creating long-lasting memories. In addition to teaching and assessment, fieldcourse leaders can schedule some fun games, shared activities such as social walks, local food and drink tasting, and group activities to create a sense of identity and belonging.

### Fieldwork Case Study: Undergraduate and Postgraduate Fieldwork at the University of St Andrews

At the University of St Andrews, a range of field trip options of varying immersive intensity have been explored across all years to support ESD. For example, the numerous first-year students are met at locations within easy walking distance of the university to discuss coastal management or new university energy projects. Second-year students meet course leaders on the golf course, where they discuss local efforts towards sustainability in practice, linking to theoretical and critical lecture content. The university is utilised as a learning space with students able to inspect water saving, renewable energy and insulation features of sustainable newbuild on campus, for formative assessment. In final years, field trips further afield have enabled students to see, discuss, contribute and research sustainability, both collectively and individually. A residential stay in an ecovillage allows students to experience social and systems thinking aspects of sustainability in practice, tree planting with a community group enables students to hear from local activists. In order to deal with carbon emission and accessibility issues, virtual field trip options were developed. Masters' students presented online on environmental issues and management using photographs taken on self-guided field trips within walking distance of their homes around the world. These examples of outdoor and indoor learning offer opportunities to explore real-world challenges and solutions and to engage students in different ways, supporting the development of normative, strategic and problem-solving competencies with assessments to strengthen learning through practical reports, reflective essays, research presentations and group project proposals.

### Fieldcourse Social Activitiy Case Study: Taskmaster at the University of Southampton

One example of a field course social activity is provided by the University of Southampton where the first-year Environmental Science residential field course has a week-long 'Taskmaster' competition. All students work in groups to complete various short-term and week-long tasks of some sustainability relevance, mixed with increasing levels of silliness, and all scored by the staff 'Taskmaster' with prizes for the winning team. This builds team skills, cohort relationships, communication and creativity, all through formative sustainability assessments played out in a fun, informal setting that makes the most of all students and staff staying together far from home. Student feedback has been consistently effusive with continuing references to the fieldcourse throughout their studies and when discussing the programme with other students and applicants. Impactful assessment does not always need to be summative.

### *The Risks of Disconnection and the Impacts of Artificial Intelligence (AI)*

Impactful, enjoyable and transformative learning and assessments are frequently those with a personal touch. However, we need to be cognisant of the increasing risks of losing that personal touch, the possibility of disconnection from each other that arises from greater integration of artificial intelligence (AI) into our educational structures and experiences. We need to build innovative assessment methods that will counter the challenge of AI in assessments. Authentic assessment has inherent sustainability benefits and is also a vital component in preventing (or limiting) the use of AI in assessments.

AI in assessment writing and submission is an area of great concern. The challenges around academic integrity (or 'Academic Responsibility and Conduct' to avoid confusion over the use of 'AI') in the age of generative AI are vast. This is beautifully captured in the celebrated paper 'Chatting and cheating: ensuring academic integrity in the era of ChatGPT' where Cotton *et al.* (2023) only revealed the paper had been written directly by ChatGPT at the very end of the article, highlighting the level of sophistication in these large language machines (LLMs) when writing academic papers and how challenging this is going to be for assessors.

AI has been identified as an inhibitor of achieving SDG4 Quality Education despite potentially acting as an enabler in 71% of the SDGs and 79% of the 169 targets (Vinuesa *et al.*, 2020). Students need to understand the implications of AI on climate action and the SDGs, and to understand how harmful biases in AI can be amplified through use in their assessments (Debnath *et al.*, 2023). It is vital that students recognise the importance of well-researched, accurate data and interpretations to feed into AI algorithms. Machine learning systems are (currently) limited in their value to a progressive sustainability agenda, as their decisions can be based on (potentially biased) human-derived data and judgements that feed their systems. As Rich and Gureckis (2019) argue, statistically biased models create socially and environmentally biased decisions, intensifying the problems that AI is considered by some to potentially prevent. Assessments explicitly addressing these challenges can be helpful to students in understanding the possibilities and constraints of AI.

## Conclusion

Assessment matters to our students. It is how they express themselves, how they show us the extent and sophistication of their understanding, how they achieve the marks that lead to the award of their degrees. We owe it to them to ensure their assessment is exciting, challenging, contemporary and transformative.

In this Chapter, we have explored the purpose and principles of assessment. We have explored how different formats of assessments can be created and delivered. We have demonstrated there is a balance between formative and summative assessments in terms of their pedagogical value to learners and the workload of educators. The need for assessments to be inclusive was emphasised, in embracing difference within groups and in format of assessment. The complexity around large language models and AI must also be at the front of our collective minds as we work to innovate around this unpredictably challenging area. We analysed the principles of assessment for ESD in particular. Authentic assessment is a strong thread running throughout the Chapter and weaving together learning in ESD; authentic not only in providing real-world context, but also our position as creators, partners, markers, feedback providers and supporters of our learners on their assessment journeys. We hope this authenticity is evident throughout this Chapter, and that readers will embrace this in their work as innovative assessors. Finally, if ESD is held around co-creation of innovative pedagogy (Chapter 6) to facilitate creative and wide scoping, relevant curricula (Chapter 5), the assessment is the keystone for learner and educator focus and learning. By adapting or developing relevant assessment, a module, programme or institution can rapidly deepen ESD engagement. Such learning can be stimulating and transformative not only for learners but also for educators, changing the perceived drudgery of 'marking' into a shared exploration of possibility.

## References


Advance HE (2012) *A Marked Improvement: Transforming Assessment in Higher Education.*

Ajjawi, R., Tai, J., Huu Nghia, T. L., Boud, D., Johnson, L. and Patrick, C. (2019) Aligning assessment with the needs of work-integrated learning: The challenges of authentic assessment in a complex context. *Assessment & Evaluation in Higher Education*, 45(2), 304–316. DOI:10.1080/02602938.2019.1639613.

Akçayır, M., Dündar, H. and Akçayır, G. (2016) What makes you a digital native? Is it enough to be born after 1980? *Computers in Human Behavior*, 60, 435–440, ISSN 0747-5632.

Arsenis, P., Flores, M. and Petropoulou, D. (2021) Enhancing graduate employability skills and student engagement through group video assessment. *Assessment & Evaluation in Higher Education*, 47(2), 245–258. DOI:10.1080/02602938.2021.1897086.

Bennett, R. E. (2011) Formative assessment: A critical review. *Assessment in Education: Principles, Policy & Practice*, 18(1), 5–25. DOI:10.1080/0969594X.2010.513678.

Black, P. and Wiliam, D. (2018) Classroom assessment and pedagogy. *Assessment in Education: Principles, Policy & Practice*, 25(6), 551–575. DOI:10.1080/0969594X.2018.1441807.

Boud, D. (2008) How can Practice Reshape Assessment? In: Joughin, G. (ed.) *Assessment, Learning and Judgement in Higher Education*. Dordrecht: Springer Netherlands, pp. 29–44.

Boud, D., and Associates (2010). *Assessment 2020: Seven propositions for assessment reform in higher education*. Sydney: Australian Learning and Teaching Council. Available from: https://www.uts.edu.au/sites/default/files/Assessment-2020_propositions_final.pdf. Accessed 30 September 2024.

Buil-Fabregá, M., Martínez Casanovas, M., Ruiz-Munzón, N. and Filho, W. L. (2019) Flipped classroom as an active learning methodology in sustainable development curricula. *Sustainability*, 11(17), 4577. DOI:10.3390/su11174577.

Cage, E., Jones, E., Ryan, G., Hughes, G. and Spanner, L. (2021) Student mental health and transitions into, through and out of university: Student and staff perspectives. *Journal of Further and Higher Education*, 45(8), 1076–1089. DOI:10.1080/0309877X.2021.1875203.

Catarci, M. (2021) Intercultural education and sustainable development: A crucial nexus for contribution to the 2030 agenda for sustainable development. *Social Sciences*, 10(1), 24. DOI:10.3390/socsci10010024.

Clouder, L., Karakus, M. and Cinotti, A. *et al.* (2020) 'Neurodiversity in higher education: A narrative synthesis'. *Higher Education*, 80, 757–778. DOI:10.1007/s10734-020-00513-6.

Cotton, D. R. E., Cotton, P. A. and Shipway, J. R. (2023) Chatting and cheating: Ensuring academic integrity in the era of ChatGPT. *Innovations in Education and Teaching International*, 61(2), 228–239. DOI:10.1080/14703297.2023.2190148.

Dacre Pool, L., Gurbutt, D., Houston, K. (2019). Developing Employable, Emotionally Intelligent, and Resilient Graduate Citizens of the Future. In: Diver, A. (eds) *Employability via Higher Education: Sustainability as Scholarship*. Springer, Cham. https://doi.org/10.1007/978-3-030-26342-3_6

Dann, R. (2014) Assessment as learning: Blurring the boundaries of assessment and learning for theory, policy and practice. *Assessment in Education: Principles, Policy & Practice*, 21(2), 149–166.

Davidson, R., Snelling, C., Karanicolas, S., Crotti, T. and Phillips, B. (2019) Authentic Assessment as a Tool to Bridge the Transition Between Learning and Work. In: Diver, A. (ed.) *Employability via Higher Education: Sustainability as Scholarship*. Cham: Springer. DOI:10.1007/978-3-030-26342-3_17

Debnath, R., Creutzig, F., Sovacool, B. K., *et al.* (2023) Harnessing human and machine intelligence for planetary-level climate action. *Npj Clim. Action*, 2, 20. DOI:10.1038/s44168-023-00056-3

Dochy, F. (2008) The Edumetric Quality of New Modes of Assessment: Some Issues and Prospects. In: Joughin, G. (ed.) *Assessment, Learning and Judgement in Higher Education.* Dordrecht: Springer Netherlands, pp. 85–114.

Ecclestone, K. (2008) Instrumental or Sustainable Learning? The Impact of Learning Cultures on Formative Assessment in Vocational Education. In: Joughin, G. (ed.) *Assessment, Learning and Judgement in Higher Education.* Dordrecht: Springer Netherlands, pp. 153–174.

Evans, C. and Robertson, W. (2020) The four phases of the digital natives debate. *Human Behavior and Emerging Technologies.*, 2, 269–277. https://doi.org/10.1002/hbe2.196

Fernandez, V., Simo, P. and Sallan, J. M. (2009) Podcasting: A new technological tool to facilitate good practice in higher education. *Computers & Education*, 53(2), 385–392. DOI:, ISSN 0360-1315, DOI:10.1016/j.compedu.2009.02.014.

Fulghum, R. (1986) *All I Really Need to Know I Learned in Kindergarten.* New York Books. ISBN 978-0-394-57102-7

Galindo-Dominguez, H. (2021) Flipped classroom in the educational system: Trend or effective pedagogical model compared to other methodologies? *Educational Technology & Society*, 24(3), 44–60. Available at: https://www.jstor.org/stable/27032855 [Accessed 31 July 2024].

García-Morales, V. J., Garrido-Moreno, A. and Martín-Rojas, R. (2021) The transformation of higher education after the COVID disruption: Emerging challenges in an online learning scenario. *Frontiers in Psychology*, 12, 616059. [Accessed 31 July 2024].

Gibbs, P. (2017) Higher Education: A Compassion Business or Edifying Experience? In: Gibbs, P. (ed.) *The Pedagogy of Compassion at the Heart of Higher Education.* Springer.

Graham, P., Kuyvenhoven, C., Upitis, R., Arshad-Ayaz, A., Scheinman, E., Khan, C., Goebel, A., Brown, R. S. and Hovorka, A. (2020) The emotional experience of sustainability courses: Learned eco-anxiety, potential ontological adjustment. *Journal of Education for Sustainable Development*, 14(2), 190–204.

Grantham Institute (2021) The impact of climate change on mental health and emotional wellbeing: current evidence and implications for policy and practice. Grantham Institute Briefing Paper 36. [online] Available at: https://www.imperial.ac.uk/grantham/publications/the-impact-of-climate-change-on-mental-health-and-emotional-wellbeing-current-evidence-and-implications-for-policy-and-practice.php [Accessed 31 July 2024].

Gulikers, J. T. M., Bastiaens, T. J. and Kirschner, P. A. (2004) A five-dimensional framework for authentic assessment. *Educational Technology Research and Development (ETR&D)*, 52, 67–86. DOI:10.1007/BF02504676.

Hall, N. M. and Jones, J. M. (2021) Student-produced podcasts as a teaching and learning tool. *American Journal of Distance Education*, 37(1), 53–65. DOI:10.1080/08923647.2021.1995256.

Harland, T. (2012) *University Teaching: An Introductory Guide*. Abingdon: Routledge.

Hetzler, S. (2010) "Brain-supporting environments for decision making in complex systems. *Kybernetes*, 39(9/10), 1551–1565. DOI:10.1108/03684921011081169.

Hillier, A., Goldstein, J., Murphy, D., Trietsch, R., Keeves, J., Mendes, E. and Queenan, A. (2018) Supporting university students with autism spectrum disorder. *Autism*, 22(1), 20–28. DOI:10.1177/1362361317699584.

Horn, A., Scheffelaar, A., Urias, E. and Zweekhorst, M. B. M. (2023) Training students for complex sustainability issues: A literature review on the design of inter- and transdisciplinary higher education. *International Journal of Sustainability in Higher Education*, 24(1), 1–27. DOI:10.1108/IJSHE-03-2021-0111.

Howell, R. A. (2021) Engaging students in education for sustainable development: The benefits of active learning, reflective practices and flipped classroom pedagogies. *Journal of Cleaner Production*, 325, 129318. DOI: ISSN 0959-6526, DOI:10.1016/j.jclepro.2021.129318.

Joughin, G. (2008) *Introduction: Refocusing Assessment*. In: *Assessment, Learning and Judgement in Higher Education* (pp. 1–11). Dordrecht: Springer Netherlands.

Keamy, R. L., Nicholas, H. R., Mahar, S. and Herrick, C. (2007) *Personalising Education: From Research To Policy And Practice*. Melbourne: Office for Education Policy and Innovation. https://www.vgls.vic.gov.au/client/en_AU/vgls/search/detailnonmodal/ent:$002f$002fSD_ASSET$002f0$002fSD_ASSET:1304418/ada?qu=Victoria.+Department+of+Education+and+Early+Childhood+Development&d=ent%3A%2F%2FSD_ASSET%2F0%2FSD_ASSET%3A1304418%7EASSET%7E265&ic=true&ps=300&h=8

Kebritchi, M., Lipschuetz, A. and Santiague, L. (2017) Issues and challenges for teaching successful online courses in higher education: A literature review. *Journal of Educational Technology Systems*, 46(1), 4–29. [Accessed 31 July 2024].

Kemp, S., Kendal, J., Warren, A., Wright, L., Canning, J., Grace, M. and Saunders, C. (2015) 'Global Consensus Is a Dream, but Twitter Is Real: Simulating a Sustainable Development Goals Summit Through Interdisciplinary Classroom Politics and Negotiation by Social media'. In: Leal Filho, W., Brandli, L., Kuznetsova, O. and Paço, A. (eds.) *Integrative Approaches to Sustainable Development at University Level*. World Sustainability Series. Cham: Springer, pp. 563–575. DOI:10.1007/978-3-319-10690-8_38.

Keyes, C. L. M., Eisenberg, D., Perry, G. S., Dube, S. R., Kroenke, K. and Dhingra, S. S. (2012) The relationship of level of positive mental health with current mental disorders in predicting suicidal behavior and academic impairment in college students. *Journal of American College Health*, 60(2), 126–133. DOI:10.1080/07448481.2011.608393.

Kibble, J. D.. (2017) 'Best practices in summative assessment', *Advances in Physiology Education*. DOI:10.1152/advan.00116.2016. [Accessed 31 July 2024].

Knowlton, J. L., Halvorsen, K. E., Handler, R. M. and O'Rourke, M. (2014) Teaching interdisciplinary sustainability science teamwork skills to graduate students using in-person and web-based interactions. *Sustainability*, 6, 9428–9440. DOI:10.3390/su6129428.

Koh, K. (2017) Authentic Assessment.*Oxford Research Encyclopedia of Education*.https://oxfordre.com/education/view/10.1093/acrefore/9780190264093.001.0001/acrefore-9780190264093-e-22.

Låg, T. and Grøm, R. (2019) Does the flipped classroom improve student learning and satisfaction? A systematic review and meta-analysis. *AERA Open*, 5(3), 1–17. [Accessed 31 July 2024].

Macaskill, A. (2012) The mental health of university students in the United Kingdom. *British Journal of Guidance & Counselling*, 41(4), 426–441. DOI:10.1080/03069885.2012.743110.

Nicholson, D. and Valeria, D. (2021) Design Principles for Assessment of Sustainability Teaching. In: *Assessment and Feedback in a Post-Pandemic Era: A Time for Learning and Inclusion* (pp. 183–195). Advance HE. ISBN 9781916359352.

Nicholson, D. and Vargas, D. (2021) *Design Principles for Assessment of Sustainability Teaching*. In: *Assessment and Feedback in a Post-Pandemic Era: a Time for Learning and Inclusion* (pp. 183–195). AdvanceHE. ISBN 9781916359352

Orana, S. (2022) What do we mean by "pedagogy" in sustainability education? *Teaching in Higher Education*, 27(1), 114–129. DOI:10.1080/13562517.2019.1699528.

Pereira, D., Flores, M. A. and Niklasson, L. (2016) Assessment revisited: A review of research in *assessment and evaluation in higher education. Assessment & Evaluation in Higher Education*, 41(7), 1008–1032. DOI:10.1080/02602938.2015.1055233.

Price, E. A. C., Nicholson, D. T., Dunk, R., Lawler, C., Carney, M., Vargas, V., Veitch, S., Leigh, S., Singleton, M. and Mottram, S. (2024) 'Enabling change agents for sustainable development: A whole-institution approach to embedding the UN sustainable development goals in higher education', *International Journal of Sustainability in Higher Education*. DOI:10.1108/IJSHE-02-2024-0112.

Price, E. A. C., White, R. M., Mori, K., Longhurst, J., Baughan, P., Hayles, C. S. and Gough, G. (2021) Supporting the role of universities in leading individual and societal transformation through education for sustainable development. *Discover Sustainability*, 2, 49. DOI:10.1007/s43621-021-00058-3.

QS Higher Education Report (2018) 'The global skills gap in the 21st century'. [online] Available at: https://www.qs.com/portfolio-items/the-global-skills-gap-in-the-21st-century/ [Accessed 31 July 2024].
Quality Assurance Agency (QAA) and Advance HE (2021) *Education for Sustainable Development Guidance*. [online] Available at: https://www.qaa.ac.uk/the-quality-code/education-for-sustainable-development [Accessed 31 July 2024].
QAA (2021) Higher Education Toolkit Part 12: Assessment. Online report by the The Quality Assurance Agency, UK. Available at https://www.membershipresources.qaa.ac.uk/docs/membership-resources/teaching-learning-and-assessment/he-toolkit-part-12-assessment.pdf?sfvrsn=dae1c781_14 [Accessed 9 January 2025].
Race, P. (2019) *The lecturer's Toolkit: A Practical Guide to Assessment, Learning and Teaching*. Routledge. [Accessed 31 July 2024].
Redclift, M. (2005) Sustainable development (1987–2005): an oxymoron comes of age. *Sustainable development*, *13*(4), 212–227.
Reyna, J. and Meier, P. (2018) Learner-generated digital media (LGDM) as an assessment tool in tertiary science education: A review of literature. *IAFOR Journal of Education*, 6(3), 93–109. DOI:10.22492/ije.6.3.06.
Rich, A. S. and Gureckis, T. M. (2019) Lessons for artificial intelligence from the study of natural stupidity. *Nature Machine Intelligence*, 1, 174–180. DOI:10.1038/s42256-019-0038-z.
Rodríguez-Chueca, J., Molina-García, A., García-Aranda, C., Pérez, J. and Rodríguez, E. (2019) Understanding sustainability and the circular economy through flipped classroom and challenge-based learning: An innovative experience in engineering education in Spain. *Environmental Education Research*, 26(2), 238–252. DOI:10.1080/13504622.2019.1705965.
Royal Geographical Society (with IBG) (2020) *Council of Heads of Geography in UK Higher Education Institutions, Principles for Undergraduate Fieldwork, version 1 (December 2020)*. [online] Available at: https://www.rgs.org/research/higher-education-resources/principles-for-undergraduate-field-courses#:~:text=All%20fieldwork%20should%20be%20planned,communities%20and%20all%20other%20stakeholders [Accessed 31 July 2024].
Ryan, A. and Tilbury, D. (2013) *Flexible pedagogies: New pedagogical ideas*. Report for The Higher Education Academy, November 2013. Higher Education Academy. [online] Available at: https://s3.eu-west-2.amazonaws.com/assets.creode.advancehe-document-manager/documents/hea/private/resources/npi_report_1568036616.pdf [Accessed 31 July 2024].
Sadler, D. R. (2008) Transforming Holistic Assessment and Grading into a Vehicle for Complex Learning. In: Joughin, G. (ed.) *Assessment, Learning and Judgement in Higher Education*. Dordrecht: Springer Netherlands, pp. 45–64.
Sadler, D. R. (2013) 'Opening up feedback: Teaching learners to see'. In Merry, S., Price, M., Carless, D., & Taras, M. (Eds.)*Reconceptualising Feedback in Higher Education: developing dialogue with students*. (Ch.5, 5463). London: Routledge.
Sandri, O. (2022) What do we mean by 'pedagogy' in sustainability education? *Teaching in Higher Education*, 27(1), 114–129. [Accessed 31 July 2024].
Shrader, A. M. and Louw, I. (2021) Using a social media project as a way to get students to communicate conservation messages to the general public. *Journal of Biological Education*. DOI:10.1080/00219266.2021.1924231
Smith, M., Polglase, G. and Parry, C.. (2017) Construction of Student Groups Using Belbin: Supporting Group Work in Environmental Management. In: *Pedagogic Research in Geography Higher Education*. Routledge.
Springett, D. (2005) Education for sustainability in the business studies curriculum: A call for a critical agenda. *Business Strategy and the Environment*, 14(3), 146–159.
Statista (2021) Number of podcast listeners worldwide from 2019 to 2024 (in millions) [Graph]. *Statista*. [online] Available at: https://www.statista.com/statistics/1291360/podcast-listeners-worldwide/ [Accessed 31 July 2024].
Statista (2022) Estimated number of podcast listeners in the United Kingdom (UK) from 2017 to 2026 (in millions) [Graph]. *Statista*. [online] Available at: https://www.statista.com/forecasts/1147560/podcast-reach-uk [Accessed 31 July 2024].
Sterling, S. (2012) *The Future Fit Framework: An Introductory Guide to Teaching and Learning for Sustainability in HE*. York: Higher Education Academy.

Students Organising for Sustainability UK (SOS-UK) (2023) *SOS-UK Sustainability Skills Survey 2022-23*. [online] Available at: https://cdn.prod.website-files.com/6008334066c47be740656954/651d7ed9dca42698cee12509_20230928%20Sustainability%20Skills%20Survey%20Final-%20HE%20only.pdf [Accessed 31 July 2024].

Students Organising for Sustainability UK (SOS-UK) (2024) *SDG Teach In 2024 report*. [online] Available at: https://cdn.prod.website-files.com/6008334066c47be740656954/66745ebcbd70a3babdf74dc3_2024%20Campaign%20Report.pdf [Accessed 31 July 2024].

Swaffield, S. (2011) Getting to the heart of authentic assessment for Learning. *Assessment in Education: Principles, Policy & Practice*, 18(4), 433–449. DOI:10.1080/0969594X.2011.582838.

Thomas, I. (2009) Critical thinking, transformative learning, sustainable education, and problem-based learning in universities. *Journal of Transformative Education*, 7, 245–264. DOI:10.1177/1541344610385753.

Tumpa, R., Skaik, S., Ham, M. and Chaudhry, M. (2023) Enhancing project management graduates' employability through group assessment innovations: An empirical study. *Project Leadership and Society*, 4, 100084. DOI:10.1016/j.plas.2023.100084. [Accessed 31 July 2024].

Vinuesa, R., Azizpour, H., Leite, I., Balaam, M., Dignum, V., Domisch, S., Felländer, A., Langhans, S. D., Tegmark, M. and Fuso Nerini, F. (2020) The role of artificial intelligence in achieving the sustainable development goals. *Nature Communications*, 11, 233. DOI:10.1038/s41467-019-14108-y.

Wakefield, A., Pike, R. and Amici-Dargan, S. (2023) Learner-generated podcasts: An authentic and enjoyable assessment for students working in pairs. *Assessment & Evaluation in Higher Education*, 48(7), 1025–1037. DOI:10.1080/02602938.2022.2152426.

Weaver, D. and Esposto, A. (2011) Peer Assessment as a method of improving student engagement. *Assessment & Evaluation in Higher Education*, *37*(7), 805–816. DOI:10.1080/02602938.2011.576309.

Wyse, D., Pandya, J. and Hayward, L. (2015) The SAGE Handbook of Curriculum, Pedagogy and Assessment. Sage Publications Ltd.

Yorke, M. (2008) Faulty Signals? Inadequacies of Grading Systems and a Possible Response. In: Joughin, G. (ed.) *Assessment, Learning and Judgement in Higher Education*. Dordrecht: Springer Netherlands, pp. 65–84.

Yorke, M. (2010) Employability: Aligning the message, the medium and academic values. *Journal of Teaching and Learning for Graduate Employability*, 1(1), 2–12.

## Appendix 1: Group Work Instructions Example

The following provides an example of group work instructions that may be useful for addressing the issue of student freeloaders in group assessments.

**Group Assessment instructions: you must read this!**

This exercise forms X% of the assessment for the whole module. It is important you attend every session (unless not possible for health or accessibility reasons) and contribute fully to all group work.

The assessment is subject to a peer-review process, based on the evidence collected through the instructions below. This can affect your mark if there has been an unequal contribution of work. Equally, students can be removed from the assessment group if found to be in breach of the instructions below.

***By registering for this module, you are agreeing to conduct all your group work according to the following requirements:***

- You are required to meet with your team to progress work in this project as agreed by the majority group consensus. These meetings can be in person or on Teams.
- You should not expect other group members to attend meetings or respond immediately to communications outside of normal working hours (09:00–18:00 weekdays).

- ***You are required to record minutes of all meetings held***. The minutes must include the names of all attendees, any apologies with reason submitted (if sensitive this should not be recorded), and any non-attendees with no reason submitted. These minutes should be posted to your group page on the module blackboard site as evidence of group work which can be used to resolve any group issues.
- If meeting on Teams, it is advised that meetings are recorded so all members have a record of their agreed tasks. However, all group members must agree to the meeting being recorded.
- ***All minutes must include all agreed actions with designated responsibility***. The minutes should then be agreed by all parties and recorded as such. Subsequent meetings will include all parties reporting back against their actions, again recorded in the minutes.
- All team members should share minute taking responsibility and are required to submit the minutes to all team members within two working days at the latest.
    - N.B. Have an agreed meeting finish time to ensure speed in the proceedings, and stick to the deadlines! Recommend a maximum meeting time of either 60 or 90 minutes.
- If a team member fails to attend a meeting or has not completed their actions without good reason, a '**first warning**' should be recorded against their name, and the module lead informed.
- If a team member fails to attend a meeting or has not completed their actions without good reason after a 'first warning' has been issued and recorded against their name, a '**conduct meeting**' should be arranged with the module coordinator and attended by the appropriate team members. Meeting minutes will be used as evidence for this meeting, and if guilty of failing to attend and contribute to the project a '**final warning**' will be issued.
- If a team member has been proven to have missed a further project, action deadline, presentation or the site visit meeting without good reason after having received a 'final warning' in the 'conduct meeting', or it is proved that a team member has made no notable contributions to the work without an approved reason (e.g. illness, family reasons, personal circumstances), the group member may be removed from the group for this Assessment and an alternative assessment based on this exercise will be allocated.

## Appendix 2: Individual Report Case Study: Sustainability Legislation and Policy Brief (University of Southampton) Additional Materials

The examples below supplement the example individual report case study for the Sustainability Legislation and Policy Brief.

A **Briefing Document Audience**

Students are required to write their Sustainability Law & Policy Briefing Document (maximum of 1500 words) for one of the following audiences (the examples for each audience area are for illustrative purposes and not an exhaustive list):

1. **Professional, Statutory and Regulatory Bodies (PSRBs)** – e.g. British Psychological Society, British Computer Society, Royal Geographical Society, The Engineering Council, Chartered Society of Designers, Royal Institute of British Architects, General Medical Council

2. **Trade & Industry Bodies** – e.g. Make UK, Federation of Small Businesses, National Farmers Union, The Food & Drink Federation, AMPS, UK Fashion & Textile Association, Federation of Master Builders
3. **Sustainability NGO** – e.g. Sustainability First, The Wildlife Trusts, Tearfund, RSPB, Friends of the Earth, Client Earth, CPRE
4. **Sustainability Professional Bodies** – e.g. British Association for Sustainable Sport (BASIS), Institute of Environmental Management and Assessment (IEMA), Nuclear Institute, Institution of Environmental Scientists (IES), Chartered Institution of Ecology and Environmental Management (CIEEM), Chartered Institution of Wastes Management (CIWM), Chartered Institution of Water and Environmental Management (CIWEM), UK Environmental Law Association (UKELA)
5. **Sustainability Consultancy** – e.g. Mott MacDonald, WSP, Ramboll, Arup, CBRE, Trium

B **Area of Sustainability Law and Policy**
After selecting their audience, students select one area of sustainability law and policy for their Briefing Document. The submission is built around one or more case studies to illustrate the key outcomes of the case(s), the relevant legislation applied in the case, the impact of the case(s) on the area of law and policy, where appropriate how the case and legislation shaped other related areas of sustainability law and policy

**Areas:**

1. Climate
2. Fair trade
3. Workers rights
4. Biodiversity and conservation
5. Waste management
6. Water management
7. Air quality

Chapter 8

# Sustainability Research, Teaching and Practice

## Towards Transdisciplinary Knowledge Co-Production in Universities

*Rehema M. White, Clare Saunders and Zoe P. Robinson*

### Introduction

The university is a social place, in which empirical experiments and in-person interactions occur; a political sphere in which power is wielded and philosophical goals pursued; an intellectual space in which ideas take shape, are moulded and solidified as publication and possibly patent; and a physical structure, which requires material resources and organisational strategies. Universities play a key role in producing, sharing and debating knowledge to understand the world and to develop technological and social solutions that incorporate philosophical and conceptual questions of what it is to be human, the social science of inequalities and injustice and the natural and physical sciences. Universities also need the arts, aesthetics and cultural engagement to enable us to envision sustainable futures, look to the past and connect with and through the humanities (Kagan 2018). External actors are generators of knowledge and can also help academic staff identify real-world sustainability challenges and assist in finding meaningful impactful channels for academic expertise to contribute to creating real change. Graduates embody knowledge and enact competencies after graduation in later professional and personal capacities. Through the interrelated, interacting and interlinking elements of research, teaching and practice, the university can be considered as a knowledge hub through which knowledge is generated, exchanged and disseminated, occasionally implemented and often evaluated.

The aim of this chapter is to explore the wider context of universities as knowledge hubs in which Education for Sustainable Development (ESD) is linked to sustainability research and the implementation of knowledge through policy and practice. First, we examine concepts of knowledge and how knowledge flows in a higher education context. We then explore sustainability research, broadly defined as research covering topics of relevance to understanding sustainability challenges and their solutions, using sustainability research attributes, such as transdisciplinary and systems thinking approaches. Our exploration of sustainability research focuses on transdisciplinary approaches, socio-ecological innovation, systems thinking, moral and ethical frameworks and the practitioner researcher. We return to the concept of knowledge flows, as articulated in knowledge management. A discussion of research-led teaching, teaching-led research, practice-led learning, research on ESD and teaching sustainability research and the sustainability *of* research practice enables further integrative analysis. We conclude that the artificial divisions between research, teaching and practice are unhelpful when we consider the roles of universities as integrated knowledge and innovation hubs for

DOI: 10.4324/9781003451563-8

sustainable futures. We offer some examples to illustrate how universities have achieved knowledge integration, and we provide some practical recommendations to strengthen knowledge generation and integration across ESD and other areas.

### *Knowledge Generation and Flows*

Most higher education occurs in universities in UK, although there are some creative arts institutions (e.g. The Royal Academy of Music, Glasgow School of Art, Chicken Shed Theatre Company) and some specialist vocational institutions (e.g. The Royal Veterinary College, London School of Hygiene and Tropical Medicine), and a growing number of further education colleges approved to deliver higher education. Much of the literature on knowledge and sustainability draws on the university context. In this chapter, we thus refer to 'universities' as the principal form of higher education institution under scrutiny. This is not to deny that other institutions have significant impacts; in fact, vocational and arts higher education institutions play highly significant roles in the theorising, practice and policy of creative arts and other professions.

Universities are believed to have a significant potential role to play in sustainability transitions, by producing, exchanging and implementing knowledge (see Chapters 1, 2). Historically, however, higher education has been part of the problem, by producing many graduates with extractive, profiteering and technical tendencies, devoid of a moral compass or ecological literacy (Orr 1994; Peters and Wals 2013). As global sustainability challenges become more critical and better realised (UN 2015; Rockström *et al.* 2023), there has been increased recognition of the role that universities must play. Interactions and integration need to occur between ESD; sustainability research; operational leadership; engagement with local communities and other stakeholders for a more positive contribution to society (Yarime et al. 2012; Sterling 2013). We consider ESD to be teaching and learning that supports graduates in active knowledge acquisition and generation, that develops specific and generic sustainability competencies and that creates opportunity for transformative learning. It is a process of critical consciousness that explores with learners what kind of futures we envision and the knowledge, competencies and practices required to journey towards these futures (see Chapter 2).

Declaring universities to be knowledge hubs is more complicated than it first appears to be. Universities can also be knowledge 'sinks', where research is undertaken and data collected, but the results do not move beyond university or academic boundaries, either through failure to publish or dissemination only via specialist, fire-walled publications. Although university research is often lauded for its societal transformation potential, it can also be extractive, in terms of both human and material resources, and there can be tensions between the educational and research missions of universities.

'Knowledge' can be understood in different ways. Knowledge can be perceived as information and facts, technical skills and knowhow, abilities to access and synthesise perspectives, experience in a particular area, or a suites of skills, capacities and competencies. Knowledge is not absolute but rather is considered to be 'justified true belief'. Knowledge is intimately linked to power (e.g. Foucault). Knowledge can be perceived as a dynamic process of debate and reflection (e.g. Miller *et al.* 2011), or a resource to be managed (e.g. Budur *et al.* 2024) or an attribute or an outcome. Knowledge is linked to beliefs and attitudes; it is normative (Miller *et al.* 2011) – what to study, who accesses knowledge and how to use knowledge all depend on moral frameworks and belief systems. Knowledge is thus also political. This complexity is important for ESD and sustainability transitions because it highlights that the type and interpretation of knowledge pursued (e.g. renewable energy technologies versus behaviour change) will reflect perspectives on sustainable development; and the choice of who is involved in such decisions will depend on power, politics and the design of participatory processes (e.g. funding decisions, governance norms).

Knowledge generation, exchange and implementation involves identifying problems and questions, gathering, analysing and interpreting data, debating results, exchanging findings, piloting utilisation and supporting how to achieve practical outcomes and impacts. This is a complex process, involving multiple actors. Academic staff, whether research or education focused, learners at all levels, professional services staff, university campus estate staff, local communities, and public and private sector members can all produce, share and utilise knowledge. ESD is essential to all of these processes, through supporting learners to develop competencies for sustainability research and practice; co-learning by staff; and creating dialogical spaces with practitioners, policy makers and the public(s).

Universities have huge potential to contribute to sustainability transitions, but they are inherently slow-moving and are not developing a future generations perspective, external engagement, values and leadership fast enough (O'Riordan *et al.* 2020). They have been poorly structured to generate and exchange knowledge for sustainability (Miller *et al.* 2011). Some recent changes in university role and function are welcome. Universities have become less loosely coupled (characterised by a high level of self-governance by academic rather than managerial staff) and have increasingly taken on more organisational, managerial characteristics (Broström *et al.* 2021). This has led to a greater emphasis on organisational professionalisation and increasing use of performance indicators to be accountable and efficient with state and other funding, along with increased competitiveness (Broström *et al.* 2021). It has also caused a shift in the purpose of universities, with increased expectations for them to address current societal problems, generate local development and deliver technological innovation (Geuna and Muscio 2009; Budur *et al.* 2024). However, such changes in the purpose and professionalism have also led to some mixed outcomes. Policy makers have increasingly sought more control over allocation of research funding, through, for example, assessment of university 'excellence' (e.g. the UK Research Excellence Framework assessment processes) or policy guidance on the subject of funding (Broström *et al.* 2021). Such processes can be positive in asking academics to consider sustainability, but if these funding calls are too specific or framed in particular ways, they have implications for how we seek sustainability. Sustainable development tends to address complex, interconnected and wicked problems (Rittel and Webber 1973; Funtowicz and Ravetz 1993) and needs broad changes across the socio-technological system to provide a holistic response to the UN Sustainable Development Goals (SDGs) (Schot and Steinmueller 2018) and beyond. In addition, attempts to commercialise research can have mixed success.

Whilst publicly funded institutions can generate financial benefits from research, such benefits have tended to be over rated, and much of the commercialisation has occurred through patents and other means derived mainly from early biotechnological successes, rather than from all kinds of research (Broström *et al.* 2021). It can be more difficult to derive commercial benefits from socio-ecological solutions that address sustainability challenges locally or globally. In addition, whilst accountability and equitable processes within universities are critical, Broström *et al.* (2021) note that the increased organisation of these more tightly coupled institutions may negatively affect the capacity of their researchers to act autonomously and entrepreneurially. The agenda for entrepreneurship is often aligned with that of ESD, in that both areas develop and require overlapping competencies and creative and design thinking. However, whilst the entrepreneurial university is able to benefit from economically rewarding knowledge areas, it is not the same as an institution that can co-produce frugal and inclusive innovation with local stakeholders (Arocena and Sutz 2021). Hence, we want our universities to be efficient and accountable, but to include flexibility and processes for creative thinking that are not associated directly with economic income. We want universities to learn from each other, yet be locally unique and globally relevant. There is no perfect blueprint for a university, or how knowledge creation and exchange should be enacted. For example, solutions from the Global North are often not appropriate for the Global South, yet it is often assumed that they should be imported unquestioningly, and at cost (Arocena and Sutz 2021)

### *Beyond Sustainability Science*

There is some debate about the relationships between research for sustainability, research on sustainability, sustainable research and sustainability science. The concept of research *for* sustainability, which is often called sustainability research, retains the normative impetus of Education *for* Sustainable Development. This concept thus recognises the multi-faceted, interconnected problems of unsustainability and aims to address them (White 2013). Research *on* sustainability implies a more neutral stance of providing information or knowledge without engaging with its use. In this Chapter, we take the view that sustainability science is a subset of sustainability research, and that they are not synonyms (see Chapter 4 for further discussion).

### *Sustainability Research*

In the same way that we can consider all teaching to have the potential to be ESD (Orr 1994), we might consider that all research could be relevant to sustainability. Research traditionally explores questions about what it means to be human; about how societies can offer social justice and live within environmental limits; and about how science can provide understanding and solutions for the major challenges we face today. Whilst these areas were once seen as separate domains of the humanities, social sciences, and natural and physical sciences, respectively, some argue that these traditional metadisciplinary fields are being replaced by interdisciplinary forms of organisation, as higher education becomes orientated towards solving pressing real-world problems, such as those posed by sustainability (Trowler 2012). We discussed in Chapter 2 how ESD includes coverage of topics relevant to sustainability, the use of innovative pedagogies and the support of competencies in learners and educators. Similarly, sustainability research can include consideration of topics, modes and outcomes (White 2013). Framing of sustainability research topics, as for ESD, often starts with a focus on discipline-specific issues or with a pre-existing holistic perspective such as the SDGs, and matures into a more integrative and interconnected consideration of the true nature of sustainability issues. For example, it is now widely recognised that the 'environmental crisis' is not a single factor but rather is a complex interrelated web of intersecting crises, including social, cultural, political and economic aspects (see, for example, Lönngren and Van Poeck 2021).

Sustainability research will exhibit at least some of the following research attributes or modes: inter- and transdisciplinarity, linking theory and practice, joining local impact with global awareness, using participatory approaches to mobilise different knowledge forms, socio-ecological innovation, systems thinking and normative awareness with exploration of the moral and ethical aspects of sustainability research (Miller *et al.* 2011; White 2013; White and van Koten 2016). We now explore these attributes.

### *Transdisciplinary Approaches in Sustainability Research*

Different disciplines use different definitions of the terms used to label different ways of working across disciplines, further complicating discussions of interdisciplinary or transdisciplinary research. Here, we describe single disciplinary research as grounded in disciplinary frames and methodologies, multidisciplinary research as involving multiple disciplines working on the same problem but with limited collaboration or integration of outputs, and interdisciplinary research as involving interaction between disciplines to produce an integrated output (Max Neef 2005). In contrast, transdisciplinarity is used here to describe the exchange and development of new paradigms and methods across disciplines, and with engagement with external non-academic actors (Max Neef 2005; Tress *et al.* 2005; White 2013). Transdisciplinary research thus enables us to draw through different disciplines to connect theory and practice and create participatory approaches across a breadth of non-academic stakeholders in research. Transdisciplinarity is particularly relevant to sustainability research because the complexity of sustainability challenges means that it is crucially important to hear, account for and build on multiplicities of knowledge (Lang *et al.* 2012). In general, transdisciplinary sustainability research has in common a dedication to developing shared (but sometimes complex) problem definitions, the co-creation or co-production of knowledge, and/or attempts to use the gleaned knowledge to solve real-world problems (Knapp *et al.* 2019). Many researchers are now exploring the potential of creative and transdisciplinary ways of working that centre different forms of knowledge (not just 'science') (Fam *et al.* 2016). Transdisciplinary research changes the role of the researcher from a generator of supposedly objective knowledge into a 'change agent, knowledge broker, reflective scientist, self-reflexive scientist and process facilitator' (Bennich *et al.* 2022, p. 1088, citing Whittmay and Schapke 2016).

Academia for change is not only a Western, nor a recent notion; Paulo Freire (Freire 1970) challenged the assumed dominance of academia with its technical and economic focus. He called for a pedagogy of the oppressed and freedom for individuals through liberal education and a different way of thinking. 'This means that the creation of a critical consciousness becomes an important content of development' (Hadorn *et al.* 2006). Many subsequent approaches arose from theoretical frameworks such as liberation theology, with a practical focus on participation (such as Participatory Rural Appraisal) in the 1980s and 1990s (e.g. Chambers 1994). Whilst participatory processes became increasingly common in developing countries, they were gradually taken up in developed countries as well (e.g. Blackstock *et al.* 2007).

Forms of deliberative participation require collaboration between academics and non-academics. Such communicative action, in which two or more actors seek to develop mutual understanding, often for purpose (Habermas), can be difficult at a fundamental level. A cognitive clash can arise between North-South relationships because of ontological or epistemological divides (Mardero *et al.* 2023). This clash can be overcome through 'reflexive learning' across 'epistemic communities' (Hadorn *et al.* 2006). There can even be epistemological incompatibility between academics, for example, across natural and social sciences, making strong interdisciplinary or transdisciplinary research and education challenging (Max Neef 2005), and speaking to the need to train a new generation of academics and researchers able to cross these divides. Such differences are mirrored in different investigatory and educational models across these arenas (e.g. hypothetico-deductive versus grounded methodologies) and explain why learners can benefit from explicit explanation of interdisciplinary processes when learning in interdisciplinary programmes. Increasingly, we see attempts at co-production of knowledge. In the context of sustainability research, co-production can be defined as 'Iterative and collaborative processes involving diverse types of expertise, knowledge and actors to produce context-specific knowledge and pathways towards a sustainable future' (Norström *et al.* 2020). These authors suggest that the impetus for co-production comes from both a descriptive goal, a more effective joint outcome through collaboration, and a normative goal, a shift towards society accepting and incorporating a plurality of perspectives. They propose that successful co-production should thus be pluralistic, but also context-based, goal-oriented and interactive. Bennich *et al.* (2022) argue that transdisciplinary research is particularly useful at the project scoping stage. They recommend interviewing appropriate stakeholders before even setting research questions. Such scoping can help develop causal loop diagrams: identify linkages between different parts of sustainability systems as a way to tackle them holistically; and map gaps in knowledge.

The emphasis of sustainability research has thus shifted from producing technical solutions towards a 'social resolution' of problems through participatory processes, social learning and co-production among academic and non-academic participants (Funtowicz *et al.* 1998, p. 104). The arts and humanities are critical in enabling imaginaries and facilitating creative forms of co-production and transdisciplinarity (Kagan 2018). The processes of mobilising knowledge are reflective and self-reflexive, generating new senses of self-awareness that are linked to learning (White 2013). Hence, research and education are intertwined in mutual learning journeys. Sustainable development is well suited to this model of academia, since it is not merely about producing solutions but also about transformational change, equity across groups of people and pursuit of 'the common good' rather than merely private and commercial interests (Hadorn *et al.* 2006). Transdisciplinary contexts thus shift perceptions of knowledge as being suites of 'value-neutral objective truth' (Hadorn *et al.* 2006) towards a constructivist view of scientific knowledge that has value associated with its social relevance (Funtowicz and Ravetz 1993; Nowotny *et al.* 2001) – indeed, a 'post-normal science' (Funtowicz and Ravetz 1993).

Transdisciplinary research that recognises a multiplicity of voices for the delivery of sustainability has deep resonance with efforts to 'decolonise the curriculum'. This challenging initiative requires thinking deeply about and redressing the damage caused by western scientific models to people and their environments in developing countries. This involves foregrounding minority and silent voices that have been marginalised due to colonial and Westernised enlightenment thinking. Indigenous and traditional knowledge forms need to be respected and included in sustainability solutions (Mardero *et al.* 2023). Fortress conservation, which involved setting aside nature reserves, for example, was a well-meaning science-driven attempt to protect wildlife, but it had negative consequences, including cutting Indigenous peoples off from their life support systems, destroying cultures and causing more damage from poaching and tolerated game sports (Siurua 2006).

Environmental injustices, race and class are tightly interwoven (Pellow 2000), and it must be recognised that they are perpetuated by some forms of education and research and left unchallenged by others. It is important to address equality, diversity and inclusivity issues in sustainability research (Rowe and Schuster-Wallace 2023). Not only is this ethical, but it also leads to better outcomes by enabling different voices.

Despite recognition of the importance of transdisciplinary research, it remains marginalised as an academic priority due to the structure of many university systems (the separation of academics into subject-specific departments and faculties, the ongoing dominance of subject-specific degree offerings, subject silos, research monitoring exercises and norms of scientific journals with limited areas of expertise) as well as the challenges of achieving it in practice (e.g. Miller *et al.* 2011; White 2013). Transdisciplinary studies are challenging because of different languages and scientific/disciplinary practices, different conceptual frameworks, working across different perspectives and different ideas of its purpose. For example, they enable us to scope out a research area by way of problem definition, to generate systematic knowledge, and to implement knowledge in meaningful ways. There are also challenges and tensions around how engaging it needs to be to practitioners and to what extent it needs to be oriented towards particular forms of 'impact' (Brandt *et al.* 2013; and see discussion below). Results may not emerge in expected formats and can sit dormant whilst waiting for publication in peer reviewed literature. Ultimately, in addition to these practical and epistemological issues, transdisciplinary approaches are difficult because they are not merely about tweaking methods but rather they envisage a new education-innovation system with universities as their big driver (Hadorn *et al.* 2006). We now explore aspects of innovation for sustainability.

### *Socio-ecological Innovation*

Knowledge is critical for social innovation (Gibbons *et al.* 1994) and universities should be major contributors (Hadorn *et al.* 2006). Social innovation has been understood in different contexts but can usefully be defined as being 'A novel solution to a social problem that is more effective, efficient, sustainable or just than existing solutions and for which the value created accrues primarily to society as a whole rather than private individuals' (Phills *et al.* 2008, p. 36). Social innovation is a process and not only an output, because of its intended participatory nature (Arocena and Sutz 2021).

Social innovation is required within our institutions to enable them to change (Miller *et al.* 2011), but our higher education institutions also need to stimulate social innovation in local communities and wider society. Sustainable development explicitly addresses inter-and intra-generational justice as well as environmental conservation; hence, social innovation can help address poverty and inequality (Posch and Steiner 2006). Partnerships between universities, communities and other actors can go beyond social innovation to generate socio-ecological innovation (social change occurring within environmental limits) and leverage sustainability transitions (White and van Koten 2016). Knowledge and practice innovation can address social and environmental problems (Posch and Steiner 2006), but there is sometimes a tendency for universities to emphasise economic forms of innovation.

Universities can stimulate regional economies, firstly through direct impacts of employment and the provision of services for a university population and, secondly, via innovation, the growth of the local knowledge economy and development of a learning region (Karatzoglou 2013). If such economic stimulation supports more sustainable economies, such as sharing or circular models, this is in line with ESD and sustainability research, but if it exacerbates extractive, inequitable models of capitalism, or focuses on only economic dimensions of engagement, this can be problematic. Indeed, a focus mainly on economic aspects of innovation has been critiqued from the Global South. Arocena and Sutz (2021) point out that universities tend to concentrate knowledge generation activities, and that this concentration is more prominent in today's knowledge-based capitalist society. They call for universities that promote development with inclusive and frugal innovation, aligning well with the notion of the community or civic university. They suggest that all universities can learn from forms of social innovation that are directed to a particular cause or tackle as yet unknown goals; that are value-oriented, whether radical or mainstream in focus. Universities in the Global North often lead on national needs, but South universities exhibit good capacities to hold endogenous research knowledge.

There are a number of different approaches that have been identified to develop social innovation and transdisciplinary knowledge using co-production in responsible research innovation approaches (Wakunuma *et al.* 2021). These include capital-oriented approaches which are competitive, driven by policy makers, and not fully inclusive, and livelihood-oriented approaches which are usually less techno-economic, and are context-based, draw on informal and community-based organisations, and inclusive policies. The focus and form of such innovation can be driven via democratic processes for the common good, but power asymmetry can divert benefits to existing elites. Wakunuma *et al.* (2021) suggest that sustainable development requires an integrated version of these perspectives in all countries to enable marginalised voices to be heard, to address inequalities and to include local as well as global concerns. The Wellcome Trust Concordat for the Environmental Sustainability of Research and Innovation Practice is a recent practical effort to enhance research responsibility (see Box 8.1).

**Box 8.1 Universities Are Seeking to Enhance the Sustainability of Research Operations**

University College London (UCL), for example, has committed itself to being a single-use plastic free campus by 2023. It writes on its website that:

> UCL will not consume or purchase any non-essential single-use plastics on campus by 2024. This includes recyclable plastics, compostable plastics and hygiene plastics, e.g., hand sanitiser. Essential single-use plastics which currently have no accessible, safe or sustainable alternatives will still be used at UCL, but will be optimised and reduced (https://www.ucl.ac.uk/sustainable/staff/plastic-free-ucl).

Leeds University also made a pledge, in 2019, to become plastic free by 2023. The success rate was hampered by COVID-19, but there has been some degree of success: single use bags have been eliminated from all procurement processing, laboratories have sourced multiple-use plastic weighing boats and petri-dishes, the University has adopted the use of glass syringes, and reusable cups and face-masks have also been heavily promoted (https://sustainability.leeds.ac.uk/news/2023plasticfree-the-story-so-far/).

Social innovation, and more so socio-ecological innovation, can thus be undertaken to support sustainability transitions and transform local and international practices. There is learning across Global South and North to ensure that we develop locally relevant and globally inclusive research with ontological plurality, that focuses on sustainability issues and does not merely support economic growth. Finally, piecemeal social innovation efforts may be contradictory or partial, and socio-ecological innovation should be combined with wider systems perspectives such as the multi-level perspective (a framework for sustainability transition) to enable a more holistic effort (Arocena and Sutz 2021). We now explore the benefits of systems thinking in knowledge for sustainability.

### *Systems Thinking in Sustainability Research*

Universities need to transcend their mono-disciplinary research projects and adopt a paradigm shift that enables a holistic, problem-solving approach through inter- and transdisciplinarity and systems thinking (Posch and Steiner 2006). Sustainability research is often holistic, using systems thinking to locate and link research questions, processes and outputs. Systems thinking helps people to break out of conventional belief systems by seeing the bigger picture. Without recognising links between different parts of a system, solutions-oriented sustainability research is at risk of generating new and unanticipated problems. For example, much of the dialogue and focus on 'smart city' initiatives as solutions for addressing sustainability challenges in cities, predominantly focus on the role of digital technology and may deliver 'smartness' (technological linkages) more than the green outcomes they are purported to address (Kutty *et al.* 2020). By thinking through and beyond issues inherent in business-as-usual models, we can reveal that current policy approaches tend to provide short-term gain to small proportions of the population at the risk of longer-term failure for a majority (Garrity 2018). Systems thinking can help us work towards providing both short-term and longer-term solutions. Systems thinking also helps to address the complexity of sustainability wicked problems (Rittel and Webber 1973; Buchanan 1992) and the uncertainty inherent in multi-faceted, multi-stakeholder issues.

### *Moral and Ethical Concerns of Sustainability Research*

The complexities of doing research in partnership with others require moral, ethical and practical considerations (White 2013). For example, holistic, transdisciplinary research on sustainability does not lend itself to straightforward ethics protocols, because the research can unfold in unexpected directions and the researcher needs to be open to the inputs of non-academic partners, or the different positionalities of the researcher themselves. Likewise, it can be paradoxical to target outcomes and estimate numerical outputs when a researcher is focusing on participatory, flexible modes of action research (White 2004).

The positionality of sustainability researchers also needs attention when considering moral and ethical challenges. In sustainability research, researchers may have multiple roles and act the part as practitioners as well as researcher. Such mixed roles and identities are referred to variably in different literature as 'pracademics' (e.g. Panda 2014), practitioner-researchers (e.g. Heikkinen *et al.* 2016) or scholar-activists (Derickson and Routledge 2015). In many cases, the literature on these hybrid identities focuses on particular professions, such as architecture or education, where research becomes embedded into practice. For many ESD researchers, they may likely have this dual role even if they do not explicitly identify as such, as both practitioner and researcher. Where the 'practitioner-researcher' role extends beyond academia, these roles may provide important 'boundary spanning' contributions (Panda 2014) helping ensure the wider impact of sustainability research. The 'insider' positionality of such roles provides useful perspectives to research, alongside ethical and moral dilemmas around the boundaries between practice and research, and research participants and consent.

Other moral and ethical concerns may include the nature of partners involved in transdisciplinary research (e.g. oil and gas companies, who may engage researchers in green transition technology research), how research outputs are used and by whom, how the time and inputs of community-based researchers is compensated, and the moral imperative to ensure publication and dissemination of research funded by public bodies and contribute to by the wider public (to avoid becoming a knowledge 'sink'). As part of the quest for 'useful' research, it is especially important for research resources to be made openly available to scholars in developing countries to improve the quality of education and research (Kanwar *et al.* 2010).

### *Operational Sustainability of Sustainability Research*

The sustainability of operational aspects of research is under increased scrutiny and pressure (Hugé *et al.* 2016; Menon and Suresh 2020; Box 8.2). Research activities themselves can generate immediate, unsustainable impacts, such as plastic waste, the energy use of vast computer servers as well as the rather brutal human resource consequences on gig economy researchers. Academics and conference organisers are being asked to consider the impacts of travel, in terms of carbon and finance, but also wider accessibility and inclusivity issues (yet promotion criteria may still reference the need to demonstrate international standing and networks, difficult to achieve without international travel). Whitmarsh *et al.* (2020) ironically found that climate change researchers fly more than other researchers, which raises some difficult questions and needs to be considered against benefits and forms of global fieldwork and cooperation. Academic work has traditionally included substantial travel (Baer 2019). Some funders demand or support sustainable travel for data collection, such as train travel, which can be more expensive than flying over medium distances, and takes longer, hence needing to be placed within increasingly time pressured academic life, alongside personal life pressures. The use of more sustainable resources, such as reduction of single-use plastics and energy efficient and environmentally friendly practices in laboratories, is encouraged in some institutions. Many universities are working on the challenge of generating sustainable laboratories.

Whilst the reduction in paperwork (paper and printing) and increase in online processes is seen by some to be more sustainable, there is increasing realisation of the energy, space and resource costs of information technology and associated massive servers. In the words of Natalie Pollard:

> Online meetings, streamings, and purchases rely on vast racks of plugged-in, stationary servers, situated in real places across the planet. These huge data farms are connected across continents via submarine fiber-optic cables (Starosielski 4). It is not a cloud but these cables—snaking beneath the oceans—that carry 99 percent of global Internet communications.
>
> (Pollard 2022, p.1)

**Box 8.2 Concordat for the Environmental Sustainability of Research and Innovation Practice**

The voluntary 'Concordat for Environmental Sustainability of Research and Innovation Practice' co-developed by the Wellcome Trust in consultation with the UK research and innovation sector was launched in the UK in 2024 to address the sustainability implications of research delivery, and change the way we conduct research to achieve a transition to sustainable practices. The Concordat goes beyond the oft discussed issues of academic travel to consider infrastructure and equipment sharing. The Concordat covers six areas: leadership and system change; sustainable infrastructure, sustainable procurement, emissions from business and academic travel, collaborations and partnerships, environmental impact and reporting data. The launch of the Concordat, along with creating a new focus on improving the sustainability of research practices, provides an additional route to consider research connections with ESD and the need to ensure that undergraduate and postgraduate learners, from the start of their research careers, consider and work to mitigate the negative sustainability impacts of their research (see: https://wellcome.org/who-we-are/positions-and-statements/environmental-sustainability-concordat).

In fact, we have seen talk of 'data furnaces', when data centres acknowledge and marketise the excess heat produced by servers. This emphasises their extreme energy use (and inefficiencies) but also the potential for waste heat recovery, where servers can be farmed out to heat office or residential buildings (Judge 2014).

**Box 8.3 Transdisciplinary Research Generating Multiple Forms of Impact**

One of the authors of this chapter (CS) led the Arts and Humanities Research Council funded Designing a Sensibility for Sustainable Clothing project. This project drew on social practice theory, co-created design and the theory of affect to encourage more sustainable clothing choices. In tune with practice theory, we provided participants with the stuff (e.g. fabric, sewing machines, thread, scissors), the competence (we taught them skills in making and mending clothes) and meaningful networks of new friends to encourage pro-environmental change over a series of 40 one-day workshops with skilled instructors. Following social design principles, the workshops were co-created with input from the 40 participants, allowing them to have a say in shaping their own experiences. The theory of affect was used to recognise, celebrate and work with the emotional connections that people have with their clothing. Our work found that making, mending and modifying workshops had a significant impact on the sustainability of participants' clothing choices. They tended to purchase fewer new items, to make more careful purchasing decisions with quality fibres and to develop new senses of identity by being brave at developing their own styles with individualised forms of clothing (West *et al.* 2021; Willett *et al.* 2022; Saunders *et al.* 2024).

*Knowledge Management*

The relationship between research, teaching and practice is important, and we need to enhance knowledge management processes in universities for sustainability outcomes. Knowledge management includes the management of integrated activities and processes associated with knowledge production, codification, storage, sharing and utilisation (Demir *et al.* 2023 in Budur *et al.* 2024). The concept and practice gained traction in the 1990s as a way to enhance intra-organisational knowledge flow and increase external impact whilst adding value to knowledge generated (Martins *et al.* 2019). Whilst it is seen to reflect integrated and collaborative processes (Martins *et al.* 2019), the economic focus of early efforts means that some universities still appear to emphasise the economic gains from knowledge management rather than wider sustainability goals. A sustainable development perspective shifts the focus of knowledge management from economic gain to wider social and environmental benefits (Martins *et al.* 2019). At the same time, active knowledge management is crucial to ensure that knowledge production, exchange and implementation for sustainability occurs (Budur *et al.* 2024). Enhanced knowledge management for sustainability in universities could generate positive outcomes. These could include improved operational sustainability within the institution; ESD of learners and of other university staff, including researchers; co-production and implementation of knowledge regionally with relevant stakeholders; and a novel research and teaching agenda for innovation for sustainability (Karatzoglou 2013). Networks and alliances with the relevant regional stakeholders are strengthened via RCEs in ESD (Karatzoglou 2013).

Such knowledge management includes tacit and explicit knowledge (Budur *et al.* 2024). Research engagement and action on real-world issues may require a multi-level approach that is not mediated only by a central technology transfer office, and that recognises the ways in which external engagement goes beyond commercial partnerships with industry firms. It would thus involve interaction with the third sector to address non-financially beneficial sustainability challenges (Knudsen *et al.* 2021). These authors suggest an ecosystem model in which research competence is leveraged to interact with local and global issues, rather than a commercial transfer of technology or knowledge as in recent university commercialisation frameworks. Developing countries tend to have less well-honed knowledge management processes (Budur *et al.* 2024) and more quantitative and rigorous monitoring and evaluation are required (Karatzoglou 2013). Further research is required to explore how university governance can enable collaborative approaches to most effectively exchange knowledge for sustainable development and other societal needs (Broström *et al.* 2021). This may include consideration of the implications of more centralised approaches to partner management including increased resilience to partnerships if academic staff leave, but is a step removed from the 'on-the-ground' relationships needed to connect the curriculum and research with partners, versus the more individual academic-focused approach to working with partners, which builds on trusted relationships between individuals, but are less resilient to changes in staffing, or broadening new opportunities from partnerships.

Staff training in universities can enhance knowledge management for sustainability (Budur *et al.* 2024). Knowledge production and exchange requires staff to acquire or strengthen social competences to develop relationships and processes with appropriate stakeholders (Posch and Steiner 2006). However, not all academics can shine in all areas of activity (teaching, research, impact, administration) and Brand and Karvonen (2007) define an 'ecosystem of expertise' required for these different aspects of research. They suggest that different people will have strengths in interdisciplinarity, technical implementation of knowledge, public deliberation or other aspects. However, as is the case of practitioner-researchers/pracademics/scholar-activists (see above), researchers can also hold several concurrent roles.

### *Knowledge Mobilisation and the Impact Agenda*

The field of knowledge management is often framed as supporting universities to maximise transfer of their research for their benefit as well as benefit of their regions. However, there has been an increasing call for universities to be accountable to external state and private funding by achieving and demonstrating 'impact'. The 'impact agenda' in higher education requires scholars to consider the utility of their research for society. This agenda has been evolving in universities in the UK and Australia since the early 2010s and is reflected in research quality assessment exercises, in specific funding calls and in altered expectations. The concept of research impact aligns with some of the sustainability research attributes outlined above, in that it encourages engagement with real-world issues and external stakeholders. Aspects of this impact drive are thus welcome for sustainability research, as it encourages universities to participate in the innovation knowledge shift for a sustainability transformation and pushes towards transdisciplinary approaches. The positive consequences of this agenda are that it encourages more challenge-focused research with greater emphasis on co-design and interdisciplinarity as well as diverse modes of knowledge exchange. Different forms of knowledge production have been described, with Mode 1 knowledge production focusing on the development of traditional disciplinary contributions and Mode 2 being reflexive, accountable and participatory, and in which knowledge originates from reflecting on or tackling real-world problems, not those that arise from disciplines (Gibbons *et al.* 1994; Nowotny *et al.* 2001; Hessels and Van Lente 2008). Impact on disciplinary development is stronger in Mode 1 research, which is perceived to be a safer home for a risk-averse or career-focused academic. Impact on the sustainability of society is likely to be more significant from Mode 2 research (Rau *et al.* 2018), and may become more significant over time as we train a new generation of academics and the systems of reward and recognition slowly start to shift.

The impact agenda is also changing as academics have started to think more creatively about cultural and societal impacts (Chubb and Reed 2017). Some projects, for example, generate impact on the public via sensibilities of sustainability, drawing on behaviour change theory to encourage people to think, feel and act in more environmentally sustainable ways. These were initially not recognised as important impacts, unlike new products and services or new laws or policies, but are crucial to achieving sustainability. Whilst impact was initially defined in narrow frames around economic benefits, wider impact frameworks have now been realised. Impact can be instrumental, conceptual, policy related, connective, capacitive or relational (Meagher *et al.* 2008), and includes cultural, social and environmental as well as economic impacts.

There are, however, potential negative aspects to the impact agenda. A neoliberal underpinning to impact seeks particular kinds of measurable, economic impact rather than a holistic contribution to support the common good. The first iterations of impact were symptomatic of an overly marketised university system. There has also been some resistance to the 'impact agenda' because of the way it challenges epistemological purity

(Smith *et al.* 2020). In addition, not all impacts will support a more sustainable world; as we noted above, knowledge outputs can actually be destructive (Orr 1994; Sterling 2001), and it remains unclear how negative impacts of research are captured in current evaluation exercises. However, researchers are increasingly coming to terms with the more nuanced 'impact agenda', and this will continue to develop with suitable funding and promotion incentivisation and through new generations of, and perhaps even a 'new type' of academic. Academics are keen to demonstrate that their work has some value, even though this may be harder for scholars in some areas than others. Those in the environmental humanities may struggle to explain to others the value of their work more than scholars in environmental engineering, for example, in a society which preferentially celebrates scientific endeavours.

Whilst universities still need to engage more in epistemological pluralism and reflexivity (Miller *et al.* 2011), we can see that sustainability research is shifting towards Mode 2 (Gibbons *et al.* 1994), transdisciplinary, forms of knowledge co-production, exchange and impact, with different possible roles for researchers within the required ecosystem of expertise (Brand and Karvonen 2007). Crucially, for this Chapter, we see such research as a form of social, mutual and problem-based relational learning in which divisions between research and education are blurred. We now explore some of the specific areas of overlap between research, teaching and practice (also see Chapter 3).

### *Challenges for Sustainability Research*

There are a number of challenges in undertaking sustainability research, some of which we touched on in the sections above. First, it often addresses, or it could be argued *must* address, complex, unpredictable, real-world challenges. Second, it is often, although not always, transdisciplinary, or at least interdisciplinary, drawing on appropriate knowledge paradigms and processes to address the relevant challenge. Third, it requires critical

#### Box 8.4 Community engagement through the Civic University Network

One example of how community engagement can be promoted is the Civic University Network (civicuniversitynetwork.co.uk), which is encouraging universities to do this work through focusing on places, publics, partnerships and impacts. The commitment to place ensures that universities work with their local communities to prioritise economic, social, environmental and cultural life. The work involves publics in ensuring that the work universities do is informed by the voice of local communities. Wider partnerships are used to help communities to overcome specific challenges they face and impact is measured in a way that helps understanding what has been achieved, and how things can continue to be improved. Currently, in the UK, the following Universities have published Civic Partnership Agreements: Sheffield Hallam, Newcastle, the five universities in Manchester, the two universities in Nottingham, the two universities in Southampton, Goldsmiths, Exeter, Sheffield, Lincoln, Keele, Queen Mary, Derby and Leicestershire and Rutland.

questioning of the normative and moral framing of the research. Fourth, it needs to navigate the practical structures of academic funding, publication, impact and reward. Within such structures, individual researchers must navigate plural identities of researcher, practitioner and/or activist. These challenges are unpacked, but not fully resolved, below.

Addressing real-world challenges may initially seem straightforward. However, sustainability research requires that academics consider the boundaries and wider implications of their research. For example, research in chemistry to enhance battery storage capability could also consider sources of rare metals and the processes and human rights issues relating to their extraction and transport. This may provide a rationale for research (i.e. to provide alternatives) or contribute to unanticipated negative consequences (new areas of extractions and human exploitation). Interdisciplinary or transdisciplinary research requires the integration of different disciplines in the framing and pursuit of particular research questions and an intentional systems thinking lens to consider less visible consequences and implications.

Transdisciplinary research, as discussed above, requires sustainability researchers to work across disciplines and with other actors, such as policymakers, community members or private sector representatives. If the disciplines span an ontological or epistemological divide, this presents fundamental issues such as the way that reality is seen to be constructed (Burrell and Morgan 1979). Mixed methods research is often appropriate to address real-world problems, using quantitative methods to explore patterns and consequences, and qualitative methods to gain rich, deep understanding of human actions. To engage with other actors, academics must learn how to facilitate dialogical processes, how to undertake stakeholder analyses and even how to manage conflicts. This deepens the need for a meaningful engagement with ontology and epistemology, as well as practical methodological skills. For example, working across very different perspectives, such as those offered by Indigenous Peoples, demands a sophisticated ontological flexibility, along with respectful and rigorous data collection and interpretation. Researchers need to strengthen their normative, collaborative, interdisciplinary and self-awareness competencies to develop ontological maturity, appreciation of different perspectives and the ability to work with conflict rather than being threatened by it. This process may evoke difficult emotions, where identities are challenged. Traversing knowledge paradigms can be personally as well as professionally challenging.

When undertaking sustainability research, we are not merely answering a list of questions on the latest research agenda. We are critically and concurrently assessing moral, social and environmental issues. In this way, academics need to strengthen the ethical and moral frameworks of sustainability research and other knowledge activities (see Peters and Wals 2013; Chubb and Reed 2017; Miller *et al.* 2011). A systems approach is also needed, but the complexity can be overwhelming when researchers first explore research for sustainable development. We have to appreciate global drivers, whilst focusing on contextualised local issues.

Next, academia has a structural and procedural framework that can inhibit sustainability research within or across disciplines. The tighter coupling of universities as organisations has led to efficiencies and accountability measures with positive and negative consequences (Broström *et al.* 2021). It is good that increased transparency supports academics and learners who may have been overlooked in prior nepotistic and network-based decision-making. Women, non-binary gendered individuals, ethnic minorities and those of lower socioeconomic status may now have more opportunities than previously. Universities can now not only recognise different systems of privilege and disadvantage but also consider how they interact. Health, citizenship status, sexuality, gender, race, class and other markers of privilege and disadvantage are interconnecting and not standalone categories. Universities must thus engender respect for intersectionality as well as develop strategies to mitigate the resultant power differentials (Roth 2020). Yet despite these positive developments, many academics are still severely constrained by time, and manage high workloads (Dowd and Kaplan 2005; White 2014; Fetherston *et al.* 2021), and therefore, the research system continues to privilege those with the flexibility to carry out research outside of their contracted working hours.

Research rewards for the individual academic have tended to be for discipline-specific journals, mainstream funding grants and quantitative metrics of citation, research graduates and income. Income metrics tend to be deemed more important than the purpose or impact of research, perhaps, as they are so much easier to measure, or perhaps because this reflects the increasing marketisation of universities. Rewards for institutions have often been within discipline boundaries, such as the Research Excellence Framework of UK. Interdisciplinary and collaborative research and pedagogies that traverse learning and research, disciplinary norms, academic and non-academic actors can take more time, and require additional attributes, such as the capacity to develop relationships and trust (White *et al.* 2023). Research that impacts local communities and the university region requires staff to build and maintain trusted relationships in those areas, and therefore necessitates a culture that encourages such academics to stay in the same institution, rather than need to seek advancement through movement to another institution.

Despite these challenges, there are some ways in which sustainability research is being supported. For example, a growing list of interdisciplinary journals are seeking to encourage innovative research that is broadly around sustainability, or more focused on particular topics. The impact agenda can be employed productively. Some funders are promoting individual or collaborative interdisciplinary funding schemes. The Research Excellence Framework in UK encourages narratives around interdisciplinarity, even if it is not yet clear how this will be assessed in future.

**Box 8.5 Examples of sustainability facing journals.**

Sustainability facing journals are interdisciplinary or encourage practitioner voice, e.g., *The Journal of Transdisciplinary Environmental Studies*. The latter states that it is

> an international journal that focuses on transdisciplinary environmental studies of relevance to planning and regulation.__The target group of the Journal encompasses both academic scholars and practicing professionals. The focus of the journal is on environmental issues, especially articles integrating the natural and social sciences in the field of environmental management and planning. Consequently, we will emphasise theory, methodology, and practical experience in transdisciplinarity relevant to these areas.

We also start to see an increase in journals encouraging the 'practitioner' voice, for example, Local Environment.

### Research-Led Teaching and Teaching-Led Research

At universities, we are expected to offer research-led teaching, in which our own research areas, traditions and results inspire and inform our teaching and mentor learners to become researchers. However, we also see in many institutions a separation of responsibilities between research and teaching that is reflected in separate research and teaching contract routes. ESD can be enhanced if we can draw on our own experiences of sustainability research or discipline-based research, or our experiences as practitioner-researchers, to do this. The contested nature of some debates in sustainability research can create an exciting but potentially difficult context for ESD. For example, traditional macroeconomics research may seek to maximise economic growth, but in ESD, learners are encouraged to critically interrogate an economic growth paradigm and consider alternatives such as circular and shared economies or degrowth.

Despite many scholars identifying as systems-thinkers in their research, there is still a gap in systems-level teaching at universities. Many academics still tend to think in linear terms and lack awareness of the complexity of dynamic systems. Effective ESD that traverses systems often needs to be interdisciplinary, involving psychology, sociology, political science, law and the humanities as much as natural science, engineering and technological science (Voulvoulis *et al.* 2022). Teaching programmes struggle to add such breadth and depth with constrained timetables and benchmark requirements. Increased breadth at the expense of depth raises concerns for some about how 'generalism' is valued compared to specialism, in a society that glorifies the specialist. These concerns possibly reduce the appeal for some learners of broader, systems-framed degrees, such as those focused on sustainability, while also challenging the sustainability researcher, who in connecting with disciplines beyond their own expertise, exists forever in a state of discomfort, whilst always learning.

Teaching-led research can also support our academic framing of sustainable development (Posch and Steiner 2006). When teaching, we are often required to read more widely or more specifically about particular topics on the edge of our research experience; we are forced to articulate our ideas clearly to a new and non-specialist audience; we engage in discussion with learners and sometimes other stakeholders in new ways. This process can also lead to new research ideas and projects. The critical engagement with learners around topics such as economic growth, for example, may feed back into and shape the framing of this topic in research proposals. Increasingly, universities are recruiting international learners, allowing us to hear a diversity of voices that might facilitate holistic problem definition and generate systems-thinking questions and research projects together.

### Research on ESD

There has been much greater research in and on ESD over the past decade, with many more academics identifying as sustainability scholars or sustainability scientists and with an increase in the number of degree programmes focusing partially or entirely on sustainable development. Subject benchmark statements in UK now require inclusion of ESD in teaching programmes (Price *et al.* 2021). Recognition of pedagogical research in higher education is increasing, with more education focused lecturer tracks and encouragement of early career staff to do qualifications in teaching at Higher Education, often including some ESD. It is thus useful and logical for staff to rigorously evaluate impacts of ESD interventions. However, those for whom ESD is not their discipline face challenges because the system of rating and rewarding research in the UK is still disciplinary-focused; therefore, ESD and interdisciplinary sustainability-focused research may not be seen as being of equal merit (Bessant and Robinson 2019). At times, these authors observed active discouragement of ESD research, in preference for more traditional disciplinary-focused research. In Chapter 13, we identify potential rich future areas of research for ESD.

### *Teaching Sustainability Research*

Teaching sustainability research, for example, within Honours research methods or dissertation classes, is an area of ESD that is rarely discussed. As outlined above, sustainability research can be challenging for academics, and these challenges can be exacerbated for the academics teaching sustainability research, and even more so for learners, within their short timeframe and defined curriculum. It takes time and effort for staff and learners to engage in real-world problems and with external stakeholders, particularly when educators are given lower 'work load allocations' for teaching preparation and delivery. Yet connecting learners with real-world problems to explore learning in sustainability research is both immensely rewarding and necessary to develop a new generation of researchers and ethically minded and responsible practitioners. While not without its challenges, when undertaken effectively, bringing together learners and external stakeholders can help understand and address local challenges whilst learning about and contributing to a more sustainable society (Brundiers and Wiek 2011).

It is appropriate that procedures in teaching are subject to stringent audit. However, the commodification of education, extreme managerial processes and audit and funding mechanisms can cause difficulties for transdisciplinary, real-world knowledge production by learners. Universities seek to market themselves and to head up league tables, and they court learner satisfaction metrics that can promote short-term gains to the failure of independent deep learning. The sort of transdisciplinary learning that can lead to transformative learning and subsequent personal and societal change is supported by authentic, collaborative pedagogies (Chapter 6) and assessments (Chapter 7). When learners prioritise grades or effort ratios, such learning environments are not always appreciated by learners at the time and can lead to lower articulated metrics of satisfaction. The commodification of education can also bias resources and attention towards teaching programmes with high market potential or perceived economic gain, and lead to neglect of arts and humanities. In addition, bureaucratic procedures and resource constraints can stifle more time intensive innovative pedagogies or limit fieldtrips and experiential learning opportunities.

Teaching sustainability research has the potential to become a component of every departmental research training, from art history to zoology, or it may remain focused within sustainable development degrees. All learners of all disciplines could have the opportunity to consider their roles as sustainability researchers, and this could be encouraged as more staff see their own disciplinary research contributions through the lens of sustainability, modelling disciplinary contributions to sustainability and developing confidence in supervising learners in this area. In addition, explicit requirements for learners to consider the sustainability relevance and implications of their research projects, as well as connections with sustainability-focused research institutes, networks or programmes such as those designed to support ESD across a university will all strengthen the training of emerging sustainability researchers.

Specific pedagogies can support learning of sustainability research. For example, social design can be used in the classroom: introducing learners to a general idea and letting them explore it in their own ways (rather like the S4S project on clothing mentioned earlier, but with learners rather than members of the general public). In this way, education can generate individualised and therefore meaningful sensibilities for sustainability. Approaches such as the Living Lab, in which learners engage in local projects, can be advantageous for learners to investigate campus operations, to engage with communities or to evaluate sustainability action locally (Jain *et al.* 2013). Supporting sustainability scientists and engineers in practical activities with real-world contexts and stakeholder engagement can help to broaden learners' perspectives and developed communication and leadership capacities and competencies (Roy *et al.* 2020). In these examples, learners have reported enjoying such learning, as well as achieving learning outcomes.

We have seen in previous chapters how ESD is not merely learning *about* the acquisition of information about sustainable development but also learning *for it*, and the building of competencies to enable graduates to develop their potential and have a positive impact on the world. Teaching sustainability research is ultimately about building the capacities of learners to ask interesting questions of the world, to interrogate those questions with normative sensitivity, intellectual agility, ethical rigour and the capacity to work with others, and position their interpretations within a systemic, global as well as specific, local context. Teaching sustainability research thus aligns naturally with a competencies approach. It can also inspire learners with a sense of agency and better prepare them to be change agents when they graduate (Brundiers and Wiek 2011).

## Doctoral Research for Sustainable Development

The practice and research of ESD has been dominated by a focus on undergraduate learners. PhD learner identities lie in the fuzzy, and often overlooked world, between learners, staff and independent researcher, with different levels of support and integration into wider university life dependent on learner, supervisor, institution and funding streams. We see a growing cohort of PhD learners who are engaging specifically with sustainability research, but whatever the area of research, within PhD programmes, there are many opportunities to support them through ESD and to ensure that, as these doctoral students begin to teach, they adopt ESD practices and principles.

Embedding ESD in doctoral research programmes presents similar educational questions to that of ESD for undergraduates: To what extent should sustainability research be within every doctoral programme or seen as a separate learning opportunity? How do we integrate across formal and non-formal modes of learning and specific and within discipline modes of sustainability research support? We are now seeing some options to undertake doctoral studies (PhD) in sustainable development or a closely related topic, celebration of sustainability research through university or regional initiatives, interest within disciplines and opportunities for doctoral students to attend workshops or conferences on sustainability research. Some provision is dependent on supervisor and learner research interests and funding and can thus differ extensively in format, although we also see training on sustainability implications of research embedded into PhD training programmes irrespective of subject. Some interdisciplinary doctoral programmes and projects have been developed, for example, cross-School scholarships at University of St Andrews and the interdisciplinary programme of the Scottish Graduate School of Social Sciences. An example of an interdisciplinary doctoral programme is the Sustainable Futures programme in Penryn at the University of Exeter.

There are different opinions as to whether a PhD should be interdisciplinary or not, with some academics supporting proficiency in one area and others promoting early flexibility in thinking and an ability to work across disciplines. Learning whilst doing a doctorate can be enhanced through dialogue across university structures, facilitated by networks or clusters. Institutional or regional centres in doctoral training can support ESD in the form of teaching sustainability and sustainability research. There is a range of internships available, with policy or private sector, to enable doctoral students to understand how to produce or translate research for policy makers or practitioners, some of which focus on sustainability. This increasing number of opportunities with government, NGO or industry during doctoral programmes is facilitating a new generation of doctoral graduates with better understanding of partner needs and processes.

We suggest that all doctoral research needs to consider what kind of future we want and how to best get there, to some extent. Not all doctoral students stay in academia, but those who do emerge as the new generation of academics, and are thus worth significant focus and investment to leverage progress in the future of ESD and sustainability research. Others will take their knowledge, skills and capacities into other sectors and be able to promote sustainability transitions from different positions.

## Integrated Knowledge Generation, Exchange and Implementation

We have discussed knowledge generation, flows and management within research and across some of the blurred areas between research and teaching for sustainability. We now consider how ESD can both stimulate and benefit from an integrated approach across teaching, research and practice.

Such integration can be achieved, for example, through the use of sustainability research results to frame theories and methods for case study teaching, or through the possibilities for new research prompted by continuous reflection on interaction with regional stakeholders through teaching activities (Posch and Steiner 2006), as discussed above. However, Posch and Steiner (2006) warn that such integration does not happen automatically. They call for 'goal-oriented systematic action' (Posch and Steiner 2006, p. 289) with commitment throughout the institution, adaptation of curricula and pedagogies and highly motivated and trained staff.

ESD influences sustainability science and sustainability research partly through its emphasis on self-awareness and individual behaviours, and the role of learning and key competences in this process (Barth and Michelsen 2013). These authors also suggest that the importance of education for societal change is enabled partly through social learning mediated forms of organisational change. Thirdly, they propose that learning about inter- and transdisciplinary approaches in learning and education contexts can inform such processes in research contexts, partly through situated learning, development of communities of practice and conflict management when perspectives differ widely.

It has been argued that an integrated approach to sustainability education, research and practice demands a new 'relational paradigm' (Walsh *et al.* 2021). This means exploring relationships and interactions across and within systems. This is another way of rejecting the idea of technocratic solutions that only address certain parts of the system. Walsh *et al.* (2021) propose relational ontologies, relational epistemologies and relational ethics to collectively explore our assumptions about the world, how we know the world and what we feel to be morally right in the world. Relational thinking negates some of the binary divisions in our perspectives. For example, rather than seeing social and ecological dimensions of sustainable development as being separate, relational approaches explore processes and relationships (West *et al.* 2021). Examples of this approach include New Materialism, which sees all human and more-than-human entities and their interactions as assemblages (Mannion 2020). This integrated, relational approach is more akin to Indigenous views of humans within nature as opposed to the dualism of Descartes, Bacon, Kant and more (Griffin 2001 in Walsh *et al.* 2021). These philosophical thinkers created divisions and paved the way for nature exploitation and the supremacy of 'man'. Relational approaches thus help us to break down divisions between research and education in universities and to see them as integrated processes that facilitate people to develop competencies that can enable them to work collaboratively, to the common good, to fulfil their potential and to develop a critical consciousness as well as producing 'products' and technical solutions.

In practice, integrated approaches will depend on the university, context and staff and learner aspirations and skill sets. One example, where a key postgraduate programme was developed to engage with local issues and stakeholders, inspired a student-led sustainability strategy for the campus (Jain *et al.* 2013).

## Recommendations to Integrate Knowledge for Sustainability

We suggest some example activities to support integration of ESD with other forms of knowledge generation and exchange (Table 8.1).

*Table 8.1* Areas of sustainability knowledge exchange and suggested example activities.

| *Area of knowledge exchange* | *Suggested example activities* |
|---|---|
| Research-led ESD | Bring contested concepts from research into your ESD teaching<br>If you attend a workshop or conference on an aspect of sustainability, discuss it in your ESD teaching<br>Subject to ethical approval, use research framing and your data, such as interview transcripts, soil cores, to present the complexity of a real-world research project<br>Develop undergraduate dissertation research to be the capstone that integrates knowledges and enables demonstration of competencies by learners<br>Bring front-line case studies from experiences as a practitioner-researcher into the classroom<br>Require learners to consider the sustainability implications of their dissertation/independent research projects as part of their initial research proposal |
| Real-world problems | Discuss a recent event (e.g. a COP event, wildfires, policy change) that is relevant to your research or practice with your learners in class |

*(Continued)*

*Table 8.1* (Continued)

| *Area of knowledge exchange* | *Suggested example activities* |
|---|---|
| | Set an assignment for learners to design research to address pre-set questions of operational sustainability at your university, e.g., offering sustainable and attractive food menus in university cafés |
| Inter/transdisciplinarity | Introduce a guest speaker into a module to give a wider perspective on a subject |
| | Do an exchange lecture with another colleague from a different discipline across your modules in a similar topic and discuss together |
| | Encourage different perspectives within a class through role play, film, field trip, research |
| Teaching-led research | Design an evaluation of your ESD intervention, present it internally within your university and consider publishing it |
| | Set an essay on a sustainability topic of interest in your research field and use the opportunity for you to read around the issue and debate it with learners |
| | Frame a module around a sustainability issue or case study and use the experience to inform a future research grant application |
| Knowledge integration | Seek funding to employ one or two learners as interns or research assistants |
| | Publish in popular, non-academic places as well as peer-reviewed journals |
| | Assess the impact of your research on external stakeholders and on ESD gains of your learners. You could use tools from Chapter 11. |

## Conclusions

The challenges to ESD and to sustainability research can seem overwhelming without further considering the wider framing of universities simultaneously (and paradoxically) becoming more constrained by neoliberal processes of commodification (Broström *et al.* 2021); re-orienting as civic and community-facing institutions (Arocena and Sutz 2021); and reconfiguring as engines of sustainability innovation (Hadorn *et al.* 2006). Whilst demonstrating significant societal and economic impacts (Rau *et al.* 2018), universities also need to develop frugal and inclusive forms of innovation (Arocena and Sutz 2021) and find ways to measure, articulate and value the purpose of research rather than simply income. Our institutions must embrace greater epistemological plurality (Nörstrom *et al.* 2020) whilst considering local knowledge forms and issues (Wakunuma *et al.* 2021).

It is difficult to navigate a path for integrated knowledge for sustainability through this changing academic landscape. However, change also offers opportunity, and there is potential now to undertake intellectually exciting, meaningful, engaging ESD and sustainability research. This is not a time for despair but rather a time of innovation and opportunity (Miller *et al.* 2011). At a time when justification, truths and beliefs of knowledge are being questioned through the dominance and abuse (by some) of social media,

AI and disrespect for 'experts', academia needs to make itself heard in relevant ways. Change can be difficult for senior management, who like to see clear plans, and for staff, who can be resistant to change, especially when the current situation appears positive (Miller *et al.* 2011). The institution and not only individual staff and learners need to embrace such change, in promotion, tenure and audit processes. Additional efforts may be required, including knowledge brokering, facilitation, interdisciplinary debate and collaborative, dialogical spaces (Miller *et al.* 2011). Despite significant contributions of universities and other higher education institutions to sustainability through research, it has been suggested that their greatest contribution is through ESD and the potential of our graduates (Karatzoglou 2013). By linking learners, whether undergraduate or postgraduate, into processes of critical sustainability research, we further enhance their self-awareness, cultural, normative, problem solving, collaborative, critical/systems/future thinking competencies and capacities to be change agents for a more sustainable world (see Jain *et al.* 2013).

This shift in approach towards a more conscious and integrated form of knowledge generation and implementation for sustainability is pioneering the manifestation of new knowledge formats. The more democratic, collaborative, relational, interdisciplinary knowledge paradigm that has been suggested (Gibbons *et al* 1994; Hessels and Van Lente 2008; Funtowicz and Ravetz 1993; Nowotny *et al.* 2001) is finally being enacted in the pursuit of sustainability.

## References


Arocena, R. and Sutz, J. (2021) Universities and social innovation for global sustainable development as seen from the south. *Technological Forecasting and Social Change*, *162*: 120399.

Baer, H.A. (2019) The elephant in the sky: On how to grapple with our academic flying in the age of climate change. *Anthropology Today*, *35* (4): 21–24. DOI: 10.1111/1467-8322.12518.

Barth, M., & Michelsen, G. (2013). Learning for change: an educational contribution to sustainability science. *Sustainability Science*, *8*, 103–119.

Bennich, T., Maneas, G., Maniatakou, S., Piemontese, L., Schaffer, C., Schellens, M. and Österlin, C. (2022) Transdisciplinary research for sustainability: Scoping for project potential. *International Social Science Journal*, *72* (246): 1087–1104.

Bessant, S. E., & Robinson, Z. P. (2019). Rating and rewarding higher education for sustainable development research within the marketised higher education context: experiences from English universities. *Environmental Education Research*, *25*(4), 548–565.

Blackstock, K. L., Kelly, G. J., & Horsey, B. L. (2007). Developing and applying a framework to evaluate participatory research for sustainability. *Ecological Economics*, *60*(4), 726–742.

Brand, R., & Karvonen, A. (2007). The ecosystem of expertise: complementary knowledges for sustainable development. *Sustainability: Science, practice and policy*, *3*(1), 21–31.

Brandt, P., Ernst, A., Gralla, F., Luederitz, C., Lang, D.J., Newig, J., Reinert, F., Abson, D.J. and Von Wehrden, H. (2013) A review of transdisciplinary research in sustainability science. *Ecological Economics*, *92*: 1–15.

Broström, A., Buenstorf, G. and McKelvey, M. (2021) The knowledge economy, innovation and the new challenges to universities: Introduction to the special issue. *Innovation*, *23* (2): 145–162.

Brundiers, K. and Wiek, A. (2011) Educating students in real-world sustainability research: Vision and implementation. *Innovative Higher Education*, *36*: 107–124.

Buchanan, R. (1992) Wicked problems in design thinking. *Design Issues*, *8* (2): 5–21.

Budur, T., Abdullah, H., Rashid, C.A. and Demirer, H. (2024) The connection between knowledge management processes and sustainability at higher education Institutions. *Journal of the Knowledge Economy*, 1–34.

Burrell, G., & Morgan, G. (1979).*Sociological paradigms and organisational analysis: Elements of the sociology of corporate life*. Heinemann Books, London, UK.

Chambers, R. (1994) Participatory rural appraisal (PRA): Analysis of experience. *World Development, 22* (9): 1253–1268.

Chubb, J. and Reed, M. (2017) Epistemic responsibility as an edifying force in academic research: Investigating the moral challenges and opportunities of an impact agenda in the UK and Australia. *Palgrave Communications, 3* (1): 1–5.

Derickson, K.D. and Routledge, P. (2015) Resourcing scholar-activism: Collaboration, transformation, and the production of knowledge. *The Professional Geographer, 67* (1): 1–7.

Dowd, K.O. and Kaplan, D.M. (2005) The career life of academics: Boundaried or boundaryless? *Human Relations, 58* (6): 699–721.

Fam, D., Palmer, J., Riedy, C. and Mitchell, C. eds. (2016) *Transdisciplinary Research and Practice for Sustainability Outcomes*. Taylor & Francis.

Fetherston, C., Fetherston, A., Batt, S., Sully, M. and Wei, R. (2021) Wellbeing and work-life merge in Australian and UK academics. *Studies in Higher Education, 46* (12): 2774–2788.

Freire, P. (1970) *Pedagogy of the Oppressed*. Seabury Press, New York.

Funtowicz, S.O. and Ravetz, J.R. (1993) Science for the post-normal age. *Futures, 25* (7): 739–755.

Funtowicz, S., Ravetz, J. and O'Connor, M. (1998) Challenges in the use of science for sustainable development. *International Journal of Sustainable Development, 1* (1): 99–107.

Garrity, E.J. (2018) Using systems thinking to understand enlarge mental models: Helping the transition to a sustainable world. *Systems, 6*: 15. DOI: 10.3390/systems6020015.

Geuna, A. and Muscio, A. (2009) The governance of university knowledge transfer: A critical review of the literature. *Minerva, 47*: 93–114.

Gibbons, M., Lomoges, C., Nowotny, H., Schwartzman, S., Scott, P., & Trow, M. (1994). *The New Production of Knowledge: The Dynamics of Science and Research in Contemporary Societies*. Thousand Oaks, California: SAGE.

Hadorn, G.H., Bradley, D., Pohl, C., Rist, S. and Wiesmann, U. (2006) Implications of transdisciplinarity for sustainability research. *Ecological Economics, 60* (1): 119–128.

Heikkinen, H.L., de Jong, F.P. and Vanderlinde, R. (2016) What is (good) practitioner research? *Vocations and Learning, 9*: 1–19.

Hessels, L.K. and Van Lente, H. (2008) Re-thinking new knowledge production: A literature review and a research agenda. *Research Policy, 37* (4): 740–760.

Hugé, J., Block, T., Waas, T., Wright, T. and Dahdouh-Guebas, F. (2016) How to walk the talk? Developing actions for sustainability in academic research. *Journal of Cleaner Production, 137*: 83–92.

Jain, S., Aggarwal, P., Sharma, N. and Sharma, P. (2013) Fostering sustainability through education, research and practice: A case study of TERI university. *Journal of Cleaner Production, 61*: 20–24.

Judge, P. (2014) Germans get free heating from the cloud. Published by Data Centre Dynamics (DCD). Available at: https://www.datacenterdynamics.com/en/news/germans-get-free-heating-from-the-cloud/ [Accessed 31 July 2024]

Kagan, S. (2018) Culture and the arts in sustainable development: Rethinking sustainability research. In *Cultural Sustainability* (pp. 127–139). Routledge.

Kanwar, A., Kodhandaraman, B. and Unmar, A. (2010) Towards sustainable open education resources: A perspective from the global South. *The American Journal of Distance Education, 24* (2): 65–80.

Karatzoglou, B. (2013) An in-depth literature review of the evolving roles and contributions of universities to education for sustainable development. *Journal of Cleaner Production, 49*: 44–53.

Knapp, C.N., Reid, R.S., Fernadez-Gimenez, M.M., Klein, J.A. and Galvin, K.A. (2019) Placing transdisciplinarity in context: A review of approaches to connect scholars, society and action. *Sustainability, 11* (18): 4899.

Knudsen, M.P., Frederiksen, M.H. and Goduscheit, R.C. (2021) New forms of engagement in third mission activities: A multi-level university-centric approach. *Innovation: Organization and Management, 23* (2): 209–240.

Kutty, A.A., Abdella, G.M., Kucukvar, M., Onat, N.C. and Belu, M. (2020) A system thinking approach for harmonizing smart and sustainable city initiatives with United Nations sustainable development goals. *Sustainable Development*, *28*: 1347–1365.
Lang, D., Weik, A., Bergmann, M., Stauffacher, M., Martens, P., Moll, P., Swilling, M. and Thomas, C.J. (2012) Transdisciplinary research in sustainability science: Practice, principles and challenges. *Sustainability Science*, *7* (1): 25–43.
Lönngren, J. and Van Poeck, K. (2021) Wicked problems: A mapping review of the literature. *International Journal of Sustainable Development & World Ecology*, *28* (6): 481–502.
Mannion, G. (2020) Re-assembling environmental and sustainability education: Orientations from new materialism. *Environmental Education Research*, *26* (9–10): 1353–1372.
Mardero, S., Schmook, B., Calmé, S., White, R.M., Chang, J.C.J., Casanova, G. and Castelar, J. (2023) Traditional knowledge for climate change adaptation in Mesoamerica: A systematic review. *Social Sciences & Humanities Open*, *7* (1): 100473.
Martins, V.W.B., Rampasso, I.S., Anholon, R., Quelhas, O.L.G. and Leal Filho, W. (2019) Knowledge management in the context of sustainability: Literature review and opportunities for future research. *Journal of Cleaner Production*, *229*: 489–500.
Max-Neef, M.A. (2005) Foundations of transdisciplinarity. *Ecological Economics*, *53* (1): 5–16.
Meagher, L., Lyall, C. and Nutley, S. (2008) Flows of knowledge, expertise and influence: A method for assessing policy and practice impacts from social science research. *Research Evaluation*, *17* (3): 163–173.
Menon, S. and Suresh, M. (2020) Synergizing education, research, campus operations, and community engagements towards sustainability in higher education: A literature review. *International Journal of Sustainability in Higher Education*, *21* (5): 1015–1051. DOI: 10.1108/IJSHE-03-2020-0089.
Miller, T.R., Muñoz-Erickson, T. and Redman, C.L. (2011) Transforming knowledge for sustainability: Towards adaptive academic institutions. *International Journal of Sustainability in Higher Education*, *12* (2): 177–192.
Norström, A.V., Cvitanovic, C., Löf, M.F., West, S., Wyborn, C., Balvanera, P., ... and Österblom, H. (2020) Principles for knowledge co-production in sustainability research. *Nature Sustainability*, *3* (3): 182–190.
Nowotny, H., Scott, P. and Gibbons, M. (2001). *Re-Thinking Science: Knowledge and the Public in an Age of Uncertainty* (p. 12). Cambridge: Polity.
Orr, D. (1994) *Earth in Mind: On Education, Environment, and the Human Prospect*. Island Press.
Panda, A. (2014) Bringing academic and corporate worlds closer: We need pracademics. *Management and Labour Studies*, *39* (2): 140–159.
Pellow, D.N. (2000) Environmental inequality formation: Toward a theory of environmental injustice. *American Behavioural Scientist*, *43* (4): 581–601.
Peters, S. and Wals, A.E. (2013). Learning and knowing in pursuit of sustainability: concepts and tools for trans-disciplinary environmental research. *Trading zones in environmental education: Creating transdisciplinary dialogue*, 79–104.
Phills, J.A., Deiglmeier, K. and Miller, D.T. (2008) Rediscovering social innovation. *Stanford Social Innovation Review*, *6* (4): 34–43.
Pollard, N. (2022). Where "the cloud" touches the ground: Electronic poetry, digital infrastructures and the environment. *ISLE: Interdisciplinary Studies in Literature and the Environment*, *31* (1), 46–71: https://doi.org/10.1093/isle/isac039
Posch, A. and Steiner, G. (2006) Integrating research and teaching on innovation for sustainable development. *International Journal of Sustainability in Higher Education*, *7* (3): 276–292.
Price, E.A., White, R.M., Mori, K., Longhurst, J., Baughan, P., Hayles, C.S, ... and Preist, C. (2021) Supporting the role of universities in leading individual and societal transformation through education for sustainable development. *Discover Sustainability*, *2* (1): 1–16.
Rau, H., Goggins, G. and Fahy, F. (2018) From invisibility to impact: Recognising the scientific and societal relevance of interdisciplinary sustainability research. *Research Policy*, *47* (1): 266–276.
Rittel, H.W. and Webber, M.M. (1973) Dilemmas in a general theory of planning. *Policy Sciences*, *4* (2): 155–169.

Rockström, J., Gupta, J., Qin, D., Lade, S.J., Abrams, J.F., Andersen, L.S., Armstrong McKay, D.I., Bai, X., Bala, G., Bunn, S.E. and Ciobanu, D. (2023) Safe and just Earth system boundaries. *Nature*, *619* (7968): 102–111.

Roth, S. (2020) Intersectionality and coalitions in social movement research – A survey and outlook. *Sociology Compass*, *2021* (15): e12885.

Rowe, A. M., & Schuster-Wallace, C. (2023). Implementing EDI across a large formal research network: contributing to equitable and sustainable water solutions for a changing climate. *Geoforum*, *147*: 103881.

Roy, S.G., de Souza, S.P., McGreavy, B., Druschke, C.G., Hart, D.D. and Gardner, K. (2020) Evaluating core competencies and learning outcomes for training the next generation of sustainability researchers. *Sustainability Science*, *15*: 619–631.

Saunders, C., Griffin, I., Hackney, F., Barbieri, A., Hill, K.J., West, J. and Willet, J. (2024) A social practices approach to encourage sustainable clothing choices. *Sustainability*, *16*(3), 1282; https://doi.org/10.3390/su16031282

Schot, J. and Steinmueller, W.E. (2018) Three frames for innovation policy: R&D, systems of innovation and transformative change. *Research Policy*, *47* (9): 1554–1567.

Siurua, H. (2006) Nature above people: Rolston and" fortress" conservation in the South. *Ethics and the Environment*: 71–96.

Smith, K.E., Bandoloa-Gill, J., Meer, N., Stewart, E. and Watermeyer, R. (2020) *The impact agenda: Controversies, consequences and challenges*. Policy Press, Bristol, UK.

Sterling, S. (2001). *Sustainable education: re-visioning learning and change*. Totnes: Green Books for the Schumacher Society.

Sterling, S. (2013) The sustainable university: Challenge and response. In *The Sustainable University* (pp. 17–50). Routledge.

Tim, O'Riordan, T., Jacobs, G., Ramanathan, J. and Bina, O. (2020) Investigating the future role of higher education in creating sustainability transitions. *Environment: Science and Policy for Sustainable Development*, 62 (4): 4–15. DOI: 10.1080/00139157.2020.1764278.

Tress, G., Tress, B. and Fry, G. (2005) Clarifying integrative research concepts in landscape ecology. *Landscape Ecology*, *20*: 479–493.

Trowler, P. (2012) Introduction. In: Trowler, P. Saunders, M. and Bamber, V. (eds) *Tribes and Territories in the 21st Century*. Rethinking the significance of disciplines in higher education. Routledge.

United Nations (UN) (2015) Transforming our world: the 2030 Agenda for Sustainable Development. https://sdgs.un.org/2030agenda

Voulvoulis, N., Giakoumis, T., Hunt, C., Kioupi, V., Petrou, N., Souliotis, I. and Vaghela, C.J.G.E.C. (2022) Systems thinking as a paradigm shift for sustainability transformation. *Global Environmental Change*, *75*: 102544.

Wakunuma, K., Castro, F.D., Jiya, T., Inigo, E.A., Blok, V. and Bryce, V. (2021) Reconceptualising responsible research and innovation from a global South perspective. *Journal of Responsible Innovation*, *8* (2): 267–291.

Walsh, Z., Böhme, J., & Wamsler, C. (2021). Towards a relational paradigm in sustainability research, practice, and education. *Ambio*, *50*(1), 74–84.

West, J., Saunders, C. and Willett, J. (2021) A bottom up approach to slowing fashion: Tailored solutions for consumers. *Journal of Cleaner Production*, *296*, 126387.

White, R.M. (2004) A paradox for environmental education: How can we 'deliver training to targets' using 'participatory, reflective approaches'? *Southern African Journal of Environmental Education*, *21*: 81–93.

White, R.M. (2013) *Sustainability Research: a Novel Mode of Knowledge Generation to Explore Alternative Ways for People and Planet. Chapter in The Sustainable University: Progress and Prospects*. Ed. Sterling, S., Maxey, L., Luna, H. Abingdon: Routledge

White, R.M. (2014) *Who Am I? The role(s) of an academic at a 'sustainable university'*. In W. Leal Filho *et al.* (eds.), *Integrative Approaches to Sustainable Development at University Level*, World Sustainability Series, DOI 10.1007/978-3-319-10690-8_46.

White, R.M., Schmook, B., Calmé, S., Giordano, A.J., Hausser, Y., Kimmel, L., Lecuyer, L., Lucherini, M., Méndez-Medina, C. and Peña-Mondragón, J.L. (2023) Facilitating biodiversity conservation through partnerships to achieve transformative outcomes. *Conservation Biology*, e14057. https://doi.org/10.1111/cobi.14057

White, R.M. and van Koten, H. (2016) Co-designing for sustainability: Strategising community carbon emission reduction through socio-ecological innovation. *The Design Journal*, *19* (1): 25–46. DOI: 10.1080/14606925.2015.1064219.

Whitmarsh, L., Capstick, S., Moore, I., Köhler, J. and Le Quéré, C. (2020) Use of aviation by climate change researchers: Structural influences, personal attitudes, and information provision. *Global Environmental Change*, *65*, 102184. https://doi.org/10.1016/j.gloenvcha.2020.102184.

Willett, J., Saunders, C., Hackney, F. and Hill, K. (2022) The affective economy and fast fashion: Materiality, embodied learning and developing a sensibility for sustainable clothing. *Journal of Material Culture*, *27* (3): 219–237.

Yarime, M., Trencher, G., Mino, T., Scholz, R.W., Olsson, L., Ness, B., Frantzeskaki, N. and Rotmans, J. (2012) Establishing sustainability science in higher education institutions: Towards an integration of academic development, institutionalization, and stakeholder collaborations. *Sustainability Science*, 7: 101–113.

Chapter 9

# Leadership and Governance for Education for Sustainable Development

## Engagement, Strategy and Transformation

*James W. S. Longhurst, Zoe P. Robinson and Elizabeth A. C. Price*

### Introduction

Universities have a significant role to play in considering and pursuing more sustainable futures (Sterling *et al.*, 2013), since higher education can create the attitudes, changes, and leadership necessary for the transformation of societies (Pee and Vululleh, 2020). High-level institutional support for embedding Education for Sustainable Development (ESD) has been identified as critical to the success of ESD in higher education (Fiselier *et al.*, 2018; Leal Filho *et al.*, 2019). Strong sustainability leadership can help promote action around a shared vision of ESD (SDSN, 2020). However, sustainability leadership can involve ambiguity and complexity in relation to the scope and level of commitment relevant to a university, how success is measured and how leadership for sustainable development can be delivered (Sheil, 2013; Haddock-Fraser and Gorman, 2020). ESD offers two major challenges to higher education leadership: those of *paradigm*, demanding a shift in the way we perceive education, and of *provision*, offering processes, resources, and support for the embedding of ESD within and across our universities (Sterling, 2004). In this chapter, we will explain the role and importance of leadership for ESD in higher education and explore different models and levels of leadership. We will then outline a range of tools for leadership of ESD and consider approaches that can be effective in a range of institutional contexts.

### The Role and Importance of Leadership for ESD in Higher Education

> Many things on which your future health and prosperity depend are in dire jeopardy: climate stability, the resilience and productivity of natural systems, the beauty of the natural world, and biological diversity.
>
> It is worth noting that this is not the work of ignorant people. It is, rather, largely the result of work by people with BAs, BScs, LLBs, MBAs, and PhDs.
>
> (Orr, 1991)

Society faces a set of profound sustainability challenges – a grossly unequal global society, an industrial system in urgent need of de-carbonisation, a rapid decline of biodiversity, an increasing problem of air pollution, a global society living beyond planetary boundaries, extreme globalisation, the need for reparation, effects of climate change and

DOI: 10.4324/9781003451563-9

biodiversity loss felt most by the most vulnerable. These are the systemic realities of an unsustainable model of development.

The UN Sustainable Development Goals (UN DESA, undated) represent society's best hope for avoiding catastrophic change. Higher education must and will play a leading role in plotting the route to a sustainable future and guiding society's adaptation to living sustainably within the limits of the planet. Humanity is in the midst of a climate and environmental emergency where the capability of the planet to support our demands upon it is increasingly problematic. Current and future students understand this and expect their institution to act (UNESCO, 2024).

Higher education can be a powerful vehicle for sustainable development but much of higher education creates graduates who perpetuate current models of unsustainable behaviours and damaging environmental impacts. Of course, sustainability already matters for many higher education institutions but by no means all. Orr (1991) made his observations more than 30 years ago and in that period much has changed, but for many institutions, the basic premise of Orr remains the same. Graduates are produced who have disciplinary knowledge but who lack the broader context of how that discipline affects sustainability and lack awareness, skills, or knowledge about how they can contribute to the development of a more sustainable future.

Higher education has a significant role to play in guiding society towards a sustainable future through research, community engagement, and by developing the knowledge, skills, and attributes of students so that they are aware of the global sustainability challenge. Education enables students to take responsibility for their lifestyles and can nurture a healthy human–nature relationship (Fiselier *et al.*, 2018) and helps develop critical thinking to help question unsustainable norms and narratives. Some but by no means all institutions have recognised the adverse impacts that their approach to higher education creates. Many more of the higher education providers in the UK need to consider how their different domains of activity, including, curriculum, research, estate management, and community engagement actions, can contribute to the creation of a more sustainable society. Universities, with their scale of resource and potential for positive impact across all 17 of the UN Sustainable Development Goals, are well placed to strategically and practically support a sustainable development pathway but also to critically engage with concepts and directions for sustainability. Higher education not only is capable of supporting a sustainable future but also arguably has a moral responsibility to its students, future graduates and to their wider communities and regions to exercise sustainability leadership. Higher education institutions, no matter their size, capacities, and capabilities, need to engage strategically and operationally across all domains of activity, not as a 'nice to have' but as a 'core business' organising purpose. To do so requires senior staff understanding and the exercise of leadership.

By virtue of its size, distribution across the nation space and through its financial resources, the higher education sector is uniquely placed to advance sustainability. In 2021–2022, there were over 2 million students studying at UK higher education providers which employed nearly 240,000 staff, some 3.6% of the UK population (UUK, 2024). Not only does the sector have scale it also has a substantial financial resource with a combined annual income of almost £44 billion in 2021–2022 (UUK, 2024). How these resources and capabilities are deployed across the teaching and research missions and in support of civic engagement and campus developments can either advance or retard achievement of a more sustainable future. Increasingly, external accreditations of sustainability in higher education are assessing how leadership of an institution is enabling the development of a sustainable institution. Examples of this include Responsible Futures (SOS-UK, 2023), the Sustainability Leadership Scorecard (EAUC, 2024), or the annual People and Planet University League (People and Planet, 2023). The international Environmental Management System standard ISO 14001-2015 (ISO Standards, undated), under which a number of universities in the UK are certified, also sets expectations for the role of leadership in supporting and enabling effective and sustainable environmental management of the organisation. Recruitment agencies specialising in HE senior leadership appointments are increasingly recognising the importance of sustainability awareness within the candidates for such roles; see, for example, Odgers Berndtson (2024).

Universities already produce large quantities of data to show how they are contributing to such a future. Many higher education institutions now produce a range of policy, strategy, and annual reporting that addresses sustainability issues. UUK (2023) report that 96% of their member universities have a clear, publicly available strategy to reduce carbon emissions and 97% have sustainability information openly available on their website. However, it is questionable as to whether the necessary step of placing sustainability as a central consideration in the institutional decision-making process has been achieved. Indeed, Fiselier and Longhurst (2018), in a survey of 139 higher education institutions' websites to identify institutions' engagement with the 2014 version of the national ESD guidance (QAA and HEA, 2014), found a variety of mostly general sustainability information to be present but only limited information on the role of ESD. Mostly lacking was reference to ESD in the specification of the graduate learning outcomes and in the approach to teaching, learning, and assessment. Interestingly, the 2014 guidance made little reference to the role of leadership in enabling and promoting implementation of ESD. The incorporation of ESD into the mainstream of the higher education system is necessary in order for the higher education sector to transition away from a model that perpetuates an unsustainable set of social and economic relations and which contributes to the exceedances of planetary environmental boundaries and further embeds gross global inequalities.

Critical to that change is developing curricula that embed the ideas of ESD into taught programmes. In 2021, the QAA and Advance HE published the second iteration of the ESD guidance for higher education. The important role of leadership in creating circumstances in which ESD can be implemented is foregrounded in this guidance. ESD is described as a process that equips learners across all disciplines with the knowledge, skills, attributes, and values required to pursue sustainable visions of the future and address complex problems. ESD allows students to identify how they can contribute to solutions that address environmental and social justice issues. The guidance advises universities to design their educational offer so that ESD is present in all programmes of study. The guidance recognises that ESD is best achieved when ESD objectives, targets, and KPIs are part of the institution's strategic priorities, strategies, and policies. This institutional leadership support will allow ESD to be considered in the validation of new courses and in the review of existing courses. This, in turn, requires that ESD is articulated within quality assurance and enhancement processes (QAA, 2024), and that appropriate staff development is in place to enable staff to engage in ESD at an institutional level (Chapter 10).

Higher education institutions in the UK are operating with an increasingly difficult financial environment, with a declining unit of resource and for some, a difficult student recruitment market. In such a resource-constrained environment, institutional leaders may struggle to see the importance and opportunity provided by ESD especially when sector support agencies, themselves operating in a resource-constrained manner, only are able to provide advice and guidance rather than substantial new resources. As Fiselier *et al.* (2018) note, the longer-term solution to integrating and embedding ESD in a university mission is providing staff with the time and resources to engage with the concepts of ESD within the context of their own discipline. In so doing, staff will challenge prevailing orthodoxies and consider new pedagogic practices. The role of leadership in a resource-constrained environment is twofold. Firstly, to empower staff to engage and explore ESD through legitimising engagement and secondly, to recognise that ESD engagement is not, necessarily, about new resources but can be achieved with a redirection of existing resources.

As a sector dedicated to knowledge and thought leadership, it is essential that we contribute to achieving the SDGs, reversing biodiversity loss, and reaching net zero emissions. These outcomes are essential, they are feasible and achievable, and the sector has a responsibility to engage wherever and however it can. Students are acutely aware that they will live their lives as the climate and ecological crises play out. A typical student leaving a UK university this year might expect to live at least another 60 years (ONS, 2024); a life course in which they will experience wide ranging, adverse climate and ecological changes. They rightly ask how their educational experience will prepare them for the challenges that they will encounter in their professional and private lives, a future that will not be business as usual. Thanks to the long running sustainability skills surveys conducted by SOS-UK (undated a) over more than a decade, there is a substantial evidence base of student concern about these matters. The Times Higher Education Pulse Survey (Times Higher Education, 2021) indicated that 82% of students wanted to live in a way that was consistent with sustainable citizenship. Respondents wanted their institution to demonstrate how they are making progress against the UN's Sustainable Development Goals across education and research and for their institution to exhibit good practices in their civic engagement. Numerous surveys (e.g., Zurich Insurance, 2020) indicate that future cohorts of students will be much more concerned about the climate and ecological emergency. They will expect their institution to take the climate and ecological emergency seriously, to manage their estate wisely, to include ESD within the formal and informal curriculum and to prepare them for the challenges they will face across their life course, both professional and private, as they live through a changing climate. Future students might not use the term 'ESD' but increasingly will come to expect that the ideas and principles of ESD are present in their educational experience. Furthermore, they will expect that their institution will embody these issues in the way the institution is managed. Institutional leadership will need to respond to these expectations. The changing world of work is creating new expectations and opportunities for the deployment of ESD knowledge, skills, and competencies. Employers are recognising the need for capacity to deal with complexity and uncertainty, areas that those with competencies in ESD are well suited to address.

Current and future graduates will inherit the changing climate of tomorrow. Institutions have a responsibility to prepare them for that future whilst using their research activities and policy advice to help mitigate future emissions and to support society in preparing and adapting for the unavoidable changes that are to come. The higher education sector has many good examples to draw upon, from mitigation and adaptation of estates, to curriculum developments, research and civic engagement, but it is not widespread nor always core business nor effectively built into leadership and governance structures. There exists a gap between the need for mobilising institutional resources and the reality of day-to-day business. A gap exists in the required leadership and action for universities to take their place in catalysing a sustainable future, and until it is closed, the higher education sector cannot claim to be preparing its students for the changing climate of the 21st century.

Institution leaders will need to understand the challenges of an increasingly unsustainable world and appreciate the deeply held concerns of students for action. These concerns are not those of students alone, as many staff want to their institution embrace ESD and to provide training and support for engaging in ESD. Institutions will need to respond by developing and implementing the changes needed across all domains of activity so that higher education can play its proper part in developing a sustainable future. As Orr (1991) and others have argued, the current higher education system is failing to prepare students for the intricacies and challenges of the 21st century and is in fact creating graduates who go into society living and promoting highly unsustainable ways of living.

Sterling (2004) argued that ESD is 'not just another issue to be added to an overcrowded curriculum, but a gateway to a different view of curriculum, of pedagogy, of organisational change, of policy and particularly of ethos', but institutions have struggled to create the conditions in which this can be realised. As Weiss *et al.* (2021) observe, senior leadership can be both a barrier to change and a driver of change. Strong university leadership imposing change from the top, without careful consultation and the building of organisational trust, can create a barrier to desired change by initiating resistance to the intended institutional goal by those unconvinced of the change or disaffected. However, leadership support for ESD in higher education is a necessary precondition for action at the scale of an institution and a driver of change through provision of resources, communication strategies, coordination of activities at various scales, and inclusion in the high-level strategic plan of an institution. So far, this chapter has largely discussed the role of senior leadership, yet leadership is not the preserve of the senior team, rather actions at all levels from students, faculty staff, and professional services can together create conditions where institutional engagement with ESD is enabled and enriched. This, in turn, can create opportunities for change and movement towards a whole institution engagement with ESD where the curriculum, research agenda, civic engagement, and campus development and management of the institution are aligned with the goal of ESD.

## Different Models and Levels of Leadership

> Anyone seeking to influence another is a potential leader.
>
> (Haddock-Fraser and Gorman, 2020)

Leadership is an essential condition of achieving sustainability within higher education institutions, and of creating 'the conditions conducive to the possibility of improving teaching and learning' (Blackmore, 2013: 139). Leadership for sustainability in higher education is influenced by the complexity of universities, the 'multifaceted sub-cultures, influencers and viewpoints across staff, students, government, business and alumni' as well as the culture of academic freedom and gap between the professional services and academic staff worlds (Haddock-Fraser and Gorman, 2020: 3). As the quote at the start of this section highlights, this leadership can take many forms, from a single, senior position with legitimacy and expectation for leadership from their title, who sets out strategy and directives for others to follow; to leadership within 'bottom-up' movements often advocating for change from the senior leaders; to leadership from the 'middle-out' (Shiel and Jones, 2016; Zohar *et al.*, 2021), which may comprise academic or professional services staff implementing and driving change in their own spheres of influence, maybe while supporting and developing bottom-up leaders, and attempting to influence senior leaders. Spillane *et al.* (2004) argue that leadership should be assessed as 'an organisational quality', and that a focus on 'leadership activity' rather than individual leaders is more important in educational settings, where both formal and informal leadership is inevitably shared among multiple interacting members of the institution.

There are myriad models and theories of leadership and sustainability leadership and increasingly, sustainability leadership in higher education settings, although this latter is still viewed as limited in volume and quality (Aung and Hallinger, 2022). The complexity of the university system, and the requirement for transformation for sustainability across the whole institution requires a leadership approach which is ambitious, holistic, and integrative in nature (Avissar *et al.*, 2018), as well as requiring leadership for sustainability transformation at different levels. This chapter does not seek to provide a comprehensive review of all possible leadership models but explores some different models of viewing leadership of particular pertinence to the transformation of higher education settings to achieve sustainability.

### *Bottom-up, Top-down, Middle-out Leadership*

In the context of sustainability in higher education, bottom-up leadership is often taken to refer to the student voice (Brinkhurst *et al.*, 2011; Mazon *et al.*, 2020), while top-down leadership is from senior executive level. In the context of sustainability in universities, top-down leadership has largely been seen as the integration of sustainability as part of executive-level thinking and decision making in general, rather than related to specific executive-level responsibility and roles for sustainability, although such named roles are becoming more common. Senior-level leadership is often viewed as setting strategy for others to follow yet is equally important in 'unblocking' obstacles to change experienced by others. In Senge's seminal work on learning organisations, he argues for new views of leadership, claiming that the traditional 'individualistic' view of leadership 'is based on assumptions of people's powerlessness, their lack of personal vision and inability to master the forces of change' (Senge, 1990: 340 in Smith, 2001). In contrast, he describes a new view of leadership where leaders are designers, stewards of a vision for the organisation that they manage for the benefit of others, and teachers with responsibility for building organisations where people continually expand their capabilities (Smith, 2001).

While bottom-up leadership is often viewed as lacking in power and hence focused around advocacy to influence senior-level decision making, within university settings, 'the bottom' (students) have a very powerful role, particularly as the narrative of students as customers becomes more embedded in university culture, and the minds of the students themselves. However, often students are not aware of the power to influence change that they hold, nor do they have the agency to negotiate the traditional systems of power within the university setting. Less discussed as a level of leadership is the 'middle out' (Brinkhurst *et al.*, 2011; Shiel and Jones, 2016), seen in the context of universities as staff driving change within their own spheres of influence. Within higher education institutions, many named sustainability professionals (e.g. Sustainability Managers) sit in 'middle-out' positions, requiring development to enable participation at a strategic level (Haddock-Fraser and Gorman, 2020), although there is a trend for the creation of more senior executively linked positions. The middle-out also have an important advocacy role, often having less transience in universities than students or senior leaders, as demonstrated by a quote from a senior leader highlighting the key leadership role played by motivated individuals in advocating for whole institution change and prioritisation of sustainability (Box 9.1):

> You need 'thorns in your side', you need people who repetitively say the same thing until it becomes common practice...You need that constancy and repetition.
>
> (Dooris *et al.*, 2018)

Each of these different levels of leadership are intersecting and interdependent, and any discussion of leadership for sustainability transformation within universities must include consideration of these levels. The bottom up cannot by themselves secure the level of transformation required, but are essential in creating 'demand' to influence senior leaders. Middle-out academics can support students through the curriculum to develop agency and understanding of change management. Top-down senior leaders are needed to establish a culture to legitimise middle-out leadership in driving sustainability initiatives within their

**Box 9.1 Case Study: 'A Thorn in the Side' – A Personal Story of Navigating Leadership Roles**

The Dooris *et al.* (2018) quote above resonates strongly with me. For over 18 years at Keele University, I have tried to be that 'thorn in the side' in both formal and informal leadership roles. I need only to raise my hand in a meeting for people to know that I will be questioning how we drive sustainability in whatever initiative is being discussed.

When asked about how to develop the agency to drive sustainability in universities, my response is usually 'just do it', or at least, if permission is needed, 'offer to do it.' From 'offering' informally to help embed sustainability in the curriculum and wider student experience, I spent 10 years with the title as 'Director of Education for Sustainability' with that responsibility. As I saw it, a large part of that role was to listen. To try to understand different disciplines, to understand where the sustainability hooks lay, and to bring examples of sustainability transformation in their disciplines, and to connect them with disciplinary experts doing this work. To listen to what new change initiatives were on the way within my university and build sustainability into those.

What I have realised is that change never stops, it is impossible to think the job is done – the next initiative will come round the corner, with new opportunities to ensure sustainability is embedded, while some of those great initiatives from the past, fall away into history. I still need to be that thorn. But as more and more people develop their own sustainability lens, more people become confident to be those thorns, until we're not thorns at all, but just part of a 'community of values' (White and Harder, 2013, see discussion above) so important to driving the change needed.

own sphere of influence, and to establish communication and collaboration processes to enable genuine co-production of top-down commitments, structures, and decisions.

Reliance on any one area of leadership leads to a lack of resilience in maintaining positive change, for example, the potential for changing commitments to sustainability brought about through regular changes in senior leadership with different priorities and agendas (Shiel and Jones, 2016). Transformation of every aspect of a university's operations and activities (Chapter 3) requires 'local leadership' as well as senior-level leadership. Universities perhaps more than other organisations can encourage independence and autonomy that can stimulate organically generated local leadership. Leal Filho *et al.* (2020) assert that anyone in the university can become a sustainability leader. People with personal commitments to sustainability look to bring that into professional lives and drive change within their own sphere of influence becoming sustainability leaders no matter their role. White and Harder (2013) talk of a 'community of values' within universities as important in driving sustainability – where different 'levels' of leadership, as well as traditionally divided groups such as students, academic, and professional services staff come together through a shared personal conviction to drive sustainability within their university. White and Harder (2013) argue a university needs to foster this internal community of values, and that through enabling their staff and student communities to act to drive sustainability, 'the university becomes more than a place of work – it becomes a place of discussion and mutual and collective action' (p.146), and hence a powerful force to lead transformation.

### *Transformational vs Transactional vs Radical Leadership*

ESD and whole-institution change is explicitly a transformational agenda, and hence requires transformational leaders. It is unlikely that any person who views themselves as a leader would aspire to anything other than transformational leadership, and yet studies of leaders demonstrate a prevalence of transactional, often seen as 'macho' leadership approaches being carried out (Shiel and Jones, 2016). Transformational leadership is associated with fairness, honesty, and responsibility, mobilising the energy of others to enable transformation. Bass (2000) describes transformational leaders as those who 'raise the awareness of their constituencies about what is important, increase concerns for achievement, self-actualization and ideals. They move followers to go beyond their own self-interests for the good of their group, organization or community, country or society as a whole'. In contrast, he describes transactional leaders in terms of reinforcing behaviours which meet the commitments to the leader or organisations, positive (e.g., praise and rewards) or negative approaches (e.g., negative feedback and disciplinary action). Thus, transactional and transformational leadership are not seen by Bass (2000) as a different ends of a spectrum, but as being conceptually independent.

Few senior leaders in higher education would probably identify themselves as radical leaders, in part due to the pragmatism borne of the need to balance financial realities and wider vision and the 'straitjacket' imposed on leadership styles due to larger external contexts such as neoliberalism and associated new public management practices in universities (Blackmore, 2014; White and Burkinshaw, 2019). Yet, it can be argued that the scale of the systems change needed requires radically new forms of leadership (Shiel and Jones, 2016). Writers on ESD suggest that bold leadership, those leaders willing to transform structures, cultures, and processes, are uncommon in universities (Tilbury, 2013). Shiel and Jones (2016) describe effective sustainable leaders as those challenging silo mentalities, facilitating new processes to encourage synergies across university functions, and striving to re-align systems 'towards the common endeavour of sustainability'. Maybe one aspect of radical leadership is, in recognition of the scale of transformation required, and the need to concentrate on leadership as a team, leadership that integrates across bottom-up, middle-out, and top-down leadership, rather than individual endeavour.

### *Diversity and Leadership*

Sustainability transformation of higher education institutions requires ways of thinking and working that challenge conventional wisdom and approaches. Studies of the qualities of effective sustainable leaders identify, alongside general qualities of leadership (see Yukl, 2006), greater levels of emotional intelligence, openness, integrity, empathy and humility, and more holistic and inclusive ways of working (Shiel and Jones, 2016). Women are still under-represented in higher education leadership (White and Burkinshaw, 2019), hence Shiel and Jones (2016) question whether predominantly male teams, more used to deploying transactional and adversarial approaches to thinking, interaction and decision making, and the typical gender imbalance in senior teams may inhibit more transformational ways of working. Women tend to favour more democratic rather than autocratic and participative rather than directive styles of leadership (Eagly and Johnson, 1990). Hence, more gender diversity at all levels of leadership may enhance the capacity for delivering transformational change within universities.

Diversity comes in many different forms. The environment and conservation professions are amongst the least diverse in the UK (RACE report, 2022), while there is an acknowledged dearth of representation regarding Black and Ethnic Minorities in senior leadership roles within higher education (Arday, 2018), and hence, we can assume a lack of racial diversity in sustainability leadership within higher education, particularly at more senior levels. Diversity within higher education settings also includes disciplinary differences, with STEM academics more likely to be appointed to leadership positions in higher education (White and Burkinshaw, 2019), inevitably influencing worldviews and approaches to problem-solving and leadership. It is unusual to have flexible working at senior levels, barring those requiring or desiring more flexible working practices from entering senior leadership positions (White and Burkinshaw, 2019). Although there is increasing scholarship around neurodiversity in organisations, there is limited research into how neurodiverse characteristics may influence leadership behaviours (Roberson *et al.*, 2021), and a paucity of literature exploring links between neurodiversity and sustainability leadership. Some of the most well-known faces of sustainability leadership, most notably Greta Thunberg, are publicly neurodiverse and are recognised for their effective yet unconventional leadership (Roberson *et al.*, 2021), demonstrating potential leadership strengths associated with neurodiverse characteristics. As difficulty with communication and social interaction is a common neurodiverse characteristic despite each condition being characterised by different sets of behaviours, it also highlights a danger of placing too much emphasis on empathic communication as a sustainability leadership panacea.

Another area of diversity where there is clear under-representation at senior levels due to challenges and barriers in the workplace, is from Lesbian, Gay, Bisexual, Transgender, and Queer or Questioning and others (LGBTQ+) communities (Swank, 2018; Baillinson *et al.*, 2020; Federo, 2024). In addition to the value that diversity and diverse experiences and perspectives brings to leadership, in the context of sustainability leadership,

LGBTQ+ communities are more likely to engage in environmental (and social) activism compared to their heterosexual counterparts (Castruita and Fassina, 2024) and therefore enter leadership positions with already formed commitments to these areas. Castruita and Fassina (2024) attribute this to the LGBTQ+ community's heightened awareness of, and commitment to, addressing social inequities, making environmental issues a natural extension of LGBTQ+ activism.

There is substantial educational research that recognises the positive influence of different forms of cultural diversity and the need to lead in ways that recognise and value difference within universities, and this is clearly the case in driving sustainability transformations (Blackmore, 2013). Leadership for sustainability in our higher education institutions therefore needs to ensure inclusive policies and supportive workplace cultures in order to address systemic challenges influencing the diversity of voices contributing to leadership. Deeply considering, not just diversity, in terms of under-represented groups, but *intersectionality*, (the interconnected nature of social categorisations such as race, class, and gender), is essential to leadership and the climate change discourse. As Castruita and Fassina (2024) write, 'recognizing the overlapping and cumulative impacts of these identities contributes to crafting solutions that are truly inclusive and just'. Chapter 3 provides an example of how diversity can be brought into university decision making through the use of a 'shadow' board of students with the exclusive purpose of highlighting Equity, Diversity, and Inclusion implications of university business.

### Distributed Leadership

Distributed leadership is seen as enabling change in an organisation's internal culture with respect to mainstreaming sustainability, encouraging collaboration, and the development of diverse bottom-up and top-down structures in the organisation (Avissar *et al.*, 2018). Distributed leadership recognises the complexity of higher education institutions, and the need for a sense of ownership to embed change in long-term practice (Blackmore, 2013). Distributed leadership can be intentionally actioned or it can informally arise, with individuals taking on their own agency as leaders (Jones *et al.*, 2014). Even intentionally actioned distributed leadership can take different forms from more controlled distribution with centralised visions or goals where individuals are given tight parameters to work within and may be monitored against particular performance metrics, to a more independent model where individuals have the freedom to develop practices which align broadly with organisational values, with no requirement to report or even disseminate back to other areas of the organisation. Blackmore (2013: 151) writes that truly distributed leadership requires a re-distribution of power and resources and 'not just delegation down the line from management of more work, risk and responsibility' perhaps cautioning against too tight control, while also acknowledging the weaknesses of too little centralisation and communication.

Importantly, distributed responsibility can help ensure resilience of sustainability governance within organisations. Several sustainability 'leaders' at different levels provides resilience against individually committed individuals leaving the organisation. If a key individual leaves in one area, there is still sufficient activity in other parts of the institution to maintain momentum and culture (Robinson and Laycock Pederson, 2021).

However, distributed models of leadership are somewhat at odds with what is purported to be highly centralised leadership in higher education institutions (Gronn, 2008), while the need for holistic approaches to sustainability leadership is at odds with the highly segregated and siloed nature of universities (Moore, 2005). Effective distributed leadership needs to challenge the normative views of success within a university setting measured, for academics by research funding and publications, which is at odds with the more practical orientation of embedding sustainability (Bessant and Robinson, 2019), and to develop values and incentives for academics and professional service staff alike to lead sustainability initiatives within their own spheres of influence. Without support for leadership including incentives and developmental support (see Avissar *et al.*, 2018), leading sustainability initiatives at any level will only ever be the domain of those personally committed to driving sustainability transformation, and with the personal circumstances to enable the capacity to do so.

### *Compassionate Leadership*

Leadership skills need to be responsive to the changing nature of universities and we have seen them adapt to meet the needs of increasing marketisation (Lee, 2021). Yet, in acknowledging the negative impacts for sustainability of the increasing marketisation we see within our universities, we need also to ensure the space for leadership which can challenge these narratives and consequences. The COVID-19 pandemic raised awareness of global and institutional inequalities and heightened awareness of the need for compassionate leadership (Ramachandran *et al.*, 2023; Hashemi Toroghi *et al.*, 2024) and compassionate pedagogies (Andrew *et al.*, 2023). Compassionate leadership, and 'organizational compassion' is a means to enhance sensitivity to EDI (Hashemi Toroghi *et al.*, 2024) to create a more humane and supportive higher education environment. Andrew *et al.* (2023) argue that exploring discourses of compassion and care in higher education and highlighting that higher education has a relational element encompassing purposeful and trusting relationships, can mean that interactions start to hold more meaning and benefit. Ramachandran *et al.* (2023) identify six critical dimensions of compassionate leadership, namely: empathy; openness and communication; physical, mental health and well-being; inclusiveness; integrity; respect and dignity. They present a definition for compassionate leadership that emphasises the role of leadership in supporting the growth of individuals – 'compassionate leadership can be conceived as a personality encompassing the traits and behaviours of compassionate love, care, selflessness, wisdom, integrity, empathy, accountability, authenticity, presence, dignity, self-compassion and self-cultivation as a matter of inducing, motivating, influencing, persuading people to achieve their personal and organizations growth'. The discourse above, highlighting the importance of diversity and need for distributed leadership from all levels, as well as the need for a counterbalance to the negative implication of increasing marketisation in our universities for staff and student well-being, as well as sustainability, maybe above all suggests we should look to establish models of compassionate leadership whatever the leadership role.

## Tools of Leadership for ESD

A range of tools are available to support leadership and governance of sustainability initiatives in universities, including policy, strategy development, implementation, engagement, and monitoring (McCoshan and Martin, 2014; Reeves *et al.*, 2023) (Figure 9.1). Strategy is the design of action and the identification of the necessary timescale to achieve policy intentions. Crucially, engagement and monitoring have a role at every stage of enabling ESD. Aspects of implementation, engagement and monitoring are developed further in other chapters.

*Figure 9.1* Drivers of leadership and governance enabling ESD include policy and strategy, implementation, engagement and monitoring.

Institutional context and culture are key factors influencing what is possible in terms of enabling ESD in a particular university (Niedlich *et al.*, 2020). This includes the nature and degree of strategic commitments to ESD, capacity of staff and students to implement ESD across an institution and inclusion of ESD in engagement and monitoring processes (Reeves *et al.*, 2023).

### *Governance*

Governance provides a framework for managing organisations that encompasses processes and results. Governance can operate at multiple, interacting levels of an organisation to guide collective behaviour toward more sustainable outcomes (Clark and Harley, 2020). Universities may operate under different governance systems, but the scope of governance generally includes setting strategy, monitoring performance, and ensuring accountability (Haddock-Fraser *et al.*, 2018). In order to meet the ambitious agenda set by the SDGs, UNESCO (2019) advocates a whole-institution approach to ESD which is best supported by senior leadership and governance mechanisms to ensure that institutional ESD commitments are explicit and achieved (Price *et al.*, 2021). In addition, reflexive governance that questions core commitments in navigating uncertainty is seen as increasingly important (Clark and Hartley, 2020). Reflexive governance arrangements benefit from participation that engages diverse viewpoints and ensures continual learning since universities differ in their forms, student populations, size, specialisms, national context, and institutional cultures (White and Harder, 2013) and thus will vary in how they perceive and provide governance supporting ESD (Clark and Hartley, 2020).

### *Strategy and Motivation for ESD*

Strategic commitment to embed ESD can provide structure and impetus to support the roll-out of ESD across institutions. Prior to developing a strategy to address ESD, it is worth considering if the ESD agenda aligns strongly or weakly with institutional context in terms of overall strategy or priorities for teaching and learning (Reeves *et al.*, 2023). A recent survey of UK universities with 84 respondents from 34 institutions revealed that 75 (89%) reported an institutional strategic commitment to sustainable development to some degree (Reeves *et al.*, 2023), while in a worldwide survey of representatives of universities engaged in sustainability networks, only 43% indicated that their university had made the strategic decision to embed the SDGs in their curriculum (Leal Filho *et al.*, 2019).

Once institutional context is understood, it can be worthwhile engaging key stakeholders with the drivers for action on ESD articulated in Chapter 1 in order to formulate strategy. Key stakeholders are not only people with authority in an institution, but also those with influence, such as staff, students, alumni, and external partners. An exploration of ESD in UK universities identified a division in approaches between institutions. One group of institutions applied a top-down approach while the other group relied on their institutional identity to drive ESD. Both approaches achieved successful outcomes, but the authors concluded that the culture of an institution will determine which approach is most likely to succeed in each context (Fiselier *et al.*, 2018). Despite this, the value of a whole institution approach to progressing sustainable development and ESD and the important role of senior leadership teams, staff and students in enabling development of a positive culture that recognises and addresses sustainable development imperatives across all areas of activity cannot be over emphasised (UNESCO, 2019; Advance HE/QAA, 2021). ESD forms a central aspect of holistic, whole institution approaches to sustainability in universities (Price *et al.*, 2021).

### *Engaging Stakeholders in Strategy Development and Organisational Change*

A variety of approaches can be employed to engage stakeholders in strategy development, but building internal support for organisational change is key whatever the context through addressing six components of institutional culture: legitimacy, ownership, relevance, attainability, authenticity, and impartiality (Figure 9.2; Box 9.2; Olsen, 2023; Price *et al.*, 2024).

### *Strategy Implementation*

A strategic commitment to embed ESD represents an important recognition of its value, as well as a significant logistical challenge. Reeves *et al.* (2023) identified some overarching principles that are of use in any setting to make progress on ESD which include adopting an approach aligned with institutional strategy (recognising that ESD may align strongly or weakly with stated strategic goals), aiming to empower staff and students, and adopting an incremental approach so ESD engagement unfolds over time for individuals and is increasingly embedded within formal processes. Many aspects of this are identified in the UK ESD guidance (Advance HE/QAA, 2021). Reeves *et al.* (2023)

*Figure 9.2* Supporting organisational change through addressing six components of institutional culture. (*Source*: Adapted from Olsen, 2023.)

**Box 9.2 Informing Strategy Through Consultation (Price *et al.*, 2024)**

To develop a new sustainability strategy and address the six components of institutional culture (Olsen, 2023) at Manchester Metropolitan University, UK, different engagement activities were employed in a consultation process (Price *et al.*, 2024):

a Leadership training: training was delivered by staff, students, and alumni to about 100 leaders from across the University and Students' Union. This training led to a heightened awareness, better understanding of aspects of sustainable development, and positive engagement from leadership teams. In turn, this strengthened *ownership* of sustainability and development of the new strategy.

b Engagement: Students were involved in the creation of a short video as a communication piece to inform staff, students, and external stakeholders about strategy development, to illustrate *relevance* of the process and encourage engagement with it.

c Consultation: A range of consultation activities were undertaken with staff, students, and external stakeholders to capture ideas on what Manchester Met should be doing by 2030 if it were to be a leading sustainable university. This facilitated *legitimacy*, *ownership*, *relevance*, *authenticity*, *attainability*, and *impartiality* of the process.

 1 Online survey: A short online survey collected feedback from internal and external stakeholders on what the university's key sustainability priorities should be.

2 Interactive online workshops: Workshops open to all staff and students were delivered across the three themes of *Place* (exploring campus sustainability), *People* (exploring social responsibility), and *Impact* (exploring ESD and research that supports global sustainability agendas).
3 Social media campaign: A student-led campaign on Instagram and Facebook also served to identify sustainability priorities for students.

d Practice review: A best practice review, consultation with external partners, and horizon scanning were undertaken to ensure *legitimacy* and *relevance* of outcomes.
e Dialogue: Engaging leadership teams through conversations about delivery in their areas to support sustainability ambition facilitated *ownership*, *attainability*, and *authenticity*.
f Endorsement: Endorsement and associated *legitimacy* was sought from those at the most senior levels of leadership and governance.

The findings from all aspects of the stakeholder consultation were considered alongside sector guidance and examples of best practice to develop a Leadership in Sustainability Strategy with four strategic areas: (1) Leadership in Sustainability, (2) Academic Innovation and Impact, (3) Sustainable Campus and Practices, and (4) Engagement and Partnerships (Manchester Metropolitan University, 2022).

explore scenarios based on working with different levels of strategic commitment to ESD (high priority or lower priority). Embedding ESD into roles, structures, and decision-making processes (Box 9.3) can enable regular dialogue and vigilance to ensure a commitment to ESD is maintained and opportunities for enhancement are taken (Reeves *et al.*, 2023).

**Box 9.3 Idealised Governance Checklist for ESD**

Idealised governance checklist for embedding sustainability and ESD into roles, structures, and decision-making processes. What is the approach to governance for sustainability and ESD of your university? To what extent do you see that played out in the everyday?

- Clarify responsibilities for sustainability and ESD within the University's governance, leadership, and management structures.
- Arrange briefings for senior Academic and Professional Services colleagues on ESD and its implications for the university.
- Develop training (possibly online) on ESD.
- Involve the Students' Union in discussions on the implications of ESD.

- Identify and update relevant policies, procedures, and Codes of Practice to ensure they are coherent, and in alignment with sustainability in areas such as education (e.g., graduate attributes, quality assurance processes and student voice), research, international, partnerships, campus and practices, staff contracts, recruitment and appraisal policies for staff members and Governors, etc. Make policies and procedures relevant to sustainability publicly accessible.
- Include consideration of the impact of new policies and procedures on sustainability as part of their approval process.
- Annually review sustainability issues as part of the review process for policies, practices, and procedures.
- Arrange an annual standing item on the key principles of sustainability in appropriate University committees, e.g., Education Committee, EDI Strategy Board, People Strategy Board, etc.
- Schedule discussion on sustainability at the Board of Governors to agree the issues to be covered within institutional practice.
- Incorporate sustainability into the induction process for staff and students and start of year information for returning students.

### *Framing Success in ESD*

Monitoring performance offers internal and external validation and assurance about the effectiveness of ESD implementation. Internal approaches include measuring progress against targets, embedding in quality assurance processes and student voice. External measures of success include indicators of esteem such as accreditation and rankings. Although addressing ESD in performance monitoring is an important component of its mainstreaming across an institution, it is likely to be ineffective without a wider enabling environment that motivates and empowers staff and students to understand the agenda and put it into practice (Reeves *et al.*, 2023). This includes reinforcing the value that sustainability can add to academic activities, including to student experience, graduate attributes, and opportunities for staff development and recognition (Price *et al.*, 2024). Developing an enabling environment though professional development is addressed in Chapter 10.

A recent survey of UK institutions revealed that whilst strategic commitments to sustainability or ESD are increasingly frequent, explicit inclusion of ESD in quality assurance and student voice processes is still rare, revealing a misalignment between strategic commitments to ESD and effective quality assurance processes to address it and evidence impact (Reeves *et al.*, 2023). Universities are increasingly being compared or ranked by engagement with sustainability (SDSN, 2020). However, a challenge faced by universities in implementing ESD is ambiguity in how sustainability outcomes relate to individual organisational success (Haddock-Fraser and Gorman, 2020). There remains a lack of sector-wide agreed metrics for ESD and sustainability in higher education with recognition achieved by a range of awards, accreditations, league tables, and frameworks that attribute varied significance to ESD (Haddock-Fraser and Gorman, 2020).

A recent analysis of six of the most popular sustainability assessment and reporting frameworks used by higher education concluded that all the frameworks examined align with the UN SDGs in some way and that challenges of participation are likely to be outweighed by the advantages. Challenges include the complexity of participation and data gathering, the time, financial and resource commitment required, ability to align to the SDGs, and eligibility and applicability. Advantages include demonstrating a commitment to transparency and accountability, helping institutions gain recognition for their sustainability efforts, and generating opportunities for partnerships and influence (Elsevier, 2023). Thus, they can serve to address the components of institutional culture: legitimacy, ownership, relevance, attainability, authenticity, and impartiality (Olsen, 2023). In some cases, reporting frameworks can not only measure success, but they can also act as change programmes to support embedding ESD across all aspects of student learning and supporting bottom-up, top-down, middle-out leadership (Boxes 9.4 and 9.5; Figure 9.3; SOS-UK, 2023, 2024). Monitoring and evaluation of ESD are explored in Chapter 11.

### Box 9.4 Responsible Futures: Working in Partnership with Students for ESD

Responsible Futures is an accreditation mark and framework that supports partnerships between students' unions and institutions through structured criteria to encourage action on embedding ESD, with interventions at different levels of an institution: top-down, middle-out, and bottom-up (SOS-UK, 2023, 2024; Figure 9.3).

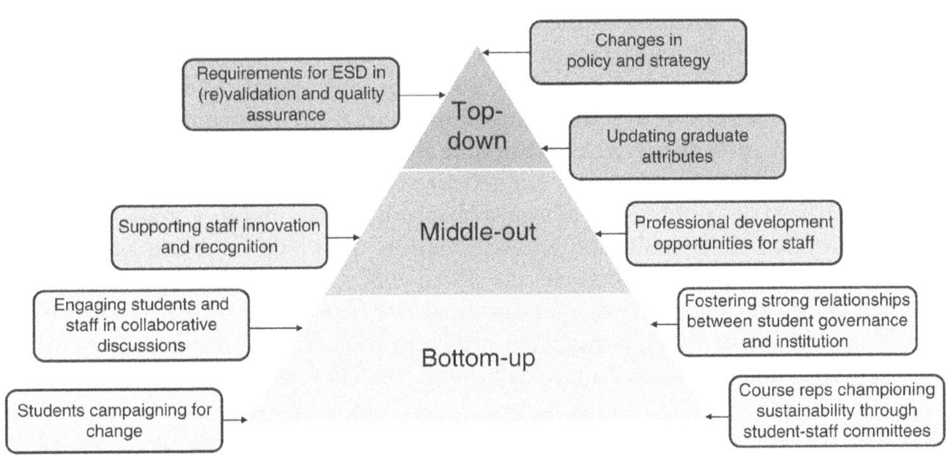


*Figure 9.3* Responsible Futures: working in partnership with students for ESD. (*Source*: Adapted from SOS-UK, 2024.)

**Box 9.5 Supporting the Students' Union (SU) at the University of the West of England (UWE) to Engage with the Sustainability Agenda**

Over the last 15 years, the university's leadership has worked closely with the SU, supporting the development of capacity and capability to engage, lead, and effect change in their own operations but also to stimulate student-led action across the university's curriculum, campus management, and wider operations. This deliberate engagement policy involving financial and time inputs has enabled the SU to work closely and effectively with university staff. Outcomes from this high level of partnership working include:

- SOS Responsible Future accreditation covering the university – SU partnership (SOS-UK, 2023)
- inclusion of the SU in UWE's ISO 14001 EMS certification covering operational and educational activities (UWE, 2024),
- top scoring SU in the NUS Green Impact scheme for 8 years in a row (SOS-UK, undated b).

## Conclusions

ESD adoption frequently appears to be an 'emerging agenda' within universities, meaning that despite student expectation and strategic commitment, there is a gap in terms of capacity to support meaningful implementation (Reeves *et al.*, 2023; SOS-UK, undated). To address the need for ESD, institutional leaders need to understand the ESD agenda and to legitimise its adoption throughout the institution that they lead. This will require support and training for staff and the development of strategies, policies, and processes enabling ESD across the range of institutional activities.

Leadership is essential to achieve ESD and a broader sustainability agenda within higher education institutions and this leadership can take many forms. Institutional context is a key factor influencing what is possible in terms of enabling ESD in a particular university, but effective measures are framed by two overarching principles that can be effective regardless of context: (1) demonstration that sustainability adds value to academic activities and (2) consultation and co-creation at all levels to build a shared vision and support for whole-institutional change (Price *et al.*, 2024). In a resource-constrained environment, legitimising staff engagement need not necessarily lead to a need for new resource but may be achieved through the redirection of existing resources.

It is likely that institutions that do not orientate the curriculum and wider activities towards ESD will find that their student body increasingly advocates for positive change. Leaders that do not engage with the ESD agenda will be failing in the responsibility that higher education has to inform, educate, envision, and pursue better futures for people and planet. Ultimately, all institutions will need to adapt their operations to embrace a more sustainable model of engagement. This new paradigm of university leadership will recognise the importance of ESD and the responsibility for leadership that higher education has in society.

## References


Advance HE/QAA (2021). Education for sustainable development guidance. Available at: https://www.advance-he.ac.uk/knowledge-hub/education-sustainable-development-guidance [Accessed 31 July 2024].

Andrew, M.B., Dobbins, K., Pollard, E., Mueller, B. and Middleton, R. (2023). The role of compassion in higher education practices. Journal of University Teaching & Learning Practice, 20(3), p. 01.

Arday, J. (2018). Understanding race and educational leadership in higher education: Exploring the black and ethnic minority (BME) experience. Management in Education, 32(4), pp. 192–200.

Aung, P.N. and Hallinger, P. (2022). The intellectual structure of the literature on sustainability leadership in higher education: An author co-citation analysis. International Journal of Educational Management, 36(5), pp. 784–799.

Avissar, I., Alkaher, I. and Gan, D. (2018). The role of distributed leadership in mainstreaming environmental sustainability into campus life in an Israeli teaching college: A case study. International Journal of Sustainability in Higher Education, 19(3), pp. 518–546.

Bailinson, P., Decherd, W., Ellsworth, D. and Guttman, M. (2020). LGBTQ+ voices: Learning from lived experiences. McKinsey Quarterly, 1(2), pp. 1–15.

Bass, B.M. (2000). The future of leadership in learning organizations. Journal of Leadership Studies, 7(3), pp. 18–40.

Bessant, S.E. and Robinson, Z.P. (2019). Rating and rewarding higher education for sustainable development research within the marketised higher education context: Experiences from English universities. Environmental Education Research, 25(4), pp. 548–565.

Blackmore, J. (2013). A feminist critical perspective on educational leadership. International Journal of Leadership in Education, 16(2), pp. 139–154. DOI: 10.1080/13603124.2012.754057.

Blackmore, J. (2014). Wasting talent? Gender and the problematics of academic disenchantment and disengagement with leadership. Higher Education Research and Development, 33, pp. 86–99.

Brinkhurst, M., Rose, P., Maurice, G. and Ackerman, J.D. (2011). Achieving campus sustainability: Top-down, bottom-up, or neither? International Journal of Sustainability in Higher Education, 12, pp. 338–354.

Castruita, B. and Fassina, N., (2024). Uplifting the critical value of the LGBTQ+ climate workforce. Available at: https://digital.sandiego.edu/cgi/viewcontent.cgi?article=1037&context=npi-sdclimate [Accessed 31 July 2024].

Clark, W.C. and Harley, A.G. (2020). Sustainability science: Toward a synthesis. Annual Review of Environment and Resources, 45, pp. 331–386. https://doi.org/10.1146/annurev-environ-012420-043621

Dooris, M., Powell, S. and Farrier, A. (2018). Healthy universities: Whole university leadership for health, wellbeing & sustainability. Leadership Foundation for Higher Education/Advance HE.

Eagly, A.H. and Johnson, B.T. (1990). Gender and leadership style: A meta-analysis. Psychological Bulletin, 108, pp. 233–256. DOI: 10.1037/0033-2909.108.2.233.

EAUC (2024). Sustainability Leadership Scorecard. Available at: https://www.eauc.org.uk/sustainability_leadership_scorecard [Accessed 31 July 2024].

Elsevier (2023). Demystifying sustainability assessment and reporting frameworks. Elsevier. Available at: https://assets.ctfassets.net/o78em1y1w4i4/vsnNF0bJcJgdMSWUJuHL0/5abac6ecfc7268caacc7d83aac4b2fbf/Elsevier_Sustainability_Frameworks_Whitepaper.pdf [Accessed 31 July 2024].

Federo, R. (2024). The rainbow glass ceiling: Breaking barriers for LGBTQ+ inclusion in board diversity. Academy of Management Perspectives, (ja), p. amp-2023.

Fiselier, E. and Longhurst, J.W.S., (2018). A critical evaluation of the representation of the QAA and HEA guidance on ESD in public web environments of UK higher education institutions. In: W. Leal Filho, ed., Implementing Sustainability in the Curriculum of Universities. World Sustainability Series. Springer, pp. 223–246. doi:10.1007/978-3-319-70281-0_14

Fiselier, E.S., Longhurst, J.W.S. and Gough, G.K. (2018). Exploring the current position of ESD in UK higher education institutions. International Journal of Sustainability in Higher Education, 19(3), pp. 393–412. DOI: 10.1108/IJSHE-06-2017-0084.

Gronn, P. (2008). The future of distributed leadership. Journal of Educational Administration, 46(2), pp. 141–158.
Haddock-Fraser, J. and Gorman, D. (2020). Building your influence: The role of The smart sustainability leader. Emerald Open Research, 2, p. 53.
Haddock-Fraser, J., Rands, P. and Scoffham, S. (2018). Leadership for Sustainability in Higher Education. Bloomsbury Academic, London.
Hashemi Toroghi, H., Denney, F. and Simpson, A.V. (2024). Cultivating staff equality, diversity, And inclusion in higher education in the post-pandemic era: An organizational compassion perspective. Frontiers in Sociology, 9, p. 1378665.
ISO Standards (undated). ISO 14001 and related standards. Available at: https://www.iso.org/iso-14001-environmental-management.html [Accessed 31 July 2024].
Jones, S., Harvey, M., Lefoe, G. and Ryland, K. (2014). Synthesising theory and practice: Distributed leadership in higher education. Educational Management Administration and Leadership, 42(5), pp. 603–619.
Leal Filho, W., Eustachio, J.H.P.P., Caldana, A.C.F., Will, M., Lange Salvia, A., Rampasso, I.S., Anholon, R., Platje, J. and Kovaleva, M. (2020). Sustainability leadership in higher education institutions: An overview of challenges. Sustainability, 12(9), p. 3761.
Leal Filho, W., Shiel, C., Paço, A., Mifsud, M., Avila, L.V., Brandli, L.L., Molthan-Hill, P., Pace, P., Azeiteiro, U.M., Vargas, V.R. and Caeiro, S. (2019). Sustainable Development Goals and sustainability teaching at universities: Falling behind or getting ahead of the pack? Journal of Cleaner Production, 232, pp. 285–294.
Lee, C. (2021). Promoting diversity in university leadership: The argument for LGBTQ+ specific leadership programmes in higher education. Perspectives: Policy and Practice in Higher Education, 25(3), pp. 91–99.
Manchester Metropolitan University (2022). Leadership in sustainability strategy. Available at: https://www.mmu.ac.uk/sites/default/files/2022-06/Leadership-in-Sustainability-Strategy-2022-2026.pdf [Accessed 31 July 2024].
Mazon, G., Pereira Ribeiro, J.M., Montenegro de Lima, C.R., Castro, B.C.G. and Guerra, J.B.S.O.D.A. (2020). The promotion of sustainable development in higher education institutions: Top-down, bottom-up, or neither? International Journal of Sustainability in Higher Education, 21(7), pp. 1429–1450.
McCoshan, A. and Martin, S., (2014). From strategy to implementation: The second evaluation of the Green Academy programme. Higher Education Academy, York. Available at: https://www.advance-he.ac.uk/knowledge-hub/strategy-implementation-second-evaluation-green-academy-programme [Accessed 31 July 2024].
Moore, J. (2005). Barriers and pathways to creating sustainability education programs: Policy, rhetoric and reality. Environmental Education Research, 11(5), pp. 537–555.
Niedlich, S., Kummer, B., Bauer, M., Rieckmann, M. and Bormann, I. (2020). Cultures of sustainability governance in higher education institutions: A multi-case study of dimensions and implications. Higher Education Quarterly, 74(4), pp. 373–390.
Odgers Berndtson (2024). Sustainability. Available at: https://www.odgersberndtson.com/insights/sustainability/ and https://www.odgersberndtson.com/insights/why-does-sustainability-matter-in-the-higher-education-sector/ [Accessed 31 July 2024].
Olsen, A.B. (2023). Getting employee buy-in for organizational change. Harvard Business Review. Available at: https://hbr.org/2023/02/getting-employee-buy-in-for-organizational-change [Accessed 31 July 2024].
ONS Life Expectancy Tables (2024). Available at: https://www.ons.gov.uk/peoplepopulationandcommunity/healthandsocialcare/healthandlifeexpectancies/articles/lifeexpectancycalculator/2019-06-07 [Accessed 31 July 2024].
Orr, D. (1991). What is education for? Six myths about the foundations of modern education, and six new principles to replace them. The Learning Revolution. Available at: https://www.context.org/iclib/ic27/orr/ [Accessed 31 July 2024].
Pee, S. and Vululleh, N. (2020). Role of universities in transforming society: Challenges and practices. In: E. Sengupta, P. Blessinger and C. Mahoney, eds., International Perspectives on Policies, Practices and Pedagogies for Promoting Social Responsibility in Higher Education. Innovations in Higher Education Teaching and Learning, Vol. 32, Emerald Publishing Limited, pp. 67–79.

People and Planet (2023). People and Planet University League: Methodology. Education for sustainable development. Available at: https://peopleandplanet.org/resources-training/people-planet-university-league/methodology/education-sustainable-development [Accessed 31 July 2024].

Price, E.A.C., Nicholson, D.T., Dunk, R., Lawler, C., Carney, M., Vargas, V., Veitch, S., Leigh, S., Singleton, M. and Mottram, S. (2024). Enabling change agents for Sustainable Development: A whole-institution approach to embedding the UN Sustainable Development Goals in higher education. International Journal of Sustainability in Higher Education, 25(7), pp. 1333–1350. doi:10.1108/IJSHE-02-2024-0112

Price, E.A.C., White, R.M., Mori, K., Longhurst, J., Baughan, P., Hayles, C.S., Gough, G. and Preist, C. (2021). Supporting the role of universities in leading individual and societal transformation through education for sustainable development. Discover Sustainability, 2, p. 49. DOI: 10.1007/s43621-021-00058-3.

QAA and HEA (2014). Education for sustainable development: Guidance for UK higher education providers. Quality Assurance Agency and Higher Education Academy. [Quality Assurance Agency, Gloucester. 28pp

Quality Assurance Agency (QAA) (2024). UK Quality Code for Higher Education. QAA, Gloucester. Available at: https://www.qaa.ac.uk/docs/qaa/quality-code/uk-quality-code-for-higher-education-2024.pdf?sfvrsn=19a5b881_32 [Accessed 31 July 2024].

RACE report (2022). 2022 report. Available at: https://assets-global.website-files.com/623c735 9fd38194a54b48eaa/6397552ecb940a007016399c_20221208_The%20RACE%20Report_2022%20Report.pdf [Accessed 31 July 2024].

Ramachandran, S., Balasubramanian, S., James, W.F. and Al Masaeid, T. (2023). Whither compassionate leadership? A systematic review. Management Review Quarterly, pp. 1–85.

Reeves, A., Gwilliam, J., Harrison, P., Price, E., Schantz, N., Ribchester, C., Hughes, T., Gretton, S., Strachan, S., Logan, L., Boxley, S., Lengthorn, E., Barrett, H. and Peres, S. (2023). Education for sustainable development and academic quality: Principles and processes for higher education providers. Quality Assurance Agency (QAA). Available at: https://www.qaa.ac.uk/docs/qaa/members/education-for-sustainable-development-and-academic-quality-principles-and-processes-for-higher-education-providers.pdf?sfvrsn=63e2ac81_8 [Accessed 31 July 2024].

Roberson, Q., Quigley, N.R., Vickers, K. and Bruck, I. (2021). Reconceptualizing leadership from a neurodiverse perspective. Group & Organization Management, 46(2), pp. 399–423.

Robinson, Z.P. and Laycock Pedersen, R. (2021). How to repurpose the university: A resilience lens on sustainability governance. Frontiers in Sustainability, 2, p. 674210.

SDSN (2020). Accelerating Education for the SDGs in Universities: A guide for universities, colleges, and tertiary and higher education institutions. Sustainable Development Solutions Network (SDSN), New York.

Senge, P. (1990). The Fifth Discipline: The Art and Practice of The Learning Organization. Doubleday, New York.

Sheil, C. (2013). Leadership. In: S. Sterling, L. Maxey and H. Luna, eds., The Sustainable University: Progress and Prospects. Routledge, London, pp.110–131.

Shiel, C. and Jones, D. (2016). Sustainability and social justice: Leadership challenges. In: L. Shultz and M. Viczko, eds., Assembling and Governing the Higher Education Institution. Palgrave Studies in Global Citizenship Education and Democracy, Palgrave Macmillan, London, pp.43–63. doi:10.1057/978-1-137-52261-0_2

Smith, M.K. (2001). Peter Senge and the learning organisation. Available at: https://infed.org/peter-senge-and-the-learning-organization/ [Accessed 31 July 2024].

SOS-UK (undated a). Sustainability Skills Survey. Available at: https://www.sos-uk.org/research/sustainability-skills-survey [Accessed 31 July 2024].

SOS-UK (undated b). Green Impact. Available at: https://greenimpact.nus.org.uk/find-out-more-students-unions/ [Accessed 31 July 2024].

SOS-UK (2023). Responsible Futures. Available at: https://www.sos-uk.org/project/responsible-futures [Accessed 31 July 2024]

SOS-UK (2024). Responsible Futures - changes and interventions from top-down, middle-out and bottom-up. Available at: https://www.sos-uk.org/resources-file/responsible-futures-changes-and-interventions-from-top-down-middle-out-and-bottom-up [Accessed 31 July 2024].

Spillane, J.P., Diamond, J.B., Sherer, J. and Coldren, A.F. (2004). Distributing leadership. In: M. Coles and G. Southworth, eds., Developing Leadership: Creating the Schools of Tomorrow. New York: Open University Press, pp.37–49.

Sterling, S. (2004). Higher education, sustainability, and the role of systemic learning. In: P.B. Corcoran and A.E.J. Wals, eds., Higher Education and the Challenge of Sustainability: Problematics, Promise, and Practice. Dordrecht: Springer Netherlands, pp.49–70.

Sterling, S., Maxey, L. and Luna, H. (2013). The Sustainable University: Progress and Prospects. Routledge, London, p. 23.

Swank, E. (2018). Sexual identities and participation in liberal and conservative social movements. Social Science Research, 74, pp. 176–186.

Tilbury, D. (2013). Another world is desirable: A global rebooting of higher education for sustainable development. In: S. Sterling, L. Maxey and H. Luna, eds., The Sustainable University: Progress and Prospects. London: Earthscan/Routledge, pp. 71–86.

Times Higher Education (2021). Students, sustainability and study choices. Available at: https://cdn.theewf.org/uploads/pdf/THE_Students-Sustainability-and-Study-Choices_Report_Final.pdf [Accessed 31 July 2024].

UN Department of Economic and Social Affairs (undated). The 17 goals. Available at: https://sdgs.un.org/goals [Accessed 31 July 2024].

UNAI (2023). United Nations Academic Impact: Why join? Available at: https://www.un.org/sites/un2.un.org/files/30-05-2023_why_join_guide.pdf [Accessed 31 July 2024].

United Nations Educational, Scientific and Cultural Organization (UNESCO) (2019). Framework for the implementation of education for sustainable development (ESD) beyond 2019. Available at: https://unesdoc.unesco.org/search/71aaa3f9-9656-43a7-a740-f3fb57e1dbc5 [Accessed 31 July 2024].

United Nations Educational, Scientific and Cultural Organization (UNESCO) (2024). Greening curriculum guidance: Teaching and learning for climate action. UNESCO, Paris, France. Available at: https://www.unesco.org/en/articles/greening-curriculum-guidance-teaching-and-learning-climate-action [Accessed 31 July 2024].

Universities UK (n.d.). Latest insights and analysis: Higher education numbers. Available at: https://www.universitiesuk.ac.uk/latest/insights-and-analysis/higher-education-numbers [Accessed 31 July 2024].

Universities UK (2023). Climate crisis: What progress have universities made? Available at: https://www.universitiesuk.ac.uk/latest/insights-and-analysis/climate-crisis-what-progress-have [Accessed 31 July 2024].

University of the West of England (UWE) (2024). ISO 14001 Environmental Management System. Available at: https://www.uwe.ac.uk/about/values-vision-strategy/sustainability/iso-14001-certification [Accessed 31 July 2024].

Weiss, M., Barth, M., Weik, A. and von Wehrden, H. (2021). Drivers and barriers of implementing sustainability curricula in higher education: Assumptions and evidence. Higher Education Studies, 11(2), pp. 42–64. Available at: https://eric.ed.gov/?id=EJ1291491 [Accessed 31 July 2024].

White, K. and Burkinshaw, P. (2019). Women and leadership in higher education: Special issue editorial. Social Sciences, 8(7), p. 204.

White, R.M. and Harder, M. (2013). The journey towards sustainability via community: Lessons from two UK universities. In: S. Sterling, L. Maxey and H. Luna, eds., The Sustainable University: Progress and Prospects. Abingdon: Routledge, pp. 146–161.

Yukl, G. (2006) Leadership in Organizations. 6th Ed, Upper Saddle River, NJ: Pearson-Prentice Hall, 2006.

Zohar, T., Parag, Y. and Ayalon, O. (2021). Of agency, action, and influence: The middle-out mechanism for promoting a low-carbon energy transition. Energy Research & Social Science, 72, p. 101900.

Zurich Insurance, 2020. Millions of young people want more climate change education. Available at: https://www.zurich.co.uk/media-centre/millions-of-young-people-want-more-climate-change-education [Accessed 31 July 2024].

Chapter 10

# Professional Development for All

## Enabling Advocates for Education for Sustainable Development

*Patrick Baughan, Elizabeth A. C. Price and James W. S. Longhurst*

### Introduction

In this chapter, we examine professional development opportunities to be considered for different groups of university staff, to equip those staff with appropriate skills and competences in Education for Sustainable Development (ESD). If our sector is to promote and develop sustainability, and our aim is to develop authentic sustainable graduates through learning, teaching and the broader student experience, our staff also need to be equipped to enable this (Reeves *et al.*, 2023; Vogel *et al.*, 2023; Varga-Atkins *et al.*, 2024; UNESCO, 2024). Indeed, 'Building capacities of educators and trainers' is one of the five priorities of the UNESCO Global Action Programme on ESD (UNESCO, 2018), and Fiselier *et al.* (2018) argue that the most critical driver of ESD integration within the curriculum is support for staff and student engagement.

> Educators in all educational settings can help learners understand the complex choices that sustainable development requires and motivate them to transform themselves and society.
>
> In order to guide and empower learners, educators themselves need to be empowered and equipped with the knowledge, skills, values and behaviours that are required for this transition.
>
> (UNESCO, 2020)

Yet, many universities currently lack the capacity to integrate ESD effectively into the training they provide for staff (Holdsworth *et al.*, 2008; Tilbury *et al.*, 2014; Mulà *et al.*, 2017; Tilbury, 2021).

In Chapter 3, we questioned whether ESD could ever be achieved without it being located in the context of a holistic sustainable university. We argue that ESD is relevant to all staff, and opportunities need to be provided for everyone to learn about and contribute to it to enact the whole-institution approach to ESD advocated by UNESCO (2019). We need to invest in, develop and enthuse our staff to enable all of them to reframe their own approaches to professional practice, regardless of role, and contribute to ESD at their institutions. Therefore, in this chapter, we will discuss the need for appropriate and diverse ESD-based professional development for all actors within higher education, be they university leaders, researchers, educators, or in professional and technical roles. We examine who might provide professional development, and how such development should work in a way that invites engagement and excitement in disciplinary

DOI: 10.4324/9781003451563-10

and professional contexts. We will also consider the importance of ensuring that professional development is inclusive and participatory, drawing on a range of voices and perspectives. Further, there needs to be alignment of professional development for staff, enabling them to work together. Finally, our professional development for ESD needs to be informed by student perspectives and experiences, utilising, for example, appropriate student partnership models (Cook-Sather *et al.*, 2014).

The complex challenges faced by societies have led to greater interest in higher education as a promoter and developer of sustainable development. This has been strongly influenced by the development of the UN Sustainable Development Goals (SDGs) (UN, 2015), with many universities now prioritising the SDGs in their curricula and other activities. The breadth of the SDGs means that they can resonate with all academic disciplines and are relevant to all roles, and thus, they provide one useful starting point in our consideration of professional development for ESD (QAA and Advance HE, 2021). There are encouraging signs of growth in professional development for ESD, and a variety of innovative opportunities exist (Tilbury *et al.*, 2014). Nevertheless, our sector is far from a position in which claims can be made that ESD is widely understood and practised by staff: there is much work to be done (Holdsworth *et al.*, 2008; Tilbury *et al.*, 2014; Mulà *et al.*, 2017). The under-researched area of professional development for ESD in higher education provides one route forward (Dumitru, 2017).

## What Is Professional Development for Education for Sustainable Development?

We are addressing here any form of ESD-focussed staff development. This can be supported through informal or formal activities delivered in person or online, such as guidance, training, mentoring, workshops, symposia, action-learning, communities of practice, micro-credential routes, projects or accreditation schemes (Tilbury *et al.*, 2014; Lambrechts *et al.*, 2017; Mulà *et al.*, 2017; Fiselier *et al.*, 2018; UNESCO 2024). Professional development for ESD should not only introduce the concepts of sustainable development and ESD but also develop the capacity to integrate these into the curriculum or professional practice (Holdsworth *et al.*, 2008).

Clearly, there will be significant variation in professional development across and within institutions, but the QAA and Advance HE (2021) ESD Guidance can play a valuable supporting role in encouraging and enabling individuals and universities to strengthen and embed ESD (Price *et al.*, 2021), regardless of context. Tilbury *et al.* (2014), Mulà *et al.* (2017) and Lambrechts *et al.* (2017) document a series of professional development for ESD initiatives that have been introduced, but these innovations are not widespread, and professional development for ESD needs a stronger profile (Tilbury *et al.*, 2014). While there is a need for more research, case studies of success and evaluation of outcomes, universities will benefit from utilising an overarching framework or development strategy for ESD, which itself needs to be inclusive and joined up, and demonstrate an authentic organisational commitment to sustainability (Price *et al.*, 2024). Our discussion of ideas for professional development opportunities for different staff, provided below, should help shape such a framework.

Having provided some context for professional development in ESD, in the next section, we examine types of professional development for different staff, under a series of sub-sections. These categorisations are not exhaustive but are made to show the variety of professional development opportunities that can be offered and give readers a range of ideas. The categories are not fixed, so there will be circumstances in which some staff may need or wish to experience a wider range of professional development opportunities. There should be something for everyone in the discussions that follow.

## Professional Development for Different Roles

### *Academic Staff*

Academics, themselves a diverse staff group, might be defined by many factors, including career stage, their discipline or field, their specific areas of expertise, and their contributions to research, teaching, leadership and citizenship. Many academics have a vital role in developing curricula and undertaking teaching and assessment, and so are in an influential position with respect to the implementation or embedding of ESD. Professional development should furnish educators with the competences they need to ensure that students are equipped to contribute to a sustainable world (McKeown, 2002; UNECE, 2012; Dlouhá *et al.*, 2017; Mulà *et al.*, 2017; Nikolic *et al.*, 2017; Scherak and Rieckmann, 2020). The competence framework for educators developed by UNECE (2012) to support professional development for ESD outlines three dimensions of educator competences: holistic, envisioning change and achieving transformation that are based on systems thinking and future-orientated action, and four learning domains: to know, to do, to live together, to be. In the resulting matrix, relevant educator competences are outlined and explained based on these principles (UNECE, 2012; Dlouhá *et al.*, 2017).

#### *Framing Professional Development for Academics*

Professional development for ESD for academic staff should take factors such as organisational culture, engagement and empowerment into account and should be clearly framed and communicated within a broader context of institutional change towards sustainability, emphasising why ESD is relevant to all disciplines and the wider agenda and priorities of the university (Verhulst and Lambrechts, 2015; Lambrechts *et al.*, 2017; Fiselier *et al.*, 2018). For example, while there can be perceived tensions between different institutional priorities, ESD is a powerful driver of student success, enhancing internationalisation, decolonisation, employability, entrepreneurship and community engagement. ESD therefore aligns with and supports other contemporary agendas and is beneficial both within and beyond institutions (Price *et al.*, 2021; Advance HE, 2024a). Professional development for ESD should reflect this complementarity and support colleagues to 'frame curricula, harmonise such activities and provide the context in which all of these institutional priorities can find expression' (QAA and Advance HE, 2021).

Furthermore, in a move to integrate ESD into curricula, universities have been challenged by the perception of some academics that ESD is simply an add-on and a threat to their traditional disciplines (Verhulst and Lambrechts, 2015; Fiselier *et al.*, 2018). To address this, professional development should recognise a plurality of views and varying personal and professional identities since addressing sustainability challenges requires multiple perspectives, experimentation and alternative ideas (Callejas Restrepo *et al.*, 2017; Melles, 2019; McCowan, 2023). This can be supported through professional development that balances autonomy with providing concrete guidelines which enable educators to embed ESD in disciplinary contexts (Lambrechts *et al.*, 2017). Highlighting that some approaches associated with sustainability competencies are already mainstream in university teaching, such as problem-based learning, real-world case studies and work with external partners can also catalyse engagement (Fiselier *et al.*, 2018; Vogel *et al.*, 2023). Ideally, capacity building for ESD should provide flexibility to suit different circumstances and needs, for example, light touch (face-to-face introduction), standard (online interactive modules) and digging deeper (online elements for more in-depth consideration) (Price *et al.*, 2024, Table 10.1).

Finally, and crucially, professional development for ESD seeks to transform practice and so should itself exhibit the characteristics of transformative ESD, that is, specific

*Table 10.1* Professional development for ESD at Manchester Metropolitan University.

| | |
|---|---|
| | *Education for Sustainable Development (ESD)* |
| Embedding ESD presentation | A short online presentation provides an overview of embedding Education for Sustainable Development (ESD) and its alignment with programmes at Manchester Metropolitan University. The presentation is also delivered face to face to introduce ESD concepts in staff meetings. |
| Embedding ESD online resource | An interactive online Embedding Education for Sustainable Development (ESD) resource is available to all staff in the Staff Resource Area. This programme introduces a structured approach for re-framing existing curriculum elements and/or designing new elements to embed key principles of ESD in varied disciplinary contexts, based on the CoDesignS ESD (2021) Framework. It is particularly relevant to academic, learner development and quality assurance staff. It was developed in consultation with staff and students from across the university to be relevant to all disciplines and the Manchester Metropolitan University context. |
| Postgraduate Certificate and Masters | Education for Sustainable Development is an option unit within the PGCert in Learning and Teaching in Higher Education and the Masters in Higher Education. The unit introduces the Education for Sustainable Development (ESD) concept and provides an overview of the debates and approaches to embedding sustainability in higher education curricula. |
| Curated external ESD resources | Curated suite of external ESD resources to support staff to incorporate ESD in their curricula. |
| Community of Practice | The Responsible Futures change programme supports valuable development opportunities for academic, professional services and students' union staff and students through a community of practice. |
| | *Carbon Literacy* |
| Carbon Literacy training for staff and students | Training available to all staff and to provide a comprehensive overview of climate change as a thematic aspect of ESD: the basic science behind it, its drivers and impacts, as well as an understanding of the actions required by individuals, communities, and organisations to avoid the worst impacts and set us on a path to a sustainable future. Staff and students are also trained to be Carbon Literacy trainers. |

(*Continued*)

*Table 10.1* (Continued)

| | |
|---|---|
| | *Carbon Literacy* |
| Teach Carbon Literacy | Teach Carbon Literacy training to enable academic staff to embed Carbon Literacy onto their courses and promote the initiative across their departments, involving a community of practice of Carbon Literacy Champions to tailor training to varied disciplinary contexts. |
| Carbon Literacy Training for University Leaders | Carbon Literacy leaders training to enable managers and senior colleagues to identify opportunities to make a meaningful difference – to challenge existing systems and processes, maintain a sense of urgency, and to translate Carbon Literacy knowledge into all areas of university business, so that we can work more sustainably and reach zero carbon. |
| | *Decolonising the curriculum* |
| Decolonising the Curriculum Toolkit | The Decolonising the Curriculum Toolkit aims to support academic staff in the process of reviewing and decolonising their teaching, seeing a just and fair curriculum as a core component of ESD. |
| | *Staff engagement* |
| Your Sustainable Journey | An online resource for all staff outlining a wide range of opportunities to get involved in sustainability and make a meaningful impact. |
| | *Staff recognition* |
| Sustainability Awards | An annual Students' Union Teaching Award for Outstanding Teaching for Sustainability and an annual University Staff Award for Sustainability reward achievement, showcase examples of good practice and raise the profile of sustainability and ESD. |

*Source*: Manchester Metropolitan University (2024a, b, c).

learning objectives for the SDGs, key competencies for sustainability and transformative pedagogies and teaching methods that engage head, heart and hands to enthuse staff, regardless of discipline or role (Chapters 2 and 6). For example, micro-lectures, curated readings, interactive discussions to encourage diverse perspectives, reflective exercises and game-based activities have proved effective in this respect (Dunk *et al.*, 2021; Nicholson *et al.*, 2024; Toro-Troconis *et al.*, 2024).

With these points made, there are a series of additional factors – and consequent recommendations – to consider.

### *Professional Development Opportunities for Academic Staff*

A range of provision of professional development approaches can empower academic staff to address ESD (Mulà *et al.*, 2017; Biasutti *et al.*, 2018).

First, *pedagogic* development of academic staff is often provided by accredited programmes of study – commonly referred to as academic practice or learning and teaching programmes. These are usually led and taught by colleagues in the field of academic and educational development, defined by Shay (2012) as 'a range of development and research practices aimed at the professionalization of teaching and learning in higher education, most commonly associated with various forms of student, staff, curriculum and policy development'. In the UK, as in other countries, many academic staff are expected to undertake a postgraduate certificate or higher postgraduate programme to develop their pedagogical expertise in areas including teaching, assessment and feedback, student support and curriculum design. Many of these programmes are accredited by Advance HE, an organisation that works with partners across the globe to improve higher education for staff, students and society (Advance HE, 2020). Advance HE is also custodian of the Professional Standards Framework (PSF) (Advance HE, 2023), a set of standards and guidelines for benchmarking success in higher education teaching and support of learning. While the current edition of the PSF does not explicitly refer to ESD, elements of the framework certainly relate to it and subsidiary guidelines connecting the PSF to ESD have recently been published (Advance HE, 2024b). Furthermore, the Quality Assurance Agency (QAA) Quality Code for Higher Education (2024a), that enables providers to see what is expected of them, makes explicit reference to ESD.

The aforementioned academic practice programmes present a valid and potentially important route to introduce staff to ESD (Dumitru, 2017). Given that such programmes normally require participants to link their learning to their own professional practice, they can provide an early opportunity to equip – and hopefully excite – academic and other staff in ESD. There may be barriers for inclusion of ESD in some such programmes (such as overcrowded curricula or poor fit with institutional aims) but several now do. There is also variation in the content of these programmes and whilst a growing number consider ESD in, for example, modules about learning and teaching, or curriculum design, or in a bespoke module, this is far from ubiquitous. There are different views about the value of such programmes and the role they should have in including ESD in their curricula (Baughan, 2015). Here, we advocate that the case for inclusion of ESD in staff development programmes is strong and supported by students (SOS-UK, 2023). There is a clear alignment between what such programmes are expected to achieve in addressing contemporary higher education agendas and the need to grow understanding and application of ESD.

Educational and academic developers are also involved in other pedagogic development activities for staff, such as bespoke modules, short courses, teaching and learning conferences and events, and faculty support. These provide other ways in which academic developers could further engage their colleagues in ESD. Academic development has not always been quick to adopt ESD, though we would argue here that it should: the educational or academic development function surely provides an excellent way to infuse expertise and ideas about ESD for academic staff as part of a broader pedagogic and curriculum offering (Tilbury *et al.*, 2014). Clearly, there are sometimes enablers and barriers to this: institutional leaders need to put in place staff development policy that acknowledges the importance of educational development, which incorporates, promotes and innovates in ESD as a part of its function and departments need to be resourced such that they can address ESD as a key part of their work (Vogel *et al.*, 2023).

Next, professional development for ESD needs other institutional drivers to ensure that it remains an ongoing concern and opportunity for academic staff. If a whole-institution approach is to be adopted, other, long-term initiatives are needed to ensure that ESD is understood and adopted in teaching and research capacities. Staff should be introduced to ESD at the beginning of the employment process, from induction, with opportunities provided to build from these starting blocks. It needs to be enhanced through regular development and review, and opportunities for involvement (QAA and Advance HE, 2021). By way of example, cascade initiatives have been successful in institutions in several countries. These usually involve networks of expertise with faculty or departmental representatives promoting institutional schemes in more local contexts, supporting programme teams to embed sustainability into curricula and in their teaching, often in innovative ways (Ferrer-Balas *et al.*, 2008; Roberts and Roberts, 2008; QAA and Advance HE, 2021). Ambassadors may be formed of staff representatives or teams, but further success can be achieved by way of student partnership (SOS-UK, 2024a). For example, Responsible Futures is a programme that supports partnerships between students' unions and institutions to encourage action on embedding ESD (SOS-UK, 2024a). Similarly, the CoDesignS ESD Framework promotes educators and students working in partnership to equip them with the tools necessary for ESD (Toro-Troconis *et al.*, 2024).

Finally, an array of guidance, symposia and external provision can support academic staff to embed ESD. As noted above, the ESD Guidance (QAA and Advance HE, 2021) provides resources which can be introduced and drawn upon in teaching of ESD, and in a way that can be applied to disciplinary contexts. Advance HE and QAA Practice Guides for ESD offer a variety of practical examples of ESD activities that institutions have engaged in from single workshops to larger-scale engagement projects. Several of them speak to themes raised in this chapter, such as staff development and working with students in progressing ESD (Advance HE, 2021; QAA, 2021). Organisations such as Advance HE (2024a), ICSE (2024), UNESCO and SDSN (2024), the UK Consortium on Sustainability Research (2024) and Universities UK (2024) offer symposia and conferences that provide fora to share learning and discuss contemporary practice and initiatives in ESD. Educators can also engage in learning programmes, such as the CoDesignS ESD Bootcamp (Toro-Troconis *et al.*, 2024). This is a UNESCO-supported programme that supports university teams to design and implement ESD in their curricula supported by the CoDesignS ESD Framework and Toolkit (CoDesignS ESD, 2021). SOS-UK (2024b) also offers a range of opportunities for ESD staff development through their Learning Academy.

To reflect variation in roles, experience and practice of academic staff, universities may opt to provide a range of programmes and development opportunities to support educators on their ESD journey, for example Manchester Metropolitan University (Table 10.1) and the University of the West of England (Table 10.2). These examples serve to illustrate that the suite of professional development offered to academic staff can be shaped by institutional context.

### *A Manchester Metropolitan University Case Study of Staff Development for ESD*

At Manchester Metropolitan University, a variety of resources are provided to support staff to embed ESD in their practice (Table 10.1, Manchester Metropolitan University, 2024a). Opportunities are available to all academic and professional services staff, those in dedicated roles, such as educators and university leaders, as well as students. ESD development resources vary in intensity from signposting ESD resources and overviews to an interactive online programme providing a structured approach for re-framing existing curriculum elements and/or designing new elements to embed key principles of

*Table 10.2* Expectations for staff development in the QAA and Advance HE (2021) ESD Guidance and the response of UWE.

| *Ensure that academics are supported and able to:* | *UWE Formal and Informal Staff Development Opportunities* |
|---|---|
| *Understand ESD and the UN SDGs in the context of their own discipline/subject area and associated professional contexts (including how their discipline/subject area may entrench and reproduce unjust and unsustainable thinking and/or practice).* | The ESD Action Plan mandates provision of staff development and activities for students to raise awareness of the SDGs supported by guidance available from Advance HE and QAA ESD initiatives.<br>Internal case studies of practice are collected for the annual ESD report.<br>Phase 2 of UWE's on-going project to map the UG and PG degree programmes against the SDGs. Mapping is course team led and develops from extensive team discussions about the subject matter and its positive or negative impacts on the SDGs. Discussions include student voices and has led to over 100 maps being produced to date (Gough, 2021). |
| *Understand the UNESCO sustainability competencies and integrate them as part of course and module outcomes.* | Through the formal adoption of the QAA and Advance HE Guidance by UWE's Learning, Teaching and Student Experience Committee the Knowledge Exchange for Sustainability Education (KESE) group is charged with facilitating staff development across the Schools of the university to support understanding of the sustainability competencies and their integration into modules and programmes through the university's Enhancement Framework (University of the West of England, undated a). |
| *Facilitate teaching and assessment approaches that support the development and assessment of sustainability competencies.* | The KESE Group facilitates discussions and sharing of practice across the different Schools of UWE with the aim of enhancing the visibility of competencies within the programmes of study. Examples are published in the annual ESD report (University of the West of England, undated b). |
| *Facilitate interdisciplinary and transdisciplinary teaching practices and assessment.* | Explored through the university's Postgraduate Certificate in Learning and Teaching in Higher Education (University of the West of England, undated a), in sessions delivered at the annual Teaching and Learning Conference and through School or College events facilitated by KESE. |
| *Create opportunities for the sharing of ESD ideas, knowledge exchange and experiences across the institution.* | KESE acts as a bridge between the Schools and Colleges and the ESD work of the Sustainability Board. Formal and informal Staff Development opportunities provided including internally produced Learning e-learning resources on sustainability topics, design guides to support the development of new modules or the review of existing curricula, Online Climate Education course available for all staff and informal Staff Development sessions such as Climate Fresk or MAKERS sessions (Making and Knowledge Exchange for Repair and Sustainability). |
| *Have conversations with key players to enable ESD learning and contribution beyond the curriculum.* | Conversations and engagement with UWE partnerships locally for example Bristol Climate and Nature Partnership and Future Leap; nationally with EAUC, Professional Statutory and Regulatory Bodies, PRME, SOS-UK, Advance HE and QAA; internationally with sector bodies and international partners. |

ESD. In addition, the Postgraduate Certificate and Masters in Higher Education include a module on ESD. Engagement with Responsible Futures (SOS-UK, 2024d) also supports valuable development opportunities for staff and students through a community of practice as a source of shared knowledge, learning and support.

Climate change is a theme in ESD (UNESCO, 2024) and Carbon Literacy training and Teach Carbon Literacy training, customisable for online, in-person or hybrid delivery, has been developed by academic staff at Manchester Metropolitan University to support colleagues in a range of roles and to train staff and students to be Carbon Literacy trainers (Manchester Metropolitan University, 2024b), with associated Toolkits freely available from the Carbon Literacy Project (Dunk *et al.*, 2021; Carbon Literacy Trust, 2023).

As noted above, ESD and decolonising curricula are complementary, contemporary agendas in higher education (QAA and Advance HE, 2021), and ESD resources include a Decolonising the Curriculum Toolkit to support academic staff in the process of decolonising their teaching (Manchester Metropolitan University, 2024a).

Finally, recognising that sustainability should be a part of professional development for everyone, opportunities for wider staff engagement are also shared, and annual staff awards reward achievement, showcase examples of good practice and raise the profile of sustainability and ESD (Manchester Metropolitan University, 2024c, Table 10.1).

### *A UWE Bristol Case Study of Staff Development for ESD*

Formally established in 2008, the University of the West of England's (UWE) Knowledge Exchange for Sustainability Education (KESE) group is a cross-university staff team that works to progress ESD in both the formal and informal curriculum (University of the West of England, undated a, Longhurst *et al.*, 2023). It does this through curriculum mapping, staff development, student engagement and celebration of activities. The group comprises a representative from each academic school, the university's sustainability team and the Students' Union. Its core purpose is to provide a means for discussion of ESD within the University. It shares examples of good practice across the institution and supports staff who are seeking to include ESD within their modules and programmes. The terms of reference for the group specify the production of an annual action plan and an annual report on progress delivered to both the Sustainability Board and to the Learning, Teaching and Student Experience Committee.

Led by the Professor of ESD, KESE takes responsibility for the annual ESD report and sets the agenda for the annual ESD Action Plan (University of the West of England, undated b). KESE reports on its activities at each meeting of the Sustainability Board.

In order to meet its terms of reference, the group holds regular cross-university meetings to discuss emergent issues, share initiatives in the university and to progress the annual action plan. Formal activities include contributions to the university's Postgraduate Certificate in Learning and Teaching in Higher Education delivered by the Professor of ESD. This session outlines the ESD expectations set out in Strategy 2030 and the role of KESE in supporting and enabling ESD practices to develop. KESE runs ESD sessions at the university's annual Teaching and Learning Conference and supports the production of e-learning modules and practice guides, particularly relating to the UWE Enhancement Framework and the opportunities for ESD to be made explicit with the framework.

KESE staff are critical to the external verification processes that assess the university's progress with its ESD commitments. Staff development sessions are run to prepare and support KESE members to engage in the ISO 14001-2015 certification process and the SOS-UK Responsible Futures accreditation. These external processes are critical events in demonstrating UWE's progress in meeting its stated ESD aims. Notably, the ISO 14001 certification covers the university's teaching and learning of ESD (University of the West of England, undated c).

A range of informal staff development activities are available to all staff. These include UWE's Climate Education course (University of the West of England, undated d), Climate Fresk sessions (Climate Fresk, undated) and the MAKERS – Making and Knowledge Exchange for Repair and Sustainability (University of the West of England, undated e) sessions amongst others.

Responsible Futures (SOS-UK, 2024d) and the NUS Green Impact Scheme (SOS-UK, 2024e) provide valuable development opportunities for students who are trained to assess the university's performance and to evaluate the claims made for ESD.

### Senior Leaders and Leadership Teams

> Climate change disruption is coming, and higher education institutions face the choice of taking the initiative or suffering the consequences of being left behind... I have been scanning recent news coverage from the sector for fundamental realignments of practices and tangible shifts in investments to make meaningful contributions... I have not found much...
>
> (Tilbury, Times Higher Education, 31.10.21)

Climate change, and other social and environmental threats, establish a vital need for our institutions to act, innovate and lead in sustainability issues. Tilbury (2021), like others, suggests that we should expect more from our universities. Leadership teams need to be involved and provide meaningful and authentic ESD-based policy and resource, but leadership teams too may benefit from intelligence and development about sustainability, as well as evidence of why they should be investing in it. The expectation that university leaders embed sustainability is growing (UUK, 2023), and leaders therefore need knowledge of the issues to ensure that sustainability goals are met.

What development do our leadership teams need? Hard evidence might be a starting point from which to build a provision: employers are asking for sustainability-literate graduates and students are asking for action on sustainability. Leadership development programmes should include sustainability as part of their core message and consider what leadership for sustainability means (Chapter 9). Leadership training opportunities include programmes to develop expertise and confidence as a strategic sustainability leader in higher education (EAUC, 2023) and Carbon Literacy training for university leaders which can be delivered internally by staff and students (Table 10.1). For example, at Manchester Metropolitan University, Carbon Literacy training was delivered by academic staff, students and alumni to about 100 leaders from across the University and Students' Union. This training led to a heightened awareness, better understanding of aspects of sustainable development and positive engagement with sustainability initiatives from leadership teams (Price *et al.*, 2024).

### *Quality Assurance (QA) Staff*

Staff working in quality assurance have an important role to play in supporting the embedding of ESD in programmes: quality processes and ESD enhancement activities need to align with one another, the former supporting the latter (QAA and Advance HE, 2021). To provide the best opportunities for this to happen, appropriate training and guidance will be necessary for quality assurance staff, demonstrating the critical nature of ESD, and how to introduce processes to promote its authentic embedding (Reeves *et al.*, 2023; White et al., 2023).

For those seeking a starting point on ESD and QA, the ESD Guidance Document (QAA and Advance HE, 2021) refers to quality assurance processes as part of a more general drive to promote ESD. The Quality Code for Higher Education and Subject Benchmark Statements are also valuable reference points in the design, delivery, review and quality assurance of academic programmes. They incorporate consideration of how practice within disciplines addresses wider social goals, including ESD (QAA, 2024a, b). In support of this, QAA have also published resources addressing quality processes for implementing ESD in curricula (QAA, 2023a). Reeves *et al.* (2023) produced academic quality (AQ) and student voice (SV) guidelines for ESD in higher education, recognising that 'Although addressing ESD in AQ and SV processes is an important component of its mainstreaming across an institution, it is likely to be ineffective without a wider enabling environment, that motivates and empowers students and staff to understand the agenda and put it into practice'. The guidelines include ideas, processes and case studies to support institutional and departmental strategies for development and advocate supporting staff through learning opportunities, exemplification, guidance and professional recognition to develop their understanding and adoption of ESD approaches. This approach is supported by White et al. (2023), who developed a handbook that includes a framework, tools and case studies to support monitoring and evaluation to strengthen the quality of ESD in universities and Price *et al.* (2024) who developed an embedding ESD resource that is particularly relevant to academic, learner development and quality assurance staff (Table 10.1).

In sum, staff working in quality assurance have an essential role to play in supporting and ensuring embedding of ESD. QA teams might benefit from periodic ESD training to consider the roll out of ESD in their own institutions, but the recent guidelines and case studies referred to above offer valuable guidance and examples from a range of institutions for those working in quality assurance (Reeves *et al.*, 2023; White et al., 2023).

### *Technical Staff*

Staff working in technical and information technology roles also need bespoke training for ESD. Technical staff undertake a wide variety of work, including providing specialist support to staff and students and the maintenance and procurement of large volumes of equipment, both linked closely to sustainability-decision making and behaviour. The Laboratory Efficiency Assessment Framework (LEAF) is an online tool that guides users through sustainability actions to save plastics, water, energy and other resources in laboratories. The Framework also offers user engagement and training (UCL, 2024). Technical teams in universities have established programmes and working groups to foster sustainability knowledge, share best practice and guidance and support student activities, using the LEAF framework as a learning tool, to increase students' sustainable skills development (NTDC, 2023; University of Nottingham, undated). Carbon Literacy training for professional services staff, including technical teams, has also proved effective in empowering participants to implement climate action in their professional lives (Table 10.1) (Dunk *et al.*, 2021; Manchester Metropolitan University, 2024a).

### Student Representatives and Partners

It is well documented that most students expect their institutions to develop their sustainability strategies and embed ESD (SOS-UK, 2023), whilst recent reports have also identified the concerns that students and young people have about sustainability-based threats, such as climate change (Whitlock, 2023). Sustainability should be present in all aspects of student life, and universities need to work with their students' unions to promote knowledge and innovation. This may include, for example, sessions for students, by students, on what sustainability is and what actions students can take to contribute at their institution (The Union MMU, 2024). Students are important drivers of curriculum quality for sustainability (Reeves *et al.*, 2023), and this provides an excellent opportunity for staff to work with students and for SVs to be heard (Nicholson *et al.*, 2024). Programmes usually feature student representatives, and part of their role should include representing SV about ESD (Reeves *et al.*, 2023). ESD should be included in agendas for Staff Student Liaison Committees, as well as at Programme Committees (and equivalent SV committees) where student representatives are present (QAA and Advance HE, 2021). Tilbury (2016) has emphasised the importance of students – on campus, as well as by way of sector-based student networks – as a route for informing professional development in ESD. Training is available for course representatives to explore how they can use their roles to progress ESD in curricula (SOS-UK, 2024c) and an anti-greenwash education kit for students uses speed-training tools to empower students to rate ESD learning in their courses (QAA, 2023b).

### Employability and Careers Teams

There is a clear linkage between the work of employability and careers services, and ESD and sustainability literacy and experience. This need for sustainability and employability to align is recognised in, for example, a recently published framework for ESD (Advance HE, 2024b). Increasing numbers of employers prefer to recruit students who are sustainability-literate (Thomas *et al.*, 2013), whilst many graduates are keen to work for employers that contribute positively to sustainable development (SOS-UK, 2023). To enact such provision, staff in Careers Offices and other sections of our universities dealing with employability might need bespoke training on ESD and sustainability issues. The evidence is that some employability services provide green career guidance (Liverpool John Moores University, 2024; Manchester Metropolitan University, 2024d; Ulster University, 2024). Of interest here is the work of Hooley *et al.* (2021) and Hooley (2021) focusing on five signposts towards socially just careers guidance: build critical consciousness; name oppression; question what is normal; encourage people to work together; and work at a range of levels. These publications demonstrate that careers advisors themselves need to understand the relevance of ESD and sustainability in contemporary workplaces and professions, and the practical and ethical dilemmas associated with sustainability issues in different sectors. Recognising this need, EAUC Scotland (2024) have published comprehensive guidance to support careers teams in understanding what a green job can look like, and some of the best ways to guide students.

Understanding green careers workshops for employability teams have also been developed (Change Agents UK, 2023).

## Evaluating Outcomes

Evaluation of professional development for ESD can provide insight into which approaches are successful in addressing effective and systemic change (Lambrechts *et al.*, 2017). While examples of explicit evaluation of outcomes are rare, Toro-Troconis *et al.* (2023) demonstrated an increase in participants' willingness and perceived ability to engage actively in embedding ESD in curriculum design following the CoDesignS ESD Bootcamp. Specifically, they found an increased perception of ESD's practical value, participant confidence in implementing it and readiness to adjust behaviours to accommodate ESD principles. Recognising the need for such evaluation, White et al. (2023) recommend that assessment of staff professional development opportunities should be a feature of strategy to enhance ESD provision.

## Conclusions

In this chapter, we have examined professional development for ESD: if ESD is to be embedded in our programmes and as part of the broader student experience, staff need to have the opportunity to learn, develop and innovate themselves. We have suggested that different staff and students in universities may have specific training and development needs: everyone requires a base level understanding but depending on roles and responsibilities, bespoke training will be needed for some. This might be through CPD, academic modules, courses and programmes, or guidance and there may also be various providers involved. Individual universities need to consider training needs in relation to their overall policies and strategies, visions and organisational cultures, but a core principle underlying such choices is that sustainability is the responsibility of everybody, and everybody should be provided with access to learn about it. Further, we would support advice by Mulà *et al.* (2017), that ESD professional development is a long-term project and one that, as has been demonstrated throughout this chapter, needs to be developed and evaluated with stakeholders. We need to be inclusive and participatory in our staff development about sustainability, to ensure that all perspectives are considered. It stands to reason that we work with students in partnership towards the best possible professional development for ESD for all, for good.

## References

Advance HE (2021). Education for Sustainable Development Practice Guides. Available at: https://advance-he.ac.uk/teaching-and-learning/education-sustainable-development-higher-education#practice [Accessed: 31 July 2024].

Advance HE (2023). Professional Standards Framework (PSF, 2023). Advance HE. Available at: https://www.advance-he.ac.uk/teaching-and-learning/psf [Accessed: 31 July 2024].

Advance HE (2024a). Sustainability Symposium 2024: From embedding to embodying: Strategies, policies and practices to advance sustainable citizenship. Advance HE. Available at: https://www.advance-he.ac.uk/programmes-events/events/symposia/sustainability-symposium-2024 [Accessed: 31 July 2024].

Advance HE (2024b). Framework for Education for Sustainable Development. York: Advance HE. Available at: https://www.advance-he.ac.uk/knowledge-hub/framework-education-sustainable-development [Accessed: 31 July 2024].

Barth, M., Michelsen, G., Rieckmann, M. and Thomas I. (2016). Routledge Handbook of Higher Education for Sustainable Development. London: Routledge. ISBN 9781138597549.
Baughan, P. (2015). Sustainability policy and sustainability in higher education curricula: The educational developer perspective. International Journal for Academic Development, 20(4), pp. 319–332.
Biasutti, M., Makrakis, V., Concina, E. and Frate, S. (2018). Educating academic staff to reorient curricula in ESD. International Journal of Sustainability in Higher Education, 19, pp. 179–196.
Callejas Restrepo, M.M., Blanco-Portela, N., Ladino-Ospina, Y., Tuay Sigua, R.N. and Vargas, K.O. (2017). Professional development of university educators in ESD: A study from pedagogical styles. International Journal of Sustainability in Higher Education, 18, pp. 648–665. doi:10.1108/IJSHE-02-2016-0031.
Carbon Literacy Trust (2023). New Carbon Literacy for Education Toolkit Materials. Carbon Literacy Trust. Available at: https://carbonliteracy.com/new-carbon-literacy-for-education-toolkit-materials/ [Accessed: 31 July 2024].
Change Agents UK (2023). Understanding Green Careers. Change Agents UK. Available at: https://www.changeagents.org.uk/green-careers-workshop [Accessed: 31 July 2024].
Climate Fresk (no date). World. Available at: https://climatefresk.org/world/ [Accessed: 31 July 2024]
CoDesignS ESD (2021). Learning Design and Education for Sustainable Development Bootcamp. Available at: https://codesignsesd.org/learning-design-and-education-for-sustainable-development-bootcamp/ [Accessed: 31 July 2024].
Cook-Sather, A., Bovill, C. and Felten, P. (2014). Engaging Students as Partners in Learning and Teaching: A Guide for Faculty. San Francisco, CA: Jossey-Bass.
Dlouhá, J., Vintar Mally, K. and Dlouhý, J. (2017). ESD principles in higher education from a perspective of Central and Eastern European countries. International Journal of Sustainability in Higher Education, 18, pp. 822–840. doi:10.1108/IJSHE-03-2016-0045.
Dumitru, D.E. (2017). Reorienting higher education pedagogical and professional development curricula toward sustainability – A Romanian perspective. International Journal of Sustainability in Higher Education, 18, pp. 894–907. doi:10.1108/IJSHE-03-2016-0046.
Dunk, R.M., Mörk, J. and Price, E.A.C. (2021). Carbon Literacy: Peer-to-peer training facilitates access for all staff and students. COP26 Universities Network Case Studies. Available at: https://uucn.ac.uk/wp-content/uploads/2022/07/Media_814591_smxx.pdf [Accessed: 31 July 2024].
EAUC (2023). EAUC Leadership Lab 2023. EAUC. Available at: https://www.eauc.org.uk/shop/mms_single_event.php?event_id=8153 [Accessed: 31 July 2024].
EAUC Scotland (2024). Showing the Path to Green Jobs – A guide for careers and student support staff in FHE. EAUC. Available at: https://www.eauc.org.uk/green_careers_guide_fhe_staff [Accessed: 31 July 2024].
Ferrer-Balas, D., Adachi, J., Banas, S., Davidson, C.I., Hoshikoshi, A., Mishra, A., Motodoa, Y., Onga, M. and Ostwald, M. (2008). An international comparative analysis of sustainability transformation across seven universities. International Journal of Sustainability in Higher Education, 9, pp. 295–316. doi:10.1108/14676370810885907.
Fiselier, E.S., Longhurst, J.W.S. and Gough, G.K. (2018). Exploring the current position of ESD in UK higher education institutions. International Journal of Sustainability in Higher Education, 19, pp. 393–412. doi:10.1108/IJSHE-06-2017-0084.
Gough, G.K. (2021). UWE Bristol and the Sustainable Development Goals (SDGs): Programme mapping portfolio. UWE Bristol. Available at: https://uwe-repository.worktribe.com/output/9912189 [Accessed: 31 July 2024].
Holdsworth, S., Wyborn, C., Bekessy, S. and Thomas, I. (2008). Professional development for education for sustainability: How advanced are Australian universities? International Journal of Sustainability in Higher Education, 9, pp. 131–146. doi:10.1108/14676370810856288.
Hooley, T. (2021). Green guidance: Why career development needs to pay attention to environmental change. Presentation for: Career Development Association of Australia. Available at: https://careerguidancesocialjustice.wordpress.com/2022/10/10/green-guidance-why-career-development-needs-to-pay-attention-to-environmental-change/ [Accessed: 31 July 2024].
Hooley, T., Sultana, R. and Thomsen, R. (2021). Five signposts to a socially just approach to career guidance. Journal of the National Institute for Career Education and Counselling, 47(1), pp. 59–66. doi:10.20856/jnicec.4709.

ICSE (2024). 6th International Conference on Sustainability Education. ICSE. Available at: https://www.icse-esd.org/ [Accessed: 31 July 2024].
Lambrechts, W., Verhulst, E. and Rymenams, S. (2017). Professional development of sustainability competences in higher education: The role of empowerment. International Journal of Sustainability in Higher Education, 18, pp. 697–714. doi:10.1108/IJSHE-02-2016-0028.
Liverpool John Moores University (2024). Get involved and get green with Student Futures. Liverpool John Moores University. Available at: https://www.ljmu.ac.uk/studentfutures/green-careers-and-sustainability-insights/get-involved-and-get-green [Accessed: 31 July 2024].
Longhurst, J.W.S., Gough, G.K. and Brooks, I. (2023). A University's Transformational Change Agenda and Impact on Local, National and International Sustainability Initiatives. In: Purcell, W. and Haddock-Fraser, J. (eds.) Bloomsbury Handbook Of Sustainability In Higher Education: An Agenda For Transformational Change. London: Bloomsbury. ISBN 9781350244344.
Manchester Metropolitan University (2024a). Education for sustainable development. Manchester Metropolitan University. Available at: https://www.mmu.ac.uk/about-us/professional-services/uta/education-for-sustainable-development#t-74256-1 [Accessed: 31 July 2024].
Manchester Metropolitan University (2024b). Carbon literacy for staff and students. Manchester Metropolitan University. Available at: https://www.mmu.ac.uk/sustainability/carbon-literacy/staff-students#ai-25947-1 [Accessed: 31 July 2024].
Manchester Metropolitan University (2024c). Staff engagement. Manchester Metropolitan University. Available at: https://www.mmu.ac.uk/sustainability/staff#ai-63036-0 [Accessed: 31 July 2024].
Manchester Metropolitan University (2024d). Green careers and recruitment. Manchester Metropolitan University. Available at: https://www.mmu.ac.uk/careers/about-us/green-careers#:~:text=The%20Green%20Careers%20Hub%20is,and%20advice%20on%20the%20hub [Accessed: 31 July 2024].
McCowan, T. (2023). Tertiary Education and the Sustainability Agenda. Centre for Global Higher Education Working Paper series, Working Paper 90. Oxford: Centre for Global Higher Education, University of Oxford. Available at: https://www.researchcghe.org/publication/tertiary-education-and-the-sustainability-agenda/ [Accessed: 31 July 2024].
McKeown, R. (2002). Education for Sustainable Development Toolkit. University of Tennessee, Knoxville, USA. Available at: http://kpe-kardits.kar.sch.gr/Aiforia/esd_toolkit_v2.pdf [Accessed: 31 July 2024].
Melles, G. (2019). Views on education for sustainable development (ESD) among lecturers in UK MSc taught courses: Personal, institutional and disciplinary factors. International Journal of Sustainability in Higher Education, 20, pp. 115–138. doi:10.1108/IJSHE-02-2018-0032.
Mulà, I., Tilbury, D., Ryan, A., Mader, M., Dlouhá, J., Mader, C., Benayas, J., Dlouhý, J. and Alba, D. (2017). Catalysing change in higher education for sustainable development: A review of professional development initiatives for university educators. International Journal of Sustainability in Higher Education, 18(5), pp. 798–820. doi:10.1108/IJSHE-03-2017-0043.
National Technician Development Centre (NTDC) (2023). Technical Services Sustainability Programme: Manchester Metropolitan University. NTDC. Available at: https://www.ntdc.ac.uk/news-and-events/older-news/technical-services-sustainability-programme [Accessed: 31 July 2024].
Nicholson, D.T., Vargas, V.R., Price, E.A.C., Himatlal, K., Campen, L., Hartley, M. and Hewitt, T. (2024). Transformative learning design for ESD in a skills-based module. Open Scholarship of Teaching and Learning, 3, pp. 21–36. Available at: https://osotl.org/index.php/osotl/article/view/76/96 [Accessed: 31 July 2024].
Nikolic, V., Milutinovic, S., Nedanovski, P. and Mrnjaus, K. (2017). ESD professional development of university educators in Serbia, Croatia and Macedonia: A comparative analysis. International Journal of Sustainability in Higher Education, 18, pp. 923–938. doi:10.1108/IJSHE-02-2016-0036.
Price, E.A.C., Nicholson, D.T., Dunk, R., Lawler, C., Carney, M., Vargas, V., Veitch, S., Leigh, S., Singleton, M. and Mottram, S. (2024). Enabling change agents for Sustainable Development: A whole-institution approach to embedding the UN Sustainable Development Goals in Higher Education. International Journal of Sustainability in Higher Education, 25 (7), pp. 1333–1350. doi:10.1108/IJSHE-02-2024-0112.
Price, E.A.C., White, R.M., Mori, K., Longhurst, J., Baughan, P., Hayles, C.S., Gough, G. and Preist, C. (2021). Supporting the role of universities in leading individual and societal transformation through education for sustainable development. Discover Sustainability, 2, p. 49. doi:10.1007/s43621-021-00058-3.

Quality Assurance Agency (QAA) (2021). Education for Sustainable Development Practice Guides. QAA. Available at: https://www.qaa.ac.uk/the-quality-code/education-for-sustainable-development [Accessed: 31 July 2024].
Quality Assurance Agency (QAA) (2023a). Resources for implementing Education for Sustainability. Available at: https://www.qaa.ac.uk/news-events/news/collection-of-resources-for-implementing-education-for-sustainability-now-available [Accessed: 31 July 2024].
Quality Assurance Agency (QAA) (2023b). Students driving curriculum quality for sustainability – Developing criteria and tools. QAA. Available at: https://www.qaa.ac.uk/en/membership/collaborative-enhancement-projects/education-for-sustainable-development/students-driving-curriculum-quality-for-sustainability-developing-criteria-and-tools [Accessed: 31 July 2024].
Quality Assurance Agency (QAA) (2024a). UK Quality Code for Higher Education. Gloucester: QAA. Available at: https://www.qaa.ac.uk/docs/qaa/quality-code/uk-quality-code-for-higher-education-2024.pdf?sfvrsn=19a5b881_32 [Accessed: 31 July 2024].
Quality Assurance Agency (QAA) (2024b). Subject Benchmark Statements. QAA. Available at: https://www.qaa.ac.uk/the-quality-code/subject-benchmark-statements# [Accessed: 31 July 2024].
Quality Assurance Agency (QAA) and Advance HE (2021). Education for Sustainable Development Guidance. Gloucester: QAA. Available at: https://www.advance-he.ac.uk/teaching-and-learning/education-sustainable-development-higher-education [Accessed: 31 July 2024].
Reeves, A., Gwilliam, J., Harrison, P., Price, L., Schantz, N., Ribchester, C., Hughes, T., Gretton, S., Strachan, S., Logan, L., Boxley, S., Lengthorn, E., Barrett, H. and Peres, S. (2023). Education for Sustainable Development and Academic Quality: Principles and Processes for Academic Providers. Gloucester: QAA. Available at: https://www.qaa.ac.uk/en/membership/collaborative-enhancement-projects/education-for-sustainable-development/esd-and-academic-quality# [Accessed: 31 July 2024].
Roberts, C. and Roberts, J. (2008). Starting with the staff: How swap shops can develop ESD and empower practitioners. Environmental Education Research, 14, pp. 423–434. doi:10.1080/13504620802318278.
Scherak, L. and Rieckmann, M. (2020). Developing ESD competences in higher education institutions—Staff training at the University of Vechta. Sustainability, 12, p. 10336. doi:10.3390/su122410336.
Shay, S. (2012). Educational development as a field: Are we there yet? Higher Education Research and Development, 31, pp. 311–323. Available at: http://dx.doi.org/10.1080/07294360.2011.631520 [Accessed: 31 July 2024].
SOS-UK (2023). Sustainability Skills Survey 2022 – 2023. SOS-UK. Available at: https://www.sos-uk.org/research/sustainability-skills-survey [Accessed: 31 July 2024].
SOS-UK (2024a). We partner students with institutions to work together to embed sustainability in all student learning. SOS-UK. Available at: https://www.responsiblefutures.org.uk/#programme [Accessed: 31 July 2024].
SOS-UK (2024b). Learning Academy. SOS-UK. Available at: https://www.sos-uk.org/learning-events [Accessed: 31 July 2024].
SOS-UK (2024c). Course reps and sustainability: an introduction to ESD. SOS-UK. Available at: https://www.sos-uk.org/learning-academy-trainings/course-reps-sustainability-an-introduction-to-esd [Accessed: 31 July 2024].
SOS-UK (2024d). Responsible Futures. SOS-UK. Available at: https://www.sos-uk.org/project/responsible-futures [Accessed: 31 July 2024].
SOS-UK (2024e). Green Impact. SOS-UK. Available at: https://greenimpact.nus.org.uk/ [Accessed: 31 July 2024].
The Union MMU (2024). Sustainability Society. The Union MMU. Available at: https://www.theunionmmu.org/groups/sustainability-society-23ac [Accessed: 31 July 2024].
Thomas, I., Barth, M. and Day, T. (2013). Education for sustainability, graduate capabilities, professional employment: How they all connect. Australian Journal of Environmental Education, 29, pp. 33–51. Available at: https://doi.org/10.1017/aee.2013.14 [Accessed: 31 July 2024].
Tilbury, D. (2016). 'Student engagement and leadership in higher education for sustainability', in Barth, M., Michelsen, G. and Rieckmann, I.T. (Eds), Routledge Handbook of Higher Education for Sustainable Development. London and New York: Routledge, pp. 241–260.

Tilbury, D. (2021). Climate Impact Forum: embed sustainability in university teaching to save the planet. Times Higher Education, 31 October. Available at: https://www.timeshighereducation.com/opinion/climate-impact-forum-embed-sustainability-university-teaching-save-planet [Accessed: 31 July 2024].

Tilbury, D., Mulà, I. and Ryan, A. (2014). UE4SD Report for Region North: Mapping Opportunities for Developing Education for Sustainable Development Competences. Gloucestershire: University of Gloucestershire.

Toro-Troconis, M., Ahmad, N. and Varga-Atkins, T. (2024). Learning Design and Education for Sustainable Development Bootcamp: Background, framework and toolkit. Open Scholarship of Teaching and Learning, 3, pp. 1–20. Available at: https://osotl.org/index.php/osotl/article/view/112/95 [Accessed: 31 July 2024].

Toro-Troconis, M., Inzolia, Y. and Ahmad, N. (2023). Exploring attitudes towards embedding education for sustainable development in curriculum design. International Journal of Higher Education, 12. doi:10.5430/ijhe.v12n4p42.

UK Consortium on Sustainability Research (UK-CSR) (2024). Upcoming and Past Events. UK-CSR. Available at: https://www.mmu.ac.uk/research/research-centres/ecology-environment/groups/zero-carbon-sustainable-futures/UK-CSR [Accessed: 31 July 2024].

Ulster University (2024). Green Careers. Ulster University. Available at: https://www.ulster.ac.uk/employability/advice/green-careers [Accessed: 31 July 2024].

United Nations (UN) (2015). Transforming our world: the 2030 Agenda for Sustainable Development. United Nations. Available at: https://sdgs.un.org/2030agenda [Accessed: 31 July 2024].

United Nations Economic Commission for Europe (UNECE) (2012). Learning for the Future: Competencies in Education for Sustainable Development. Geneva, Switzerland: UNECE. Available at: https://unece.org/fileadmin/DAM/env/esd/ESD_Publications/Competences_Publication.pdf [Accessed: 31 July 2024].

United Nations Educational, Scientific and Cultural Organization (UNESCO) (2017). Education for Sustainable Development Goals: Learning Objectives. Paris, France: UNESCO.

United Nations Educational, Scientific and Cultural Organization (UNESCO) (2018). UNESCO Global Action Programme on Education for Sustainable Development. Available at: https://unesdoc.unesco.org/ark:/48223/pf0000246270 [Accessed: 31 July 2024].

United Nations Educational, Scientific and Cultural Organization (UNESCO) (2019). Framework for the implementation of education for sustainable development (ESD) beyond 2019. UNESCO. Available at: https://unesdoc.unesco.org/search/71aaa3f9-9656-43a7-a740-f3fb57e1dbc5 [Accessed: 31 July 2024].

United Nations Educational, Scientific and Cultural Organization (UNESCO) (2020). Education for Sustainable Development: a Roadmap. Paris, France: UNESCO. Available at: https://unesdoc.unesco.org/ark:/48223/pf0000374802 [Accessed: 31 July 2024].

United Nations Educational, Scientific and Cultural Organization (UNESCO) (2024). Greening Curriculum Guidance: Teaching and Learning for Climate Action. Paris, France: UNESCO. Available at: https://www.unesco.org/en/articles/greening-curriculum-guidance-teaching-and-learning-climate-action [Accessed: 31 July 2024].

United Nations Educational, Scientific and Cultural Organization (UNESCO) and Sustainable Development Solutions Network (SDSN) (2024). UNESCO, SDSN, and Malaysia Join Forces in the ESD for 2030 Asia-Pacific Regional Meeting in Kuala Lumpur. UNESCO and SDSN. Available at: https://www.unsdsn.org/news/unesco-sdsn-and-sdsn-malaysia-join-forces-in-the-esd-for-2030-asia-pacific-regional-meeting-in-kuala-lumpur/ [Accessed: 31 July 2024].

Universities UK (UUK) (2023). Climate crisis: what progress have universities made? Universities UK. Available at: https://www.universitiesuk.ac.uk/latest/insights-and-analysis/climate-crisis-what-progress-have [Accessed: 31 July 2024].

Universities UK (UUK) (2024). Universities, sustainability and the climate emergency 2024. Universities UK. Available at: https://www.universitiesuk.ac.uk/latest/events/universities-sustainability-and-climate [Accessed: 31 July 2024].

University College London (UCL) (2024). LEAF – Laboratory Efficiency Assessment Framework. University College London. Available at: https://www.ucl.ac.uk/sustainable/take-action/staff-action/leaf-laboratory-efficiency-assessment-framework [Accessed: 31 July 2024].

University of Nottingham (no date). The Technical Sustainability Working Group. University of Nottingham. Available at: https://www.nottingham.ac.uk/sustainability/sustainable-labs/tswg.aspx [Accessed: 31 July 2024].

University of the West of England (no date a). Education for Sustainable Development. University of the West of England. Available at: https://www.uwe.ac.uk/about/values-vision-strategy/sustainability/education-for-sustainable-development [Accessed: 31 July 2024].

University of the West of England (no date b). Strategy, Leadership, and Plans. University of the West of England. Available at: https://www.uwe.ac.uk/about/values-vision-strategy/sustainability/strategy-leadership-and-plans/policy-and-strategy-documents [Accessed: 31 July 2024].

University of the West of England (no date c). ISO 14001 Certification. University of the West of England. Available at: https://www.uwe.ac.uk/about/values-vision-strategy/sustainability/iso-14001-certification [Accessed: 31 July 2024].

University of the West of England (no date d). Climate Education Course. University of the West of England. Available at: https://www.uwe.ac.uk/life/greener-future/climate-education-course [Accessed: 31 July 2024].

University of the West of England (no date e). MAKERS Project. University of the West of England. Available at: https://www.uwe.ac.uk/research/centres-and-groups/scu/projects/makers [Accessed: 31 July 2024].

Varga-Atkins, T., Toro-Troconis, M. and Ahmad, N. (2024). Editorial: Special issue on 'Learning Design and Education for Sustainable Development Bootcamp'. Open Scholarship of Teaching and Learning, 3, pp. i–xii. Available at: https://osotl.org/index.php/osotl/article/view/111/94 [Accessed: 31 July 2024].

Verhulst, E. and Lambrechts, W. (2015). Fostering the incorporation of sustainable development in higher education: Lessons learned from a change management perspective. Journal of Cleaner Production, 106, pp. 189–204.

Vogel, M., Parker, L., Porter, J., O'Hara, M., Tebbs, E., Gard, R., He, X. and Gallimore, J.-B. (2023). Education for Sustainable Development: a Review of the Literature 2015–2022. York: Advance HE.

White, R.M., Möbius, K., King, B., Leask, K., Peres, S., Walker, J. and Higgins, P. (2023). A Handbook for Monitoring and Evaluating Education for Sustainable Development in Higher Education. Gloucester: QAA. Available at: https://www.qaa.ac.uk/docs/qaa/members/handbook-for-monitoring-and-evaluating-esd-in-universities.pdf?sfvrsn=ac42af81_12 [Accessed: 31 July 2024].

Whitlock, J. (2023). Climate change anxiety in young people. Nature Mental Health, 1, pp. 297–298. Available at: https://doi.org/10.1038/s44220-023-00059-3 [Accessed: 31 July 2024].

Chapter 11

# Monitoring and Evaluating Education for Sustainable Development

## Co-Creating Quality Learning Experiences and Outcomes

*Rehema M. White, Carolyn S. Hayles and Georgina Gough*

### Introduction

As education for sustainable development (ESD) becomes more prevalent and accepted as an integral part of higher education, we need to ensure that provision is high quality, institutions continue to deepen their engagement, there is a coherent strategy for institutional support and all actors are involved in co-designing ESD with integrated monitoring and evaluation. It is thus critical that monitoring and evaluation are not left until the end, but, rather, they are part of the initial planning. We define monitoring as the tracking of activities, whilst evaluation is assessment of the quantity and quality of outcomes and impacts and whether goals are met in our institutional, national or global contexts. ESD can be complex and is dynamic, asking those involved to think critically and to engage with the non-academic as well as academic world (see Chapter 2). There are thus personal, academic, institutional, societal and environmental reasons why we need to monitor and evaluate activities in the short, medium and long term. Responsibility for evaluation lies with all of those involved, including educational agencies, senior managers and those with an interest in quality of education, but also programme directors, educators and learners, and even community groups and professional bodies. Whilst suggested monitoring and evaluation frameworks now exist, along with excellent examples and case studies, the journey of each institution or region is unique.

In this chapter, we see the progressive adoption and deepening of ESD as a journey. On this expedition of enquiry, discovery and innovation, it is useful to have a destination, a map, navigational aids and ways of ensuring that fellow travellers are well provisioned. We first discuss the purposes and context of monitoring and evaluation for ESD, then describe SDG mapping, highlight different indicator typologies and examples, and finally introduce a practical framework for monitoring and evaluation that is embedded in a participatory approach to support and strengthen ESD in higher education institutions.

### Purposes and Issues for ESD Monitoring and Evaluation

Education is fundamental to the pursuit of sustainability. However, ESD needs to be monitored and evaluated to assess progress, measure quality, check relevance and plan more appropriate curricula and pedagogies (Tilbury 2007). In addition, if participatory frameworks are used, they can enhance awareness and inspire different actors within education (Tilbury 2007) and stimulate debate about the wider purpose of ESD and meanings of sustainable development (White *et al.* 2023). Monitoring fulfils audit requirements of

DOI: 10.4324/9781003451563-11

higher education and public funding accountability, although there is a risk of efforts being co-opted by a neoliberal, overly audit-focused culture, and being deployed for 'green capitalism' (O'Neill and Sinden 2021). However, evaluation also serves deeper social justice goals in providing effective learning for all and can thus limit attempts to commodify education (Lockhart 2018). Although monitoring and evaluation are thus clearly critical to understand, implement and support ESD, overall efforts in this regard have been somewhat lacking to date (Karatzoglou 2013; Lozano *et al.* 2015).

It can be challenging to define the greater and institutional goals for ESD against which ESD must ultimately be assessed. Higher education has diverse purposes; it supports socialisation and vocational training but also permits individuals to fulfil their potential and the opportunity for transformative learning (Sterling 2001). The ultimate goals of ESD in higher education are thus to create a dialogical society in which equity and responsibility to others and the environment are emphasised; with skills and knowledge for technological, human and nature-based solutions; with happier and healthier individuals living in flourishing communities; who are change agents for a more sustainable future (see Chapters 1 and 2). It is important that we evaluate the process as well as outcomes of ESD. ESD requires a holistic and pluralistic approach that seeks to develop critical awareness of behaviours, values and actions (Ssossé *et al.* 2021). ESD must be embedded throughout higher education courses, although some studies call for a more dominant presence in courses such as teacher education, since graduate teachers then catalyse ESD in schools (Edwards *et al.* 2020). The evaluation of ESD will thus need to be multifaceted to explore the extent to which these different kinds of goals are met. Whilst it may be relatively straightforward to assess competence in vocational skills, audit measures can be limited in their capacity to evaluate movement towards some of the more diffuse goals, particularly the contribution of ESD in the transformation to a better and fairer world (Giangrande *et al.* 2019; Ssossé *et al.* 2021). In addition, since sustainable development addresses complex, wicked problems with uncertain outcomes (White 2013), and ESD is a transformative change agenda engaging student voice to co-design new understandings and solutions (Chapter 2), learning processes and outcomes are constantly shifting, making it even more difficult to evaluate ESD in higher education (Lockhart 2018).

The different potential foci of monitoring and evaluation approaches can create tensions but also positive synergies. For example, more participatory efforts generate awareness and understanding of ESD and produce results of qualitative depth (Tilbury 2007), but require more resource and time, and potentially less replicable evaluation data. Participatory approaches are in line with the ethos of ESD and can lead to greater buy in, better outcomes and social learning (Blackstock *et al.* 2007) and help to catalyse a positive cycle of action for sustainability (White and Harder 2013). All relevant actors should thus be engaged in the monitoring and evaluation, but the actor driving the process will be institutionally determined; it may be a quality assurance unit, a sustainability in the curriculum committee, a Dean's office or other unit. It is critical that whoever has the responsibility for monitoring and evaluation has the trust of those in the institution, the legitimacy to request input from educators and learners and the authority to lead a process of active reflection and adjustment of the strategy to embed ESD, based on the outcomes of evaluation. The importance of student voice in monitoring and evaluation has been increasingly recognised (Brooman *et al.* 2015). In addition, engaging educators in the process can enable assessment of educators' capacities to teach ESD, which are as important as learners' abilities to learn ESD (Edwards *et al.* 2020). Additional staff support or training can thus be provided.

There are advantages to both internal and external scrutiny (see Stukalo and Lytvyn 2021). External scrutiny is more assured of independence and can lead to comparative outcomes and sharing of lessons learned across institutions and programmes. Internal processes, if undertaken through participatory, good governance, can generate agency and empower educators and learners to make change and enhance ESD provision through their own innovation. However, processes that do not engage dialogically and empathetically with educators and learners, and that impose an additional administrative audit burden on educators, who are often already pressured by workloads and managerialism, may be resented. Such monitoring and evaluation processes are likely to meet with resistance and to impede rather than promote embedding of ESD across higher education institutions. Aspects of internal and external processes are discussed in more detail below.

We can thus see that monitoring and evaluation is essential to support, strengthen and scrutinise ESD in higher education, but that there are challenges in clarification of locally relevant goals, format, scale and responsibilities. ESD is multi-faceted and contextually diverse, so a range of monitoring and evaluation methods are likely to be needed in a given institution. Authentic monitoring and evaluation processes that are embedded in institutions and linked to educational reform and pedagogical innovation are required, but there can also be a place for external 'snapshots' and for wider comparative and auditing processes.

## ESD Monitoring and Evaluation across Scales

ESD evaluation needs to take place at multiple spatial, temporal and institutional scales (Ssossé *et al.* 2021). Regional, national and international programmes are relevant, at short term (annual, semester or less) and longer term (5, 10 or more years) periods. Evaluations of individual assessments and modules, programmes and institutional achievements to embed quality ESD across provision are also required. Assessing the extent to which the learner has met learning outcomes is an essential aspect of evaluation and may be undertaken via grading and reflection on assessments set within curricula (see Chapters 5 and 7). At a module level, we often focus on the extent to which learning outcomes are met (Lockhart 2018). We may also need to develop cross-sectoral or multiscalar evaluation procedures. We may need specific regional monitoring and evaluation frameworks that address relevant goals and cultural contexts, as illustrated, for example, by the specific indicator suites developed in India, Sri Lanka and Uzbekistan during the Decade of ESD (Lockhart 2018; UNESCO, 2007). It has been suggested that there has been more emphasis at large-scale (global) and small-scale (module) levels, with less focus on indicators for intermediate scales, at institutional and regional levels (Edwards *et al.* 2020). Much of the emphasis on global monitoring and evaluation was placed on the assessment of the Millenium Development Goals (MDGs), then the Decade of Education for Sustainable Development (DESD) and subsequently the UN Sustainable Development Goals (SDGs).

One of the earliest applications of monitoring and evaluation in ESD was during the DESD, when ESD was starting to gain traction. Indeed, monitoring and evaluation was identified as one of the seven key strategies for advancing ESD during the DESD. Tilbury (2007, 2009) describes the indicators used in the monitoring and evaluation process undertaken during the DESD and the implementation of the global monitoring and evaluation framework, which was adopted by UNESCO to review changes in context structures, processes and learning, outcomes and impacts, during the DESD. The framework was designed to raise awareness amongst stakeholders about ESD and the decade; provide opportunities for reflection and learning; monitor progress across a range of sectors; assess changes in context and structures; processes and learning; as well as outcomes and impacts; provide a regional as well as a global map of progress; and assess the contribution of UNESCO to the DESD and the lessons learnt in the process of implementation. This illustrates the value attached to monitoring and evaluating process, as well as outcomes. Whilst this evaluation was not undertaken at an institutional scale, the same type of framework can be applied at the institutional scale. Despite its framing as a key strategy, it has been argued that this DESD framework was not given the required level of attention and sufficient resources, resulting in its limited use and effectiveness (UNESCO, 2014; Wals 2009).

Many of the global efforts to monitor and evaluate ESD are universal, or focus primarily on ESD in schools rather than on higher education. For example, Lockhart (2018) describes how the UNESCO Institute for Statistics (UIS) continued its commitment as 'the official source of cross-nationally comparable data on education' and promised to undertake global comparisons on SDG4. In addition, the Global Education Monitoring team produce reports on aspects of education, published by UNESCO. The 2016 Report on *Education for People and Planet: creating sustainable futures for all* (UNESCO 2016) reported on available international data but noted the emphasis on ESD in schools. A recent example designed for systematic use across schools was an Outcome Indicator Test for six action domains and cognitive, attitudinal and behavioural outcomes linked to the SDGs (Günther *et al.* 2022). However, at higher education level, there is a Sustainability Literacy Test (SULITEST) that includes 30 questions for international standardisation to be included with 20 nationally specific questions and which can be used for institutional, regional or international comparisons (Lockhart 2018). Whilst national and international comparison monitoring is appealing, such standardised, systematic tests will never capture all aspects of complex, contextualised, relational ESD process at higher education and should thus always be accompanied by institutional, participatory approaches.

## Existing ESD Monitoring and Evaluation Frameworks

Several frameworks and certification schemes already exist to support institutions in their pursuit of and monitoring of sustainability in general and ESD in particular. For example, the Association of University Directors of Estates (AUDE) Green Scorecard, the National Union of Students (NUS) Responsible Futures accreditation, the People and Planet Green League and the Association for the Advancement of Sustainability in Higher Education (AASHE) Sustainability Tracking, Assessment & Rating System™ (STARS) offer frameworks (Gough and Longhurst 2017). However, some of these have only relatively recently added some ESD elements or focus less on ESD than other institutional aspects (e.g. Times Higher Education Impact Ranking) (Veidemane 2022).

Many countries have external monitoring for and strengthening of quality and provision of identified core aspects through national agencies. For example, UK Higher

Education quality is supported externally through the Quality Assurance Agency (QAA), Higher Education Academy, Advance HE, subject benchmarks and devolved funding councils, such as the Scottish Funding Council and the requirements of Higher Education Funding Council for England. Guidance for ESD in higher education was produced in 2021 (QAA/Advance HE 2021) and was subsequently supported by resource guides. Several Collaborative Enhancement Projects then addressed ESD, including focus on academic quality, student voice, the risk of greenwashing, phenomenon-based learning and monitoring and evaluation.

Increasingly, institutions are asked to evidence activity in relation to ESD for external agents. League tables often use educational data; such tables can be simultaneously useful drivers to encourage administrations to undertake meaningful work, and drivers of incoherent and time-consuming actions and even 'green capitalism' (O'Neill and Sinden 2021). There has thus been a mixed response to such external league tables; they can be powerful in provoking action by universities to meet particular indicators, but the indicators that league tables include are not always the most relevant for all institutions, and, as O'Neill and Sinden (2021) point out, institutions can greenwash by playing the numbers game rather than pursuing meaningful sustainability action. Some of the university ranking tables actually appear to rank institutions through anti-ESD factors, by focusing on indicators such as economic success of students, with no regard to sustainability awareness or abilities (Ssossé *et al.* 2021).

The ultimate purposes of monitoring and evaluation are to enable reflection on process and outcomes and to enable action to enhance provision of ESD. There thus needs to be some alignment of monitoring and evaluation processes with support mechanisms, to identify what actions may be undertaken (White *et al.* 2023 M&E). In the UK, the QAA Quality Code supports higher education, and it includes disciplinary specific Subject Benchmark Statements, which until recently had limited engagement with sustainability (Price *et al.* 2021), but which now require inclusion of ESD (see Chapter 4). Each academic discipline thus has some context for how ESD might be perceived and included, and hence some goals for QAA and, to different degrees, institutional strategies support educators to facilitate ESD using innovative pedagogies, through guidance such as the QAA/Advance HE Guidance on ESD (QAA/Advance HE 2021). External sector support is also provided globally by the network of United Nations University supported Regional Centres of Expertise in Sustainable Development (Dlouhá *et al.* 2023) and within UK by organisations such as Students Organising for Sustainability of NUS (SOS) and EAUC in partnership with others. Award schemes at national level (e.g. Green Gown Awards) and institutional level (e.g. University of St Andrews Golden Dandelion Awards) (Box 11.1) encourage and reward good practice. At the level at which education is often designed and delivered, in programmes and departments, individual academics and academic teams also need to be inspired and supported through examples, tools and frameworks. Whilst such schemes do not explicitly monitor and evaluate ESD, they can form part of the support part of an active reflective cycle of monitoring (White *et al.* 2023) and can generate discussion across institutions about goals and good practice for ESD.

These different frameworks illustrate how monitoring and evaluation can be undertaken internally to support strategies and action plans or by external assessors as part of wider comparative exercises. Monitoring and evaluation can be principally measurement of indicators or embedded within wider processes of engagement and support for ESD.

**Box 11.1 Combining Monitoring and Evaluation of Individual Modules with Recognition and Promotion of ESD: The Golden Dandelion Award at the University of St Andrews**

> The dandelion is ... a good symbol for seeding, nourishing and disseminating sustainability in the curriculum. At the University of St Andrews, we use it as a symbol to showcase excellent sustainability modules in the curriculum.

The Golden Dandelion Award was developed at the University of St Andrews to promote, inspire and reward ESD efforts by staff for individual modules. The Golden Dandelion certification is awarded by a judging committee that evaluates all qualifying entries, with the highest scoring entry each year being awarded the Golden Dandelion Prize. A Golden Dandelion Seed award was developed for new module applications to encourage the consideration of ESD in new modules.

An online application form asked applicants to analyse their module against the criteria of:

- Creativity and innovation
- Development of sustainability knowledge, skills and competencies
- Reflection on inter- or transdisciplinary engagement
- Engaging students with real-world examples in impacts on sustainability

Monitoring and evaluation can be a constrained audit process or a route to catalyse innovation and celebrate achievement. Monitoring and evaluation can be undertaken by learners, educators or education managers. Finally, monitoring and evaluation can be conducted by all relevant actors at different temporal, spatial and institutional scales, although integrated approaches are also required (Ssossé *et al.* 2021) (Box 11.2).

**Box 11.2 Need for National Scale, Cross-Sectoral and Independent Monitoring and Evaluation of ESD**

Singer-Brodowski *et al.* (2019) argue for the need for ESD monitoring to assess the extent and quality of ESD, in this instance, throughout the Germany education system (early childhood education, school education and higher education), which aims to implement ESD more profoundly within the structures of Germany's educational system, in response to the UNESCO Global Action Programme (GAP) on ESD.

'Against the background of the growing trend to use evidence-based approaches as a base for educational policies, there is an increasing need for independent monitoring with regard to ESD. Although an ESD monitoring has to be reflected critically in terms of neoliberal tendencies of measurability and standardisation, it can strengthen the efforts of ESD-upscaling by informing (political) decision makers about the status quo and further needs and preconditions of an effective implementation'.

## Whole Institution Monitoring

ESD is proposed to be a whole institution approach, and hence, the monitoring and evaluation of ESD also needs to consider other aspects of a higher education institution, including research, campus operations and community engagement and impact. Movement towards campus sustainability has previously been recorded, especially in Europe, North America and Australia (Gough and Longhurst 2017). Analyses of sustainability research have proved complex (Walsh *et al.* 2021; White 2013). Attempts to assess external effects of universities on local communities and on wider society have been subject to a range of approaches, including the UK REF Impact agenda, which has generated moral and emotional dissonance in some academics (Chubb and Reed 2018). There is often a disconnect between strategic statements and action at the level of departments or programmes (O'Neill and Sinden 2021). The need for fine grained monitoring should not dissuade us from imagining new, contextually relevant ways of creating sustainable universities and transformative learning (Lotz-Sisitka *et al.* 2017). Whole institution monitoring should be integrated, for example, considering the operational costs of ESD pedagogies. This can include exploring carbon and other costs of field excursions, recording travel modes to research conferences, working with learners to support sustainable campus activities, and other activities as locally relevant. One example of whole institution monitoring is supported by SOS-UK (Box 11.3).

## Types and Numbers of ESD Indicators

Many monitoring and evaluation processes have focused on the indicators measured to assess progress. ESD indicators consider information related to changes in ESD policies, programmes and actions as well as the results of their implementation. These changes

### Box 11.3 A Whole Institutional Approach to Monitoring and Evaluation Supported by Responsible Futures

#### Responsible Futures by SOS-UK

Responsible Futures is a whole institutional approach to embedding ESD. Every partnership that takes part in Responsible Futures has a working group that the programme organisers ask to be embedded within a formal structure. The partnership asks for a broad representation within the group, including academic staff, professional staff, students, trade union representatives to tackle sustainability holistically across the institution. Having one or two key contacts who specifically focus on ESD is critical. Identifying and empowering gatekeepers can also be useful. Sustainability champions can often identify and overcome local barriers. Regulations can be developed, such as a requirement for all new modules to indicate ESD engagement, or for every programme to demonstrate some core ESD. However, it is important to get the appropriate balance between regulation and encouragement. Monitoring and evaluation is required to demonstrate commitment.

and results can be related to the existence of certain efforts (measurable data) or their quality (observational data) (Gallopin 1996). Indicators should be meaningful, easy to assess and support reflection. However, not all indicators can be all of these things at once. Some will be easier to monitor (e.g. number of modules with sustainability relevant content) whilst others will be harder to measure, but more meaningful, in assessing transformative learning and its impacts (see Ssossé *et al.* 2021). Some processes distinguish indicators to recognise these differences. For example, in assessing ESD delivery and impacts, Tilbury and Janousek (2006) identified Status (Baseline), Facilitative (Context, Process, Learning) and Effect (Output, Outcome, Impact, Performance) indicators for ESD in schools.

Günther *et al.* (2022) developed a test to assess indicators of outcomes against action domains (in schools). However, their action domains were derived from the SDGs, which do not fully represent sustainable development, nor ESD (see Chapter 2 and later discussion in this Chapter). For example, they incorporate paradoxical perspectives embracing both neoliberal economic growth and more liberal models of prosperity, possibly involving degrowth (Chankseliani and McCowan 2021). In focusing on action domains, they implicitly support action competencies, rather than the greater focus on competency development in some ESD debates (e.g. Giangrande *et al.* 2019; Wiek et al. 2011). In addition, education is only one aspect leading to subsequent actions, which can be influenced by further barriers or support (Velasco and Harder 2014).

The UNESCO framework for the UN Decade for ESD used four indicator types (Tilbury 2007; 2009) (Box 11.4), following a similar framework of indicators to that of Tilbury and Janousek (2006) to assess provision, support of ESD and outcomes.

These indicators can be adapted to institutional context. An example of this is shown in Table 11.1.

**Box 11.4 Indicator Types Used by the UNESCO Framework for the UN Decade for ESD (from Tilbury 2007; Tilbury 2009)**

**Checklist Indicators:** To provide information on initial policy, legislation, regulatory and governance measures taken by a government in order to implement the strategy.

**Input Indicators:** To provide information on a broader spectrum of activities taking place to implement the strategy (e.g. amount of public authority money invested in ESD materials, and proportion of public supported research on ESD).

**Output Indicators:** To provide information on the direct results of these activities s (e.g. performance of trained educators, number of businesses involved in ESD projects and number of educators who received training on ESD issues).

**Outcome Indicators:** To provide information on the possible impact of the implementation of the strategy, particularly on values, attitudes and choices in favour of sustainable development (e.g. learning outcomes resulting from ESD partnerships, and community-based projects and business involvement).

*Table 11.1* Examples of typical indicators for an institutional five-year strategic plan for ESD, drawing on the framework of Tilbury and Janousek (2006).

| *Indicator* | *Target* |
|---|---|
| Baseline indicator | % of degree programmes that have mapped SDGs against curriculum |
| Context indicator | ESD academic lead for institution |
| Process indicator | 50% of academics have undertaken compulsory ESD training |
| Learning indicator | Learner competency surveys indicate increases in sustainability competency development; every degree programme has some assessment that includes ESD curriculum and competencies |
| Output indicator | HEI Resource training manual |
| Outcome indicator | % of academics adopting innovative pedagogies; % of modules including ESD curriculum content, pedagogies and/or focus on competencies |
| Impact indicator | Survey of sustainability awareness, skills and employment intentions (e.g. SOS student survey) |
| Performance indicator | % of educators confident in ESD; % of learners developing sustainability competencies |

Despite the tensions within the SDGs as an agenda for sustainability, there are SDG indicators that are designed to support monitoring and evaluation of ESD. At this global level, educational targets and education-related indicators are embedded within many of the SDGs and form a major component of Agenda 2030 (Cebrián *et al.* 2020). Specifically, ESD is a component of SDG 4.7 which aims to: 'by 2030, ensure that all learners acquire the knowledge and skills needed to promote sustainable development, including, among others, through education for sustainable development and sustainable lifestyles, human rights, gender equality, promotion of a culture of peace and non-violence, global citizenship and appreciation of cultural diversity and of culture's contribution to sustainable development' (UN 2015).

The particular indicator of relevance is: '4.7.1 Extent to which (i) global citizenship education and (ii) education for sustainable development, including gender equality and human rights, are mainstreamed at all levels in: (a) national education policies, (b) curricula, (c) teacher education and (d) student assessment' (UN 2015).

This SDG4.7 indicator has been critiqued for failing to capture the essence of ESD as a transformational change agenda (Giangrande *et al.* 2019; UNESCO 2016). The underpinning role of education, in all of its forms, for other SDGs is recognised. Examples where ESD explicitly underpins other SDGs include links to Goal 12 (SDG12), Target 12.8, and Goal 13 (SDG13), Target 13.3 (UN 2015, Lockhart 2018).

This discussion of indicators reveals the need for complex suites of internal and external indicators that address different elements of ESD process and impact, different scales, and that enable global comparison and assessment of progress whilst strengthening contextualised, local approaches to ESD. It is also important to measure demographic and contextual characteristics in relation to ESD indicator recording; Ssossé *et al.* (2021) note that, for example, men tended to record improvements in declarative awareness of sustainability whilst women recorded more emotional commitment to sustainable development. We now discuss mapping of SDG coverage within institutions. Indicators themselves do not comprise a monitoring and evaluation approach, and it is discussed below how indicators can be more closely embedded with dialogical processes and activities to encourage quality ESD.

## Mapping the Sustainable Development Goals (SDGs)

ESD comprises holistic and relevant curricula, strengthening specific and generic sustainability competencies, through innovative pedagogies. Initial monitoring and evaluation programmes in higher education often focus on the former of these elements; assessing topics taught, and then expand beyond this over time. Currently, the SDGs offer a first step in scoping curricular content. Higher education institutions were slow to engage with the SDGs, although it was clear that they offered promise for greater embedding of ESD (St George's House 2018). Some universities were early adopters, and it was apparent that the SDGs could provide a mechanism for collaboration with external partners and a possibility for critical analysis. Mapping activity in relation to the SDGs is thus an increasingly common activity for higher education institutions. This has been recently reinforced because one of the major league tables has currently explicitly included SDG mapping as a curricular ESD indicator (Price *et al.* 2021).

UNESCO is the United Nations leading agency for ESD and is responsible for the implementation of ESD for Agenda2030, the current global framework for ESD aligned with SDG4, which takes up and continues the work of the DESD (2005–2014) and the Global Action Programme (GAP) on ESD (2015–2019), as explained above. The SDGs are useful in that they demonstrate the wide scope of sustainable development, they provide a common suite of aspirations and target with which to discuss sustainable development with external partners and they align with regional, national and international policy direction (see Chapter 2 for more discussion). They do need to be treated with caution, however, since they include paradoxical visions of sustainable development as economic growth and liberal development (Chankseliani and McCowan 2021; Eisenmenger *et al.* 2020). A further critical aspect of SDG implementation is how to embrace their interrelationships and adopt holistic, systems thinking, rather than always addressing individual or clusters of SDGs (Fonseca *et al.* 2020). In addition, they fail to address locally contextual and Indigenous issues (Chankseliani and McCowan 2021; Eisenmenger *et al.* 2020) and pursuit of some targets can actually negatively impact other SDGs if a policy coherent approach is not employed (Eisenmenger *et al.* 2020). Despite these issues, they remain a useful and globally shared statement of ambition and action.

As a first step, mapping the SDGs can be a useful way of approaching the monitoring and evaluation of ESD (Gough 2021). It is a useful exercise as opens up dialogical spaces in the institution, engages all disciplines and raises awareness of the scope and political context of sustainable development (Price *et al.* 2021). It is important that SDGs are not cherry picked but rather seen as a systemic framing and integrated whole within, across and around which academic work can be located. Mapping can include keyword searches or engagement with academics, or use of ChatGPT to identify sustainability content, or a hybrid approach (Adams *et al.* 2023; Gough 2021). Examples of mapping using automated and participatory means is discussed in Box 11.5 and through support with training and awards in Box 11.6.

**BOX 11.5 Automated versus Participatory Means of Mapping SDGs**

Different routes to mapping SDGs have been followed. Automated investigation of programme catalogues to identify SDG-relevant content has been trialled at some institutions, such as the University of Southampton. Such processes enable broad scale coverage but are dependent on search terms used and on material available in course catalogue descriptions, which may not include details of course case studies or assessments. In future, artificial intelligence may offer wider possibilities for this approach. However, University of the West of England, Bristol, undertook a bottom up, messier but more inclusive approach for SDG mapping (Gough 2021). They initially worked with a small pilot group in a specific subject and then gradually expanded the discussion and mapping exercise until they had educators from all departments. This approach enabled SDG mapping to generate awareness and critical debate, rather than being merely a tick box activity.

## Mapping Sustainability Competencies

The specific information we need for a particular task in sustainable development, such as understanding the implications of a recycling policy or developing a form of renewable energy, changes rapidly. By equipping graduates not only with such knowledge but also with the skills and capacities to be active change agents in an uncertain, complex world, we are better preparing them for the future (Giangrande *et al.* 2019; Wiek et al. 2011). Development of these 'sustainability competencies' also overlaps with other educational agendas such as equality, diversity, inclusion and entrepreneurship.

**BOX 11.6 Mapping SDGs at University of St Andrews: Raising Awareness and Encouraging Engagement through Training and Awards**

University of St Andrews undertook a process of mapping curricula against the SDGs. As a first step, Directors of Teaching for each Department or School were asked to fill out a spreadsheet indicating which SDGs were covered in each module. Some Directors filled this out based on the module catalogue and module handbooks; others asked educators to fill out their assessment for their own modules. Awareness and critical debate of the SDGs were generated in optional staff development courses, through application for Golden Dandelion certification, in formal modules for Early Career staff training and in ESD workshops. With the assistance of an intern, different online display options were trialled. Finally, attempts were made to generate 'unexpected stories' of ways modules contributed to SDGs that might not have been expected. The visualisation of SDG mapping then generated further discussion across the institution (Figures 11.1 and 11.2).

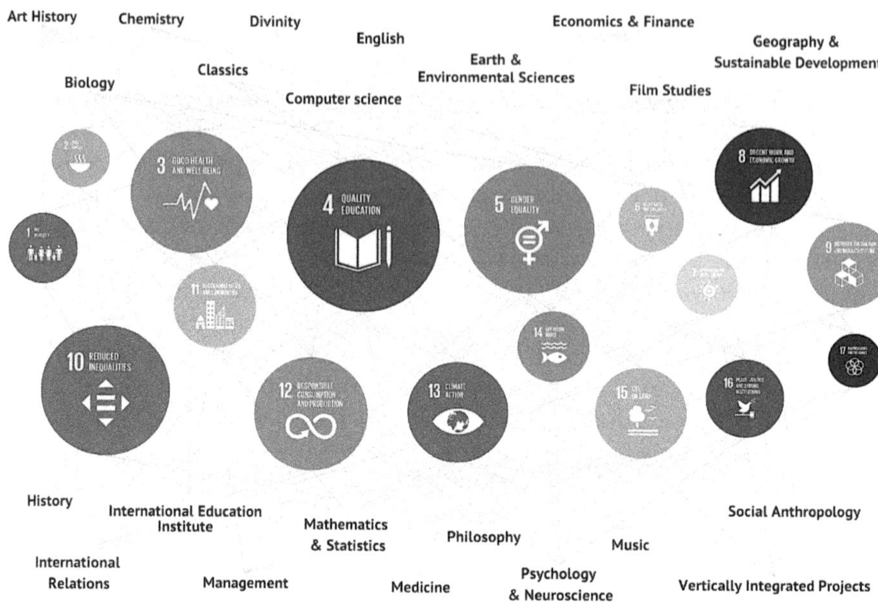


*Figure 11.1* Initial mapping of the SDGs across modules in different Schools at the University of St Andrews illustrated that all SDGs were covered in some way and identified some unexpected interactions. (*Source*: Anya Polatajko, Gosia Mitka and Rehema White: Visualising extent and form of self-reported engagement with the UN Sustainable Development Goals in the curriculum across academic Schools at the University of St Andrews, 2023. Accessible at https://sdgs.wp.st-andrews.ac.uk.)

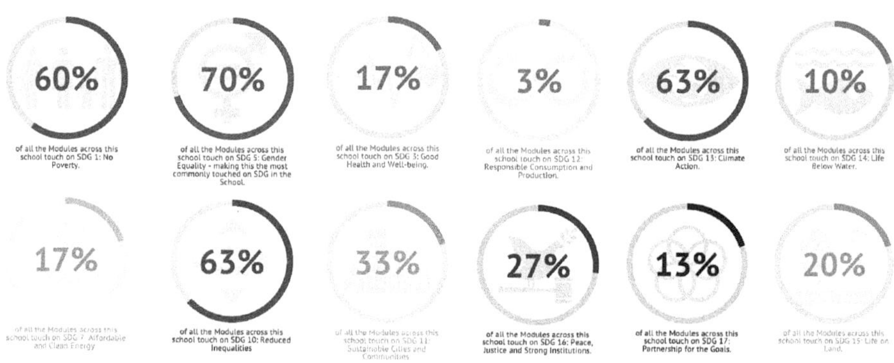


*Figure 11.2* An example of preliminary SDG mapping from the School of Classics at the University of St Andrews. Although this is not a discipline that is always believed to address sustainability, there was good coverage across the SDGs in modules mapped. (*Source*: Anya Polatajko, Gosia Mitka and Rehema White: Visualising extent and form of self-reported engagement with the UN Sustainable Development Goals in the curriculum across academic Schools at the University of St Andrews, 2023. Accessible at https://sdgs.wp.st-andrews.ac.uk/school-of-classics/.)

Sustainability competencies are 'complexes of knowledge, skills, and attitudes that enable successful task performance and problem solving with respect to real-world sustainability problems, challenges, and opportunities' (Wiek et al. 2011). The UN SDGs define a sustainability competency as an 'interplay of knowledge, capacities and skills, motives and affective dispositions' (UNESCO, 2017). The eight key sustainability competencies (see Chapter 2) are shared across all disciplines.

There has been growing recognition of the importance of competencies as a focus from ESD, and they should thus be considered in monitoring and evaluation. The competencies include cognitive and non-cognitive elements and thus can be supported not only in the curriculum but through extra-curricular activities and further life experiences (Valderrama-Hernández *et al.* 2019). For this and other reasons, it can be difficult to monitor and evaluate the development of competencies by learners and educators (Cebrián *et al.* 2020; Giangrande *et al.* 2019). Many of the tools developed to date focus on summative rather than formative and reflective evaluation (Cebrián *et al.* 2020). It can be challenging to enable reflective outputs along with the necessity for competency indicators to be relevant, valid and feasible (Roegiers 2016). Monitoring and evaluation need to accept non-cognitive as well as cognitive aspects of education, with some intrapersonal competencies being especially difficult to assess authentically (Giangrande *et al.* 2019). We need ways to gather qualitative as well as quantitative data, especially at country scales (Lockhart 2018). It is also important to note that competence is gained through practice and is not an end state, which makes it harder to assess (Vare *et al.* 2019). It has been suggested that an effective way to evaluate competencies is through self-reflective questioning, whether by learners or educators, regarding key aspects of specific and generic sustainability competencies (Giangrande *et al.* 2019). These authors pointed out that such questioning reinforces learning and can be open-ended journalling or adapted to Likert questions for analysis (see White *et al.* 2023). Critical reflection linked to such questions can form effective assessments (Zeegers and Clark 2013). Because of their complexity and different forms, it could also be better to assess competences through multiple types of assessment, possibly using Competence Assessment Programmes that include psychometric measurements (Baartman *et al.* 2007). This can be a tricky context, since we want to rigorously assess student learning, yet not succumb to the test obsession that can pervade education (McDowell 1995 in Baartman *et al.* 2007). Frameworks that combine competence assessment with domain learning are likely to be more effective, although there are still challenges in effectively evaluating higher education programmes (Valderrama-Hernández *et al.* 2019). The research on supporting and evaluating competencies provides a strong rationale for innovative assessment, as discussed in Chapters 6 and 7. In this chapter, we are more concerned with the success of the curricula and pedagogies in facilitating competence development, rather than the achievements of individual learners, although of course these outcomes overlap.

Whilst we need to discuss values and the consequences of enacting values through attitudes and behaviours, we are not trying to impose specific values or ideologies in ESD (Komasinski and Ishimura 2017). It is important that learners develop critical capacities to assess knowledge and information and are given experiences to form their own values. Monitoring should not impede the potential of ESD to facilitate creative thinking (Lockhart 2018). If we pursue targets and pre-determined outputs too rigidly, we could be in danger of a paradoxical loss of innovation, flexibility and attention to emotional connection (White 2004).

One monitoring and evaluation framework for SDG Goal 4, Target 4.7 aimed to ensure that by 2030, 'all learners acquire the knowledge and skills needed to promote sustainable development, including, among others, through education for sustainable development and sustainable lifestyles, human rights, gender equality, promotion of a culture of peace and non-violence, global citizenship and appreciation of cultural diversity and of culture's contribution to sustainable development' (UN 2015; Giangrande *et al.* 2019).

These authors offer an evaluation framework in the form of a set of questions. Learners, educators, managers and others can respond to these questions in their own self-reflection and evaluation. This question format is important. It encourages dialogue, demands a thoughtful response and consequently negates superficial 'box ticking'. Example questions are illustrated in Table 11.2.

*Table 11.2* Example self-reflective questions suggested to be appropriate to assess competencies in higher education.

| *Key sustainability competency* | *Example of competencies* | *Example evaluation questions* |
|---|---|---|
| Intrapersonal | Presencing, self-awareness, stress management, meaning making, connection with self, capacity for inner peace, mental wellbeing, self-reflection | Are learners able to be present in themselves? Can learners hold (without having to resolve them) contradictory feelings and or thoughts? Do learners practise self-awareness? Are learners able to know when they or a group is stressed and take appropriate steps? Can learners make meaning in the work they do? Do learners practise love and compassion? Are learners aware of their mental and emotional health and do they have the abilities to maintain healthy mental and emotional states? |
| Future thinking | Visioning, developing scenarios, backcasting, recognising heritage, intergenerational equity | Are learners encouraged to imagine and envision sustainable futures? Can learners effectively use backcasting and forecasting skills in planning strategic activities? Do learners connect with their heritage and culture when looking to the future? Can learners identify future scenarios and use them to inform decision making? Are learners able to apply an awareness of intergenerational fairness to decisions and planning? |
| Systems thinking | Systems thinking, working with complex problems, promoting resilience, understanding tipping points and feedback loops | Are learners able to work with interconnectedness and complexity in a systemic context? Do learners have a functional knowledge of tipping points, resilience and feedback loops? Do learners have a working concept of resilience? Can learners adopt a holistic perspective? |

*(Continued)*

*Table 11.2* (Continued)

| *Key sustainability competency* | *Example of competencies* | *Example evaluation questions* |
|---|---|---|
| Strategic | Planning, decision making, implementing, addressing challenges, organisational development, use of Kolb's action reflection cycle. | Are learners able to practise decision making and analyse consequences? Can learners use planning and assessment tools? Can learners identify and address challenges with regard to strategies and their implementation? Have learners implemented a plan they have designed? Do learners know how to use the behavioural change cycle for effective action and reflection? Are learners aware of organisational development issues and practices? |

*Source*: Adapted from Giangrande *et al.* (2019).

## A Practical Monitoring and Evaluation Framework

White *et al.* (2023), supported by QAA in UK, recently developed a practical monitoring and evaluation framework to be implemented in higher education (Figure 11.3) and produced a Handbook with practical examples to facilitate its implementation using contextually appropriate tools. This framework proposes a six-step process, spiralling through successive iterations to enable ESD to be embedded and established within an institution or programme (Table 11.3). The process is an active learning and reflection cycle drawing on Kolb and Kolb (2018). It normally begins with dialogical exchange about the meanings and

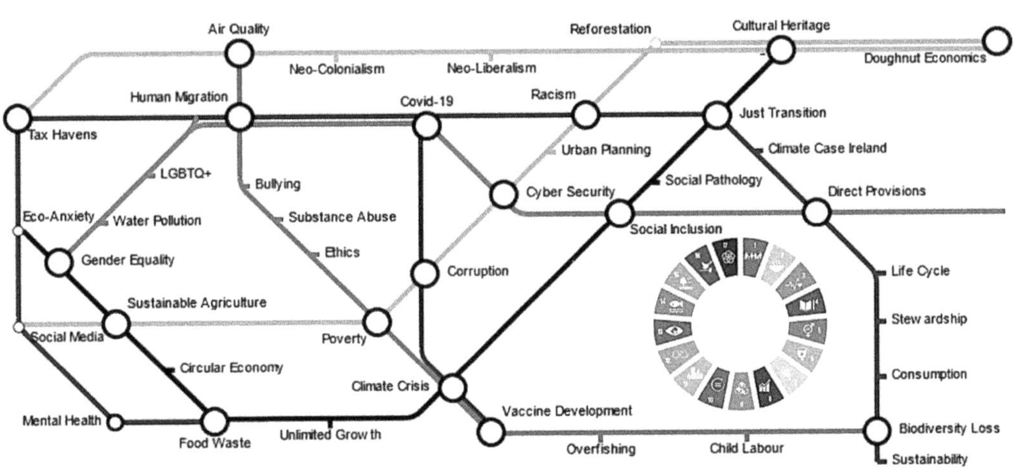


*Figure 11.3* Example of SDG mapping, demonstrating the visual output possible.

*Table 11.3* Steps involved for the framework to monitor and evaluate education for sustainable development.

| | |
|---|---|
| 1 Discuss | Debate the meanings and definitions of ESD in a particular institution and context, raising awareness amongst staff, students and other stakeholders |
| 2 Scope | Scope existing ESD themes and approaches, mapping curricular and extra-curricular activity and considering topics (e.g. against the SDGs), pedagogies and key competencies |
| 3 Plan | Collaboratively agree goals and establish targets, indicators and an action plan |
| 4 Support | Support staff, students and ESD initiatives, deepen and strengthen ESD and celebrate achievements |
| 5 Evaluate | Assess impacts of ESD in short and medium term and through graduate achievements in the long term |
| 6 Reflect | Reflect on processes, outcomes and impacts, learn from experience and others and adapt ESD support and monitoring as required |

Although the table shows a linear process, an institution or department could cycle through these steps, deepening ESD on each cycle, and the steps are thus part of an action reflection spiral of learning as illustrated in Figure 11.3.

*Source*: Adapted from White *et al.* (2023).

definitions of ESD, raising awareness among stakeholders. Secondly, stakeholders map and scope existing provision; most institutions already have pockets of excellent activity. Next, there is strategic planning to agree goals, develop an action plan and identify indicators. The fourth step provides support mechanisms to encourage and enable educators, learners and others. In-depth evaluation then seeks to go beyond quantitative indicators and assess meaningful outcomes, such as graduate behaviours. Finally, reflection enables adaptive planning and support before further discussion with stakeholders and the spiral begins again. These steps are explored in more detail below, using the metaphor of a journey to illustrate the progressive and exploratory nature of this framework. This framework is designed for integrated debate and contributions across academic staff, professional service staff, senior management, learners, professional bodies, university community groups (such as Transition) and possibly with some input from external stakeholders.

## 1 Discuss: Deciding Where to Go on a Journey

Before departing on a journey, it is good to imagine possible forms of travel and to imagine types of destination. Not everyone likes to travel at the same pace or has sufficient luggage and resources to ease the process. Sometimes, not everyone is starting from the same place. Individual, programme, institutional, disciplines and sector journeys may take different paths, even if they share a broad destination. The first step is thus to gather people together, plan collective journeying and galvanise people to join the expedition. Some agreement on purpose and meaning of travel is required.

There are many definitions of ESD, and White *et al.* (2023) also provide some common definitions (see also Chapters 1 and 2). This dialogical process enables people to share perspectives, find their own meaning and agree a common institutional definition. This discussion can include topics, competencies and pedagogies but may also expand to the need for transformative learning and graduates who can act as change agents.

## 2 Scope: Organising Provisions

Are we exploring unmapped territory? Before taking the first step, we need to gather our team for the expedition. Here, we can identify people within a programme, faculty or institution who have already started along their ESD path. We can map activities against the SDGs and scope pedagogical innovation and existing assessment of relevant indicators such as graduate attributes, educator training and assessment forms. Such mapping does not have to be perfect – taking the first step along the journey is the most important outcome. We can consider what resources we need to begin, linking back to discussions undertaken and involving stakeholders in the process. We may, for example, map modules engaging with ESD using keywords, calculate the number of learners exposed to ESD in curricula, assess the number of programmes with ESD in core compulsory modules and monitor educators' engagement in training and workshops (Table 11.4).

*Table 11.4* Different scoping approaches can be used concurrently. They vary in form from overarching assessments of typical content to detailed analysis of curricular and pedagogic content. These scoping approaches are only indicative and should be adapted to context.

| *Scoping approach* | *Possible tasks* |
|---|---|
| *Mapping curriculum* | |
| Mapping content through key word searches | Automated searches for ESD key words in module titles and module descriptors in university programme documents. Key words may differ with context; include discussion of relevant 'ESD keywords' in Step 1. |
| Mapping with academic champions | Each department or programme has an academic champion or enthusiast who works with departmental academic and service staff and learners to identify relevant examples at module or programme level. |
| Mapping with learners | Learners identify examples of ESD in their programmes. |
| Mapping pedagogies | Mapping of teaching and learning approaches can begin in this step or can be undertaken when deepening ESD in later steps. This might include a matrix of types of assessment used across a programme, or the presence or absence of particular pedagogical approaches in a programme. |
| Mapping competencies | Mapping competencies is more complex and may be undertaken later in the process. It may include a matrix of competencies completed for each programme, as discussed with programme directors, or analysis of learning outcomes or assessments for modules. |
| *Mapping extra-curricular activity* | |
| Mapping with wider groups and communities | Mapping relevant co-curricular activities together with wider university groups, including student societies, Transition University groups and other initiatives that practice or pursue sustainable development. |

(*Continued*)

*Table 11.4* (Continued)

| *Scoping approach* | *Possible tasks* |
|---|---|
| *Mapping learner or staff engagement* | |
| Mapping learner exposure | Number of learners experiencing ESD, including particular topics, pedagogies, competencies in core or option modules |
| Mapping learner exposure across core/compulsory modules | Number of learners experiencing ESD or particular topics, pedagogies, competencies in core modules and thus in programmes |
| Mapping learner exposure across programmes | Number of learners experiencing ESD or particular topics, pedagogies, competencies at different stages of programmes to illustrate progression |
| Mapping educators exploring ESD themes and approaches | Number of educators exploring ESD themes and approaches, across programmes and the institution |

*Source*: Adapted from White *et al.* (2023).

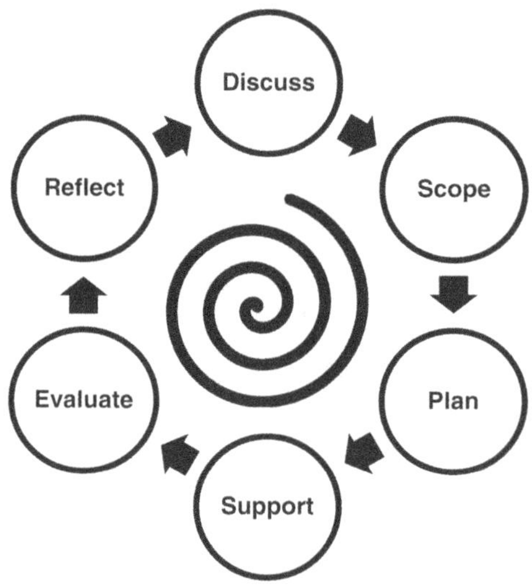


*Figure 11.4* A framework including steps to monitor and evaluate education for sustainable development, using an action reflection spiral of learning. (*Source*: Image drawn by author, adapted from White et al. 2023.) Based on a work at https://www.ucc.ie/en/sdg-toolkit/.

*Source*: This is from the excellent SDG Curriculum Toolkit by John Barimo, Catherine O'Mahony, Gerard Mullally, John O'Halloran, Edmond Byrne, Darren Reidy, Maria Kirrane, licensed under a Creative Commons Attribution-NonCommercial 4.0 International License.

A number of toolkits exist to help map the SDGs, including a tool from the University of Cork that uses a scale of 0 to 5 and includes pedagogies and interdisciplinarity, generates visuals and has a research extension (Figure 11.4).

## 3 Plan: Mapping the Monitoring and Evaluation Journey

This step includes development of an ESD strategy and action plan to support as well as evaluate ESD. Mapping the journey begins not with the first step, but with a clear destination. The goals of ESD are embedded in people and the changes they can make – learners, but also educators, university operations and engagement staff, communities, professional bodies and more. ESD supports competencies to enable individuals to fulfil their potential but also to enable societal sustainability transformation. We thus seek to produce articulate, compassionate, innovative, competent, resilient, responsible graduates who will make the world a better place. We can also see beyond the individual to society – recognising competencies for the community, and in private and public spheres. As an institution with ESD relating to community engagement and local influence, we need to think about the impacts of teaching on such areas. Whilst the emphasis of ESD is on learner development, we can see a significant impact on educators, who can also develop competencies and skills.

A logical framework (logframe) approach can help us determine our goals, and the impacts, outcomes and outputs that will be required. We can then plan activities and finally develop indicators.

Co-design and participatory processes are essential to maintain in this planning. Who do we need on the team? What kind of resources do we need to support our journey? How do we navigate our goals, milestones and travelling together? We need to enthuse learners, staff and management in planning the journey.

Remember to link your monitoring and evaluation framework to existing indicators and to relate it to other agendas for which you are gathering data, such as quality education, student welfare, ethics, diversity and inclusion, decolonising the curriculum, entrepreneurship and extracurricular sustainability initiatives. Indicators are our navigation aids.

A logframe template tool for monitoring and evaluation of ESD has been developed and is available on the project page on the QAA website to support strategic planning towards end goals (QAA 2023), with background and suggestions in White *et al.* (2023).

***When setting targets and indicators for your institution, you can ask yourselves:***

- *What targets and indicators are meaningful and should be prioritised in on our course or in our school/department or institution?*
- *How can we balance quantitative measures and qualitative stories and case studies?*
- *How can we deliver on targets yet enable a facilitated, participatory process?*
- *How ambitious should we be in setting targets and timescales to address without excessive additional workload?*
- *Who is holding us accountable to our plans and processes?*
- *Can we embed ESD within existing systems and with ongoing agendas whilst balancing transformative change?*

## 4 Support: Aiding the Journey

This step explores how to strengthen, deepen and support ESD activities at an institution or in a programme. The path will be strewn with stones and there will be mountains to climb. People will need support, resources and opportunities to celebrate achievements. This will require structural support such as University Sustainability Committees, faculty and school level committees and boards, training and resources, but also networks of people working on the ground. These may include appointed sustainability champions or self-declared sustainability enthusiasts. Induction and professional development training, certification, prizes and awards, national networks, conferences and academic mentors can all support learning and action. Internal (and external) funding for ESD research and innovation initiatives can leverage interest and action. University-wide schemes with competitive funding bids have been very successful at enthusing educators and building capacity. A distributed leadership model is critical to enable this support to be available (Price *et al.* 2021), along with a whole institution approach (Price *et al.* 2024).

## 5 Evaluate: Orienting Travel on the Journey towards Our Destination

It is important to evaluate wider ESD goals as well as to measure ESD indicators. We need to retain sight of the overall goal of transformative learning that enables graduates to be positive change agents in their personal and professional lives. The impacts of ESD can be assessed in the short and medium term through the agreed monitoring and evaluation activities, accessibility, inclusion and the quality of provision, as laid out in the ESD strategy and action plan developed in step 3. In the long term, ESD outcomes and impacts can be evaluated through graduate achievements.

### *Mapping Indicators*

Most target indicators will be relatively easy to assess, once they are well defined. These will include status and facilitatory indicators as described above.

### *Assessing Competencies*

Other targets and indicators can be more challenging to evaluate. For example, there is great interest in ways to effectively assess competencies (Giangrande *et al.* 2019; Ossessé *et al.* 2021). Specific competencies can be evaluated via assessments (see Chapter 7 for more detail), for example:

- Critical thinking – essay
- Systems thinking – systems maps and reflection
- Self-awareness – reflective diaries and essays
- Collaborative competencies – group projects

It can be more complex to assess suites of competencies across a learning unit. White *et al.* (2023) suggested reflexive questioning of both learners and educators. Whilst this could be through relatively unstructured class discussion, they developed a survey tool that enables assessment of module or programme effects on different aspects of key sustainability competencies. The survey asks learners to reflect on the extent to which they have developed or strengthened their competencies in a given module or programme and uses Likert responses against statements per competency. The tool explicitly states that not all modules will emphasise all competencies. This tool works best if learners and educators consider how learning contributes to competencies from the start of the module or programme.

**Box 11.7 Principles to Assess the Quality of ESD Being Integrated into Higher Education Institutions and to Avoid Greenwashing in ESD Claims (Ryan *et al.* 2023)**

1. Joined up sustainability learning – Sustainability must be connecting social, environmental and economic issues – mentioning the SDGS once or twice is not enough to consider a course as 'ESD'.
2. In a compulsory module – It should not be optional! We cannot ensure that everyone will make better choices if only a few learners choose the modules with the quality ESD.
3. From the first year to the final year – Really great courses will embed sustainability throughout from the first year to the final year to ensure the learning is consolidated.
4. Assessed is best! – The best skills are developed when they are applied in practice and made relevant to real-world solutions through assessments.

### *Avoiding Greenwashing*

The quality of ESD provision is important, and it is important to avoid greenwashing (see also O'Neill and Sinden 2021). A set of principles to assess the quality of ESD being integrated into HEI was developed by another QAA project led by University of Gloucestershire (Ryan *et al.* 2023; see Box 11.7). Their set of principles is applicable to any course.

### *Graduate Achievements*

In order to understand impacts of our ESD efforts, we ultimately need to gather stories of graduate achievements, including destinations, actions and impacts, and to identify the effects of ESD along with other influences on these graduates (see Chapter 12 for examples). This will require working with alumni to understand how their education affected their choices and actions, through surveys, events and highlighting individual achievements in newsletters and other publications.

## 6 Reflect: Looking Back and Preparing the Next Trek Forward

The last step completes a learning and action cycle of the spiral, seeking reflection and consideration of future practice. Time must be allocated to reflect on the activities that worked well but also those that have been challenging. It is an opportunity to explore options for the year ahead and adjust.

It is also important to combine reflection with celebration. For example, an annual workshop and celebration of activity will inspire enthusiasm and generate learning. Some universities hold annual sustainability awards events, either standalone or as part of wider HEI celebrations, in recognition of teaching and learning activities. Educators and learners may be nominated by their managers/lecturers or their peers. This sharing of good practice can help to demonstrate the value of and build a wider appreciation of ESD, establishing a reflexive process that captures learning about ESD to feed into future monitoring and evaluation plans.

### *Reporting*

This framework recognises that reporting is intended to meet both internal and external needs. As university leaders become more conscious of the need to demonstrate sustainability literacy, they will need comprehensive reports to both understand what is happening on their campuses, as well as communicate these issues with the diverse stakeholders of a contemporary higher education institution.

Reporting responsibility can be shared across the whole institution. An internal repository (held by registry, curricular support or other relevant body) can be developed so that all useful information can be appropriately stored, shared and accessed by educators and learners involved. This will encourage more educators and learners' engagement and ensure everyone can contribute to and benefit from the activities.

Reporting will improve communication between academics, departments, schools and faculties. Sharing of experiences will make it easier for all involved to see the bigger picture, identify gaps together and recognise the interconnectedness of the ESD teaching and learning experience. It is an important process for increasing data availability, mapping progress and mutual learning.

### *Governance and Accountability*

Supporting, monitoring and evaluating ESD requires resource, in terms of finance, time, tools and capacity. This demands senior leadership buy in. Ultimately, the monitoring and evaluation of ESD should enhance the quality of education as well as of ESD itself. Practising ESD can influence future education policy and practice, improve decision making and action in HEIs and serve as a means of better implementation. Monitoring and evaluation is thus a valuable tool for realising ESD and ensuring that it achieves its expected objectives.

## Conclusions

Monitoring and evaluation can sometimes be perceived as a boring necessity, demanded by external audits or required by senior management to demonstrate 'progress' in ESD. However, we have demonstrated here the complexities and nuances of monitoring and evaluation. Ultimately, such a process should ask of us the purposes of ESD in our context and spark debate on the goals of education more widely. We need to map basic metrics but also evaluate outcomes such as transformative learning and the impact of graduates as change agents in the wider world. The use of creative approaches that engage all actors will generate support and learning for ESD. For each institution, there will be diverse, contextually relevant approaches to monitor and evaluate ESD, at relevant temporal, spatial and institutional scales, for internal or external purposes.

We need to collect such data to establish a more rigorous understanding of effective strategies and activities. Monitoring and evaluation can be undertaken through a cycle of active learning and reflection that enables us to spiral impact of quality ESD throughout our institutions, as an integral part of quality education.

## References

Adams, T., Jameel, S.M. and Goggins, J. (2023). 'Education for sustainable development: Mapping the SDGs to university curricula', Sustainability, 15(10), p. 8340. DOI: 10.3390/su15108340.

Baartman, L.K., Bastiaens, T.J., Kirschner, P.A. and Van der Vleuten, C.P. (2007). 'Evaluating assessment quality in competence-based education: A qualitative comparison of two frameworks', Educational Research Review, 2(2), pp. 114–129. DOI: 10.1016/j.edurev.2007.06.001.

Blackstock, K.L., Kelly, G.J. and Horsey, B.L. (2007). 'Developing and applying a framework to evaluate participatory research for sustainability', Ecological Economics, 60(4), pp. 726–742. DOI: 10.1016/j.ecolecon.2006.05.014.

Brooman, S., Darwent, S. and Pimor, A. (2015). 'The student voice in higher education curriculum design: Is there value in listening?, Innovations in Education and Teaching International, 52(6), pp. 663–674. DOI: 10.1080/14703297.2014.910128.

Cebrián, G., Junyent, M. and Mulà, I. (2020). 'Competencies in education for sustainable development: Emerging teaching and research developments', Sustainability, 12(2), p. 579. DOI: 10.3390/su12020579.

Chankseliani, M. and McCowan, T. (2021). 'Higher education and the sustainable development goals', Higher Education, 81(1), pp. 1–8. DOI: 10.1007/s10734-020-00652-w.

Chubb, J. and Reed, M.S. (2018). 'The politics of research impact: Academic perceptions of the implications for research funding, motivation and quality', British Politics, 13(3), pp. 295–311. DOI: 10.1057/s41293-018-0077-9.

Didham, R.J. and Ofei-Manu, P. (2020). 'Facilitating collaborative partnerships in education policy research: A case of multi-stakeholder, co-investigation for monitoring and evaluation of education for sustainable development', Sustainability, 12(7), p. 2787. DOI: 10.3390/su12072787.

Dlouhá, J., White, R.M., Petry, R., Reeves, A. and Lozano, R. (2023). 'The role of the human dimension in promoting education for sustainable development at the regional level', Frontiers in Sustainability, 4, p. 1281269.

Edwards, D.B., Jr, Sustarsic, M., Chiba, M., McCormick, M., Goo, M. and Perriton, S. (2020). 'Achieving and monitoring education for sustainable development and global citizenship: A systematic review of the literature', Sustainability, 12(4), p. 1383. DOI: 10.3390/su12041383.

Eisenmenger, N., Pichler, M., Krenmayr, N., Noll, D., Plank, B., Schalmann, E. and Gingrich, S. (2020). 'The sustainable development goals prioritize economic growth over sustainable resource use: A critical reflection on the SDGs from a socio-ecological perspective', Sustainability Science, 15, pp. 1101–1110. DOI: 10.1007/s11625-020-00813-x.

Fonseca, L.M., Domingues, J.P. and Dima, A.M. (2020). 'Mapping the sustainable development goals relationships', Sustainability, 12(8), p. 3359. DOI: 10.3390/su12083359.

Gallopin, G.C. (1996). 'Environmental and sustainability indicators and the concept of situational indicators: A systems approach', Environmental Modeling & Assessment, 1, pp. 101–117. DOI: 10.1007/BF01874899.

Giangrande, N., White, R.M., East, M., Jackson, R., Clarke, T., Saloff Coste, M. and Penha-Lopes, G. (2019). 'A competency framework to assess and activate education for sustainable development: Addressing the UN sustainable development goals 4.7 challenge', Sustainability, 11(10), p. 2832. DOI: 10.3390/su11102832.

Gough, G.K. (2021). UWE Bristol and the Sustainable Development Goals (SDGs): Programme mapping portfolio. Project report for University of West of England. Available at: https://uwe-repository.worktribe.com/output/9912189 [Accessed 31 July 2024].

Gough, G.K. and Longhurst, J.W.S. (2017). 'Monitoring progress towards implementing sustainability and representing the UN Sustainable Development Goals (SDGs) in the curriculum at UWE

Bristol'. Presented at Implementing Sustainability in the Curriculum of Universities, Manchester Metropolitan University, 7 March 2017.
Günther, J., Overbeck, A.K., Muster, S., Tempel, B.J., Schaal, S., Schaal, S., Kühner, E. and Otto, S. (2022). 'Outcome indicator development: Defining education for sustainable development outcomes for the individual level and connecting them to the SDGs', Global Environmental Change, 74, p. 102526.
Karatzoglou, B. (2013). 'An in-depth literature review of the evolving roles and contributions of universities to education for sustainable development', Journal of Cleaner Production, 49, pp. 44–53. DOI: 10.1016/j.jclepro.2012.07.045.
Kolb, A. and Kolb, D. (2018). 'Eight important things to know about the experiential learning cycle', Australian Educational Leader, 40(3), pp. 8–14.
Komasinski, A. and Ishimura, G. (2017). 'Critical thinking and normative competencies for sustainability science education', Journal of Higher Education and Lifelong Learning, 24, pp. 21–37. DOI: 10.14943/J.HighEdu.24.21.
Lockhart, A.S. (2018). 'Monitoring ESD: Lessons learned and ways forward', in Leicht, A., Heiss, J. and Byun, W.J. (eds.) Issues and Trends in Education for Sustainable Development, UNESCO, p. 215.
Lotz-Sisitka, H., Mukute, M., Chikunda, C., Baloi, A. and Pesanayi, T. (2017). 'Transgressing the norm: Transformative agency in community-based learning for sustainability in southern African contexts', International Review of Education, 63, pp. 897–914.
Lozano, R., Carpenter, A. and Huisingh, D. (2015). 'A review of "theories of the firm" and their contributions to corporate sustainability', Journal of Cleaner Production, 106, pp. 430–442. DOI: 10.1016/j.jclepro.2014.05.007.
O'Neill, K. and Sinden, C. (2021). 'Universities, sustainability, and neoliberalism: Contradictions of the climate emergency declarations', Politics and Governance, 9(2), pp. 29–40.
Price, E., Nicholson, D.T., Dunk, R., Lawler, C., Carney, M., Vargas, V.R., Veitch, S., Leigh, S., Singleton, M. and Mottram, S. (2024). 'Enabling change agents for Sustainable Development: A whole-institution approach to embedding the UN Sustainable Development Goals in higher education', International Journal of Sustainability in Higher Education, Vol. ahead-of-print No. ahead-of-print. https://doi.org/10.1108/IJSHE-02-2024-0112
Price, E.A., White, R.M., Mori, K., Longhurst, J., Baughan, P., Hayles, C.S. and Preist, C. (2021). 'Supporting the role of universities in leading individual and societal transformation through education for sustainable development', Discover Sustainability, 2(1), pp. 1–16.
QAA (2023) Monitoring and evaluating ESD in higher education. Available at: https://www.qaa.ac.uk/membership/collaborative-enhancement-projects/education-for-sustainable-development/monitoring-and-evaluating-education-for-sustainable-development-in-higher-education [Accessed 30 September]
QAA/Advance HE (2021). Education for sustainable development guidance. Available at: https://www.qaa.ac.uk/quality-code/education-for-sustainable-development and https://www.advance-he.ac.uk/knowledge-hub/education-sustainable-development-guidance [Accessed 29 March 2021].
Rieckman, M. (2018). 'Learning to transform the world: Key competencies in ESD', in Leicht, A., Heiss, J. and Byun, W.J. (eds.) Issues and Trends in Education for Sustainable Development. UNESCO. Available at: https://www.researchgate.net/publication/323234910_Chapter_2_-_Learning_to_transform_the_world_key_competencies_in_ESD [Accessed 12 August 2024].
Roegiers, X. (2016). Marco conceptual para la evaluación de las competencias.
Ryan, A., Webb, M., Hughes, B., Williams, D., Stevenson, N., Davico, R., Thorne, K., Hepplethwaite, A. and Gard, K. (2023). Students driving curriculum quality for sustainability. Report for QAA CEP on ESD. Available at: https://www.qaa.ac.uk/docs/qaa/members/qaa-efs-project-report-final-july-2023.pdf?sfvrsn=2aa0ac81_2 [Accessed 12 August 2024].
Singer-Brodowski, M., Brock, A., Etzkorn, N. and Otte, I. (2019). 'Monitoring of education for sustainable development in Germany: Insights from early childhood education, school and higher education', Environmental Education Research, 25(4), pp. 492–507.
Ssossé, Q., Wagner, J. and Hopper, C. (2021). 'Assessing the impact of ESD: Methods, challenges, results', Sustainability, 13(5), p. 2854. DOI: 10.3390/su13052854.

St George's House (2018) Consultation on further and higher education and the Sustainable Development Goals. 25–26 January 2018. Report for St George's House. Available at: https://www.stgeorgeshouse.org/wp-content/uploads/2018/05/Further-and-Higher-Education-and-the-SDGs-Report.pdf [Accessed 30 September 2024]

Sterling, S. (2001). Sustainable Education: Re-visioning Learning and Change. Totnes: Green Books for the Schumacher Society.

Stukalo, N. and Lytvyn, M. (2021). Towards sustainable development through higher education quality assurance. Education Sciences, 11(11), 664.

Tilbury, D. (2007). 'Monitoring and evaluation during the UN Decade of Education for Sustainable Development', Journal of Education for Sustainable Development, 1(2), pp. 239–254. DOI: 10.1177/097340820700100217.

Tilbury, D. (2009). 'Tracking our progress: A global monitoring and evaluation framework for the UN DESD', Journal of Education for Sustainable Development, 3(2), pp. 189–193. DOI: 10.1177/097340820900300206.

Tilbury, D. and Janousek, S. (2006). Development of a national approach to monitoring, assessment and reporting on the decade of education for sustainable development. Australian Research Institute of Education for Sustainability and Australian Government Department of the Environment, Water, Heritage and the Arts.

UN (United Nations) (2015). Transforming our world: The 2030 agenda for sustainable development. A/RES/70/1. Available at: https://sustainabledevelopment.un.org/content/documents/21252030%20Agenda%20for%20Sustainable%20Development%20web.pdf [Accessed 31 July 2024].

UNESCO (2007). The UN Decade of Education for Sustainable Development (DESD 2005-2014): The first two years. UNESCO, Paris.

UNESCO (2014). Shaping the future we want: UN Decade of Education for Sustainable Development (2005-2014) – Final report. Paris: UNESCO. ISBN 9789231000539.

UNESCO (2015a). Framework for Action Education 2030: Towards inclusive and equitable quality education and lifelong learning for all (draft). Incheon: UNESCO. DOI or further access details required.

UNESCO (2016). Education for people and planet: Creating sustainable futures for all. Global education monitoring report, 2016. Paris: Global Education Monitoring Report Team. DOI: 10.54676/AXEQ8566. ISBN 978-92-3-100167-3. Available at: https://unesdoc.unesco.org/ark:/48223/pf0000245752 [Accessed 31 July 2024].

UNESCO International Bureau of Education (2016). Global monitoring of target 4.7: Themes in national curriculum frameworks. Geneva: UNESCO. Available at: http://unesdoc.unesco.org/images/0024/002463/246382e.pdf [Accessed 31 July 2024].

UNESCO (2017) Education for Sustainable Development Goals: learning objectives. UNESCO. Available at: https://unesdoc.unesco.org/ark:/48223/pf0000247444 [Accessed 10 January 2025].

Valderrama-Hernández, R., Sánchez-Carracedo, F., Alcántara Rubio, L. and Limón-Domínguez, D. (2019). 'Methodology to analyze the effectiveness of ESD in a higher degree in education: A case study', Sustainability, 12(1), p. 222. DOI: 10.3390/su12010222.

Vare, P., Arro, G., de Hamer, A., Del Gobbo, G., de Vries, G., Farioli, F., Kadji-Beltran, C., Kangur, M., Mayer, M., Millican, R. and Nijdam, C. (2019). 'Devising a competence-based training program for educators of sustainable development: Lessons learned', Sustainability, 11(7), p. 1890. DOI: 10.3390/su11071890.

Veidemane, A. (2022). 'Education for sustainable development in higher education rankings: Challenges and opportunities for developing internationally comparable indicators', Sustainability, 14(9), p. 5102. DOI: 10.3390/su14095102.

Velasco, I., & Harder, M. K. (2014). From attitude change to behaviour change: institutional mediators of education for sustainable development effectiveness. Sustainability,6(10), pp. 6553–6575.

Wals, A.E. (2009). 'A mid-DESD review: Key findings and ways forward', Journal of Education for Sustainable Development, 3(2), pp. 195–204. DOI: 10.1177/097340820900300216.

Walsh, Z., Böhme, J. and Wamsler, C. (2021). 'Towards a relational paradigm in sustainability research, practice, and education', Ambio, 50, pp. 74–84.

White, R.M. (2004). 'A paradox for environmental education: How can we "deliver training to targets" using "participatory, reflective approaches"? Southern African Journal of Environmental Education, 21, pp. 81–93.

White, R.M. (2013). 'Sustainability research: A novel mode of knowledge generation to explore alternative ways for people and planet', in Sterling, S., Maxey, L. and Luna, H. (eds.) The Sustainable University: Progress and Prospects. Abingdon: Routledge.

White, R.M. and Harder, M. (2013). 'The journey towards sustainability via community: Lessons from two UK universities', in Sterling, S., Maxey, L. and Luna, H. (eds.) The Sustainable University: Progress and Prospects. Abingdon: Routledge.

White, R.M., Möbius, K., King, B., Leask, K., Peres, S., Walker, J. and Higgins, P. (2023). A Handbook for Monitoring and Evaluating Education for Sustainable Development in Higher Education. Produced for QAA UK. Available at: https://www.qaa.ac.uk/membership/collaborative-enhancement-projects/education-for-sustainable-development/monitoring-and-evaluating-education-for-sustainable-development-in-higher-education [Accessed 31 July 2024].

Wiek, A., Withycombe, L. and Redman, C.L. (2011). 'Key competencies in sustainability: A reference framework for academic program development', Sustainability Science, 6, pp. 203–218. DOI: 10.1007/s11625-011-0132-6.

Zeegers, Y. and Clark, I. (2013). Redesigning Pedagogy to Challenge Students' Perceptions of Sustainability (Doctoral dissertation, Higher Education Academy).

Chapter 12

# Graduate Futures

## Embodying Education for Sustainable Development

*Simon Kemp*

### Defining 'Sustainable 'or 'Green' Jobs

As is still fairly typical across society, politics, media and economic analysis, writers and analysts continue to refer to sustainability through the catch-all term 'green'. Across the academic, business and especially the policy literature, the terms 'sustainability skills or jobs' and 'green skills or jobs' are used interchangeably. In this chapter, we will use the term 'sustainability skills or jobs' except for where an article or major policy report specifically adopts the term 'green skills or jobs'.

The notion of a 'green economy' goes back decades, but it came to prominence as a primary theme of the UN Conference on Sustainable Development of 2012 (Rio +20) as a response to a recovery from the global financial crisis. Although subsequent definitions have focused on carbon and environmental management, the Rio+20 requirements of a green economy were modelled on holistic sustainable development through inclusivity, economic growth, employment, poverty eradication and healthy ecosystems (UN DESA, 2023). This description of a green economy clearly aligns with the requirements of SDG8 'Promote sustained, inclusive and sustainable economic growth, full and productive employment and decent work for all' but is also seated firmly in the delivery of all other 16 Sustainable Development Goals.

The United Kingdom Office for National Statistics (ONS) defines a green job in rather more prosaic terms as 'employment in an activity that contributes to protecting or restoring the environment, including those that mitigate or adapt to climate change' (ONS, 2023, section 3). The Green Careers Guide (EAUC Scotland, 2023) offers a definition of 'Green jobs are jobs that help to benefit the environment, generally by protecting, enhancing or conserving it'. These definitions are clearly limited to the environmental dimension of sustainability, and the ONS consider this definition to be one that addresses job areas that contribute to net zero as well as the diversity of environmental employment activities. This ONS definition is also consistent with other definitions to allow temporal comparisons on a global basis, which is clearly of importance when measuring a transition to a greener economy and sustainable society.

The United Nations Environment Programme provided a wider classification in 2011 in the lead up to the UN Conference on Sustainable Development of 2012 (Rio +20), providing a definition of 'green jobs as work in agriculture, manufacturing, research and development, administrative, and service activities, that contribute substantially to preserving or restoring environmental quality. Specifically, but not exclusively, this includes jobs that help to protect ecosystems and biodiversity; reduce energy, materials and water

DOI: 10.4324/9781003451563-12

consumption through high efficiency strategies; de-carbonize the economy; and minimize or altogether avoid generation of all forms of waste and pollution' (UNEP & ILO, 2011). In terms of the skills required for this transition, the European Centre for the Development of Vocational Training provided a broad, non-academic discipline or employment sector definition of green skills as 'the knowledge, abilities, values and attitudes needed to live in, develop and support a society which reduces the impact of human activity on the environment' (CEDEFOP, 2010). The report also suggested that nearly every job will be a green job and understanding sustainable development and environmental issues must be embedded within existing education and training, as opposed to building new standards. However, a 2024 UK Parliament study found a low awareness of green skills and training opportunities across the United Kingdom, linked to uncertainty around the mixed definitions of green skills (UK Parliament, 2024). Confusion around green skills and jobs reflects the ongoing challenging discourse around sustainability, with a lack of agreement proving a difficult barrier in the transition to a cleaner and more equitable society. Higher education must provide leadership in this space rather than contributing to the proliferation of contested definitions, descriptions and targets. Collaboration with business, governments, community bodies and NGOs for consistency of message is clearly key for the achievement of sustainable graduate futures.

Economic projection models and data analysis articulate the predicted growth and importance of a green economy, the green jobs that form that economy, and therefore the roles graduates who have experienced ESD will play in that future. In 2018, the International Labour Organization (ILO) World Employment and Social Outlook projected that a net 18 million more jobs would be created if the initial UNFCCC Paris Agreement 2 degrees Celsius goal is met, with 24 million new jobs globally if sustainability is implemented within business practices, and that 1.2 billion jobs depend on a sustainable society (ILO, 2018).

These projected numbers have risen as the speed and urgency of the transition to a sustainable economy has increased. The United Nations Environment Programme 2021 publication 'Global Guidance for Education on Green Jobs' estimated an additional 60 million new jobs by 2030, recognising the importance of collaboration from the Higher Education system with business, governments, communities and NGOs to this path (UNEP 2021). The 2023 Global Green Skills Report from LinkedIn analysed workforce trends in the sustainability sector, based on the activity of over 930 million LinkedIn users (LinkedIn 2023). This report identified that approximately one in eight global workers had one or more green skill, with this considered deficient in meeting the projected demand for green skills globally.

The volume of research, definitions, and reports addressing 'green' or 'sustainable' jobs serve to demonstrate the importance attached to the careers of our current and future graduates. Whilst many of the definitions focus primarily on the environmental dimension of sustainability in terms of 'green jobs', recognising the social, cultural and economic justice elements of sustainability careers remains crucial and is the approach adopted throughout this chapter.

## The Importance of University Students and Staff to a Transformative Sustainable Future

Higher education offers students opportunities to work in partnership with highly skilled and experienced staff on a vast range of projects that can leverage significant social, cultural, economic and environmental benefits as part of the transition to a sustainable future. Student and staff collaboration is a mutually beneficial transaction, which offers unique, rich perspectives to learning and teaching design (Dickerson *et al.*, 2016; Brown, 2019; Dollinger and Lodge, 2019), providing student contributions are valued with clear communication of outputs (Martens *et al.*, 2018). These collaborations enhance knowledge exchange when working with partners outside the classroom, improving graduate skills and prospects (O'Leary, 2013; O'Leary, 2016; Hill *et al.*, 2019; Römgens *et al.*, 2019). The maturity and advanced skill sets of HE students means they can be entrusted with the futures of external partners, with the justified expectation of professional standard project outcomes.

University staff often possess many years of experience in not only their area of academic specialisation but also of community collaborations, be they charities, governments, community groups, small to medium enterprises or multinational organisations. Academics also offer a respected seal of quality and a reputation for excellence that the HE sector has earned over centuries of positive societal and economic impact, as well as the more traditional metrics of academic quality that are embedded into our cultural perspectives through centuries of work. It is only right that we in the higher education community ensure our students benefit from this historical, current and future reputation through universities opening up these rich avenues of opportunity to our students across all levels.

The scale of potential for socially and environmentally beneficial impacts (or projects) from students working with external partners is enormous. The size of the resource is staggering, with 2,862,620 students studying in UK higher education in 2021 (HESA, 2024). Activating a modest proportion of that student population across the UK and extended globally could provide potentially unimaginable positive outcomes for sustainability. The question is: how do we activate that potential?

There is undoubted power in the student population. This has been proven time and time again through the years across the globe, from the American Civil Rights Protests in the 1960s (Jennings, 2002) to the Fridays for Future climate protests in the late 2010s (Svensson and Wahlström, 2021). This power and potential for transformative change is amplified when students join with university staff to work with external partners. When collaborating with students and external partners, staff need to be confident that all partners share reasonable expectations and that students will commit themselves to the required time and quality for successful outcomes.

It is important to note that arguably the greatest beneficiaries of university – student – external partner collaborations are the students. As higher education student numbers continue to grow, so does the level of competition in the graduate employment market. There are no guarantees of the desired career outcome for graduates from solely a 'good' honours degree. A diverse and contemporary curriculum vitae (CV) or LinkedIn profile demonstrating skills and attributes beyond the curriculum has greater resonance than ever before. The opportunities university staff can offer students are potentially of great value to their futures. Equally the work they produce in collaboration with external project partners matters to future students. If a project is mismanaged through lack of application, poor quality work or simple neglect, then future students will not have access to similar opportunities which is clearly unfair in an increasingly competitive university world. This places an additional burden on university staff. Balancing the needs of current students without compromising the ability of future students to meet their own needs (apologies for the obviously deliberate sustainable development definition pun) has to be at the forefront for academic staff when offering these rich opportunities to our students.

## Sustainability Skills, Competencies and Frameworks

An exploration of green job skills by Consoli *et al.* (2016) suggested that there is application of higher-level cognitive and interpersonal skills than in non-green jobs. Kwauk and Casey (2022) group these sustainability skills into transformative (systems thinking, working within complexity, coalition building), green life skills (collaboration, leadership, problem-solving), skills for green jobs (science and engineering skills, marketing skills). Whilst a useful framework, this may only be considered a starting point through the lack of clear inclusion of social and cultural academic skills.

These frameworks clearly link to the important UNESCO (2017) 'Key Competencies for Sustainability': systems thinking, anticipation, normative values, strategy, collaboration, critical thinking, self-awareness and integrated problem-solving. Graduate competencies that are so vital in the achievement of sustainable futures. The Advance HE & QAA (2021) Education for Sustainable Development Guidance provides a valuable introduction and detail for practitioners initiating their education journey in sustainability. This ESD Guidance is framed around these UNESCO key competencies, further embedding its importance to sustainability education and graduate futures.

The curricular and extra-curricular application of these key competencies for sustainability at an institutional level can take place through 'Graduate Attributes Frameworks'. These structural models guide students through the achievement of knowledge, understanding, skills, experience and personal qualities from their university experience to give them the best opportunities for their future. Crucially, they also provide a strategic framework for academics, professional services staff and student unions to deliver the key competencies for sustainability within the infrastructure of the institution.

An example of the successful melding of the key competencies for sustainability into an institutional strategic approach is the 'Graduate Attributes Framework' at the Manchester Metropolitan University (MMU). Comprising of six 'wrap-around' themes (Digital, Connected, Interpersonal, Autonomous, Sustainable and Enterprising), these attributes combine the academic abilities, transferable skills and personal qualities that a Manchester Met student can achieve and exemplify when they graduate (Figure 12.1) (https://rise.mmu.ac.uk/lessons/attributes/).

Whilst the graduate attributes under the 'Sustainable' theme are clearly aligned with UNESCO (2017) Key Competencies for Sustainability, it would be erroneous to think sustainability attributes are consigned to one category. Box 12.1 demonstrates how the other MMU graduate attributes also align to critical sustainability competencies.

The Manchester Metropolitan University 'Graduate Attributes Framework' perfectly demonstrates how sustainability competencies, values and thinking can drive the strategic approach of creating graduates for a sustainable future, through the creative use of sustainability terminology permeating the framework without necessarily making it explicit. Education for Sustainable Development plays the most critical role in the graduate achievement of these skills and competencies and the transfer point from learning, assessment and experience to graduate contributions to a green economy.

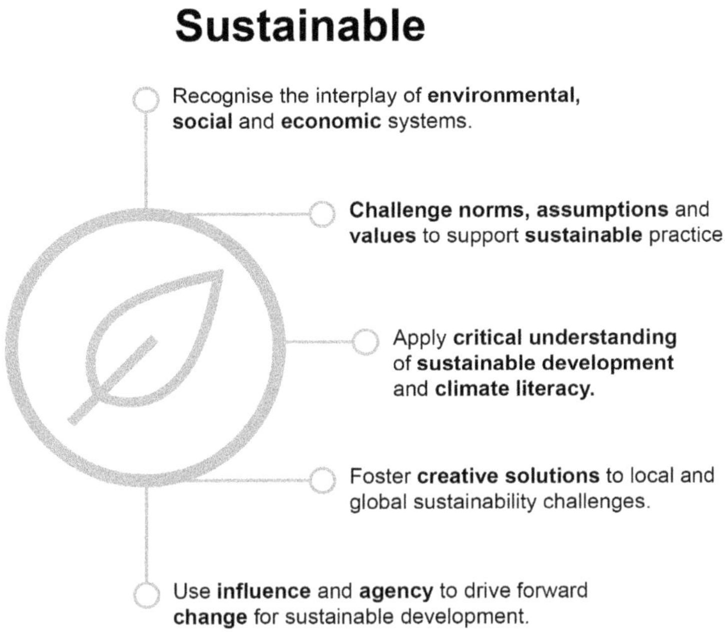


*Figure 12.1* The 'Sustainable' theme of the Manchester Metropolitan University Graduate Attributes Framework. (*Source*: Manchester Metropolitan University, 2024.)

**Box 12.1 Manchester Metropolitan University 'Graduate Attributes Framework' and the Alignment to Sustainability Competencies**

The MMU '*Connected*' attribute includes 'collaborate, forming networks to share and broaden knowledge' without which sustainability is unachievable; 'recognising and respecting diversity in cultures beyond my own', aligning with Normative Competency; systems thinking competency through 'cultivate awareness of disciplines within a wider global context'; and 'contribute positively to communities, both local and global, recognising personal impact on both' which is the optimal outcome of any of our graduates in terms of leading to a sustainable future.

The '*Interpersonal*' attribute further demonstrates how sustainability competencies can be woven into the fabric of an institution and its students. 'Draw on effective strategies for collaboration to create fair and inclusive working environments' again focuses on working together but with a link to the United Nations Sustainable Development Goals (SDG) specifically SDG 8 'Decent Work and Economic Growth' and SDG 10 'Reduced Inequalities'. Progressive and collaborative systems thinking is all about 'Challenge assumptions and seek diverse perspectives to foster equity and inclusion'. The Interpersonal attribute also includes other qualities that reflect sustainability values such as 'empathy', 'respect', 'compassion', 'empower'. The 'integrity' and 'prioritise health and wellbeing' in 'Autonomous' also reflect sustainability values.

The '*Enterprising*' attribute is especially important in terms of graduates for a sustainable future, as it fuses the UNESCO key sustainability competencies and knowledge with employability skills through 'generate creative insights into real-world opportunities and challenges' and 'demonstrate financial literacy, with sustainable solutions to challenges'.

## Project-Based Learning and Assessment – the Impact on Graduate Futures

Graduate futures are clearly linked to the award of an undergraduate or postgraduate degree as evidence of their understanding of their discipline. The distinguishing factors that present students with the opportunities to gain that first role and enhance their career opportunities lies in the application of skills and competencies-based learning and assessment, preferably through experiential learning, and increasingly through working in teams. Birdman et al. (2022) support the application of project-based learning in building competencies that can lead to graduate sustainability careers, highlighting the importance of collaboration, student autonomy and the replication of real-world challenges through what is frequently termed 'authentic assessment' (Koh, 2017). Asgarova et al. (2023) strongly advocate for an extension of the use of authentic assessments across curricula due to the potential to build sustainability skills, contribute to local communities and engagement with the SDGs. Positive social, cultural, economic and environmental outcomes from assessments is clearly very much consistent with the principle of education <u>for</u> sustainable development.

Authentic assessment as a pedagogical approach is framed and discussed in Chapter 6 'Learning and Teaching for Education for Sustainable Development', and in Chapter 7 'Innovating Assessment' where a number of examples of how authentic assessment practices have can lead to sustainability careers for university graduates can be located.

## Co-curricular Activities for Sustainable Graduate Futures

The importance of co-curricular activities to ESD is well established in the academic literature (e.g. Winter and Cotton, 2012). However, it is always worthwhile to see examples of how this can be applied in practice in sustainability.

One example of a high impact co-curricular activity is the University of Southampton Social Impact Lab (SiL), with a specific focus on social sustainability leadership. Developed by Professor Pathik Pathak, since its launch in 2017 SiL has led over 5000 unique student participants and was the first university centre in the UK dedicated to the promotion of social impact leadership through a diverse range of co-curricular activities where students gain knowledge, build skills and learn through experience to lead sustainable social change. Initially running out of the Faculty of Social Sciences, SiL operations extend across three

University of Southampton campuses, working with Schools as diverse as Electronic and Computer Science, the Winchester School of Art and the Southampton Business School. The outcomes data shows the powerful impact of student involvement in SiL with 85% feeling more engaged with their studies, 95% feeling their university experience had been enhanced and 85% feeling their wellbeing had improved. Additionally, 90% felt they had a clear sense of their career direction, and 81% believed they had improved their leadership skills. SiL has supported more than 50 students to start their own social ventures, spanning the full spectrum of social impact interventions (advocacy campaigns, activism, public policy interventions and social enterprises). These are powerful social sustainability-focused impacts with both curriculum and co-curriculum benefits.

## Student Organisations and Their Work for Sustainable Graduate Futures

There is a rich range of sustainability-focused enterprise activities that students are engaged in. Some opportunities exist as part of long-established university and student union projects. Others are hosted within national student enterprise groups partnered with corporate funders, whilst some are grassroots student groups run from a personal or collective deep-seated sense of social and or environmental justice.

### *Case Study: Graduate Futures (Students Organising for Sustainability UK)*

Graduates today must be equipped for careers in a green economy, many of which don't even exist yet. Through the work of SOS-UK with students and young people, it is clear that they want to see an education system that prepares them for careers where they can have a positive social and environmental impact.

The annual Sustainability Skills Survey shows that despite the cost-of-living crisis, and mounting student debt pressures on graduates, 75% of students say they would accept a salary £1000 lower than average to work in a company with a good social and environmental record. Importantly, this is not to say that careers in ethical organisations are always paid less but rather this challenges the dominant sector narrative that graduates prioritise pay above all else. Students' number one action that they want to see their institutions take with regard to sustainability is to 'incorporate sustainability within the formal curriculum' (70% of respondents) (SOS-UK, 2023a).

In response to this demand from students, the Responsible Futures programme was developed 10 years ago to support institutions to work in equal and active partnership with their students to embed sustainability across all aspects of students' learning experiences (SOS-UK, 2024a). To date, Responsible Futures has engaged 48 institutions, reaching over 1.1 million students globally, and training over 200 student auditors to assess and accredit their institutions' progress. The partnership between students and staff working on Responsible Futures drives transformative change. Not only is Responsible Futures transformative for the students' unions and institutions involved, it also in itself represents a transformational learning experience for students. Student auditors report development of critical thinking, communication and confidence. Importantly, the audit provides a safe space for students to challenge to their institutions to go further and faster on curriculum reform in the face of the climate and ecological emergency.

These skills are exactly those which we need all graduates, regardless of discipline, to be leaving education with. A recent global consultation of over 1000 young people across five continents, led by SOS-International and UN Environment Programme, identified that young people understand green skills to be interdisciplinary and inclusive of both technical and 'softer skills', and they see the potential for all jobs to be green jobs. However, they also identified major gaps in their own education to be equipping them with green jobs, and lack of support from government and industry to support progression into green careers (SOS-International, 2024).

This is why it is critical that universities and colleges integrate practical, hands-on, solutions-oriented sustainability education across all parts of the curriculum: students desperately need the associated skills to access the opportunities of green jobs in the future. The Global Green Skills Report by LinkedIn (2023) states green jobs have experienced a 15.2% increase over 2022–2023, despite the overall job market slowing. There is enormous opportunity to be accessed by graduates who are prepared to progress into such careers.

A further, vastly successful programme run by SOS-UK is the UNESCO award-winning 'Green Impact'. This student and staff partnership sustainability learning and awards scheme supports teams in improving the sustainability work of their institution. The most powerful element of Green Impact is the genuinely student and staff collaborative focus of the programme, offering crucial ESD competencies for all partnerships with a focus on their skills for the future. The student power behind this sector-leading programme is perfectly captured by the fact that it started with a student idea in 2006 and has since expanded into one of the most impactful sustainability engagement programmes, reaching tens of thousands of people in HE and beyond each year (SOS-UK, 2024b).

The reach and scale of positive change of the Green Impact team and the wider work of SOS-UK is vast, as demonstrated by the numbers. However, it is always vital to take a step back from the numbers and consider the transformative effect on individuals. An especially inspirational example of this is presented by Charlotte Bonner.

### *Graduate Case Study 1: The Path to Leadership in Sustainability: Charlotte Bonner, Chief Executive Officer, Environmental Association for Universities and Colleges (EAUC)*

I went to university with some vague objectives – to get a higher-level education and subsequent job, to pursue a subject I was interested in and to lean into the opportunities that being a university student provides. I'd chosen English Language and Linguistics as a subject not out of a desire for a particular vocation, but because it was broad, I enjoyed it, and it gave me flexibility in terms of what I did next.

I've always been a cyclist and use two wheels as my main form of transport as well as for leisure and exercise. When I got to university, there wasn't anywhere obviously suitable to store a bike without the high risk of it being stolen. Therefore, I started asking questions and was soon introduced to my institution's sustainability manager as well as student environmental campaigning groups.

These interactions introduced me to the social and environmental challenges we face, and I became committed to being part of the solutions to these challenges in my life and career. I tried to switch courses to environmental science but was told my humanities heavy A Levels meant that wasn't possible. I therefore sought co-curricular opportunities and was elected as one of the students' union environment and ethics officer, working voluntarily on top of my studies and employment.

While serving as a students' union officer, I met two pivotal figures in my career: John Mulholland, then director of training for NIFES Consulting Group and Jamie Agombar, who continues to champion environmental and social justice through NUS and SOS-UK. John recognised my passion and professionalism, taking a significant risk by recruiting me into my first graduate role, where he taught me invaluable lessons about management, navigating complex organisations, and the essentials of consultancy: know your brief! Jamie showed me that student-led initiatives could lead to sector-wide change and later became my boss in a role I kept for over ten years, leading behaviour change programmes like Green Impact and developing education for sustainable development (ESD) and food and farming initiatives.

My career path has been shaped by these mentors and roles. I've also spent time as Union Development Director for NUS, supporting students' unions through the pandemic, learning about organisational development and governance whilst doing so and immersing myself in the further education and skills sector whilst National Head of ESD for the Education and Training Foundation.

Now, I find myself in my dream job, heading up the Environmental Association for Universities and Colleges (EAUC). I work to support post-16 education organisations across the UK and Republic of Ireland to achieve their sustainability goals, to help accelerate ambition and impact, to create long-lasting systems change and make opportunities for historically marginalised individuals and communities to be seen, valued, heard and lead in the EAUC community. It's a privilege and a pleasure to be in this role.

I've heard the best jobs are ones you can do, want to do, and need doing. Having good mentors, asking challenging questions, being kind to colleagues, and focusing on positive impact have been key to my career to date. I am proud to have a job that aligns with my values and the future I want to see. My journey has been a mix of hard work, curiosity, taking risks, and luck. I look forward to continuing on this path.

Charlotte's story beautifully articulates how the journey to sustainability leadership is not restricted to a particular set of A-levels or equivalent qualifications, nor the degree a student studies. It is about grasping co-curricular and graduate opportunities, the importance of mentorship to build the next generation of leaders, being authentic and generous, the desire to make a positive contribution to the world, the confidence to build meaningful collaborative partnerships regardless of your point of experience, and ultimately building a career you believe in and where everyone believes in you.

Whilst Charlotte's story shines a light on important organisations in the ESD community and higher education sector, this is not a complete list. One of the many strengths of the sustainability community is the range of student and staff-focused organisations working to drive the transformation to a sustainable future with a particular focus on graduate skills, experience and positive outcomes.

Change Agents UK are an important leadership training and recruitment organisation in supporting the transition to more sustainable futures for our students. Operating as a broker between graduates (and any individual seeking a career in sustainability), Change Agents UK match applicants with defined skills and attributes to organisations in need of systems thinking employees across all areas of the sustainability sector. As an organisation with a clear mission to 'create a secure, resilient, zero-carbon and fair future for all and every candidate we place is one step closer to this goal', they also offer education and leadership skills programmes to support individuals and organisations in the adaptation to more sustainable workplaces and industries (Change Agents UK, 2024).

Enactus is a global sustainability-focused student entrepreneurial organisation with a stated mission of providing extra-curricular opportunities for students to apply sustainability academic knowledge and transferable skills, and improve their employability profiles. Students work in interdisciplinary teams, with businesses and community groups across the world for positive social and environmental change through innovation and entrepreneurship to 'solve the world's biggest problems' (Enactus, 2025). The key performance indicators (correct as of June 2024) illustrate the scale of sustainability education and entrepreneurship positive impact: 1626 team projects in 33 countries, from 1064 campus programmes, involving 42,450 student members annually, with 13.1 million lives impacted (Enactus, 2025).

## Student and Graduate Case Studies

A recent graduate who has benefitted from the entrepreneurship opportunities provided by Enactus but applied her own leadership and time management skills is Gracie Horton, as demonstrated in her graduate sustainability leadership and research case study.

### *Graduate Case Study 2: Sustainability Leadership and Research: Gracie Horton (Ex-President of Enactus Southampton and PhD Student)*

> I chose a BSc Geography degree because I wanted to see how our generation could help to tackle challenges including climate change and hydrological extremes. I learnt about current global issues, conducted fieldwork and travel, and I am now undertaking my PhD titled 'Understanding the role of social capital for climate resilience.' The skills that I learnt while studying a university degree and conducting my research will enable me to thrive, continuing to strive towards a more sustainable future for generations to come through my aim to work in the sustainability and/or disaster management sphere.
>
> My passion for sustainability stems from the two projects I created and led as President of Southampton Enactus (Seeds for Thought and Project Milan). In October 2021 our presentation came third out of thirty-three countries, meaning we were the third-best team against 1,800 global teams and 72,000 students, and in April 2022, Enactus Southampton won the Enactus UK Nationals Competition. My 'Seeds for Thought' project was pitched to leading companies such as Amazon, BIC, Unilever, and SAP, and secured over £1,000 in funding.
>
> My time as President Southampton saw me leading an organisation of over 70 people operating a portfolio of 5 businesses working towards solving the 17 UN Sustainable Development Goals. Overseeing this organisation has improved my time management and organisational skills, and required me to apply a methodical approach to problem-solving. Presenting my project at the UK National Social Entrepreneurship Competition enabled me to gain excellent verbal communication skills as I was tasked with answering questions from the 100 judges on the panel.

The case study of Gracie Horton demonstrates the high-level abilities that our students can possess whilst studying for an undergraduate degree and progressing to postgraduate research for their individual future. All of the invaluable experience and development of what are typically called 'transferable skills' from the opportunities embraced by Gracie are clearly of personal value to her, but equally they are actually the optimum graduate skills for a sustainable future.

Undoubtedly, the most transformative graduate outcome is where students break free of the potential confines of academic and institutional support, building their own destinies to demonstrate true entrepreneurial spirit, developing their own unique sustainability-focused project, product or service. An especially inspirational example of this is Harriet Noy, founder of her own sustainability business 'Hazaar'.

### *Graduate Case Study 3: Sustainability Entrepreneurship: Harriet Noy (CEO and Founder of Hazaar)*

> I graduated from the University of Birmingham with a BA degree in Economics. Driven by a passion to make sustainability accessible, easy and fun for all, I founded Hazaar, a company dedicated to integrating sustainable resource use and a circular economy approach in universities. Whilst at University I founded the Plastic Free Society and having gained rapid traction through Facebook with over 20,000 student users, Hazaar was born, developing rapidly into the only zero waste student marketplace, helping universities achieve their sustainability targets whilst creating a stronger sense of community and social impact. Currently powering circular economies for 7 universities, Hazaar has been recognised for its contribution to the sector by winning the Sustainability International impact award at The PIEoneer 2023 award.

Harriet found that students want to lead a more sustainable life whilst at University, but constraints of cost and convenience can prevent that. In addition, many universities are falling short on their sustainability targets and want new ways to embed sustainability on campus. Through Hazaar, Harriet is on a mission to integrate a circular economy into university life, ensuring every item of reusable value gets recirculated, avoids ending up in the waste stream and gets a new lease of life, whilst helping students both save money and lead a more sustainable life. Harriet's passion for sustainability, entrepreneurship and providing opportunities for as many young people as possible shows how individuals can make a profound difference in the pursuit of sustainable graduate futures.

Graduates who follow a sustainability-focused path in their studies whilst making the most of the opportunities from extra-curricular work and the 'hidden curriculum' of institutions (Winter and Cotton, 2012) are able to follow a diverse range of career routes owing to the multi and inter-disciplinary nature of their work. Students looking to a future where they can contribute to sustainability solutions do not need to feel constrained by the regular career routes typically outlined through the teaching and assessment of their degree. Sometimes students can be inspired by a single module or extra-curricular experiences with the result of realigning their career aspirations and realise there are different ways of making the critical difference. Two examples are presented by Joshua Davies and Keri Whitewood.

### *Graduate Case Study 4: A Career across Sustainable Business: Joshua Davies (Sustainability and Responsible Banking Senior Manager, Santander)*

Ever since I was young I've had a love for the outside world, and I followed this passion through my school and university studies. At university I volunteered to take part in every environmentally themed extra-curricular activity I could lay my hands on, and this led to me taking on a number of leadership roles. Example include volunteering as an 'Enviro-Champs Project Assistant' at The Environment Centre and Southampton City Council, President of the Environmental Sciences Student Society, Surveyor for the GeoData Institute, Eco-campus Officer, elected 'Ethical and Environmental Officer' for the Student Union, and 'Blackout Student Committee Chair'. Within my studies I focused on modules with real world skills-based assessment where I was able to complete environmental management work with organisations such as Old Mutual Wealth and First Wessex.

When I graduated I continued volunteering with Old Mutual Wealth to progress the work we had completed in the Environmental Management Systems module, as well as a 10-week internship with URS/AECOM. Although my internship was voluntary I was able to prove my ability to be part of their team and was then employed as a Sustainability Graduate. I was there for nearly two years where I worked on the National Industrial Symbiosis Programme (NISP), BREEAM projects, ESG annual reports, and water and carbon footprinting. My next role was as a Sustainability Manager (then Senior Sustainability Manager) with Multiplex where I led the sustainability management work for the One Blackfriars development in central London, and developed the Multiplex Net Zero Carbon programme.

Seven years after graduating I was lucky enough to be recognised for my work with a 'edie Sustainability Leaders Award – Rising Sustainability Star and 'edie 30 under 30 class of 2019'. Other than a gratefully received award, this has enabled me to become part of an even wider network of inspirational young sustainability professionals.

I am currently the Sustainability and Responsible Banking Senior Manager for Santander, a role that whilst not necessarily where I thought I might be a decade after graduating, really does reflect the skills and experience I gained through my degree, extra-curricular leadership roles, and professional career to date. Finance is one of the most vital areas as part of the quest for a sustainable future and I greatly enjoy the contributions I make through work such as ESG disclosures, sustainability linked corporate loans, and our ESG Strategy and Targets.

### *Graduate Case Study 5: Career Dreams Realigned: Keri Whitewood (Principal Solictor, Natural England)*

I have always had an interest in the environment and nature, but how it has ultimately become my career is not how I would have anticipated. Before considering university, I undertook a 10-week nature conservation volunteering programme in Tanzania, completing site surveys to collect baseline data to feed onto should be into nature conservation policy. When considering university, I wanted to learn about and encompass wider environmental issues, such as climate change and other human impacts on the planet (waste production, fuel consumption, food production, water use). During my Environmental Science course at the University of Southampton, I participated in the extra-curricular activities such as the Environmental Science Student Society and waste auditing to enhance my employability profile, but it was the compulsory 'Environmental Law and Policy' module sparked my ultimate decision to become a lawyer. That following summer, I undertook a 6 week internship at an ecological consultancy, where I completed site surveys and wrote environmental impact assessment reports as part of the planning application. Through the module and internship I saw how the practical work undertaken by so many professionals is entirely shaped by the legal framework and policy positions that underpins them. To pursue this further, I focused my Masters Dissertation on international legislation regarding invasive species and policies to prevent their introduction via shipping ports.

To become an environmental lawyer I undertook a further 2 years study, worked as a paralegal for a year and completed the 2 years training contract that was necessary to qualify as a solicitor. Initially I worked in private practice, at a corporate law firm advising clients, mainly within the agricultural sector on a range of legal areas. This included work relating to land sales/purchases, agri-environment subsidy schemes (by virtue of the Common Agricultural Policy (EU Regulations)), and other regulatory issues.

It was on joining Natural England's as a solicitor in the in-house legal team where I could really draw together my degree studies and legal career. The organisation is the government's advisor on the natural environment and inputs into government policies/initiatives, advises about the potential impacts on nature of, for example planning applications or potential developments, and is responsible for multiple regulatory matters including species licensing and designating and regulating protected areas. Through my role as Principal Solicitor I provide legal advice to help shape policy and the ongoing projects within the organisation that are driving forward nature recovery and a more sustainable future.

Most graduates aim to pursue career paths that reflect the broad term of 'graduate jobs', those roles defined as 'professional' despite the lack of specificity in the terminology and only defined by the Office for National Statistics (2018) as 'a role where the tasks require knowledge and skills gained through higher education'. However, this path can offer contradictions to sustainability value sets held by some graduates, leading to some to ultimately step away from that particular treadmill. One example is Amy Nicholass.

### *Graduate Case Study 6: A Diverse Sustainable Business, University and Community Career: Amy Nicholass (Aberystwyth University)*

I approached my studies with the aim of building a broad understanding of how a capitalist society impacts the environment and society, and the inherent interdependencies. I participated in lots of voluntary work to build my non-academic skills, knowing from previous experience that employers favour applicants with practical experience. Examples included volunteering with Sustrans on local cycling related community projects, conservation work, organising events for Green Action student's union group, and helping to set up a food cooperative. I ran a Climate Forum festival event for Student Hubs which included talks, live music and a vintage fashion show in collaboration with a local vintage clothes shop, Winchester School of Art and Solent

University, which is when I developed my love of collaborative engaging events to communicate sustainable development issues. I also had a work placement and employment with New Leaf Sustainable Development in Hereford. As a lifelong learner in sustainability, post-graduation I continued to expand my skills with Forum for the Future: Systems Change practitioner's course and certificates with the Sustainable Development Goals Academy, plus training in facilitation and co-production.

My graduate role was with Sustrans as a Workplaces Project Officer advising small businesses on sustainable transport, followed by Project Manager for Go Green, working with 1000 small, medium and large organisations across Bristol for its year as European Green Capital. I then worked in sustainable finance as Project Manager for ClimateWise, working with the insurance industry on climate change at the Cambridge Institute for Sustainability Leadership (CISL), followed by freelance work as a sustainability consultant working with the Banking Environment Initiative also at CISL. Returning to Bristol, I became Senior Consultant at Eunomia Research and Consulting in the policy team, project managing work on topics such as climate change, waste reduction and circular economy with councils, NGOs and DG Env of EU Commission. Now working in Wales for Aberystwyth University as Project Officer for the 'Transport and Health Integrated research NetworK' (THINK), I arrange hybrid events for a wide network of organisations to promote sustainable transport, social justice and health and systems thinking.

Having developed a successful and varied career across all elements of sustainability, I give my unpaid time to the community. I advocate for the power of using comedy and humour to communicate sustainability issues, having completed a Sustainable Stand-Up course and I am a member of the Humour and Creativity Research Group at Aberystwyth University. I also uses my project management skills from my work to organise a Repair Café in my local community, and I am setting up a local Library of Things and community electric car club as well as growing veg in my allotment.

Amy offers an inspirational example of the diversity of roles and sectors available to proactive graduates with the generosity, skills and competencies to contribute to a sustainable future but also that a graduate role is certainly not restricted to the traditional 'professional' sectors.

## A Challenging and Unpredictable Future

Living in this complex, rapidly changing world with increasingly intertwined challenges poses considerable personal and professional difficulties for all of us, but especially for our current and future students. There is a growing body of work illustrating the emotional impacts of knowing and experiencing environmental change has on individuals and communities across the world. The Grantham Institute (2021) demonstrated the negative impacts on the mental health and wellbeing of people from climate change, with young people more likely to experience mental distress even if not directly affected. An increasingly recognised condition termed as 'eco-anxiety' or 'ecological grief and anxiety' defined as the distress from climate change knowledge leading to people being anxious about their future (Cunsolo *et al.*, 2020; Coffey *et al.*, 2021). Individual actions to respond to sustainability challenges, especially climate change, have been shown to have a positive mental health impact on those actors, creating a valuable output of mutually beneficial gains for people and planet (Costello *et al.*, 2011; Bouman *et al.*, 2020). This transfers further from one-off actions to the greater benefits from developing life-long careers in sustainability where the wellbeing and climate impacts are continual, deeper and lasting decades rather than days.

However, whilst pursuing action and a career-tackling sustainability challenge can have these co-benefits, there can be difficult decisions to make. A potentially problematic area of graduate futures is whether individuals looking for a more sustainable future should work with or for petrochemical and exploitative industries. Students Organising for Sustainability UK research in 2023 indicated only 16% of students would consider a job or career with a company funding the fossil fuel industry, whilst 79% state working with an organisation that makes a difference to sustainability issues is an important career consideration for them (SOS-UK, 2023b).

The idea of considering whether to work with or for industries that have contributed so much to the climate crisis and a myriad of other sustainability impacts is a deeply challenging and problematic concept for the majority already working in the sustainability sector, whilst new or future graduates with sustainability values as part of their compass may decide against this route. However, it may be considered by some that the scale of capital investment and research and development required for a full transition to a green, low carbon or sustainable future can arguably only be achieved through financial commitments and full participation from those multinational conglomerates that did so much to create the impacts. As much as sustainability advocates of all generations might wish for national governments to lead the political agenda and allocation of finances to tackle this multifarious problem, the reality is that there is no firm evidence of voters and taxpayers being willing to elect political leaders, or that they support the scale of societal and industrial change at the financial or regulatory level required for this challenge. Research published by the Climate Engagement Partnership (2021) suggested that the UK public supported most net-zero policies until personal behaviour restrictions and especially financial costs were proposed, a finding supported by Brock *et al.* (2023) in the paper '"I'll take the easiest option please". Carbon reduction preferences of the public'.

This is an ethically contentious issue for many but might be an area of significant employment in the future for our graduates. We need to question whether or not we develop the necessary skill sets for students to work in these fields, and whether we facilitate the networks to encourage graduates to pursue these career routes. Can it be argued that as unpalatable as it may be to many people, there is a need for highly qualified and skilled, new and experienced graduates to work with and/or for the organisations that have contributed so much to the crisis we find ourselves in? Some will say no, that it is a line in the sand that cannot be crossed. They will understandably refuse to compromise and will not consider following this path. Others might accept the need for a problematic form of pragmatism, and may attempt to support and lead a sustainability revolution from within these organisations and industries. These potential career routes raise passionate opinions. The question is if we accept the sustainability paradox can only be solved by deep and total collaboration across all communities and industries, should graduates who choose careers in these sectors and companies for sustainability reasons (despite their personal misgivings) be demonised for these decisions, or should they be supported, or even celebrated as part of collaborative solutions for graduate futures? A deeply difficult question to resolve, but an important one to be aware of the deeper we proceed into the decarbonisation of our economy and society in particular.

As we write this book, we stand on the precipice of arguably the most uncertain future for our graduates ever. Aside from the rapidity and ferocity of our changing climate and the ecological emergency, artificial intelligence (AI), and in particular generative AI is changing the graduate employment landscape in ways we do not yet fully comprehend. Thousands of leading AI developers, thinkers and practitioners called for a pause in the unprecedented speed of development of AI in an open letter in 2023 (Future of Life Institute, 2023) stating that 'Advanced AI could represent a profound change in the history of life on Earth, and should be planned for and managed with the commensurate care and resources'. These warnings have not been heeded and we are heading to an unpredictable future that we do not understand, whilst Geoffrey Hinton (one of the renowned 'Godfathers of AI') suggested it might be the greatest threat to humanity, stating concerns of a possible threat from AI if machines achieved higher intelligence than humans, taking control of the planet.

Generative AI has vast electricity requirements which are only projected to considerably increase in the short term, threatening our ability to transition to a lower Carbon economy. For example, Google reported a 48% in greenhouse gas emissions in 2023 compared to 2019 data due to the processing power and electricity consumption required for AI, threatening its net zero emissions by 2030 target (Google Report 2024), with Microsoft reporting similar concerns regarding their net-zero aspirations.

Many of the current jobs employing graduates may become redundant in the near future due to AI, with Suleyman and Bhaskar (2023) highlighting the risk to 'cognitive labour'. There are also potential sustainability advantages from advancements in AI. Taghikhah et al. (2022) have written about the potential of AI to contribute to sustainability solutions such as through supporting and developing interventions for the promotion of pro-environmental behaviour in societies, along with efficiencies in renewable energy production and managing wildfires, highlighting the possible ability of AI to contribute data-led interventions and strategies to advance progress in tackling the climate crisis. Bibri *et al.* (2024) outline how the combination of AI and artificial intelligence of things (AIoT) may be important in addressing environmental complexity in smart cities to advance sustainability goals, whilst also presenting considerable challenges particularly around ethics and the urgency of regulation.

However, the progressive work around AI generally does not consider the potential impact on sustainability work conducted by individuals, internal collaborative projects and larger scale external programmes. Where data analysis was previously conducted by individuals or teams of analysts, does that work become obsolete in an AI dominated near future? A vital question we need to ask ourselves as educators is are we preparing our students and graduates not just for a more socially, economically and environmentally disrupted future, but for a future where employment, professional development, and career stability are uncertain in ways we do not yet understand? ESD teaches students critical skills and competencies that will increase their resilience in an increasingly uncertain and volatile future, but is it enough?

## Conclusion

Quite simply, when pursuing a lifelong development path that has been shaped by social and environmental justice values, it is personal fulfilment that is the most vital outcome for graduate futures, and that is down to the individual. All we can do as educators is provide the ideas, opportunities, collaboration, mentorship, emotional and professional support to help our graduates be the best people they can be, working with us to transform our collective futures.

## References

Asgarova, R., Macaskill, A. and Abrahamse, W. (2023). 'Authentic assessment targeting sustainability outcomes: a case study exploring student perceptions', International Journal of Sustainability in Higher Education, 24(1), pp. 28–45. DOI: 10.1108/IJSHE-07-2021-0266.

Bibri, S.E., Krogstie, J., Kaboli, A. and Alahi, A. (2024). 'Smarter eco-cities and their leading-edge artificial intelligence of things solutions for environmental sustainability: A comprehensive systematic review', Environmental Science and Ecotechnology, 19, p. 100330. DOI: 10.1016/j.ese.2023.100330.

Birdman, J., Wiek, A. and Lang, D. (2022). 'Developing key competencies in sustainability through project-based learning in graduate sustainability programs', International Journal of Sustainability in Higher Education, 23(5), pp. 1139–1157. DOI: 10.1108/IJSHE-12-2020-0506.

Bouman, T., Verschoor, M., Albers, C.J., Böhm, G., Fisher, S.D., Poortinga, W., et al. (2020). 'When worry about climate change leads to climate action: how values, worry and personal responsibility relate to various climate actions', Global Environmental Change, 62, 102061.

Brock, A., Williams, I. and Kemp, S. (2023). '"I'll take the easiest option please". Carbon reduction preferences of the public', Journal of Cleaner Production, 429, p. 139398.

Brown, N. (2019). 'Partnership in learning: how staff-student collaboration can innovate teaching', European Journal of Teacher Education, 42(5), pp. 608–620. DOI: 10.1080/02619768.2019.1652905.

CEDEFOP (2010). Skills for Green Jobs. Available at: https://www.cedefop.europa.eu/en/publications/3057 [Accessed 31 July 2024].

Change Agents UK (2024). Sustainability Leadership Skills Programme. Available at: https://www.changeagents.org.uk/sustainability-leadership-skills [Accessed 31 July 2024].

Climate Engagement Partnership (2021). Net Zero Policies – ahead of COP26, how do the UK public view net zero policies?. Available at: https://www.ipsos.com/sites/default/files/ct/news/documents/2021-11/net-zero-policies-ipsos-cep-october-2021.pdf [Accessed 31 July 2024].

Coffey, Y., Bhullar, N., Durkin, J., Shahidul Islam, M. and Usher, K. (2021). 'Understanding eco-anxiety: A systematic scoping review of current literature and identified knowledge Gaps', The Journal of Climate Change and Health, 3, p. 100047. DOI: 10.1016/j.joclim.2021.100047.

Consoli, D., Marin, G., Marzucchi, A. and Vona, F. (2016). 'Do green jobs differ from non-green jobs in terms of skills and human capital?, Research Policy, 45(5), pp. 1046–1060. DOI: 10.1016/j.respol.2016.02.007.

Costello, A., Maslin, M., Montgomery, H., Johnson, A.M. and Ekins, P. (2011). 'Global health and climate change: moving from denial and catastrophic fatalism to positive action', Philosophical Transactions of the Royal Society A: Mathematical, Physical and Engineering Sciences, 369(1942), pp. 1866–1882. DOI: 10.1098/rsta.2011.0007.

Cunsolo, A., Harper, S., Minor, K., Hayes, K., Williams, K. and Howard, C. (2020). 'Ecological grief and anxiety: the start of a healthy response to climate change?, The Lancet Planetary Health, 4(7), pp. e261–e263. DOI: 10.1016/S2542-5196(20)30144-3.

Dickerson, C., Jarvis, J. and Stockwell, L. (2016). 'Staff–student collaboration: student learning from working together to enhance educational practice in higher education', Teaching in Higher Education, 21(3), pp. 249–265. DOI: 10.1080/13562517.2015.1136279.

Dollinger, M. and Lodge, J. (2019). 'Understanding value in the student experience through student–staff partnerships', Higher Education Research & Development, 39(5), pp. 940–952. DOI: 10.1080/07294360.2019.1695751.

EAUC Scotland (2023). How to find a job that's good for you and the planet. A Green Careers Guide. Available at: https://www.eauc.org.uk/green_careers_guide [Accessed 31 July 2024].

Enactus (2025). Enactus: what we do. Available at: https://enactus.org/what-we-do/ [Accessed 10 January 2025].

Future of Life Institute (2023). Pause giant AI experiments: An OPEN letter. Available at: https://futureoflife.org/open-letter/pause-giant-ai-experiments/ [Accessed 31 July 2024].

Google (2024) Google Environmental Report 2024. Published July 2024. Available at: https://www.gstatic.com/gumdrop/sustainability/google-2024-environmental-report.pdf [Accessed 30 September 2024].

Grantham Institute (2021). The impact of climate change on mental health and emotional well-being: current evidence and implications for policy and practice. Available at: https://spiral.imperial.ac.uk/bitstream/10044/1/88568/9/3343%20Climate%20change%20and%20mental%20health%20BP36_v6.pdf [Accessed 31 July 2024].

Higher Education Statistics Agency (HESA) (2024). Who's studying in HE?. Available at: https://www.hesa.ac.uk/data-and-analysis/students/whos-in-he [Accessed 31 July 2024].

Hill, M.A., Overton, T.L. and Thompson, C.D. (2019). 'Evaluating the impact of reflecting on curriculum-embedded skill development: the experience of science undergraduates', Higher Education Research & Development, 39(4), pp. 672–688. DOI: 10.1080/07294360.2019.1690432.

International Labour Organisation (ILO) (2019). Skills for a Greener Future: A Global View. Available at: https://www.ilo.org/sites/default/files/wcmsp5/groups/public/@ed_emp/documents/publication/wcms_732214.pdf [Accessed 31 July 2024].

Jennings, M.K. (2002). 'Generation Units and the Student Protest Movement in the United States: An Intra- And Intergenerational Analysis', Political Psychology, 23, pp. 303–324. DOI: 10.1111/0162-895X.00283.

Koh, K. (2017). Authentic Assessment, Oxford Research Encyclopedia of Education. DOI: 10.1093/acrefore/9780190264093.013.22 [Accessed 31 July 2024].

Kwauk, C.T. and Casey, O. M. (2022). "A green skills framework for climate action, gender empowerment, and climate justice,"Development Policy Review, Overseas Development Institute, vol. 40(S2), October. DOI: 10.1111/dpr.12624.

LinkedIn (2023). Global Green Skills Report 2023. Available at: https://economicgraph.linkedin.com/en-us/research/global-green-skills-report [Accessed 31 July 2024].

Manchester Metropolitan University (MMU) (2024). Manchester Met Attributes. Available at: https://rise.mmu.ac.uk/lessons/attributes/ [Accessed 31 July 2024].

Martens, S.E., Spruijt, A., Wolfhagen, I.H.A.P., Whittingham, J.R.D. and Dolmans, D.H.J.M. (2018). 'A students' take on student–staff partnerships: experiences and preferences', Assessment & Evaluation in Higher Education, 44(6), pp. 910–919. DOI: 10.1080/02602938.2018.1546374.

O'Leary, S. (2013). 'Collaborations in Higher Education with Employers and Their Influence on Graduate Employability: An Institutional Project', Enhancing Learning in the Social Sciences, 5(1), pp. 37–50. DOI: 10.11120/elss.2013.05010037.

O'Leary, S. (2016). 'Graduates' experiences of, and attitudes towards, the inclusion of employability-related support in undergraduate degree programmes; trends and variations by subject discipline and gender', Journal of Education and Work, 30(1), pp. 84–105. DOI: 10.1080/13639080.2015.1122181.

Office for National Statistics (ONS). (2018). 'One in eight young people without degrees work in graduate jobs'. Available at: https://www.ons.gov.uk/employmentandlabourmarket/peopleinwork/employmentandemployeetypes/articles/oneineightyoungpeoplewithoutdegreesworkingraduatejobs/2018-09-18 [Accessed 31 July 2024].

Office for National Statistics (ONS). (2023). 'Green jobs' update, current and upcoming work: March 2023'. Available at: https://www.ons.gov.uk/economy/environmentalaccounts/articles/greenjobscurrentandupcomingwork/march2023#green-jobs-definition [Accessed 31 July 2024].

Quality Assurance Agency (QAA) and Advance HE (2021). Education for Sustainable Development Guidance. Available at: https://www.qaa.ac.uk/the-quality-code/education-for-sustainable-development [Accessed 31 July 2024].

Römgens, I., Scoupe, R. and Beausaert, S. (2019). 'Unraveling the concept of employability, bringing together research on employability in higher education and the workplace', Studies in Higher Education, 45(12), pp. 2588–2603. DOI: 10.1080/03075079.2019.1623770.

Students Organising for Sustainability International (SOS International), United Nations Environment Programme (UNEP) (2024). International Green Skills and Green Jobs for Youth Consultation Report 2024. Available at: https://sos.earth/green-skills-and-green-jobs-report/[Accessed 31 July 2024].

Students Organising for Sustainability UK (SOS-UK) (2023a). SOS-UK Sustainability Skills Survey 2022-23. Available at: https://cdn.prod.website-files.com/6008334066c47be740656954/651d7ed9dca42698cee12509_20230928%20Sustainability%20Skills%20Survey%20Final-%20HE%20only.pdf [Accessed 31 July 2024].

Students Organising for Sustainability UK (SOS-UK) (2023b). Student perspectives on careers, banking and finance, and the fossil fuel industry. Available at: https://www.sos-uk.org/research/student-opinion-careers-and-the-fossil-fuel-industry [Accessed 31 July 2024].

Students Organising for Sustainability UK (SOS-UK) (2024a). Responsible Futures Impact Report 2014-2024. Available at: https://cdn.prod.website-files.com/652055b7884ba1306a5baac6/664cddbea501f424103e4a6a_Responsible%20Futures%20Impact%20Report%202014-2024_compressed.pdf [Accessed 31 July 2024].

Students Organising for Sustainability UK (SOS-UK) (2024b). Green Impact. Available at: https://www.sos-uk.org/project/green-impact [Accessed 31 July 2024].

Suleyman, M. and Bhaskar, M. (2023). The Coming Wave. Bodley Head. ISBN 978-1847927484.

Svensson, A. and Wahlström M. (2021). Climate change or what? Prognostic framing by Fridays for Future protesters. Social Movement Studies. DOI: 10.1080/14742837.2021.1988913.

Taghikhah, F., Taghikhah, E., Bakhshayeshi, I., Tayari, S., Karatopouzis, A. and Hanna, B. (2022). 'Artificial intelligence and sustainability: solutions to social and environmental challenges', in Asadnia, M., Razmjou, A. and Beheshti, A. (eds.) Cognitive Data Science in Sustainable Computing, Artificial Intelligence and Data Science in Environmental Sensing, Academic Press, pp. 93–108. DOI: 10.1016/B978-0-323-90508-4.00006-X.

United Kingdom (UK) Parliament POST (2024). Green skills in education and employment POSTnote 711. Available at: https://researchbriefings.files.parliament.uk/documents/POST-PN-0711/POST-PN-0711.pdf [Accessed 31 July 2024].

United Nations Department of Economic and Social Affairs (DESA) (2023). Green economy. Available at: https://sdgs.un.org/topics/green-economy [Accessed 31 July 2024].

United Nations Educational Scientific and Cultural Organisation (UNESCO) (2017). Education for Sustainable Development Goals Learning Objectives. Available at: https://unesdoc.unesco.org/ark:/48223/pf0000247444 [Accessed 31 July 2024].

United Nations Environment Programme (UNEP) (2021). Global Guidance for Education on Green Jobs: Connecting Higher Education and Green Opportunities for Planetary Health. Available at: https://wedocs.unep.org/bitstream/handle/20.500.11822/35070/GGEGJ.pdf [Accessed 31 July 2024].

United Nations Environment Programme (UNEP) and International Labour Organisation (ILO) (2011). Green Jobs: Towards Decent Work in a Sustainable Low-Carbon World. Available at: https://sdgs.un.org/publications/green-jobs-towards-decent-work-sustainable-low-carbon-world-17491 [Accessed 31 July 2024].

United Nations Sustainable Development Solutions Network (UN SDSN) (2024). Goal 13 for Universities competition. Available at: https://irp.cdn-website.com/6f2c9f57/files/uploaded/Universities%20for%20Goal%2013%20-%20Competition%20Brief%202024_v0.pdf [Accessed 31 July 2024].

Winter, J. and Cotton, D. (2012). 'Making the hidden curriculum visible: sustainability literacy in higher education', Environmental Education Research, 18(6), pp. 783–796. DOI: 10.1080/13504622.2012.670207.

Chapter 13

# Conclusions

## Creating Hope Through Education for Future Generations

*Rehema M. White*

### Introduction

At the time of writing, there is concern over a decline in butterflies, conflict in the Middle East and fears that new renewable energy infrastructure will damage the few relatively wild places we have in the UK. Global sustainability challenges manifest temporally and spatially in everchanging ways. Yet, there is also much to celebrate. Over the past 20 years, we have seen mainstreaming of many sustainable development issues. Practices and policies that once seemed radical have entered the public domain. For example, abolition of modern slavery, regenerative agriculture, community energy and peat bog restoration have become widely supported activities. Individuals, groups and governments have designed and applied brave projects. Education is crucial in generating and enacting hope for sustainable futures, by inspiring care for our collective future, and developing knowledge, skills and competencies to understand and address sustainability issues.

Higher education matters. The number of students enrolled in universities globally has doubled over the last 20 years and is now approximately 254 million students: an enrolment ratio of around 40%, albeit with large regional differences (UNESCO 2024). Higher education is critical in providing education for vocational and professional requirements, for socialisation, for personal fulfilment and for transformative learning (Sterling 2001). Higher education institutions are important in the development of citizens, professionals, leaders and activists who can create new possibilities for the ways we live. Higher education can inspire, disrupt or reduce aspirations and abilities towards sustainability.

This book has explored the reorientation of higher education through Education for Sustainable Development (ESD). It is not a matter of *whether* or *when* we reorient education – it is a matter of *how*, and *now*. This intention does not merely add a further topic to packed curricula; it is not an add-on or accommodation into existing education (Sterling 2024), it encourages a critical consciousness, through dialogical, experiential and authentic learning. Teaching and learning in higher education can thus develop understanding of the current interconnected climate and nature crises, social inequality and conflict, yet move beyond documenting despair to pursue socio-ecological-technological solutions. However, this book has also demonstrated that ESD is both an aspiration of and a route towards quality education. Many of the principles and approaches discussed across Chapters represent excellent pedagogical practice and align well with other progressive educational agendas.

The aims of this book were to offer a critical debate on ESD, linking theory and practice, and to encourage those with an interest in higher education to explore or deepen

DOI: 10.4324/9781003451563-13

engagement with principles and perspectives of ESD. This book is for everyone – academic staff, professional service staff, senior management, operations managers, students, professional bodies and external stakeholders. It is not designed to narrow ESD debate into a niche, specialist field, but rather to provide entry points or provocations for a wide range of actors to be curious and to advance their interests in this area.

Throughout the book, we navigated tensions between theory and practice, intending to offer a critical viewpoint in each area whilst offering approaches, tools and examples to encourage readers to support ESD in their teaching, institutions and organisations. The book was thus designed to be a catalyst to deeper reflection, whilst also providing useful guidance to enhance teaching and learning practices. It was created to push conceptual boundaries but also so that some people would take their first step, perhaps including a new case study or widening the context of an assessment.

Whilst we focus on ESD in higher education institutions, we understand that learners experience different forms of ESD through lifelong learning (White *et al.*, 2023a). ESD in higher education thus needs to be dynamic to connect with learning within schools in diverse educational systems. ESD needs to support graduates to be fulfilled individuals, responsible societal contributors and change agents as they move into employment in private sector, government or civil society; as they become entrepreneurs, community activists or homemakers; as they develop as leaders, carers or creators. Learning for sustainability also occurs in wider settings, through informal learning, such as in communities, and non-formal exposure to media and other cultural influences. Learners will thus also develop through co-curricular activities such as regenerative community groups or student societies.

The differences in learning experience over time, place, discipline and institution mean that ESD is highly contextual. ESD practice needs to reflect the different capacities and interests of educators and different biocultural, disciplinary and graduate destination contexts. In this book, we have tried to identify opportunities for diverse contextually relevant ideas, routes and approaches for ESD. We hope that further research and exchange in this area will develop the debate around the relevance of particular options.

In this last Chapter, a brief summary of the key points identified in each chapter is now undertaken. Overarching themes are then highlighted, and future research areas are identified. Finally, it is concluded that profound changes are required in the higher education system. Every individual has the capacity to take immediate, small steps, but collectively we need to pursue transgressive pedagogies for radical change in ideas, individuals and institutions.

## Chapter Highlights

Chapter 1 (Kemp 2024) outlined the rationale for this book. There was a plea for engagement with ESD because of the urgent global crisis and disturbing local manifestations of sustainability challenges, but also because ESD is good education. We called for greater critical understanding of ESD and growth of this field of enquiry and practice in a way that strengthens theory-action links. It was noted that this book emerged after the authorial team, with others, developed the UK ESD guidance for QAA and Advance HE (QAA/Advance HE 2021), in an attempt to provoke greater critical engagement with the ideas and approaches within and underpinning that document.

In Chapter 2 (Price and White 2024), the evolution of models of sustainable development over time was followed. Sustainable development does not merely focus on the environment, it tackles the, at times, difficult relationships between environmental integrity and social justice, in the understanding that human wellbeing is dependent on nature, and we need to act accordingly (e.g. Martin *et al.* 2024, Redclift 2005). Current unsustainable human actions require change, and a normative outlook is required as we navigate towards sustainable futures. Education will be fundamental to this change, through awareness, dialogue, knowledge and developing capacities. ESD is not education *about* sustainable development, it is thus education *for* sustainable development. It has emerged from environmental education and covers a wide range of topics, currently framed by, but also more than, the UN Sustainable Development Goals (SDGs) (UN 2015); and seeks to develop specific and key sustainability competencies in learners through innovative pedagogies. ESD aims to open up debates rather than close down conversations through rigid definitions. ESD is a whole institution approach that enhances the experience and outcomes of education, aligning with several other topical educational agendas. Through ESD, we can be attentive to nature and enhance joy in education. We can maintain rather than increase staff workload through adoption of existing tools and resources and careful embedding of ideas within curricula and assessment. Whilst practical ideas for ESD were offered, the Chapter called for a reorientation of higher education.

Chapter 3 (Robinson *et al.* 2024) explored ESD as a whole institution venture. The Chapter tracked the history and evolution of higher education and universities, highlighting the complexity of these institutions. Universities are acknowledged to be important actors within their regions and nationally, stimulating economies, providing employment and infrastructure and enriching intellectual and cultural capital. However, an increasingly neoliberal, managerialist framing of higher education has been fuelled through competition, quasi-markets, audit culture and commodification (such as seeing learners as 'customers') (e.g. Bessant *et al.* 2018). Whilst some enhanced professionalism and efficient bureaucracy is welcome, critical pedagogical theorists seek alternatives to the neoliberal university. The Chapter explored dangers of some models of ESD being complicit in current context, for example, through greenwashing, and a disconnect between the rhetoric of ambitious university sustainability statements and the reality on the ground. The pursuit of a sustainable university requires radical change, to support local and global impacts, outstanding leadership, active student voice, a sustainable campus and integration of teaching, research and operations.

Chapter 4 (White and Preist 2024) demonstrated that ESD is relevant to all academic disciplines, and, in the UK, Subject Benchmark Statements require the adoption of ESD principles and approaches. Academic disciplines are thought domains, comprising suites of intellectual frames, methods and debates, useful for organising within complex institutions, for communicating across institutions and for supporting vocational learning. Many examples were provided, demonstrating innovative ways to engage with ESD. These included case studies with altered assessment focus, reshaped modules or programmes pivoted around ESD. An interesting outcome for educators was the offering of enhanced learning opportunities; ESD did not clutter the curriculum or detract from core material. It was argued that the emerging discipline of sustainability science does not comprise all intellectual or normative aspects and that a wider, shared, interdisciplinary field of enquiry and practice exists. Real-world problems are not confined to single disciplines, and multi- or interdisciplinarity can be useful to engage learners early in their degree programmes. However, transdisciplinary approaches offer enhanced potential for learning and action, generating more opportunity for transformative learning for learners, educators and external stakeholders (e.g. Baumber 2022). Such approaches can be challenging to implement, as they traverse epistemological as well as practical barriers, but the rewards can be substantial.

Curriculum is often the entry point for those supporting or deepening an ESD approach. In Chapter 5 (Gough and Kemp 2024), theories of teaching and learning framed different ways to include ESD topics and approaches. Curriculum design was explored and the need for inclusive, compassionate and authentic curricula was emphasised. The competencies can be supported in learners through effective curriculum design but also educators who develop competencies can better design curricula with positive outcomes for ESD. Drivers for ESD inclusion in curricula were unpacked and case studies of relevant curricular innovation were provided.

Whilst curriculum is the foundation of teaching and learning, pedagogy brings this to life and Chapter 6 (White *et al.*, 2024) explored modes of teaching and learning. Whilst innovative pedagogies are encouraged, many of the listed pedagogical approaches have long been employed in quality education. Paulo Freire (1970) called for critical pedagogies to liberate the oppressed. Heart-hand-head (Geddes 1949) pedagogical approaches acknowledge affective, physical and cognitive domains of learning. A relational approach is required in ESD because of the relationships between people who hold different perspectives, the interconnected nature of sustainability challenges, the recognition of Indigenous ontologies with humans in nature and the need for transdisciplinarity and cross-sectoral working. Relational pedagogies and eco-pedagogies support this approach (Walsh *et al.* 2021). Compassionate pedagogies encourage us to be inclusive and kind in our collective learning experience, especially since transformative learning can be disorienting and difficult. Student voice again emerged as essential in learner – educator – place interactions and for collaborative, cooperative and independent work.

Assessment is often the key focus of learners. Chapter 7 (Kemp and White 2024) explored how assessment *for* and *as* learning has shifted from earlier notions of only assessment *of* learning. Key principles for assessment included validity, transparency, reliability, authenticity, manageability, inclusiveness, with appropriate feedback being critical to fully achieve learning outcomes, to be kind and to limit educator workload and stress. For ESD, assessment needs to include learner-centred, flexible, future thinking, experiential, collaborative, interdisciplinary, authentic, affective, enquiry-based (Nicholson and Vargas 2021) and also creative attributes, not all necessarily in the same piece of assessment. Authentic assessment needs to not only address real-world context but also permit true-to-self engagement by learners and genuine support and honest, but kind, feedback by educators. Assessment supports development of competencies as well as knowledge. Different assessment formats were analysed, including essays, reports, podcasts and fieldwork, with examples to illustrate innovation across different disciplines and study levels.

Higher education institutions are not only for teaching and learning but also support research and the dissemination and implementation of knowledge. Chapter 8 (White *et al.* 2024) discussed the university as a knowledge hub, including aspects of knowledge management. The commodification of universities, directed funding and audit culture constrain research areas, create strong drivers for certain kinds of impact, and cause competition for international students. These pressures are not all bad for ESD, because academics are engaging with the SDGs, addressing real-world problems and undertaking more transdisciplinary research, but there are concerns around the globalised neoliberalism of the higher education sector. The field of enquiry and practice of sustainable development is being rapidly shaped through sustainability research. Aspects explored in more detail included transdisciplinarity, social innovation, systems thinking and the navigation of moral and ethical frameworks. These research attributes reflect a wider shift to Mode 2, democratised, post-normal science (Funtowicz and Ravetz 1993, Gibbons *et al.* 1994, Nowotny *et al.* 2001). Teaching-research-practice links highlighted included the need for more research on ESD, enhanced teaching and learning of sustainability research for undergraduates and postgraduates, and teaching and learning connecting with real world. There was discussion of how we can each support change and find our role in the ecosystem of expertise of sustainability knowledge (Brand and Karvonen 2007).

Supporting, enhancing and embedding ESD in higher education institutions requires leadership. Chapter 9 (Longhurst *et al.* 2024) explored how leadership can alter institutional paradigms and provision. Whilst reorienting the system of higher education is proposed, this requires ambitious and courageous governance from the highest level. Leaders set key goals and support strategies and action plans to embed ESD, with consultation, and often adopting external frameworks or support systems. Ultimately, leaders have responsibility for reporting, and they create externally facing narratives. Governance should engage internal and external stakeholders and provide top-down support for SD enthusiasts to create a virtual cycle of community values and action. Models of sustainability leadership can be bottom up, top down, middle out or distributed. Leadership should be transformational, and may be transactional or radical, depending on individual proclivity, context and timing. Diversity and inclusion are fundamental and compassionate leadership can facilitate inclusion and wellbeing.

All staff within higher education institutions need to be supported to facilitate ESD, and Chapter 10 (Baughan *et al.* 2024) explored the role of professional development. This is one of the fundamental issues for ESD, because learners and leaders are demanding ESD content, but many educators feel ill equipped to address ESD topics and explore new pedagogies. If ESD is to be a core aspect of teaching and learning in higher education, resources and courses are required for academic and support staff. Early career academics are now developing greater sustainability awareness; hence, the capacity for ESD teaching and learning may be changed in future generations. Institutions are increasingly providing induction and professional development training, within the general shift in higher education to more curricular and pedagogic support. It is critical that higher education leaders and quality assurance staff also gain professional development in this area. The Chapter concluded that sustainability is the responsibility of everyone in the institution, but curricula, confidence and competencies needed to be supported to enhance ESD provision.

As the case for ESD has been built, most higher education institutions have begun their journey embedding ESD, and there have been growing calls for mechanisms to enable effective monitoring and evaluation for quality provision. In Chapter 11, White *et al.* (2024) explored how ESD progress can be monitored and how quality can be evaluated. It is important to be clear about the purpose and goals of ESD, to evaluate and review process as well as outcome, and to gain support and motivation for ESD. Monitoring and evaluation differ across scales and are required at module, programme, institution, national and global levels. Suites of indicators appropriate to scale and context can be developed to understand baseline, progress and outcome measures. Because ESD is a whole institution initiative, monitoring and evaluation often link to research, impact and operations actions and metrics. A practical framework was introduced that seeks dialogue, scoping, planning, supporting, evaluation and reflection (White *et al.* 2023b). Practical tools can help map SDGs against curriculum and to assess pedagogical uptake, but it can be harder to assess competencies and to gather meaningful data on long term graduate outcomes.

Ultimately, successful ESD will enable learning that supports positive graduate futures as well as enriching the personal and professional capacities and outputs of academic staff and local stakeholders. In Chapter 12, Kemp (2024) explains several of the programmes supporting green jobs and green skills, which are terms currently used interchangeably with sustainability employment and skills. Many universities aim for variations of graduate attributes, which align broadly with sustainability competencies, although are usually less numerous and specific. Attributes and competencies can be developed through quality ESD, including relevant curricula, pedagogies, authentic assessment and extracurricular activities. We need to consider that many future green careers do not yet exist, and we need to develop learner capacities for adaptation and resilience in a world beset by complex, uncertain challenges, often with no obvious solution. Many graduates seek employment with meaning and purpose and are willing to accept less pay for this. Students consistently request ESD in surveys of higher education, student-led organisations and UNEP have identified gaps in education for green skills, and employers seek sustainability skills and competencies, hence higher education must support this agenda. Individual graduate stories illustrated how a combination of influences, including formal, non-formal and informal curricula and activities, mentorship and new opportunities led to them becoming change agents for sustainability after graduation.

## Overarching Themes

The critical analysis across this book revealed several overarching themes of importance for ESD in higher education but also more widely for education and for sustainable development, and for the role and practices of higher education institutions now and in the future.

### *Compassion over Commodification*

Higher education institutions, and specifically universities, are under pressure in the UK and across the Western world. Commodification and neoliberal regimes (Bessant *et al.* 2018) have caused a narrowing of intellectual focus to courses that pay, precarity for staff on temporary contracts and a scramble for research and other funding options, including international students. Many staff are demoralised and feel pressured by high workloads. These pressures make it difficult to introduce what are sometimes seen to be additional agendas, such as ESD. In addition, the global picture of higher education in UK has shifted because of political changes, eroding our connections with Europe, but providing greater opportunities with Asia and other regions. However, we can make the most of the positive consequences of these sector-wide pressures. The rise in professionalisation can counteract nepotistic or discriminatory recruitment or practices. The presence of international students in classrooms creates fantastic opportunities to widen debates and offer different perspectives in ESD. In places where higher education was the privilege of the elite, and at a time of austerity, it is right that higher education institutions are as self-supporting as possible. ESD aligns with several other topical agendas, and clever strategic planning can support mutualisation and synergy between positive, progressive agendas to reduce pressures on academic and support staff. For example, ESD aligns well with agendas for quality education, inclusive education, authentic learning, decolonisation of the curriculum, entrepreneurship, innovative digitalisation and more. ESD can offer greater purpose and hope for learners and educators alike, but must be supported sensitively in contexts where staff are disillusioned or stressed. Higher education institutions still need to inspire innovation and spaces for creativity, intellectual discovery and personal fulfilment of educators as well as learners. Compassionate leadership is required to appreciate and defend students and staff (Toroghi *et al.* 2024).

### Democratisation and Digitalisation of Knowledge

Along with these pressures on universities are pressures on knowledge. The democratisation of knowledge and the shift to greater participation and co-production of knowledge (Functowitz and Rabowitz 1993, Gibbons *et al.* 1994, Nowotny *et al.* 2001) have led to some people having contempt for 'the expert' and threatens to move us beyond post-normal science to a post-truth era. What people believe, and want to believe, can be reinforced within online bubbles of indignation. Teaching and learning in our higher education institutions needs to create safe spaces to learn how to gather, analyse and interpret information. ESD can contribute to this through innovative pedagogies, by enabling collective and individual critical analysis of real-world case studies and by strengthening critical, systems and future thinking, along with normative, collaborative and self-awareness competencies. This is an example of how ESD is a form of quality education.

One aspect of this knowledge revolution is the exponential growth in use of digitalisation and AI. The former creates greater immediate access to information, but not necessarily accurate, ethical or unbiased information, requiring an emphasis on source and moral context and not merely on assimilation. Currently, higher education institutions are grappling with how to ensure work submitted is produced by learners and not AI. The material environmental impacts of AI are also significant, with vast data centres and infrastructure required to support the innocuous sounding 'cloud'. In the future, there is hope for use of AI in particular ways to enhance learning (Debnath *et al.* 2023). For example, second language learners can enhance language skills and read more through AI tools; AI can search larger data sources; AI can support administrative or managerial tasks; AI can support learning practices for some forms of neurodiversity. However, we are not there yet, and the use of authentic, verbal, critical assessments in ESD offers immediate methods to address some of the concerns raised by the rapid rise of AI.

### Plurality, Inclusion and Wellbeing

ESD demands consideration of a plurality of perspectives and thus invites and celebrates diversity in all forms – gender, age, ethnicity, nationality, culture, socio-economic status, neurodiversity and more. Creating safe, compassionate spaces for different people to express themselves in respectful ways in ESD activities and assessments supports inclusion, sharing of perspectives and development of emotional as well as intellectual maturity in individuals and university communities. Mutual understanding and respect counteract conflict, and ultimately sustainable development both requires and supports peace, at local and global scales.

Inclusion also mandates that different voices, especially those of marginalised or power limited groups, are heard in the design of curricula, pedagogies and assessment. The importance of student voice in ESD design and development was raised across most Chapters. In addition, active engagement by local and international stakeholders was seen to be important. Such participation needs to be meaningful contribution rather than tokenistic consultation. Learners, local community and other stakeholders can also enhance future research agendas through ESD.

Inclusion relates to wellbeing. Learning can assist self-fulfilment and enable each individual to reach their potential, but these effects will be stronger if all individuals feel supported and able to flourish. If kindness and compassion are present within ESD approaches, they facilitate feelings of acceptance and self-worth. Across several Chapters, there were calls for compassionate leadership, compassionate pedagogies, compassion for others and compassion for nature in ESD. The physical, mental, emotional and spiritual wellbeing of learners, educators and other staff, families and communities is important. Learners in higher education often have employment or caring responsibilities in addition to learning tasks. ESD can support these needs in practical ways through enhancing employability and life skills, but also through developing understanding of other perspectives, collaboration, self-efficacy, agency and self-expression.

One aspect of wellbeing of particular relevance to ESD is eco-anxiety (Graham *et al.* 2020). Many learners, and often educators, feel despair and a sense of hopelessness when facing the severity of the climate and nature crises. Whilst ESD curricula facilitate understanding of the causes and magnitude of these issues, ESD is also normative and future facing, seeking to explore and share solutions at local and systems scales to address such crises. As several Chapters noted, it is important that active hope is pursued.

### *Every Institution Is Unique*

A further theme that emerged across all Chapters is the need to recognise and celebrate the uniqueness of each higher education institution. Whilst institutions can learn from each other, they also need to recognise their local landscape, community, employers, cultures, academic specialisms, history and other aspects of 'context'. The authentic learning, holistic outlook and normative intention common in ESD allow for different possibilities to be explored. Each institution can pursue its own route to sustainability, for and with ESD (White and Harder 2013). Some institutions are primarily vocational, providing learning for vocational professions. Others have developed reputations for learning in the liberal arts and humanities. Supporting institutional identity, creating a sense of community and pursuing local strengths requires excellent leadership along with grassroots enthusiasm.

Monitoring and evaluation are essential within and across institutions. There is a need to balance quality assurance with the expression of different learning experiences across institutions, relevant to context. Some ESD indicators will need to be widely applicable, but others will be unique to context. The current strong influence of league tables (e.g. People and Planet) in university rankings can be welcome when indicators are relevant and achievable by all, but can sometimes have a perverse effect on emphasis within particular institutions. Higher education institutions need to play the game carefully, ensuring that appropriate indicators are assessed for local benefit whilst being able to demonstrate engagement with wider sectoral measures.

### *Curricula, Pedagogies and Competencies*

Bizarrely, generations of 'educators' in higher education began their teaching careers with no, or almost no, training as an educator. This is partly a reflection of the privileged status of research over teaching (see below) and a throwback to the history and evolution of universities towards mass teaching models. The sector is now better at supporting learning in teaching than previously, but many educators begin with research qualifications and very little teaching experience. The new generation of academic staff is encouraged to undertake professional development, including postgraduate certificates in academic practice, and to apply in UK for Fellowship of the Higher Education Academy, but there remains a cohort of academic staff who are learning by doing teaching. In such contexts, ESD can sometimes be the 'Trojan mouse' (phrase courtesy of Zoe Robinson) into educational purpose theory and practice for educators. Across this book, theory and approaches of ESD through curricula, pedagogies, assessments and competencies were provided. Educators can start small, by using a case study to inform learning, or adapting an assessment. The UN Sustainable Development Goals (SDGs) (UN 2015), whilst not constituting all of the possible curricular topics, comprise an existing framework with several excellent resources to start engaging with topics, case studies and theory-policy-practice examples. However, a more nuanced route to explore curriculum and pedagogy emerges through investigation of the interconnectedness and relationships between SDGs and between other elements of interest in ESD. Taking a holistic, systems approach can be empowering for learners and educators. An interesting theme to emerge is the liberation of relational and eco-pedagogies. Exploration of such approaches can engender paradigmatic change in the way teaching and learning, and also research, are understood. Not only can the relationships between topics, sectors or actors be explored, but by accepting that humans are part of nature, the boundaries of the traditional Social, Economic and Environmental dimensions of sustainable development are eroded. The 'epistemological error' of a reductionist perspective is changed to a holistic perspective (Sterling 2024). This approach offers new possibilities to understand and resolve existing challenges through reciprocity and respect (Kimmerer 2013), although tensions between different elements in sustainable development often remain.

The emphasis on competencies can also be illuminating for educators. Whilst curriculum is important, and pedagogy enables, the notion that we are seeking to develop capacities and skills as well as knowledge shifts the emphasis of learning in some disciplines. Of course, many disciplines have packed curricula and benchmarks and have long outlined specific competencies (e.g. Medicine, Engineering), but other programmes support a wider liberal arts education. As universities have emphasised graduate attributes, the parallel debate of key sustainability competencies is timely.

### *Progression and the Individual*

Throughout this book, there has been discussion of groups and practices, standards and values. However, learning is experienced by individuals. ESD is embedded in process but becomes embodied in people. It is important to consider progression, in lifelong learning, within degree programmes and across the institution, and how and when each person learns.

Individuals learn throughout their lives and from formal but also informal and non-formal contexts. In Scotland, for example, it is a requirement that every school learner experiences ESD and outdoor learning, and that ESD is included in teacher training and professional development. Even early years education is strengthening ESD provision. Many young people have been inspired by youth activism. We need to consider how to deepen ESD experience throughout the higher education degree programme, and how to respond to changing needs and expectations from the new learners entering our degree programmes and from employers and others seeking particular graduate attributes.

Within degree programmes, there may be a formal embedding of approaches and principles across the years, but ESD in higher education is often championed by individual educators and the learner experience can thus be serendipitously influenced by the educators they have. As we develop ESD capacity in higher education institutions, it will be important to map competencies as well as curriculum and to deepen learning experiences through the degree programme.

The importance of the whole institution approach to ESD was reiterated across Chapters. Progression in learning should also be cognisant of the co-curricular experience. First-year learners may be exposed to 'new' norms of recycling, energy sparing and sustainable transport through operational sustainability in higher education institutions. Second and third years may undertake internships in sustainability areas, or contribute to societies with a sustainability focus, or lead community regenerative action. We can provide greater responsibility through the degree to reflect this extra learning and offer opportunities for explicit reflection on this learning in formal curricula.

Self-awareness is a competency that is sought in ESD. Knowledge of self, self-compassion and self-efficacy will be required for our graduates to gain the most from their learning experience, to be able to effectively interact with others and to be the change agents we envisage. Co-curricular and optional experiences and courses can support learners and staff in this process.

### *Knowledge Production and Exchange*

There were references throughout Chapters to the continued tension between research and teaching in higher education institutions, especially universities, and the frequent privileging of research in terms of time, funds and status. This perceived and enacted tension has made it more difficult to emphasise effort and quality in education, including ESD. However, as discussed in Chapters, ESD can be an entry point to sustainability for many academics and can thus enhance research focus and gains. Teaching can be a form of self-discovery, as well as academic learning, for educators as well as learners. Hence, ESD can erode some of the longstanding tension between these areas and demonstrate how knowledge production and exchange can happen across domains of activity in higher education institutions.

Universities have made grand claims about their effects in local regions and contributions to national economies. Some of these claims can be validated and shift towards sustainable economic models through genuine pursuit of sustainable development in teaching and learning as well as research. There is possibility for institutions to close the gap between rhetoric and reality in university mission statements and delivery. Producing graduates with the awareness, knowledge, skills and capacities for a just sustainability transition is an essential contribution of higher education institutions. This focus is strengthened through incentives (e.g. league tables, awards) and regulations (e.g. benchmark statements, funding and professional requirements).

There has been some excellent scholarship in the field of ESD. However, much of this has been either intensely theoretical, or practical (reporting case studies) rather than integrating theory and practice. There are notable exceptions, but the field will benefit from greater theorisation in connection with practice and impact. We hope to have achieved this within this book.

### *Resilience, but also Transformation*

Throughout this book, there were references to the Covid-19 pandemic and responses to it. Whilst this was a prominent moment in time for humanity, there will be other crises to come and to overcome. Climate change, biodiversity loss, globalisation, military conflict and more are causing disruptions in societies and planetary processes.

We face many such wicked problems, denoted by complexity, unpredictability and intractability, as outlined across Chapters. ESD needs to support learners to develop key sustainability competencies but also overarching abilities for adaptation and resilience. Resilience is important at a personal level, to enable learners, and educators, to understand sustainability crises, yet not be paralysed by despair. Resilience is important at institutional levels, and ESD provides a dynamic framework through which to engage academic debate and support active engagement with sustainability challenges. Resilience is important for communities, and for industry. However, there has been some resistance to the emphasis on resilience, which implies the need to absorb and valiantly accommodate sustainability issues. Whilst an element of resilience is beneficial, critics call for transformation of wider systems that currently manifest and maintain unsustainability (e.g. Voulvoulis *et al.* 2022).

Chapters consistently noted the intention of transformative learning through ESD. Transformative learning usually derives from a paradigm change that often, but not always, is provoked by a disorienting dilemma (Mezirow 2018). Individuals experience a dramatic change in view and, in theory, adopt more sustainable values and practices. The implications from ESD are that such learners can then become change agents in their academic disciplines, communities and careers, and can work to catalyse wider sustainability transformations, through individual efforts, leadership or collective impact.

There are three difficulties with this pleasant image. The first is that transformative learning can be disruptive for learners, because having one's worldview challenged is rarely easy. This can be a negative experience, at least initially. Not only do we have to support emotional and mental wellbeing of our learners through such experiences, but institutions can be wary of the initial learner discomfort leading to negative feedback from students (which ultimately links to league tables). Second, transformed learners seeking to transform societal systems may become frustrated with their intransigence and resort to activism, rather than the action and advocacy we encourage. Activists can tread a careful line between legal and illegal activities, purpose and burnout. Whilst we might be proud of our graduates challenging unsustainability in this way, a perceived need to fight *against* rather than *with* the system is not always conducive to flourishing, post-graduation livelihoods. Finally, as each Chapter highlights, sustainability challenges are significant. We may begin to erode unsustainable practices, as the volume of ESD-enhanced graduates increases, but it will take both the reorientation of higher education and the disruption of the current turbocapitalist, power-fuelled socio-economic system to achieve sustainability transformation. The enormity of this challenge will not be possible through higher education alone. It will take collaboration with other sectors – government, private sector and civil society, across sustainability areas, with grassroots support and global partnership.

The origins of sustainable development discourse referred to the needs of future generations. The moral imperative to achieve sustainability for intergenerational equity has been set in legislation in some countries. Change must also be equitable within current generations, and the focus on a just sustainability transition needs to be emphasised in ESD teaching and learning. Intergenerational discourse can help to mediate change, whilst retaining connections to land, heritage and identity.

Every classroom has different views on whether we should pursue sustainability through reformist means, or radical action. ESD does not resolve this question but rather opens it up for debate. A further question is whether ESD should be reformist or radical. In this book, we encourage staff and students to join the conversation, and we suggest first steps for those beginning to consider future facing higher education, whilst also calling for reorientation of the higher education system. It is clear that systemic transformation is required (Sterling 2024). At least some learning will need to be not only transformative, but transgressive, disrupting current paradigms, processes and practices to gain traction for change (Sterling 2024; Lotz-Sisitka *et al.* 2015).

## Future Research Areas

Many of these overarching themes raise more questions than they answer and provide fertile soil for future research areas. The capacity of ESD to present novel questions creates an exciting field for exploration from different disciplines and perspectives and combinations thereof. Some potential research issues raised through the debates in this book are highlighted here, but they are not all encompassing.

In this book, we recognised the huge wealth of different perspectives in and from the Global South, non-Western and Indigenous cultures (e.g. Kimmerer 2013, Vásquez-Fernández and Cash Ahenakew 2020), but we did not have the authority nor space to speak to them at length in this volume. We thus note the need for biocultural diversity and alternative intellectual and ontological debates to inform our thinking. Different linguistic traditions tend to carry diverse meanings of sustainability and ESD, and we also look forward to mutual translation of language and ideas through future research and knowledge exchange.

We consistently note the benefits of acknowledging and strengthening human-nature relationships, yet the majority of higher education learning takes place in lecture theatres, seminar rooms or laboratories in urban areas. There is evidence for the wellbeing benefits of nature connectedness (e.g. Martin *et al.* 2020) and the learning and wellbeing benefits of ecological and architectural design (e.g. Orr 2006). Future research could explore how enhanced nature exposure and experience may support ESD, wider learning and wellbeing in higher education institutions within the context of the whole institution and the green estate.

An additional wellbeing issue requiring further research is eco-anxiety. We need greater understanding of the causes, which appear to be a logical response to sustainability crises, and we need carefully evaluated routes to support affective engagement in formal learning and for adjacent programmes to create active hope in learners, all university staff and local communities.

The SDGs comprise the current policy aspiration and action plan for sustainable development, but there will be a modified suite of goals will have emerged in 2030. Higher education institutions need to actively contribute to this policy debate and to research the implications for knowledge production and exchange in higher education institutions.

There is much research to be undertaken around curricular enhancement, pedagogical approaches and combinations of specific and key sustainability competencies. As noted above, greater linkage of theory and practice is required to underpin the field of enquiry and practice of ESD. For example, the form and context of ESD in postgraduate learning and research needs to be further investigated. We need to test the validity of sustainability competencies and investigate how to facilitate them and how to assess them.

There is some evidence of benefits of ESD, but there is a need to monitor and evaluate ESD approaches, in the short, medium and long term, and to investigate relationships between ESD and quality education, and other agendas, as noted above.

The humanities have much to contribute to ESD, and additional research in this area is required. Fundamentally, ESD is a personal and collective investigation of what it might mean to be human, with, in and for nature, and of our place in the universe. The creative arts, craft and design have significant roles in expression and exploration of our humanity, but have both been underemployed and underexplored in ESD to date.

Finally, this book has identified many questions about the role of higher education institutions. What will the role of universities be over the next decades, and into the next millennium? Higher education institutions have the potential to be knowledge brokers in society, but with that right comes responsibility. The role of ESD within programmes, institutions and the sector is currently unclear, but research could identify significant functions and values through ESD. Within this context, each of us needs to identify our individual strengths and purpose within the ecosystem of expertise of sustainability knowledge.

## Conclusions

Freire called for a critical consciousness (Freire 1970) to identify and change social inequality and environmental degradation through individual and collective learning and action. ESD enables this critical consciousness, causing us to question, to critically analyse and to be able to make value and action judgements. ESD is not just for learners – it is a journey for educators, other academic and support staff, communities, employers and the state.

Higher education supports learners to acquire knowledge, skills, capacities and competencies to be change agents in the world. ESD can help them be change agents for good, within the complex, contested world they will inhabit. They may be reformist or radical, transformative or transgressive. With access to and the privilege of learning comes responsibility. We hope that our graduates can develop the wisdom to use their learning and power in positive ways. We hope that educators can be (re)inspired to see meaning and have fun when teaching. We hope our higher education institutions can fulfil their potential in society. We hope that this book will make a difference in facilitating sustainability transformations in individuals, institutions and society. Such transformation may be our only hope.

## References


Baumber, A. (2022). Transforming sustainability education through transdisciplinary practice. *Environment, Development and Sustainability*, *24*(6), 7622–7639.

Bessant, S. E., Robinson, Z. P., & Ormerod, R. M. (2018). Neoliberalism, new public management and the sustainable development agenda of higher education: history, contradictions and synergies. In *Neoliberalism and Environmental Education* (pp. 129–144). Routledge.

Brand, R., & Karvonen, A. (2007). The ecosystem of expertise: complementary knowledges for sustainable development. *Sustainability: Science, practice and policy*, *3*(1), 21–31.

Debnath, R., Creutzig, F., Sovacool, B. K., & Shuckburgh, E. (2023). Harnessing human and machine intelligence for planetary-level climate action. *npj Climate Action*, 2(1), 20. DOI: 10.1038/s44168-023-00056-3

Freire, P. (1970). *Pedagogy of the Oppressed*. New York: Seabury Press.

Funtowicz, S. O., & Ravetz, J. R. (1993). Science for the post-normal age. *Futures*, *25*(7), 739–755.

Geddes, P. (1949). *Cities in Evolution*, new and revised edition. London: Williams and Northgate.

Gibbons, M., Lomoges, C., Nowotny, H., Schwartzman, S., Scott, P., & Trow, M. (1994). *The New Production of Knowledge: The Dynamics of Science and Research in Contemporary Societies*. Thousand Oaks, California: SAGE.

Graham, P., Kuyvenhoven, C., Upitis, R., Arshad-Ayaz, A., Scheinman, E., Khan, C., Goebel, A., Brown, R. S., & Hovorka, A. (2020). The emotional experience of sustainability courses: Learned eco-anxiety, potential ontological adjustment. *Journal of Education for Sustainable Development*, *14*(2), 190–204.

Kimmerer, R. (2013). *Braiding Sweetgrass: Indigenous Wisdom, Scientific Knowledge and the Teachings of Plants*. Milkweed editions.

Lotz-Sisitka, H., Wals, A. E., Kronlid, D., & McGarry, D. (2015). Transformative, transgressive social learning: Rethinking higher education pedagogy in times of systemic global dysfunction. *Current opinion in environmental sustainability*, *16*, 73–80.

Martin, A., Gomez-Baggethun, E., Quaas, M., Rozzi, R., Tauro, A., Faith, D. P., ... & Pascual, U. (2024). Plural values of nature help to understand contested pathways to sustainability. *One Earth*, *7*(5), 806–819.

Martin, L., White, M. P., Hunt, A., Richardson, M., Pahl, S., & Burt, J. (2020). Nature contact, nature connectedness and associations with health, wellbeing and pro-environmental behaviours. *Journal of Environmental Psychology*, *68*, 101389.

Meyerricks, S., & White, R. M. (2021). Communities on a threshold: climate action and wellbeing potentialities in Scotland. *Sustainability*, *13*(13), 7357.

Mezirow, J. (2018). Transformative learning theory. In *Contemporary Theories of Learning* (pp. 114–128). Routledge.

Nicholson, D., & Vargas, V. (2021) Design principles for assessment of sustainability teaching. In: *Assessment and Feedback in a Post-Pandemic Era: a Time for Learning and Inclusion*. AdvanceHE, pp. 183–195. ISBN 9781916359352

Nowotny, H., Scott, P., & Gibbons, M. (2001). *Re-thinking science: knowledge and the public in an age of uncertainty* (p. 12). Cambridge: Polity.

Orr, D.W. (2006). *Design on the Edge: the Making of a High-performance Building*. MIT Press.

Quality Assurance Agency (QAA) and Advance HE (2021). Education for Sustainable Development Guidance. https://www.qaa.ac.uk/the-quality-code/education-for-sustainable-development

Redclift, M. (2005). Sustainable development (1987–2005): an oxymoron comes of age. *Sustainable Development*, *13*(4), 212–227.

Sterling, S. (2001). *Sustainable education: re-visioning learning and change*. Totnes: Green Books for the Schumacher Society.

Sterling, S. (2024). *Learning and Sustainability in Dangerous Times: the Stephen Sterling Reader*. Agenda: Newcastle-upon-Tyne, UK.

Toroghi, H., Denney, F., & Simpson, A. V. (2024). Cultivating staff equality, diversity, and inclusion in higher education in the post-pandemic era: An organizational compassion perspective. *Frontiers in Sociology*, *9*, 1378665.

UNESCO (2024). *What you need to know about higher education*. https://www.unesco.org/en/higher-education/need-know Accessed 25 September 2024

United Nations (UN) (2015). Transforming our world: the 2030 Agenda for Sustainable Development. https://sdgs.un.org/2030agenda

Vásquez-Fernández, A. M., & Cash Ahenakew, P. T. (2020). Resurgence of relationality: reflections on decolonizing and indigenizing 'sustainable development'. *Current Opinion in Environmental Sustainability*, *43*, 65–70.

Voulvoulis, N., Giakoumis, T., Hunt, C., Kioupi, V., Petrou, N., Souliotis, I., & Vaghela, C. J. G. E. C. (2022). Systems thinking as a paradigm shift for sustainability transformation. *Global Environmental Change*, *75*, 102544.

Walsh, Z., Böhme, J., & Wamsler, C. (2021). Towards a relational paradigm in sustainability research, practice, and education. *Ambio*, *50*(1), 74–84.

White, R. M., & Harder, M. (2013). The journey towards sustainability via community: Lessons from two UK universities. In: S. Sterling, L. Maxey and H. Luna, eds., *The Sustainable University: Progress and Prospects*. Abingdon: Routledge, pp. 146–161.

White, R. M., Kockel, U., King, B., Leask, K., Higgins, P., & Samuel, A. (2023a). The future starts in the past: embedding learning for sustainability through culture and community in Scotland. *Frontiers in Sustainability*, *4*, 1128620.

White, R. M., Möbius, K., King, B., Leask, K., Peres, S., Walker, J., & Higgins, P. (2023b). *A Handbook for Monitoring and Evaluating Education for Sustainable Development in Higher Education*. Gloucester: QAA. Available at: https://www.qaa.ac.uk/docs/qaa/members/handbook-for-monitoring-and-evaluating-esd-in-universities.pdf?sfvrsn=ac42af81_12 [Accessed 31 July 2024].

# Index


academic discipline xv, xxii, 22, 59, 61, 65, 66, 67, 68, 69, 70, 71, 74, 116, 233, 256
academic staff preface, glossary, 43, 61, 65, 78, 81, 111, 123, 162, 164, 173, 193, 213, 215, 216, 235, 219, 217, 244, 258, 275, 279, 282
accreditation 61, 73, 77, 91, 204, 205, 206, 212, 220, 232
active hope 111, 281, 286
active learning xix, 71, 79, 110, 113, 115, 116, 117, 119, 120, 134, 243, 251
activism 147, 198, 261, 283, 284
adaptation xi, xv, xvi, 61, 63, 64, 91, 96, 123, 134, 181, 190, 192, 264, 279, 284
agency xxi, 20, 41, 50, 96, 111, 117, 123, 135, 136, 139, 141, 147, 180, 194, 195, 198, 231, 238, 281
artificial intelligence xv, xviii, 2, 114, 130, 154, 239, 270
assessment as learning xvi, 132, 134
assessment criteria 131, 132
assessment value principles 133
Association for the Advancement of Sustainability in Higher Education Sustainability Tracking, Assessment and Rating System™ 232
Association of University Directors of Estates Green Scorecard 232
audit 40, 48, 144, 179, 184, 229, 230, 231, 234, 261, 276, 277
authentic assessment xv, xvi, 87, 96, 103, 114, 130, 140, 141, 143, 144, 145, 151, 154, 155, 260, 277, 279

barriers (to change) iv, 37, 81, 94, 119, 143, 149, 197, 216, 235, 236, 277
behaviour change xxii, 147, 149, 164, 174, 263
behavioural (hands) learning domain xv, 24, 26, 117
behaviourism None found
biodiversity crisis xx, 2
blended learning xvi, 36, 49
bottom-up leadership 194

campus and operations 38, 40, 41, 45, 50, 53
Carbon Literacy 120, 214, 215, 219, 220, 222
careers iv, 6, 36, 42, 44, 59, 65, 131, 143, 145, 172, 222, 223, 255, 256, 260, 261, 262, 269, 279, 282, 284
change agents xvii, 21, 29, 59, 96, 108, 166, 180, 184, 230, 239, 244, 248, 250, 275, 279, 283, 284, 286
civic engagement 28, 190, 192, 193
climate change xi, xii, xv, xvi, xvii, xx, 9, 11, 13, 17, 20, 21, 62, 63, 64, 67, 70, 91, 101, 108, 137, 140, 149, 171, 189, 198, 214, 219, 220, 222, 255, 264, 266, 268, 284
climate-anxiety 3, 137
co-creation xvi, 38, 100, 123, 135, 155, 206
CoDesignS ESD Framework 26, 27, 28, 100, 121, 217
cognitive (head) learning domain xv, 23, 26, 117, 118, 119, 121, 122, 123, 135, 215
community of practice 214, 215, 219
compassionate pedagogy / pedagogies xvi, 110, 129, 199, 277, 281
competencies i, ii, xv, xvi, xvii, xx, 5, 6, 9, 21, 23, 24, 25, 26, 29, 49, 59, 66, 68, 69, 70, 71, 72, 73, 78, 79, 92, 94, 97, 99, 100, 103, 108, 109, 112, 117, 118, 121, 122, 130, 132, 134, 136, 140, 141, 142, 143, 147, 151, 152, 153, 162, 163, 164, 165, 176, 180, 182, 184, 192, 214, 215, 218, 234, 236, 237, 238, 239, 241, 242, 243, 244, 245, 246, 247, 248, 258, 259, 260, 262, 268, 270, 274, 276, 277, 278, 279, 280, 282, 283, 284, 286
Concordat for the Environmental Sustainability of Research and Innovation Practice 42, 169, 172
constructive alignment 87, 90, 116

constructivism xxi, 109
critical consciousness 2, 163, 166, 182, 222, 286
curriculum content 46, 87, 101, 237
curriculum design ii, xix, 4, 6, 7, 26, 49, 50, 65, 87, 88, 89, 90, 91, 92, 93, 94, 95, 96, 97, 98, 99, 100, 101, 103, 216, 223, 277

Decade of Education for Sustainable Development 22, 231, 236
decolonisation 15, 23, 63, 113, 213, 280
decolonising learning 28
degree iii, iv, xv, xvi, xvii, xviii, xix, xxi, xxii, 4, 9, 38, 43, 44, 46, 59, 60, 61, 73, 74, 76, 78, 79, 82, 87, 88, 89, 99, 101, 137, 138, 145, 148, 152, 168, 169, 178, 218, 237, 257, 284, 263, 264, 265, 266, 267, 277, 282, 283
democratisation of knowledge 280
design principles 87, 134, 135, 147, 172
dialogical process 15, 20, 244
digital technology 80, 130, 140, 150, 151, 170
disciplinary ii, 17, 29, 41, 43, 54, 59, 60, 61, 64, 65, 74, 75, 76, 77, 78, 79, 80, 81, 82, 91, 109, 129, 135, 148, 152, 166, 168, 170, 174, 177, 179, 190, 190, 196, 197, 211, 214, 215, 233, 265, 275
disciplinary learning 77
distributed leadership 198, 199, 248
diversity and leadership 197
doughnut economics xvii, 11, 13, 114
drivers (of change) 12, 61, 91, 92, 94, 96, 97, 103, 176, 200, 201, 214, 216, 222, 233, 277

eco-anxiety 3, 50, 111, 147, 268, 281, 285
eco-pedagogies xxi, 112, 120, 277, 282
EDI (equality, diversity, and inclusion) xvii, 48, 72, 139, 199, 204
education and student-facing services 39, 49, 53
Education for Sustainable Development, definition xvii
employability xviii, 3, 6, 28, 67, 72, 91, 143, 144, 145, 146, 151, 213, 222, 223, 260, 264, 267, 281
employability and careers teams 222
employers i, 22, 65, 98, 101, 146, 192, 220, 222, 267, 279, 281, 283, 286
enterprise xxi, xxii, 28, 37, 44, 72, 74, 112, 261
entrepreneurial university 39, 165
environmental education xviii, 4, 18, 19, 76, 276
environmental stewardship xviii, 10, 11, 12
epistemology xviii, 77, 176
essays 63, 80, 130, 135, 140, 148, 149, 151, 153, 248, 277
ethical 66, 67, 70, 73, 75, 118, 162, 166, 168, 170, 171, 176, 180, 182, 222, 261, 266, 278, 280
evaluation xv, xviii, xx, 5, 15, 48, 49, 54, 88, 101, 129, 131, 175, 183, 205, 212, 221, 223, 229, 230, 231, 232, 233, 234, 235, 237, 238, 241, 242, 243, 244, 246, 247, 248, 250, 251, 278, 279, 281
external scrutiny 231
extra-curricular activities 111, 143, 241, 267

feedback xv, xvi, xviii, 46, 49, 89, 92, 93, 114, 119, 129, 130, 131, 132, 133, 136, 137, 138, 141, 142, 144, 149, 154, 155, 196, 202, 216, 242, 277, 284
fieldwork xx, 89, 90, 152, 153, 171, 264, 277
flipped classroom 138, 139
formal learning xvii, xix, 22, 88
formative assessment xviii, 137, 138, 139, 153
framing 4, 9, 17, 19, 20, 22, 23, 26, 40, 72, 74, 108, 112, 150, 165, 176, 178, 182, 183, 204, 213, 214, 217, 232, 238, 276

global awareness 166
global citizenship xix, 19, 29, 69, 237, 242
Global South 61, 64, 165, 169, 170, 285
governance x, 12, 36, 37, 40, 41, 44, 47, 48, 54, 82, 119, 164, 173, 189, 192, 198, 199, 200, 203, 231, 236, 250, 263, 278
graduate achievements 244, 248, 249, 258
graduate attributes xviii, 204, 245, 258, 259, 279, 282, 283
graduate futures i, x, 151, 255, 256, 258, 260, 261, 265, 269, 270, 279
graduate outcomes 265, 279
graduates xiii, xvii, xviii, xxii, 4, 5, 6, 21, 29, 38, 59, 68, 69, 70, 71, 73, 91, 92, 98, 99, 101, 108, 131, 143, 145, 151, 162, 163, 177, 180, 181, 184, 190, 192, 193, 211, 220, 222, 239, 244, 247, 248, 249, 256, 257, 258, 259, 260, 261, 262, 263, 265, 267, 268, 269, 270, 271, 275, 279, 283, 284, 286
Green Gown Awards xvii, 233
Green Impact 50, 206, 220, 262, 263
green jobs 5, 222, 255, 256, 258, 262, 279
greenwash xviii, xxii, 29, 222, 233, 249, 276
group assessment 130, 132, 140, 141, 146, 147, 151, 159

hidden curriculum xvii, xviii, 88, 102, 103, 265
human-nature relationships 285

impact agenda 174, 175, 177, 235
inclusive practice 119
indicators xxiii, 13, 62, 74, 164, 204, 231, 232, 233, 235, 236, 237, 238, 241, 244, 245, 247, 248, 264, 278, 281, 282
Indigenous cultures 285
Indigenous knowledge 15, 63, 64, 75, 112
inequalities xvii, xxii, xxiii, 9, 10, 13, 20, 21, 29, 59, 64, 70, 76, 91, 93, 101, 108, 114, 119, 162, 168, 169, 191, 199, 259, 274, 286
informal learning xvii, xviii, xix, xx, 22, 88, 111, 275
innovative assessment 5, 88, 130, 139, 140, 151, 154, 241
interdisciplinarity xv, xix, 17, 70, 78, 79, 81, 135, 174, 177, 246, 276
internationalisation 28, 40, 146, 213
ISO 14001 144

knowledge exchange 5, 75, 151, 174, 182, 183, 218, 219, 220, 257, 285
knowledge generation 75, 163, 164, 169, 181, 182, 184
knowledge management 162, 173, 174, 277

leadership x, 5, 6, 21, 23, 25, 29, 38, 40, 41, 47, 48, 49, 53, 54, 89, 163, 164, 172, 180, 189–206, 213, 220, 248, 250, 256, 258, 260, 261, 262, 263, 264, 266, 268, 276, 278, 280, 281, 284
league tables 40, 45, 179, 204, 233, 238, 281, 284
learner centred xix, 94, 109, 114, 134, 135, 277
learners xiv, xv, xvii, xviii, xix, xx, xxi, xxii, 9, 17, 18, 19, 20, 21, 23, 24, 26, 29, 36, 59, 60, 61, 62, 63, 64, 65, 69, 73, 76, 77, 78, 79, 80, 81, 82, 83, 90, 91, 95, 96, 97, 100, 108, 109, 110, 111, 112, 113, 114, 117, 118, 119, 120, 121, 123, 129, 130, 131, 132, 134, 135, 136, 137, 139, 141, 142, 145, 146, 147, 148, 150, 151, 155, 163, 164, 165, 167, 172, 173, 176, 178, 179, 180, 182, 183, 184, 191, 211, 229, 230, 231, 234, 235, 237, 241, 242, 243, 244, 245, 246, 247, 248, 249, 250, 275, 276, 277, 278, 280, 281, 282, 283, 284, 286
learning activities 27, 89, 90, 112, 115, 116, 117, 118, 122, 249
learning design 108, 115, 116, 117, 118, 119, 121, 122, 123
learning domains 23, 27, 117, 118, 121, 122, 213
learning environment xvii, xx, 20, 21, 29, 36, 70, 73, 90, 108, 109, 114, 116, 118, 119, 179
learning for sustainability xix, 4, 20, 55, 76, 275
learning objectives for the SDGs 23, 26, 27, 100, 108, 121, 122, 215
learning outcomes 25, 26, 66, 73, 77, 81, 87, 89, 90, 91, 92, 93, 94, 97, 99, 101, 102, 103, 116, 133, 139, 140, 147, 148, 149, 180, 191, 231, 232, 236, 245, 277
liberationist 109, 123
living lab xix, 43, 46, 72, 90, 135, 143, 144, 180

manage 4, 52, 96, 176, 177, 192, 194
management xviii, xx, 6, 38, 45, 47, 48, 50, 51, 54, 64, 65, 80, 96, 144, 147, 150, 153, 161, 162, 173, 174, 177, 181, 184, 190, 191, 193, 195, 196, 198, 203, 206, 242, 244, 247, 250, 255, 263, 264, 266, 275, 268, 278
mapping xx, 99, 117, 135, 145, 218, 219, 229, 237, 238, 239, 240, 244, 245, 246, 248, 250
mental health 3, 96, 129, 137, 146, 199, 268
middle-out leadership 47, 194, 195, 197, 205, 278
mission statements 6, 37, 50, 55, 283
mitigation 192
models of leadership 198
monitoring xx, 5, 48, 49, 54, 64, 88, 149, 168, 173, 199, 200, 204, 205, 221, 229, 230, 231, 232, 233, 234, 235, 237, 238, 239, 241, 242, 243, 244, 246, 247, 248, 250, 251, 278, 279, 281
monitoring and evaluation framework 232, 242, 243, 247
moral and ethical concerns 170, 171
more-than-human xx, xxi, 14, 112, 113, 182
multidisciplinary (learning) 3, 4, 5, 166

nature xiii, xiv, xx, xxi, xxii, 5, 7, 9, 10, 14, 17, 18, 19, 20, 26, 29, 39, 46, 47, 49, 54, 59, 61, 63, 64, 66, 70, 74, 81, 82, 91, 99, 101, 110, 112, 113, 120, 121, 129, 141, 148, 152, 165, 168, 171, 178, 182, 190, 194, 198, 199, 200, 218, 221, 230, 244, 265, 266, 267, 274, 277, 281, 282, 285, 286
neocolonialism xxi, 18
neoliberal xviii, xx, 37, 40, 54, 174, 183, 230, 234, 236, 276, 279
non-formal learning xix, xx, 22, 88
normative xx, xxii, 15, 24, 25, 61, 69, 71, 76, 81, 94, 95, 108, 110, 112, 141, 142, 152, 153, 163, 165, 166, 167, 176, 180, 184, 199, 258, 259, 276, 280, 281

online learning 131
ontology xx, 77, 112, 176
operational sustainability 80, 111, 171, 173, 183, 283
outreach xx, 6, 38, 40, 41, 44, 52

paradigm shift xx, 51, 54, 55, 170
participatory i, xiv, 25, 26, 46, 64, 68, 75, 82, 118, 123, 164, 166, 167, 168, 170, 174, 212, 223, 229, 230, 231, 232, 238, 239
partnership ii, xx, 3, 15, 21, 37, 41, 45, 64, 80, 81, 129, 136, 170, 175, 205, 206, 212, 217, 218, 223, 235, 233, 256, 261, 262, 269, 285
pedagogies i, xiv, xv, xvi, xvii, xx, xxi, 3, 4, 9, 21, 23, 26, 27, 29, 49, 59, 60, 65, 76, 90, 108, 109, 110, 111, 112, 113, 114, 115, 116, 117, 118, 119, 120, 121, 129, 131, 134, 136, 165, 177, 179, 180, 181, 199, 215, 229, 233, 235, 237, 238, 241, 244, 245, 246, 275, 276, 277, 278, 279, 280, 281, 282
People and Planet University / Green League 191, 232, 282
planetary boundaries xvii, xxi, 11, 12, 13, 101, 114, 189
planning 46, 69, 89, 93, 101, 121, 152, 177, 229, 242, 243, 244, 247, 267, 279, 280
postcolonialism xxi
postgraduate xvii, 23, 81, 109, 153, 172, 182, 184, 214, 216, 218, 219, 260, 265, 278, 282, 286
post-normal science xxi, 167, 278
professional development 36, 60, 204, **211–228**, 248, 270, 278, 282, 283

QAA/Advance HE ESD Guidance 99, 233, 275
quality assurance xx, xxi, 7, 87, 88, 99, 100, 101, 102, 103, 191, 204, 214, 221, 230
Quality Assurance Agency (QAA) xviii, xxi, 4, 90, 91, 140, 191, 216, 233, 281
quality assurance staff 214, 221, 278
quality education 3, 4, 20, 29, 37, 113, 123, 136, 154, 247, 251, 274, 277, 280

radical xxi, xxii, xxii, 14, 29, 38, 40, 46, 54, 64, 109, 114, 123, 138, 169, 196, 197, 274, 275, 276, 278, 285, 286
reflective learning 139
reformist xxi, 109, 285, 286
relational paradigms 181
relational pedagogies xxi, 110, 112, 113, 114, 120, 136, 277
research and innovation 38, 39, 41, 52, 169, 172, 248
research led teaching 43, 88, 90, 162, 178
resilience 96, 143, 152, 173, 189, 196, 198, 242, 264, 270, 279, 284
Responsible Futures 191, 205, 214, 217, 219, 220, 232, 235, 261

senior leaders 49, 191, 193, 194, 195, 196, 197, 201, 220, 250
social constructivism xxi
social responsibility xxi, 4, 45, 203
socio-ecological innovation 114, 162, 166, 168, 170
socio-emotional (heart) learning domain 26, 117, 118
staff development 131, 191, 204, 211, 213, 214, 215, 217, 218, 219, 220, 239
staff engagement 42, 77, 98, 192, 193, 200, 201, 202, 206, 211, 213, 215, 219, 220, 246, 247
staff recognition 178, 204, 215, 221, 234
stakeholder engagement 44, 97, 163, 174, 180, 201, 202, 281
strategy 15, 18, 37, 43, 45, 47, 92, 98, 189, 191, 194, 199, 201, 202, 203, 204, 219, 223, 230, 236, 248
strategy implementation 199, 200, 201, 232
student centred xix, xxi, 94, 109, 114, 117, 121, 134, 135, 144, 277
student entrepreneurship 213, 264, 265, 280
student partners xx, 123, 133, 143, 205, 206, 212, 217, 222, 223, 235, 257, 261, 262
student representatives 47, 217, 222
student voice 40, 43, 53, 73, 100, 111, 123, 131, 194, 204, 230, 233, 276, 277, 281
students (definition) xxii, *passim*
Students Organising for Sustainability (SOS-UK) 140
students' unions 50, 205, 217, 222, 261, 263
subject benchmark statements xxii, 66, 67, 68, 69, 70, 71, 72, 77, 91, 92, 103, 178, 221, 233, 276
summative assessment 130, 132, 139, 145, 146, 153, 154, 241
sustainability (definition) xxii, *passim*
sustainability jobs 255, 256, 258, 262, 263, 265, 266, 267, 279
Sustainability Literacy Test (SULITEST) 232
sustainability practice 4, 119, 141
sustainability research xxii, 42, 74, 75, 76, 77, 152, 162, 164, 165, 166, 167, 168, 170, 175, 176, 177, 178, 179, 180, 181, 183, 217, 235, 278
sustainability science xxii, 41, 74, 75, 76, 181, 276

sustainability skills 139, 192, 255, 258, 260, 261, 279
sustainability skills surveys 192
sustainable development xxii, 9, 10, 11, 14, 15, 17, 18, 21, 22, 23, 26, 29, 41, 60, 68, 69, 74, 80, 95, 108, 112, 117, 119, 143, 147, 148, 149, 164, 167, 168, 169, 173, 179, 180, 182, 189, 190, 201, 211, 220, 222, 229, 230, 233, 236, 238, 255, 256, 268, 274, 276, 278, 281, 282, 283, 285
Sustainable Development Goals xxiii, 4, 13, 15, 16, 17, 45, 66, 67, 68, 69, 70, 90, 91, 98, 108, 121, 138, 143, 164, 190, 192, 212, 231, 238, 240, 255, 276, 282
sustainable university xxii 5, 36, 37, 38, 40, 41, 44, 45, 50, 51, 54, 55, 98, 202, 211, 276
syllabus 89, 92, 93, 101, 103
systems change 41, 54, 196, 263, 268

teaching-led research 162, 178, 183
technical staff 221
theory of ESD, especially **9–35**
threshold concepts 87, 93, 101, 102, 103
Times Higher Education Impact Ranking 232
tools of leadership for ESD 189, 199, 200
top-down leadership 194, 197
transdisciplinarity xxii, 59, 77, 78, 79, 81, 82, 83, 166, 167, 177, 183, 277, 278
transdisciplinary learning xxii, 28, 39, 80, 81, 82, 179
transdisciplinary research 166, 167, 168, 170, 172, 176
transformative learning xxii, 18, 23, 26, 80, 81, 82, 83, 94, 100, 109, 110, 111, 113, 114, 115, 117, 121, 123, 141, 146, 154, 163, 230, 235, 236, 244, 248, 250, 274, 277, 284
transformative pedagogies 21, 26, 27, 29, 108, 117, 118, 119, 121, 215
transgressive learning xxii, 26, 275, 285, 286
turbocapitalism xxii, 109

values 14, 17, 18, 20, 24, 25, 26, 29, 48, 50, 55, 87, 88, 89, 90, 93, 94, 102, 111, 117, 118, 137, 143, 164, 191, 195, 196, 198, 199, 211, 230, 236, 241, 256, 258, 260, 263, 269, 270, 278, 282, 284, 286

whole-institution approach 22, 48, 119, 200, 211
wicked problems 51, 64, 102, 146, 164, 170, 230, 284
work placements 69, 145, 146
workload 28, 130, 131, 136, 137, 155, 177, 231, 247, 276, 277, 279

For Product Safety Concerns and Information please contact our EU
representative GPSR@taylorandfrancis.com
Taylor & Francis Verlag GmbH, Kaufingerstraße 24, 80331 München, Germany

www.ingramcontent.com/pod-product-compliance
Ingram Content Group UK Ltd.
Pitfield, Milton Keynes, MK11 3LW, UK
UKHW050232200926
475702UK00020B/2992

* 9 7 8 1 0 3 2 5 8 8 0 1 8 *